JOHN HORRY DENT

John Horry Dent (1815-1892) as a young man
(Courtesy of Marshall Wellborn)

JOHN HORRY DENT

SOUTH CAROLINA ARISTOCRAT
ON THE ALABAMA FRONTIER

RAY MATHIS

Published under the Sponsorship of
The Historic Chattahoochee Commission by
The University of Alabama Press
University, Alabama

TO
Mary Kathryn Pugh Mathis

Library of Congress Cataloging in Publication Data

Mathis, Gerald Ray, 1937-
    John Horry Dent, South Carolina aristocrat on the Alabama
frontier.

    Bibliography: p.
    Includes index.
    1. Dent, John Horry, d. 1892. 2. Farmers—Alabama—Barbour Co.
—Biography. 3. Barbour Co., Ala.—Biography. I. Historic Chat-
tahoochee Commission. II. Title.
S417.D43M37   976.1'32 [B]   78-10693
ISBN 0-8173-5263-5

HISTORIC CHATTAHOOCHEE COMMISSION

Board of Directors
1978-1979

Mrs. Florence Foy Strang
Mr. Robert Bennett, Sr.
Mrs. Claude Milford
Mrs. Charles Crump
Mr. Glenn L. Wells
Mr. Creel Richardson
Mr. William W. Nordan
Mr. George Grimsley
Mrs. Elaine Johnson
Mr. Larry Register
Dr. Allen M. Pearson
Mrs. Jan Dempsey
Mr. Charles Tigner
Mr. Reginald Cain
Mrs. Tay Howell
Ms. Celia Doremus
Lt. Colonel (Ret.) Dick Grube
Mrs. Ann Singer
Mrs. Jenny Copeland

Past Board of Directors

Mrs. Hortense Balkcom
Dr. H. Floyd Vallery
Mrs. Ann Smith
Mr. Harold Coulter
Mrs. Dorothy Powell
Mr. W. V. Neville, Jr.
Mr. Edward W. Neal
Mrs. J. Walter Jones
Mr. Sam S. Singer
Mr. Fred Watson
Mr. Steve Elliott
Mr. Gary Ford
Mrs. Alice Doughtie
Mr. Marvin Singletary
Mrs. Agnes Halstead
Mrs. Charlotte Northrup
Mr. C. A. Blondheim, Jr.
Mrs. Sara Beasley
Mrs. Roy Greene
Mrs. W. T. Ventress

Georgia Advisory Members
1978-1979

Mrs. Pam Lindsey
Mrs. Bruce Mann
Mr. George Phillips
Mrs. Florence Moye
Mrs. Marion Roberts
Mrs. Janice Biggers

Past Georgia Advisory Members

Mrs. J. Turner Killingsworth
Mrs. Yates Cathrall
Mrs. Elizabeth Stapleton
Mrs. W. Norton Roberts
Mrs. India Wilson
Mrs. Victoria Custer
Judge Julian Webb

HCC Officers
1978-1979

Lt. Colonel (Ret.) Dick Grube, Chairman
Mrs. Claude Milford, Vice-Chairman
Mrs. Jean D. Robinson, Secretary
Mr. James S. Clark, Treasurer
Mr. Douglas Clare Purcell, Executive Director

CONTENTS

ILLUSTRATIONS

MAPS

CHARTS AND TABLES

PREFACE

John Horry Dent (1815-1892) was a South Carolina planter of moderate means, who was descended from the eminent American families of seventeenth-century founders like Judge Thomas Dent of Maryland and Elias Horry, a South Carolina Huguenot. In 1837, at the age of twenty-two, John Horry Dent moved his young wife, Mary Elizabeth Morrison, and their infant son, from the comfortable but economically depressed rice-planting district of Colleton, South Carolina, to the new Alabama frontier in Barbour County and northern environs, an area recently wrested from the Creek Indians. Financing this frontier venture in cotton planting from his wife's inheritance of forty-five slaves, and commencing the task during a depression year and the subsequent recession, Dent prospered and was a wealthy planter-financier by the time of secession and the Civil War.

Having lost at least three-quarters of his $200,000 fortune during and immediately following this war, the discouraged but determined Dent abandoned Alabama in December, 1866, for his recently purchased 400-acre "farm" near Cave Spring in Floyd County, Georgia. He lived at this Van's Valley Refugee Cottage until his death in 1892. Here in north Georgia, the self-styled "Major" Dent was a successful and influential farmer and agricultural reformer; a prosperous miller and shrewd financier-investor; as well as an active Bourbon Democrat, county commissioner, and chairman of the trustees of the progressive school for the deaf in Cave Spring. This study of Dent's life and thought is not a complete biography. Rather, it presents his seaboard origins and Alabama period, emphasizing the years 1837 through 1866, the time he resided in Barbour County.

About 1837, Dent began keeping a daily farm journal, which he continued until a few months before his death. Although he destroyed most of his correspondence, and the journals and accounts from 1843 through 1850 have not as yet surfaced for use (if indeed they still exist), the journals for 1840 through 1842 and from 1851 through 1892 are almost complete and are now available. These diaries and financial records have been the primary source for the study and the major influence on its organization. Along with daily entries, Dent also penned numerous short essays on a wide variety of topics such as crops, slaves, overseers, agricultural reform, weather, income, expenses, capital gains, loans, family, health, religion, reminiscences, sectional crises, war, emancipation, and so on, for a rich compendium of fact, opinion, and analysis.

When Dr. Floyd Vallery of the Historic Chattahoochee Commission asked me to prepare some of these materials for publication, we agreed the format would be that of a sourcebook of Dent's comment. I have, however, with the commission's consent, subsequently broadened the sourcebook approach to include enough historical background, chronological development, and interpretive analysis to make the study a type of intellectual biography, with numerous quotations from Dent. Because his essays were short and topical, they lend themselves to chronological and analytical presentation. For the sake of clarity, I have substituted a more nearly standard punctuation in place of his overuse of commas and dashes, but I have retained his idiosyncrasies of spelling and capitalization. For example, his prose, "In the Summer of 1835, a Courting I begun, I thought I..." becomes "In the Summer of 1835, a Courting I begun. I thought I...."

There has also been the problem of balancing my analysis against Dent's repetitious and sometimes ambiguous comment. Here the rule has been to let him speak openly, albeit ambivalently, on the subjects that most concerned him. I have met the question of interpretation by allowing the man's complexity to emerge through his own words. Because the study is a general one, it is not simply social, intellectual, literary, political, or economic history. Yet I have tried to utilize some of the methods of each.

With Dent's comment as the pattern, each chapter is organized around a central issue and related problems. Thus, chapter one traces his family background and experience to 1837, the year in which he moved to Alabama. This chapter also explores the sources of his self-concept as a member of the privileged upper class in which he was determined to gain a more secure position.

Chapter two treats the Alabama frontier and Dent's economic progress in Barbour County in the matters of purchasing five separate plantations, planting them, improving them, and trading them—for profits that he invested in short-term, high-interest loans, as well as in banking and other business interests. The second chapter also presents his eclectic and functional agrarianism, which transcended the simplistic typology of the yeoman versus the large planter. As a self-conscious agrarian, he was ambivalent toward both the frontier and the mature plantation, fearing the cultural deprivation of the former and the economic liability of the latter. While Dent wrote much on scientific agriculture, he was less committed to its practice than he believed, and his attitude was very negative toward the white overseers upon whom he depended for the direct management of his numerous slaves.

Dent's agrarianism simply assumed plantation slavery, the subject of chapter three, which treats his conception of the institution and his indirect management of chattels through transient overseers. This master's lack of self-consciousness about slavery confirms Louis Rubin's view that southern whites could easily ignore slaves, especially in matters of human rights. Conversely, Dent was less like Lewis Simpson's construct of antebellum whites who needed to justify slavery in a manner similar to George Fitzhugh's.[1] Dent's plantation journals discuss slavery from the perspective of marketplace profits, rather than from that of the master-slave relationship.

The fourth chapter portrays in composite fashion Dent's personal direction of the planting year, which began in January and continued with month-to-month tasks. Summarized broadly, these were clearing new ground, planting, cultivating, jobbing, harvesting, processing, transporting, and selling appropriate crops.

Chapter five, on the family, treats Dent's home life and shows that patriarchy in the abstract did not concern him enough to be worthy of discussion. He was secure as family head and often wrote of his love for home in a way that emphasized the nuclear family but did not negate the extended one. In regard to fatherly responsibility, his major anxiety was modern man's universal one of providing financial security and opportunity for his children. While he expressed some misgivings about wives' being too independent, children spoiled, and the frivolity of modern education—Dent, a chauvinist but no martinet, was content and comfortable with his family life.

Finally, chapter six depicts Dent's conservative responses to the crises of the 1850s and 1860s. As the sectional controversy over slavery moved toward secession and war, Dent was what Carl Degler has helpfully termed a "conditional Unionist."[2] Dent later became a reluctant Confederate and a pessimistic southern nationalist. Following emancipation and the trauma of planting with free labor, he tried to escape to north Georgia, a region that he temporarily idealized as a land of small farmers. Here he hoped to dramatize yeoman agrarianism, the faith that helped sustain him through war, stay laws, inflation, military defeat, emancipation, financial losses, and the other socioeconomic "revolutions" he despised. An admirer of the North, he also manifested much continuity between the Old and New South.

John Dent was apparently typical of that antebellum class of large southern planters who comprised less than 1 percent of the landowners in the gulf states of Alabama, Mississippi, and Louisiana. In fact, his unwillingness to plow all earnings back into land and slaves; his insistence on surplus capital for small loans, bank stocks, and other investments; his care to cultivate advantageous friendships and partnerships and marriages of daughters to well-connected businessmen; his several links to the outside world; and his commercial attitude toward planting indicate that Dent was much like those Natchez nabobs portrayed by Morton Rothstein in his essay "The Antebellum South as a Dual Economy: A Tentative Hypothesis." Within Rothstein's paradigms, the above characteristics made Dent more the modern capitalist in a dual economy than the traditional planter, who has been stereotyped as the member of a "disembodied, static group, withdrawn from concerns with sordid affairs of the market place, isolated from his fellows except for casual social meetings, and caught in the ruthless grip of a marketing system that drew off most of the profits in cotton for the merchant-shippers of New York and Liverpool."[3] Still, whatever Dent has to say, he is here a "case study," a single, if somewhat representative, spokesman who carefully set his views down on paper while tending plantations in southeastern Alabama.

JOHN HORRY DENT

CHRONOLOGY

1815 John Horry Dent is born, Newport, Rhode Island.

1823 His father, Captain John Herbert Dent, Colleton District, South Carolina, dies.

1835 John Dent marries Mary Elizabeth Morrison of Colleton.

1836 Dent raises rice crop in South Carolina.

1837 Dent moves to Barbour County, Alabama, and begins temporary residence at Clayton and Mount Andrew.

1838 Dent moves to Good Hope plantation on Johnson's Creek, a tributary of South Cowikee.

1839 Dent travels to Mobile.

1842 Dent moves to True Blue plantation, at present Comer, Alabama, on South Cowikee.

1849 Dent returns to enlarged Good Hope (called Miller's plantation).

1853 Dent's wife, Mary Elizabeth, dies at Good Hope-Miller's plantation.

1854 Dent marries Fanny Whipple of Richmond, Vermont.

1854 Dent moves to Johnson's plantation on Chewalla Creek.

1855 Dent moves to DeWitt's plantation, called Bleak House, on Barbour Creek.

1856 Dent's mother, Anne Horry Dent, dies.

1859 Dent visits Texas.

1860 Dent visits Tennessee.

1861 Dent visits Mississippi.

1864 Dent's eldest son, Horry, dies.

1866 Dent plants at Bleak House, using free labor, and moves to north Georgia, where he resides at Refugee Cottage (also called Cottage Home), two miles north of Cave Spring until . . .

1892 John Horry Dent dies at Cottage Home.

1

SOUTH CAROLINA HERITAGE

John Horry Dent considered himself one of the "better people" among antebellum southern whites. His self-concept was one of country squire or gentleman, although he preferred the more democratic phrase, "a man of honor." Secure in his sense of being of the upper class, he knew by early manhood that his small ruling group held a position of authority and power by virtue of birth *and* wealth, and knew also that the first condition did not remove the need for the second. That is, legitimate birth into the ruling classes of tidewater Virginia or Maryland or of the South Carolina rice district provided no sure exemption from the necessity of maintaining one's upper-class status with a regular flow of profits from the marketplace. [1]

It was in this light that young John Horry Dent viewed himself as a child of privilege who needed a fortune. In 1853 he described his youthful status as one "who had been accustomed to every comfort and everything at hand, prepared by those who had bequeathed it as an inheritance." [2] Perhaps he exaggerated, for while born into the upper class, his inheritance was largely of status and not of wealth. On the other hand, the privileges and opportunities of his family were considerable.

The full extent of John Dent's knowledge of family history is unknown. He was at least aware that both the Dents and Horrys had been prominent in the early history of Maryland and South Carolina, respectively. The founder of the paternal line in Maryland was Judge Thomas Dent, who in the mid-seventeenth century began what is alleged to be "the most distinguished branch of that name in America." According to the family genealogist, this forebearer was the progeny of a long line of gentlemen and squires reaching back to the twelfth-century town of Dent in Yorkshire, northern England. Thomas Dent's conservative Anglicanism helps explain his emigration to St. Mary's, Maryland, during the 1650s, when Oliver Cromwell's Puritan Commonwealth ruled England. Furthermore, the youthful Thomas, in his twenties and unmarried, was not the eldest son, who would inherit the bulk of his parents' wealth. The New World thus attracted this enterprising youth. Here, his legal training at the Inns of London, his five indentured servants, and appreciation for a good marriage laid firm foundations for worldly success. As a lawyer, merchant, and planter, Thomas Dent of St. Mary's accumulated additional land, indentured servants, Negro slaves, capital, political offices, and judicial appointments. Before his death in 1676, he almost embodied the Cavalier myth, which held that colonial aristocrats were titled Royalists who fled the Parliamentary regime. For while Thomas was not of noble birth, his successful business interests meant that his descendants were children of privilege, American "aristocrats."[3]

Of Thomas' six children, the eldest was William (1660-1704), the namesake of his maternal grandfather, the Reverend William Wilkinson, an Anglican priest. Favored generously by the will of this wealthy grandparent, William Dent also inherited from his father sizeable estates along the Potomac River in both St. Mary's and Charles counties. Owing to these inheritances and subsequent favors from the royal governor (who may have been a distant relative), William's land holdings amounted to thousands of acres and were the largest of any Dent's in the line of descent traced here. William, like his father, Thomas, was also a merchant, lawyer, and a member of the colonial assembly. After 1698, William became the Crown's attorney general for Maryland.[4]

William Dent's fifth child and fourth son, George (1690-1754), was the next person in this line of direct descent. George inherited a thousand acres of land, some slaves, silver plate, personal items, and one-half his father's library. The library included a large number of lawbooks, and George understandably continued the family tradition in that profession, where we are told, "In one way, he excelled his distinguished father, in as much as he became Chief Justice of Maryland, the highest judicial honor in the Province." George also enlarged his estate on the Potomac where he was "intimate with the Washington and Fairfax families" who lived on the Virginia side of the river.[5]

Among Chief Justice George Dent's offspring was John Dent (1733-1809), the fifth child and second son. This planter, John Dent of Pomonkey Hundred on the Mattawoman, received from his father a respectable inheritance of 1,280 acres of land, seven Negroes, some livestock, and household furniture. But John neglected planting in favor of politics and the local militia. During the American Revolution, he was a member of the state assembly, signer of the Association of Freemen of Maryland, a member of the Council of Safety, and briefly in 1776 "Brigadier-General in command of all militia of the Lower District on the Western Shore." In August of that year, however, he resigned the military command, explaining he was not equal to the task, and preferred to resume his seat in the state legislature. Perhaps the Dent blood was beginning to run thin. At any rate, the family's agricultural base was shrinking. In 1783 John's 1,280 acres were reduced by 200, and in 1785 he deeded almost 600 acres to his first son, George, who was already a veteran of the War for Independence and a member of the Maryland legislature.[6]

Congressman George Dent (1758-1813), like his father, John, was more politician than planter. It is, perhaps, significant that these Dents' home on the Mattawoman carried the "fanciful English name" of Windsor Castle. During the War for Independence, George rose to captain, and in

1782 he was elected to the Maryland legislature, where he served as speaker from 1788 to 1791. In 1792 he sat in the state senate before entering the United States House of Representatives the following year. He was regularly returned to Congress until he declined reelection in 1802. It was during Thomas Jefferson's and Aaron Burr's contest for the presidency in 1801 that George Dent is supposed to have worked zealously for Jefferson's election, expecting a high appointment in return. Instead, Dent received a relatively insignificant post as marshal of the District of Columbia, which he held for a brief period before resigning in disgust. He then liquidated his modest holdings in Maryland and moved to a plantation near Augusta, Georgia.

The impression of George Dent's seeming pettiness in the matter of his appointment as marshal of the District of Columbia is reinforced by two or three small incidents that, taken separately, would signify little. Although the combination of these incidents is not the whole truth, it is nevertheless revealing of one side of the man that the congressman's father willed the bulk of his estate directly to his grandson, United States Navy Captain John Herbert Dent (1782-1823), the first child of George Dent. Perhaps there was an irreparable breach between George Dent and this son. After the congressman's accidental death in 1813, it was revealed that his will did not mention Captain John Dent, although this father had provided for his wife, three other sons, a brother, and a woman "of no stated relationship." It was also with patent sarcasm that he left his one daughter a mere "twenty-five cents for reasons she will duly appreciate."[7] Finally, John Horry Dent, the subject of this study, mentioned his grandfather, Congressman George Dent, only once in the course of his voluminous journals, and then only in passing.

On the other hand, John Horry Dent was almost as reticent about his own father, Captain John Herbert Dent, whom we know largely from his official record in the United States Navy. Born in Charles County, Maryland, in 1782, John Herbert was the first child of George and Anne Magruder Truman Dent. The son began his naval career in 1798, when sixteen years of age. At that time, George Dent was in Congress, a fact which probably assisted young John's appointment as midshipman on the frigate *Constellation* under the able command of Captain Thomas Truxtun. Although this John deviated from the family's traditional professions of law and politics, the times were propitious for the nation's embryonic navy and for a young midshipman of good family connection and ample courage.[8]

No sooner had Midshipman Dent joined the *Constellation* than she was engaged in successful action against the French frigate, *Insurgente;* this was in February, 1799, during the undeclared naval war with France. He was also present a year later when the *Constellation* defeated the French *Vengeance.* Young Dent saw less than one year's active service

DIRECT DESCENT OF
JOHN HORRY DENT*

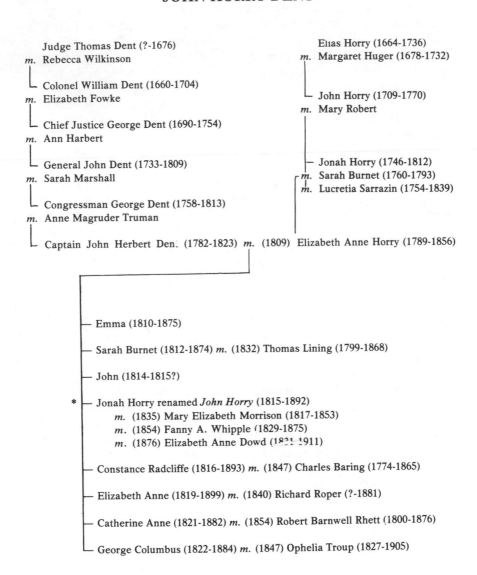

Judge Thomas Dent (?-1676)
m. Rebecca Wilkinson

Colonel William Dent (1660-1704)
m. Elizabeth Fowke

Chief Justice George Dent (1690-1754)
m. Ann Harbert

General John Dent (1733-1809)
m. Sarah Marshall

Congressman George Dent (1758-1813)
m. Anne Magruder Truman

Captain John Herbert Dent (1782-1823) m. (1809) Elizabeth Anne Horry (1789-1856)

Elias Horry (1664-1736)
m. Margaret Huger (1678-1732)

John Horry (1709-1770)
m. Mary Robert

Jonah Horry (1746-1812)
m. Sarah Burnet (1760-1793)
m. Lucretia Sarrazin (1754-1839)

Emma (1810-1875)

Sarah Burnet (1812-1874) m. (1832) Thomas Lining (1799-1868)

John (1814-1815?)

* Jonah Horry renamed *John Horry* (1815-1892)
   m. (1835) Mary Elizabeth Morrison (1817-1853)
   m. (1854) Fanny A. Whipple (1829-1875)
   m. (1876) Elizabeth Anne Dowd (1821-1911)

Constance Radcliffe (1816-1893) m. (1847) Charles Baring (1774-1865)

Elizabeth Anne (1819-1899) m. (1840) Richard Roper (?-1881)

Catherine Anne (1821-1882) m. (1854) Robert Barnwell Rhett (1800-1876)

George Columbus (1822-1884) m. (1847) Ophelia Troup (1827-1905)

SPOUSES AND OFFSPRING
OF
JOHN HORRY DENT

John Horry Dent (1815-1892) *m.* (1835) Mary Elizabeth Morrison (1817-1853)
    Robert Morrison (1836-1837)
    Emma Julia, "Minna" (1838-1919) *m.* (1857) M. B. Wellborn (1825-1885)
    John Horry (1840-1864)
    Mary Elizabeth, "Lizzie" (1842-1870) *m.* (1861) Whitfield Clark (1827-1875)
    John Herbert (1845-?) *m.* (1869) Anna Virginia Petty (1848-1889)
    Anne Horry (1847-1889) *m.* (1870) Whitfield Clark (1827-1875)
    Charles Baring (1849-?) *m.* (1884) Georgia Studemire
    Sarah Lining (1851-1866)
    Kate Constance (1853-1919)

John Horry Dent (1815-1892) *m.* (1854) Fanny A. Whipple (1829-1875)
    Fanny Whipple (1856-1892) *m.* (1875) Elbert Wiley Jones
    George Columbus (1858-1879)
    Lucy Gertrude (1861-?) *m.* (1883) Justus Collins
    Helen Almira (1865-1872)
    Carrie Mae (1868-1910) *m.* John H. Henley
    Infant daughter (1875)

John Horry Dent (1815-1892) *m.* (1876) Elizabeth Anne Dowd (1831-1911)
    no issue

before he was promoted to lieutenant, and by 1803, at twenty-one years of age, he was experienced enough to join Commodore Edward Preble's squadron in the Mediterranean, where events had patterned themselves for the Tripolitan War. In this theater, Preble's flagship was the *Constitution,* a vessel destined for special reverence in American history as "Old Ironsides." Once during the commodore's brief absence from the *Constitution,* Lieutenant Dent was given temporary command of her. Later, in one of the several assaults on Tripoli, young Dent directed affairs on the quarter-deck of the *Constitution.* But his most significant service during this war was the able command of a bomb vessel during four attacks on the North African city. Preble and Congress formally commended Dent's gallantry and skill in the bomb vessel.[9]

Following the Tripolitan War, the recently promoted Master Commander Dent passed rapidly through successive commands of the *Scourge* and the *Nautilus* to that of the *Hornet.* As master of the *Hornet,* a brig, Dent served in Commodore John Rodger's Mediterranean squadron until November, 1807, when he returned with his ship to the United States under orders to Charleston, South Carolina. This assignment initiated the second phase of Dent's naval career, which centered around Charleston and was largely inactive. In January, 1808, he was "Instructed to consider himself Senior Officer at Charleston until otherwise ordered." This instruction could have related to President Jefferson's controversial Embargo Act, which attempted to keep United States merchant ships from European ports in efforts to maintain neutrality during the Napoleonic Wars. But Dent's stationing in Charleston was also convenient to his family, who had moved to Augusta, Georgia. And 1807 was the year he received a few slaves from the will of his maternal grandmother, Elizabeth Gordon Truman.[10]

As one would expect, Charleston's upper class was receptive to this twenty-six-year-old naval officer and hero, whose family name rendered him an exceedingly eligible bachelor. Thus it transpired that Commander Dent met, wooed, and wed with seeming ease one of the city's attractive belles, Elizabeth Anne Horry. Of legendary beauty, she was descended from a distinguished Huguenot family. Elizabeth Anne and her younger sister, Mary Lynch, were the only surviving children of Jonah and Sarah Burnet Horry.[11]

Jonah Horry (1747-1812), of Charleston and the Colleton District, was a wealthy rice planter in St. Bartholomew's Parish near the summer resort of Walterboro, fifty miles southwest of Charleston. Jonah's privileged status of Charleston gentleman was based on eminent family, important friends, and large plantations, at a time when Europe's Great Wars made rice production very profitable. He was of the elite Huguenot stock of French Protestants who fled Roman Catholic persecution after 1685. These able and ambitious Calvinists quickly became a dominant force in the ruling class of South Carolina, as the family names of Marion, Moultrie, Legaré, Poinsett, and Huger indicate. Jonah Horry was a grandson of the seventeenth-century immigrant, Elias, whose own father, Jean Horry, was martyred in France. In South Carolina, the immigrant Elias married Margaret Huger, a daughter of the founder of that prominent American line. One of their offspring, John Horry, married Mary Robert, a direct descendant of Pierre Robert, an important minister of the French Protestant Church in South Carolina. Jonah was a younger son of John and Mary Robert Horry.[12]

In 1788 Jonah Horry married Sarah Burnet. Elizabeth Anne and Mary Lynch were born of this union, in 1789 and 1791, respectively. The mother, Sarah, died in childbirth in 1793 and her infant son did not survive. Six months later, Jonah married Lucretia Sarrazin, who was childless but an excellent mother to young Anne and Mary. The family was apparently a happy one. Jonah's will left Lucretia one-third of his holdings and named her coexecutor of the estate and guardian of Anne and Mary during their minorities. Lucretia, a devoted wife and mother, was much loved, especially by Anne.[13]

Still Jonah, the patriarch, was careful to name coexecutors in the persons of powerful and influential men. Lucretia was "executrix" and guardian in company with "my said Brother General Peter Horry and my friends Elias Horry (son of my Cousin Thomas Horry) Nathaniel Heyward and John Julius Pringle." The list is one of imposing personalities. Jonah's brother, Peter Horry, was a Revolutionary hero who ranked not far behind the Swamp Fox, Francis Marion, whom he assisted. The friend and cousin, Elias Horry, was the successful Charleston businessman who became president of the South Carolina Railroad.[14]

Nathaniel Heyward, Jonah's neighbor in the Combahee River region of the rice district, had the largest rice-planting operation in America of that day. When Heyward died in 1851, his holdings were valued at two million dollars. John Julius Pringle, a lawyer of impeccable pedigree, was also a neighbor at his Colleton plantation of Runnymede. The closeness of Jonah's tie with the Heyward and Pringle families led him to this precaution in his will: "In case my said Wife [Lucretia Horry] should die during the Minority of my daughters it is my desire that they may reside either with Mrs. John Julius Pringle or Mrs. Nathaniel Heyward as they may choose." Actually, Lucretia lived until 1835, long after the girls' majorities were attained.[15]

Jonah Horry's plantations, which lay between the Combahee and Ashepoo rivers, were modest compared with the baronial estates of friend Heyward. Of Jonah's "Negroes & Land," his brother, Peter, estimated them in 1812 at "about 15 Thousand acres of the Latter & between 2 & 3 Hundred Slaves." But there was some indebtedness, which Peter (who was jealous of Jonah) may have exaggerated. At the

news of Jonah's death in 1812, the embittered general wrote harshly: "I
fear it will be found he owed much more than was Expected—he was too
Penurious & Grasped at too much—Say Spiculated on Negroes & Lands
the Latter Inferior Inland Swamp.... Yet he Got in debt himself tho' I
made use of Every Argument to Prevent his doing it.... he Seldom or
Ever made Good Crops. he died abt. 66 years of age—to his wife's family
he was Generous. but to his own, he was... unjust in many Particulars."[16]

Jonah, then, was a gentleman planter who tended to neglect his
business and to indulge his immediate family and in-laws. In spite of
debts, however, he was financially solvent in life and death, leaving an
estate sizeable enough to satisfy all claims and to maintain separate
households for his heirs. There is evidence, however, that paying these
debts lowered the family's living standard. Not that they were extravagant during his lifetime—conspicuous comfort is a better way to describe
the mature plantation society of this low-country gentry. While a few rice
planters built rural mansions, the majority of them, particularly the lesser
gentry, were content with adequate country homes, especially since their
lifestyle required a summer residence away from the plantation, often in
Charleston.[17]

Because of the danger of malaria and yellow fever from the low-lying
rice fields and adjacent swamps, it was customary for a planter's family to
"winter" for six months on the plantation during the "healthy" season
and to leave about April for a safer summer's habitation. White residents
of Colleton plantations spent six-month "summers" at some nearby
sandy-soiled, pineland resort such as Walterboro, or at Charleston, or
even at one of the more fashionable vacation spots such as Saratoga or
Newport. In winter, however, the Horrys were in Colleton, enjoying the
closely knit rural society of family, neighbors, and friends with their
visiting, feasting, drinking, hunting, church-going, and attendance at the
race track of Jacksonboro. Come April, however, the Horrys, like the
Heywards and other prominent neighbors, moved to Charleston for its
six-month social season, even though that city was not a great deal
healthier than the countryside.[18]

The rice plantations' summer work (and entire work year, if one
wished) was usually left under the direction of white stewards or super-
intendents who were markedly more efficient, and expensive, than up-
country plantation overseers.[19] The system was costly, but it afforded
the leisure of Jonah Horry and his family, which the daughter, Elizabeth
Anne, described in her 1802 diary. She was a precocious twelve years
and apparently in a Charleston boardinghouse when she wrote under the
date of Monday, April 20:

Awoke at nine o'clock. Kitty brought me my breakfast in bed. Papa came

up stairs with a letter from Mary, heard it read, then stayed and talked untill 12. Did not get down stairs untill half an hour after. Intended to go out
and make some visits but was prevented by the rain; therefore went up
stairs to condole with Mrs. Barlowe on her friends departure for New York.
Some men called and stayed untill dinner, during which time did three rows
of netting to my purse and scraped a bit of whale bone. Dinner not very
good. Raining still. Mr. Coles dined at home, joked me about rising so
early. After dinner laughed and talked with him at the back door, playing
with little Gibson; almost put out my eye with a branch of a cherry tree.
Went up stairs, began a letter to my sister. Weather beginning to clear up,
put on my bonnet intending to make a visit.... Found Miss C. unwell...
returned home, took a walk, then went with Papa to drink tea at Mrs.
Mease's. After tea, went home, found the men so noisy in the parlour,
chose to go up stairs to eat my supper and then to bed. N. B. first wrote
my journal.[20]

It was almost six years from the time of these entries by Anne Horry
that Commander John Herbert Dent was designated senior officer at
Charleston. A coquette at twelve, Anne matured becomingly and at
eighteen was a fitting match for the eligible naval officer. They were
married in February, 1809, one year after Dent's arrival in Charleston.
The circumstances of their courtship were romantic enough to produce a
family legend that Ophelia Troup Dent set down in her "Memoirs" of
1902. Ophelia's description of her mother-in-law portrayed the force and
flavor of Anne's personality: "Elizabeth Anne Horry was most carefully
educated by French abbes driven to Charleston by the French Revolution.
She was highly accomplished, with charming manners and appearance.
Her father thought she should be the wife of an ambassador, but she fell
in love with a naval officer."[21]

In addition to her "generous love and high ideals," Anne was said to
be of unusual beauty. Ophelia Dent also related some words of Washington Irving that have been mistakenly applied to Anne Horry Dent.[22] Irving, who was briefly associated with Commander Dent, once wrote: "I
have been introduced to Mrs. D by her husband. I won't speak all that I
think of her; you would accuse me of hyperbole; but, to say that I admire
her would be too cold, too feeble. I think she would be a belle in heaven
itself."

Irving's compliment continued and was high praise indeed, except that
he penned it in 1807, before Dent arrived in Charleston, and supposedly
before he knew the Horrys. Furthermore, the time of the casual Dent-
Irving relationship was 1805, in the Mediterranean, during Irving's Grand
Tour of Europe. One of the author's most vivid impressions concerning
Dent was of the commander's beautiful Sicilian mistress, an opera star in
Syracuse. The family tradition of Irving's praise of Anne, however, has
fulfilled the proper role of legend, in suppressing the base, highlighting

the beautiful (which Anne must have been), and finally preserving for family history Dent's relationship with the famous author.[23]

No legend, though, completely obscures its subject. For example, Ophelia Dent related little of her father-in-law except his valor at Tripoli. Yet she unintentionally imparted two hints of character flaw. The first was Jonah Horry's desire that Anne "be the wife of an ambassador," a statement which could have stemmed from disapproval of the commander. The old Huguenot *did* wait until the day of the wedding to change his will, making John Herbert Dent an equal heir with Anne. Ophelia's second hint related to the commander's carelessness of personal possessions. He lent the valuable sword presented him by Congress to the "great tragedian of the day, Cooper, to play Othello" and "*sailor-fashion*, he did not recall it until too late . . . it was lost."[24]

Despite misgivings in some quarters, Commander Dent and Anne Horry were wed on February 7, 1809. During their courtship, James Madison had secured the presidency, keeping Jefferson's Republican Party in power, even though the controversial embargo on American shipping was increasingly unpopular. Soon the embargo would expire, abandoned by Congress, but the problems which motivated President Jefferson's policy continued, and the country drifted into a controversial war with Great Britain, from 1812 to 1815.[25]

Meanwhile, the charms of cosmopolitan Charleston and the picturesque countryside of handsome homes, manicured rice fields, and dreamlike swamps of moss and black water were offset somewhat for Commander Dent by uncertainty about his career. Though it is impossible to read his mind, one can trace some vacillation. A full month before the wedding, Dent was "Ordered to prepare *Hornet* immediately" for a cruise to New Orleans. The commander, however, dallied for weeks before leaving and did not complete the short mission until May 3. By the end of May, he was "Furloughed for 3 months," probably at his own request, even though it meant detachment "from *Hornet* at Charleston."

Then, what began as a three-month leave stretched into a full year. In February, 1810, after twelve months of marriage, Dent "Wrote from Charleston requesting orders to join a ship." But now the Navy Department delayed six months before directing him to Norfolk, Virginia, to assume command of the *John Adams*. This time the commander did not tarry; he made the trip to Norfolk and was back in Charleston with the *John Adams* in under six weeks.

At this juncture, Dent's orders reflect the Navy Department's concern at his spending so much time in port. Yet efforts to keep him at sea along the Atlantic coastline were to little avail, and once again he was slow to execute orders for a European cruise. Upon Dent's return from France in August, 1811, his major concern was getting to Washington, D. C., to lobby his promotion to captain. After surrendering command of the *John*

Adams and rushing to the capital, Dent again returned to Charleston to await orders. Subsequent assignments were a few brief and routine inspections. Yet John Herbert Dent was commissioned captain in June, on the eve of war with Britain.

Throughout the War of 1812, Captain Dent never left Charleston in an official capacity, and his orders indicate an inactive status. This could have been related to his father-in-law's death in the summer of 1812; Dent's services may have been required on the plantations. Yet one doubts that he was indispensable here, given the tradition of responsible stewards. And no sooner was peace established in 1815 than the captain "Wrote from Charleston requesting orders to active service." More specifically and less obviously, he wanted assignment to a northern port for the purpose of a vacation. Now, a minor survey assignment in Baltimore became the means whereby Dent and his wife, Anne, enjoyed extended stay in New York and in Newport, Rhode Island. This was his last active duty, although he tried and failed to secure a command in 1819.[26]

The role of Anne Horry Dent in her husband's plummeting naval career is not known. Given her strength of character, which is known, she surely was not a passive pawn in the matter. Late in life, she wrote of her "utmost disappointments and disgrace" in a way that suggested careless habits on the part of her husband. And there is some hearsay evidence, based on another family legend, that she came to detest her husband's naval career, especially when it meant his going to sea and leaving her. The family's account of Anne's negative response to her son John Horry's desire for a naval career reads: "One sailor in the family had been enough for her, she said, and she did not propose for her son to sail away into oblivion as his father had done." Actually, Captain Dent died of malaria on the plantation in 1823, but the family tradition concerning Anne's views on her son's naval career is probably correct.[27]

Another fact that points toward Anne's desiring the captain's constant company was her willingness to accompany him in the summer of 1815 when the birth of her fourth child was imminent. Her compliant bearing of healthy children at conventional one- and two-year intervals also indicates a general satisfaction with spouse and motherhood. In fourteen years of marriage, she bore eight children, of whom seven survived; and each of those led a long, active life of more than sixty years. Apparently all of the children were born in South Carolina except John Horry, who was born at Newport, Rhode Island, on August 5, 1815, during his parents' postwar vacation in the North. Initially, this son was named Jonah Horry, for his maternal grandfather. But when an older brother named John died, little Jonah was the eldest living son and his name was changed to John Horry Dent. Over the next seven years, he and his older sisters, Emma and Sarah Burnet, were joined by siblings Constance

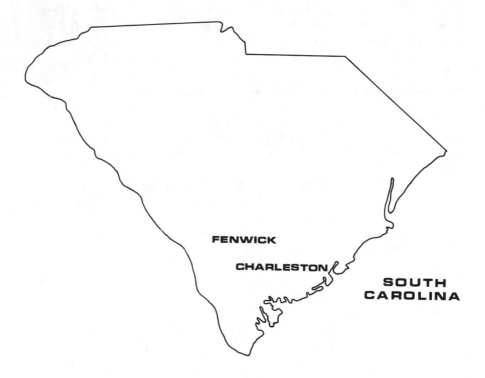

FENWICK

CHARLESTON

SOUTH
CAROLINA

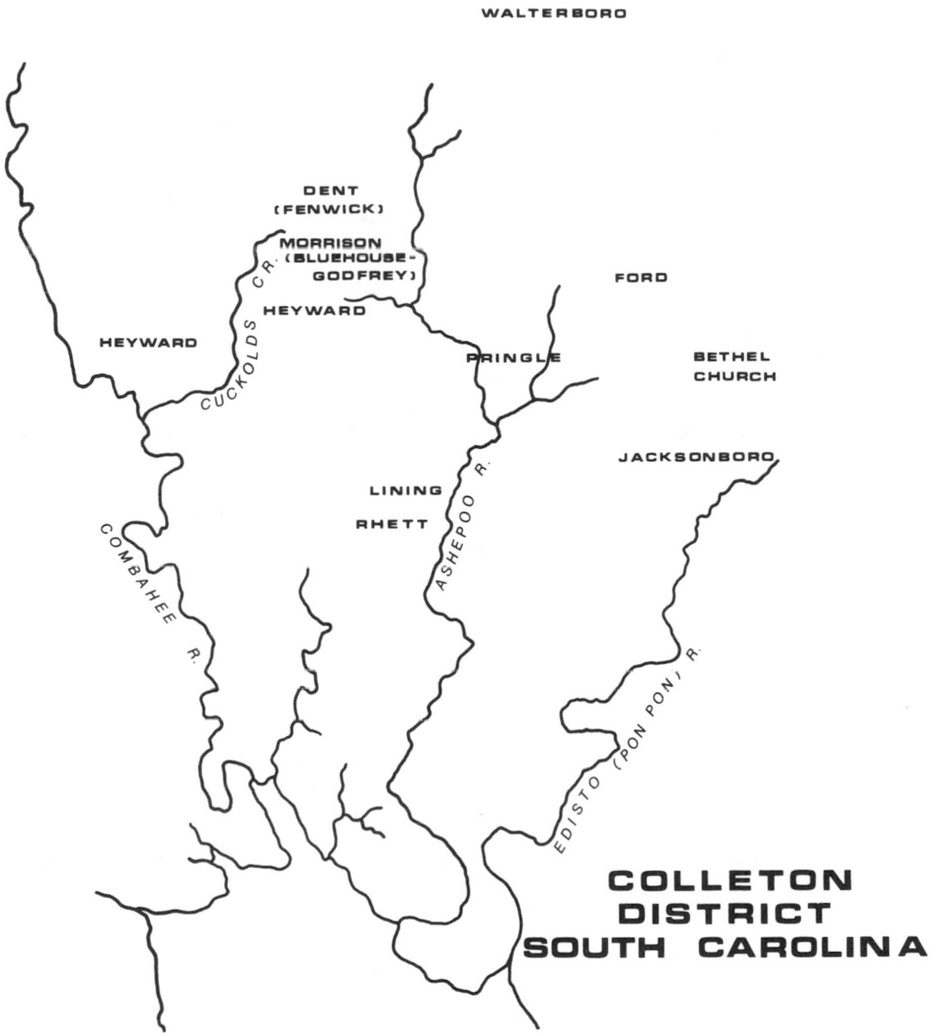

WALTERBORO

DENT
(FENWICK)

MORRISON
(BLUEHOUSE-
GODFREY)

HEYWARD

HEYWARD

FORD

PRINGLE

BETHEL
CHURCH

JACKSONBORO

LINING

RHETT

CUCKOLDS CR.

COMBAHEE R.

ASHEPOO R.

EDISTO (PON PON) R.

**COLLETON
DISTRICT
SOUTH CAROLINA**

Radcliffe, Elizabeth Anne, Kate Anne, and finally George Columbus.[28]

The family was large and basically happy, enjoying its lifestyle, which was the legacy of Jonah Horry. Although John Horry Dent would refer to his "father's plantation," he knew it was inherited from Jonah Horry, the real source of the family's comfortable estate. Despite the inheritance of Fenwick plantation in Colleton and the use of grandmother Lucretia Horry's Charleston townhouse, the Dent family nevertheless "contended with great debts," which resulted from their lifestyle and the South Carolina depression. These debts were especially pressing after Captain Dent's death in 1823.[29]

Still, John Horry Dent would later recall his early years as happy ones. In 1880 he wrote:

> About three or four months after my birth [in Newport] I was taken to their home in South Carolina (Charleston), and raised partly on their Plantation, known as Fenwicks hall, situate on the head Waters of the Combahee River, on Godfreys Savannas, fifty miles by land from the City of Charleston. My Winters were spent on the plantation and My Summers in the Village of Walterborough, until they year 1823, when my Mother changed her Summers Residence to Charleston for the education of her Children, 7 in number. In July 1823 my Father died of Malarial fever on his plantation, so after that period in my 8th year, I was raised entirely under a Mothers care and directions.[30]

The reference to Fenwick Hall on the headwaters of the Combahee River is ambiguous. The fertile rice plantation was actually west of the Ashepoo River and on Cuckold's (or Bluehouse) Creek, which empties into the Combahee. Fenwick was fifteen miles south of Walterboro near the Bluehouse Tavern and post office, which served the public road between the Ashepoo and Combahee rivers. While the plantation residence was sufficient for Anne Dent's pride, this Colleton Fenwick should not be confused with the imposing mansion of that name on the Edisto River near Charleston.[31]

In Colleton, the Dents were a part of the Ashepoo River society that served as the basis of William Gilmore Simms' historical novel *Woodcraft*. An early map shows that in addition to the Heywards and Pringles, prominent neighbors also included the Lowndes, Linings, Rhetts, Barings, Elliots, Morrisons, Radcliffes, Glovers, and Pinckneys. Here the Dent family was socially secure, as the children's marriages indicate. But following the captain's death, Anne was economically more dependent on Lucretia Horry, especially in the matter of educating her children. Though the widow and her brood lived with Lucretia during the unhealthy season, Anne was nevertheless secure and sufficiently solvent to avoid the several perils of remarriage. Another financial help was her inheritance of the bulk of the stepmother's estate in 1835.[32]

John Dent's statement that he was "raised entirely under a Mothers care and directions" was largely true. This condition and the eldest son's independence were the sources for a covert power struggle of several years' duration. John was too independent and rustic in outlook to adjust to Charleston and formal education. This was a major cause of conflict with his mother, who valued good education as a basic instrument for maintaining social status. She believed it was the means for a well-born youth "to win a high position in the community" and to "fill that station in their country to which they have a right from their birth." These convictions led her to sacrifice for the children's education. But the obstreperous John Horry would not be persuaded, at least not while he was young enough to take full advantage of opportunities. He disliked school and dreaded having to board away from home.[33]

In 1880 John Dent recalled his indifference as a scholar:

The first School I ever went to was to a Mrs Adcock in Walterborough, where I was taught my letters. And the next School was to a Mr Green also in Walterborough where I was taught reading and Writing. After that my education was pursued in Charleston, beginning at Miss Blemyers in St Phillips Street. In 1824 I was placed in the Grammar Scholl attached to the Charleston College. My teacher was Thomas Young who afterwards became a Minister of the Episcopal Church. My education was in the Charleston Grammar School and College, excepting in the Summer of 1826 when I went to School in Pendleton Village in the North Western Corner of the State of South Carolina, to one McClintock, and in 1831 I went to Mr W. H. Crouch and Brother in Charleston, who taught in Queen Street. At this school I completed what education I received.[34]

In the long run, however, Anne Dent carried her point, because John later admitted:

My greatest misfortune was when young I did not take advantage of the opportunities given me by Mother . . . [to study] when at School. I was placed at the best Schools, under the best of teachers, but I never applied myself to study, hence the 12 years I was at School I dragged through learning but little, and when through I knew no more than a studious boy would have learned in two years, the result was, I felt my ignorance throughout my life, and nothing bore me out but hard natural sense which God gave me. My natural abilities, my talent, I folded in a napkin.

In this capitulation, Dent exaggerated two points. First, he was not so ignorant as this implies. Second, he was always ambivalent on the relative merits of formal education as opposed to natural ability. Dent came closest to the truth when he acknowledged compensatory self-improvement: "Reading and association was my education." And his was a considerable learning.[35]   It was about 1830 when Anne Dent allegedly prevented him from realizing his aspirations for a naval career. This date would coincide with his leaving school in 1831, perhaps to retaliate. Dent's obsession with the sea never subsided. He sketched numerous types of ships and myriad scenes of naval battle all his life through. But at age sixteen, he took to the woods, to begin his railroad period.

"In 1831," he later recalled,

> I went on the Charleston and Hamburg R Road as Rodman to Lieut Edward Watts, U. S. Army, who was one of the Engineers who assisted in the Surveying and building of this Road, being one of the first Rail Roads built in the United States. I served as Rodman about 13 months under Lieut Watts. When he was ordered off to join his Regiment, I then left the Road and made my Way on foot to Fenwicks Hall. I liked the Rail Road life as Rodman very much. We lived in the Woods and to ourselves, Slept in tents... free from all the restraints and tom foolery of Civilization.[36]

The railroad's right-of-way was not far north of the plantation. And it was significant that Anne Dent's cousin, Elias Horry, was president of the South Carolina Railroad, which included the Charleston and Hamburg line.[37]   John could neglect school against his mother's wishes; there were other opportunities for young gentlemen. Yet he refused formal education, gave up his opportunity to learn surveying, and rejected the polite society of urban Charleston as the needless "restraints and tom foolery of Civilization."

While young Dent preferred the rural environment of Fenwick over Charleston, he could be enticed to take the "Great Northern Tour," a relatively painless, albeit expensive, means to smooth the feathers of a fledgling gentleman. "The Winter of 1833," John wrote,

> I spent at Fenwicks Hall. And in the Summer of 1833 With my Mother and Sister Constance travelled North. . . . In that Summers trip North our journeys were made in Sailing Ships, first from Charleston to New York, and then in Steam Boats, Canal boats, and Stage Coaches. Our tour that Summer extended up the Hudson River to West Point, Albany and to Saratoga, thence by the great Erie Canal to Bufalo, thence by Stages to Niagara falls and by Steam Boats and Stages to Montreal, and by Steam Boat to Quebec in Canada. Returning by Montreal we took a steamer down Lake Champlain to Burlington, Vermont, where we then took the Stage across Vermont, New Hampshire, and Massachusetts to Boston. We were three days and nights making the trip from Burlington to Boston which was then called the fast line of Stages, opposition being none. From Boston, we took Stage to Providence, thence Steamers to New Port and to New York. That rout was then Considered the great Northern tour. . . . Then (1833) the tourist saw the Country mile by mile and came in contact with the people of

all classes as travelling was then by slow stages.... In the fall of 1833 returned to Charleston, South Carolina, Sailing from New York in the Ship ... [of] Capt. N. Cobb.[38]

Dent's love of travel is obvious. The tour probably heightened his sense of social class. But Charleston proved to be no more attractive than before. Thus his stay there was brief, as he soon left for Colleton, having achieved a measure of *détente* with his mother. The arrangement was an interesting one.

The Winter of 1834 I spent at Fenwicks as a kind of Superintendent of the plantation. Most of my time was spent in hunting. And the Summer of 1834 I spent in Walterborough living with General [Malachi ?] Ford. This was the beginning of my life in the Country, which I have lived ever since, having no fancy whatever for a village, town or City life. The Winter of 1835 also the Summer, I spent as in 1834 on the plantation and in Walterborough as superintendent of Old Fenwicks. Those were the only two years of leisure and pleasure I ever enjoyed in my life, having no cares or responsibilities on my mind, as Bunting was my Mothers [white] Overseer and directly responsible for the practical management of Old Fenwicks. And there was never a man I ever knew who I was more attached to than Old Bunting. He was a man after my own heart, rough and ready and true and faithful to his friends.[39]

Here one has in microcosm the subtle and fluid nature of social influence and consciousness in the antebellum South. Young Dent, an hereditary "aristocrat," had taken Bunting, the trusted family steward, as an influential role model. After all, Captain Dent was eleven years dead. And, while Anne Dent recognized and sometimes regretted her son's identification with this social inferior, she could not do much about it. She was dependent on Bunting and also admired him. Furthermore, she needed a young superintendent to assist and eventually replace the aging steward. John's plantation apprenticeship seemed a happy compromise. He had spurned urban society and the learned professions and was proving a ready student of the complexities of rice production.[40]

The intricacies of rice planting included diligent inspection and repair of the earthen dams and large wooden sluice boxes ("trunks"), which utilized the coastal river's flow and ebb of fresh waters to flood and drain the fields at precise intervals. There was also the supervision of each Negro hand's planting and cultivation of about four acres of rice. Once the cereal ripened, it had to be cut on the stalk, stacked, bundled, transported to a barnyard, threshed, pounded free of the outer hull, polished, and finally loaded aboard ship to be sent to market.[41] After this orientation to detail, which he enjoyed, it is little wonder the mature John Dent mastered the minutiae of planting cotton and other crops.

Rice planting was pleasurable, yet Dent refused to live by his mother's crops alone. "In the Summer of 1835," he explained, "a Courting I begun. I thought I ought to Marry and set up for myself. I was tired of the dependent life I was living. And so I set to work in dead earnest to get a wife. I had the Girl in my eye, and I wanted her or none. I courted, was accepted, and on the 30th December 1835, I married Miss Mary Elizabeth Morrison. The ceremony was performed by the Rev. Robert . . . Boyd of the Methodist Church. I married the right Girl, in the right place, which our married life proved." [42]

Compared with the Dents and Horrys, Mary Elizabeth Morrison was of less prestigious—Scotch-Irish—descent. According to one sketchy family account, her impecunious grandfather, John Morrison, had, at an undetermined date, emigrated from County Down, Ireland, to Newburgh, New York. From these modest circumstances, John Morrison's son, Robert, moved to Colleton District, South Carolina, where he "served during the Revolution," and gradually accumulated a sizeable estate, of about 2,000 acres and 140 slaves. When the "self-made" Robert Morrison died in 1821, he was survived by his wife, Mary, a son, James Hamilton, and two daughters, Mary Elizabeth and Julia. By the 1830s the widowed Mrs. Morrison was married to Sampson W. Leith, a physician and state senator. Hamilton Morrison, upon reaching his majority, had taken his portion of the father's estate and moved to the newly opened Indian lands in Barbour County, Alabama. The daughters, Mary Elizabeth and Julia, were to inherit an attractive dowry upon marriage or majority. [43]

Gentleman that he was, John Horry Dent usually neglected to mention Mary Elizabeth's pecuniary attractions. He preferred to emphasize her romantic charms, which were apparently as real as the financial ones. It was for him a particularly happy coincidence of beauty and property, quite similar to his father's experience with Anne Horry, except that the Horry name was more socially prominent than that of Morrison. One might say that John Horry Dent married a social inferior, except that social status was not clearly separate from wealth. The groom brought nothing to the union except his name and reputation, a valuable birthright, nonetheless.

Family approval of marriages involving such property was often important, especially when bride and groom were minors. Elizabeth was eighteen, John twenty. From the Morrison-Leith point of view, Dent's advantages were his family and his enterprising nature. There is some evidence that John deliberately contrived to convince the Morrisons of his competence to manage Mary Elizabeth's portion of the estate. If so, it was an honest act. Although the groom was a minor, the marriage contract granted him full rights of an adult husband over his young wife's property. [44]

As for the Dent family's response, Anne approved the marriage contract, accepted Mary Elizabeth, attended the wedding, bestowed her blessing, and exacted the newlyweds' promises to be a "good Boy and Girl." Yet she was not singularly impressed with the Morrisons' social status. She liked Mary Elizabeth but disapproved of Hamilton and Julia Morrison.

Anne Dent's other children all married "higher" or "better" than John. For example, the second daughter, Sarah Burnet, wed Dr. Thomas Lining, a Colleton physician and sometime planter of distinguished lineage. Another daughter, Elizabeth Anne, married wealth and prestige in Richard Roper of the Charleston mercantile family. Constance Radcliffe wed Charles Baring, the eccentric Englishman whose family included nobility. This American planter not only built St. John's in the Wilderness at Flat Rock, North Carolina, but also was old enough to be Constance's grandfather. Kate Anne Dent was more moderate in accepting the secessionist, R. Barnwell Rhett, in his fifty-seventh year; she was a daughterly thirty-three and could not resist his grief for his first wife and the needs of his several young children. Strong concern for social status apparently motivated these marriages with elderly men and helps explain why the oldest daughter, Emma, never married. [45]

Finally, Anne Dent's successful management of her younger son, George Columbus, is perhaps indicative of her master plan for John, which, as we have seen, he stymied at several points. Being critical of George's "associates," who she believed would "turn out badly," Anne scrimped to remove her youngest to the Hofwyl School in Switzerland. Upon his return home with a "proper" education, Anne succeeded in marrying him "well" to Ophelia Troup, daughter of Dr. James Troup of Darien, Georgia, and niece of the state's governor, George M. Troup. Moving to her new Cedar Hill plantation near Darien in 1844, Anne made George her superintendent and kept him economically dependent upon her until her death in 1856. [46]

Anne Dent's treatment of John and George should not be construed as cruelty. She simply lacked sufficient property both to maintain her expensive tastes and to establish her sons' economic independence. Since she was without the means or the inclination to promote John's personal planting operation in 1835, she was surely amenable to bringing hundreds of additional acres and forty-five more slaves under the family's hegemony. Also Mary Elizabeth Morrison's Godfrey Savanna and Bluehouse plantations adjoined the Fenwick place. Thus Anne's vision of an economically independent older son being near enough to supervise her plantation dispelled any reservations she may have had about Elizabeth Morrison's social status. Furthermore, the two families had been neighbors for years. And the entire community, including Anne Dent, knew that young John was no polished Charlestonian. [47]

In this way, the "right girl in the right place" became his wife. But of Mary Elizabeth's thoughts on the subject, aside from her consent, we know nothing. She must have been as quiet as she was dutiful. Given the male domination of that day, the young wife probably appreciated her marriage and the settlement of her property, for several reasons, not the least of which would be the death of her mother in January, 1836, only a few days after the wedding. This development, Hamilton Morrison's absence, and Julia Morrison's minority, left young John Dent the considerable responsibility of managing the entire estate.[48]

In 1853 he recalled that heady experience: "In the year of our Lord One thousand Eight Hundred and thirty Six, I commenced business on my own account, having married on the 30th December 1835. My first commencement was in managing the property of my Wife and her Sister Julia J Morrison, now Mrs [Edward] Gantt. We planted on the Estates heired from their father, known as the Savanna and Blue House plantations. My success, being my first effort was crowned with prosperous results, having made a very fine [rice] crop, and all things in a thriving condition around us."[49]

The autobiography of 1880 also recounts this success and captures Dent's youthful compulsion to "independence": "In 1836 we lived on the Godfrey Savanna plantation, being her [Mary Elizabeth's] home, and where she was born and raised. And immediately after our Marriage, we set in regularly to business and went to work to try to make a comfortable home and independence. That year we made our first crop and Summered it in the Pinelands adjoining the plantation."[50]

The crop was profitable, and Dent manifested a sign of his mature frugality. It was cheaper to summer on adjacent pinelands than to move to Walterboro or Charleston. Furthermore, he needed all surplus capital he could muster to implement the plan, which Mary Elizabeth allegedly helped formulate: "In turning over in our minds the future and our future prospects, we concluded the little we had was not sufficient to commence life surrounded by a rich and showy people. So we Concluded to move West to a new rich land Country and commence life in earnest. We were both young and hearty and had the Will and enterprise to start life on the frontier among the Indians. We cared nothing about Civilization. We wanted a fair start in lifes journey."[51] The western destination was Barbour County, Alabama. But the Dents' motives for moving to this frontier were more complex than this explanation indicates. Nor is the above statement so simple as it initially appears. As one would expect, Dent offered various explanations in different stages of the journal's evolution. The move to southeastern Alabama became a vital idea, which he nourished for as long as he lived. The adventure was a part of his identity, a piece of living history he had to examine periodically for meaning and self-understanding. Thus, in another context, he explained the move as the simple magnetism of virgin land: "We were dazzled by the great temptations the far West was represented to hold in her bowels, only awaiting the hands of the laborer to possess it."[52]

Learning the truth of this virgin land required a prophet, who in this case was Hamilton Morrison, Elizabeth Dent's brother. On one occasion, John claimed they moved to Alabama because his wife wanted to join her brother in Barbour County. Perhaps this was partially true, but Anne Dent accused John of being the one who followed Hamilton. There was also friction between the Dents and Julia Morrison Gantt. The difficulty stemmed from the sisters' inability to arrive at a satisfactory division of the property they held in common. This conflict probably contributed to the Dents' desire to leave, and it might explain why they departed without selling the plantation or residence.[53]

There was also John's unspoken desire to remove himself from Anne Dent's designs. This was not simple escapism. And if it was unconscious, it was nevertheless as real as his mother's vocal disbelief that he could "bury" himself and his young family in the "wilds of Alabama." After flaying him verbally for settling in the "poorest and most savage part" of that state, Anne Dent revealed the core of their relationship in one artful act of passive aggression. She was the helpless female manipulating for John's return when she wrote: "My spirits are so harassed with hearing of mismanagement and my plantation dropping to pieces for want of the eye of a master that I can say no more at present, except love to Elizabeth." Yet Dent's desire to weaken maternal pressures was only a part of the attraction of Barbour County.[54]

Actually the motive for moving was more than fabled profits from virgin land, family problems, the natural restlessness of youth, or even the rejection of civilization. Dent's criticism of "civilization" notwithstanding, he enjoyed the genteel associations of a mature plantation society. True, he did not care for urban Charleston, but he loved rural and "cultured" Colleton. Perhaps he admired "rich and showy" people so passionately that he could not bear living "beneath" them, a status his mother's debts and the rice planters' economic depression seemed to dictate.[55] In Dent's mind, a secure upper-class status depended on a larger measure of wealth than he possessed. If he was to get a fortune, it would be in the West. Thus he moved, not, perhaps, to gain a "fair start in life's journey," as he wrote, but to brave the temporary loss of civilization in order to build a financial base for living the planter ideal as he conceived it.[56]

In 1837 this member of the lesser gentry was clearly on the economic make. And he could sound the part of an entrepreneurial pioneer: "So in January 1837, we left our Carolina home and by wagons and a Carry all started for the Promised land which was in the Creek Nation in Alabama ...just then settling up by the Whites. Barbour was then one of the newly laid out Counties and *Irwinton*, now *Eufaula*, was the town laid out on the Chattahoochee river as its future commercial emporium.'' [57] Also giving some thought to the problem of gentleman as frontiersman, Dent decided his upper-class manners could survive the southwestern frontier, provided he was the right kind of agrarian.

2

FRONTIER ALABAMA

When John Dent left Colleton District, South Carolina, he was confronted by a frontier that he both appreciated and feared. This ambivalent response to the Alabama frontier reflected an eclectic agrarianism. Henry Nash Smith has argued that the frontier, as virgin land, led Americans by 1830 to a distinction between the western yeoman's agrarianism and that of the southern planter. According to Smith, yeoman agrarians defined land as the major source of wealth and virtue, and idealized the hard labor of the small, independent farmer as the best way of life. Contrasted with this, planter agrarianism supposedly perceived wealth as more than land (e.g., slaves), viewed planting as a means, not an end, and idealized the cultured leisure of the slave-owning "aristocracy" as the highest form of social achievement. [1]

While Smith's literary distinctions are abstract, they help one understand John H. Dent, who occasionally assumed two separate agrarian ideologies but usually behaved as if they were one and the same thing. Dent's easy union of yeoman and planter is most evident in his self-concept as a frontier gentleman and scientific farmer who desired to work a large slave force without a white overseer.

Although Dent's agrarianism was an unstructured cluster of images and ideas, his most basic need was for "independence," or wealth, based on an agricultural way of life. Because farming or planting was the "best" means to that independence, the youthful Dent was willing to move to a frontier that he viewed as an economic opportunity and a cultural threat. He claimed that frontier barbarism threatened his upper-class manner and self-concept. As a balance to the frontier, however, he assumed (as we shall see) that the plantation was both civilizing and exploitative, tending toward culture and economic liability. [2] In this milieu, Dent's goal was to wrest enough financial security from one frontier to enable him to avoid moving to another.

His dual perception of the frontier allowed John Dent to admit the harshness of his early years in Alabama. About 1853, sixteen years after the fact, he recalled the move to Barbour County, a task that consumed the better part of six months. He was twenty-one years old, and Mary Elizabeth nineteen, when "Early in February 1837 we packed up... but few articles necessary merely to avoid exposure, leaving a fine and comfortable house...unsold.... I embarked in Wagons with the negroes, leaving my dear Wife and little son," Robert Morrison, "to remain until I could go and return from the land of promise and provide for the negroes for that year by making support" from a corn crop "for the next year with a part and hireing out the remainder to the best advantage."

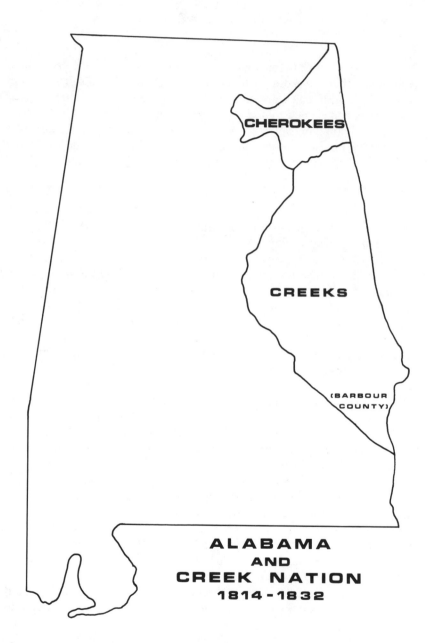

CHEROKEES

CREEKS

(BARBOUR
COUNTY)

ALABAMA
AND
CREEK NATION
1814-1832

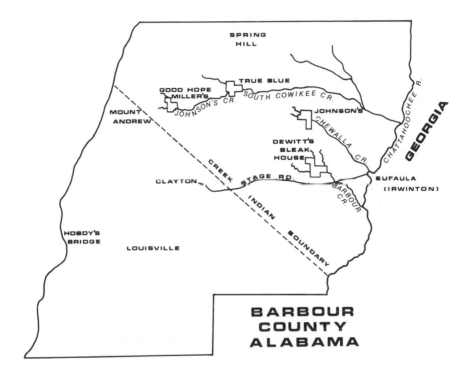

SPRING
HILL

TRUE BLUE

GOOD HOPE
MILLER'S

SOUTH COWIKEE CR.

JOHNSON'S CR.

JOHNSON'S

CHEWALLA CR.

CHATTAHOOCHEE R.

GEORGIA

MOUNT
ANDREW

DEWITT'S
BLEAK
HOUSE

CREEK

CLAYTON

STAGE RD.

EUFAULA
(IRWINTON)

BARBOUR CR.

INDIAN

HOBDY'S
BRIDGE

BOUNDARY

LOUISVILLE

**BARBOUR
COUNTY
ALABAMA**

Dent and the blacks were "a little over three Weeks in making this journey the days being short."[3] It was an overland trip across Georgia and the Chattahoochee River into southeastern Alabama.

Dent knew some local history, but he probably summarized all his knowledge of it when he generalized: "The County of Barbour was constituted in the year . . . [1833] and formed out of a part of Pike [County] and a part of the lands belonging to the Creek Indians. It was named in honor of James Barbour of Virginia, its County seat after Judge [Augustin S.] Clayton of Georgia, two distinguished States Rights men of the Jeffersonian school of politics. Lawson J. Keener, who was the Senator in the State Legislature representing this new County and Russell, proposed the naming of the County and the County seat, which was accepted and confirmed." Here Dent's reaction to the Creek Indians was one of indifference. He made few direct references to them. They were no threat to him or his family, a fact that supports the argument that Barbour County whites' final victory over the Creeks at the Battle of Hobdy's Bridge occurred in March, 1836, rather than one year later, as it is often reported.[4]

By the time of Dent's arrival in 1837, the power of the Creeks was broken and, for him, a matter of past history. It was not a happy story of white-Indian relations. Since the Treaty of Fort Jackson in 1814—whereby the Creeks, recently defeated at Horseshoe Bend, were forced to cede most of the interior portion of Alabama—whites had illegally but persistently encroached upon the remaining Creek domain in eastern Alabama. The last of the Creek Nation in Alabama lay east of a crescent formed by the Coosa River and a line southeastward from the vicinity of Wetumpka to Fort Gaines on the Chattahoochee. The southern portion of the nation included the Indian town of Eufaula and much of the present county of Barbour.[5]

The lands of the southern region were among those most attractive to white settlers. And they came, from Virginia, the Carolinas, Georgia, and especially from the counties of Henry and Pike in Alabama. In addition to isolated conflicts and small skirmishes, there was an "Intruders War" in 1827, a relatively modest affair that changed nothing. By 1832 there were some 30,000 intruders in Creek country. But now the intruders were at home; the Indians had become aliens in their own land. White settlers and speculators were determined to remove the Creeks west of the Mississippi as quickly as possible. In 1832 white men's political pressure eventuated in a new treaty, that of Cussetta, which assigned the lands to individual tribesmen and facilitated whites' purchase of private property from naive aborigines, who did not understand deeds and the legal necessity of vacating lands because of a parchment claim and right. It was all very complicated and tragic, as the inevitable clash of two alien cultures dictated the removal of the less sophisticated one, but not before one last bit of resistance, the Creek War of 1836.[6]

Following the Treaty of Cussetta, whites violated its terms and rushed into Indian country, buying up the land, organizing counties, laying out towns, reducing the forests' game, felling trees, plowing the land, building roads, and terrifying the Indians in numerous ways. Securing no satisfactory redress from local, state, or federal governments, the desperate Creeks retaliated with arms in a pathetic effort that cost some whites' lives and the destruction of the town of Roanoke on the Chattahoochee. For Barbour countians, the most significant event was the March, 1836, Battle of Hobdy's Bridge on the Pea River, in which General William Wellborn led a party of some one hundred whites in the successful capture of encamped Indians said to be traveling south to unite with the Seminoles. The capture of this Indian camp resulted in "indiscriminate slaughter of women, children, old men, and warriors." Estimates of Indian casualties ranged from 50 to 150. No warrior was taken prisoner. Some surviving women and children were enslaved.[7]

Now Indian removal was assured, and Dent was among the last of the influx of white pioneers. Already men like Eli Shorter had demonstrated their mettle as land speculators who amassed innumerable acres from the Indians for sale to immigrating whites. William Irwin had come to Eufaula from Henry County in 1832 and was so important in developing trade on the Chattahoochee that the town bore his name, as Irwinton, until 1844. General John Linguard Hunter arrived at Irwinton from South Carolina in the early 1830s and immediately set about raising its educational and cultural standards. Hunter was reputed to be a relative of the J. H. Dents. There were also the L. J. Keeners and Green Beauchamps. (Keener's role in naming the county and county seat was noted above.) And Beauchamp, a merchant-politician from Henry County, was another founding father whom Dent admired. There were also the planters, large and small, who were primarily interested in cotton production. Barbour's best cotton lands were north of Eufaula in the Cowikee country along the three forks of the creek by that name. Earlier, Dent's brother-in-law, Hamilton Morrison, had settled there, near the small community of Spring Hill.[8]

Preferring the Cowikee country, Dent, the ambitious planter, initially eschewed the progressive Irwinton of bustling commerce, which would soon have a river ferry, post office, newspaper, broad streets, fine homes, churches, academies, and benevolent and literary societies. Having identified Charleston with expensive living and debts, he disliked, perhaps even feared, urban life. This youthful response was reinforced by shocking frontier prices. "Corn was scarce, as well as all kinds of Provisions, the country then being New, and under the difficulties of an

Indian War, which was about ending. Corn $2½ pr Bushel. Meat 25 cents pr pound, and every thing else held in same proportion. Lands in the woods $10 pr Acre, rented at $3½ pr acre." In this situation, Dent promptly "hired out" his slaves, retaining either four or six blacks to plant a corn crop on a piece of land he rented in the former Creek Nation. The crop was probably planted near Morrison's place so that he could supervise it during Dent's forthcoming absence.[9]

No sooner were the slaves "settled" than Dent "returned to Carolina to make speedy arrangements for moving my family out in May. This was accomplished in due time. . . . We were now fairly embarked in a life of hardships, trials, and every deprivation of accustomed comforts and habits." Indeed, Dent remembered that "Everything" in Barbour was "in a Wild unsettled condition. My prospects ahead were dark and gloomy, but I was blessed with a stout heart and strong resolution to do my best and contend against difficulties." This "Herculean task" for one so "young and unexperienced" was rendered even more difficult by the decision to bypass the less isolated Irwinton for a temporary residence in the modest village of Clayton, the county seat, which was situated twenty miles west of the emporium on the Chattahoochee.[10]

The primitive Clayton, as Dent recalled, "was then in embryo. The Court house was a small one room log house. The Jail was a pit in the ground with a heavy log superstructure." The indispensable "tavern" was small; there were but "three or four stores and but a few residences." In spite of its roughness, however, this village was preferable to the wilderness, at least temporarily. Thus immediately upon arrival, Dent "also hired a one room shanty in Clayton for our residence, paying $10 a month for it when the house was actually not worth $20. We adopted this course in order my wife would not be isolated in the woods among the roughest class of frontiers men ever seen. Besides there was some Indians still remaining in the Nation. And it gave me ample time to look about for a home."[11]

Strangely enough, Dent's search for a plantation home took him first to Tuscaloosa, Alabama. Perhaps he required a personal loan to make downpayment for land. He did visit relatives there. Or maybe he simply wanted to see the central and western portions of the state that had been open for whites' settlement since the treaty of Ft. Jackson in 1814. With meager explanation, he wrote, "After settling" the slaves "for the year and making all things as snug" for the family "as possible, in June, on horseback, I set out to see my Uncle Dennis Dent who lived in Tuscaloosa, then the capitol of Alabama. It was a long hot ride. The ride through the Nation was a solitary journey until I fell in with Green Beauchamp who was a member of the Legislature on his way to Tuscaloos[a] also to attend a call session to pass some relief laws for the people, owing to the failure of the United States Bank. This was in June 1837.''[12]

The economic Panic of 1837 was no small matter, even though Dent's blaming the bank as the cause was overly simple and misleading. His openness to ''relief laws for the people'' at that time also accorded with his debtor status, which lasted several years. Furthermore, he admired Beauchamp, probably because he was rough and ready, like Bunting, and because Beauchamp, like Dent, was of Huguenot stock and Maryland ancestry. Dent remembered him as a comfortable traveling companion: ''I did not make all the journey on horeseback. As we [were] going to Tuscaloosa, Beauchamp and myself found it so hot and our horses suffered so much we put them up in a livery Stable in Montgomery and took the Stage for Tuscaloosa. There was not a Rail Road in Alabama at that time. Travelling was done on horseback, Stages, and Steam-boats.''[13]

Uncle Dennis, whom John Dent visited in Tuscaloosa, was also a native Marylander. He was the youngest brother of Captain John Herbert Dent. In west Alabama, Dennis was a successful planter-politician. His imposing Tuscaloosa mansion bespeaks a comfortable existence, impressive to his nephew, who recalled ''remaining in Tuscaloosa for two weeks, where I enjoyed a pleasant visit with my Uncle and relatives.'' The trip from Clayton to the capital and the pleasant association with upper-class kin stimulated Dent to draw a retrospective contrast between old settled Alabama and his new uncivilized county.[14]

The contrast showed sensitivity to social class and frontier barbarism. ''Old Alabama,'' he wrote,

> was then a rich and beautiful Country, settled by an intelligent enterprising population that were wealthy from Cotton planting. Tuscaloosa was noted for its refined population, fine Schools, both for males and females. And the State University was ... located there. Old Alabama, then (contrasted with the Indian Nation just incorporated as a part of the State), presented an appearance of wealth, refinement and elegance in comparrison with the new territory, yet to be cleared up, built up, and settled by civilized people, its present population being Adventurers, Speculators, and pioneer farmers who were moving in to settle fresh plantations to make cotton.[15]

Finding the Black Belt civilization of wealthy plantations preferable to Barbour County's unpolished adventurers, speculators, and pioneer farmers, Dent hastened to identify with an upper-class immigration that he described more sympathetically: ''Up to 1837 Cotton brought a high price, which induced a large emigration from the States of Virginia, North and South Carolina, also from Kentucky and Tennessee, to settle on the rich praries of Alabama and Mississippi for the purpose of planting Cotton. This class of emigrants were wealthy and refined. And it was that population that made Alabama and Mississippi what they turned out to be, first class States. And among all the Southern States, Alabama has no superior.''[16]

In a recollection of 1853, Dent also distinguished among three separate "classes" of settlers in Barbour County. "The first Pioneers" were "fond of hunting and trading with the Indians, by far the most of them detesting an abode among civilized and moral society. . . . The second class of adventurers" was "a set of Men whose whole object" in life "is to make money by trading and Speculation." While some speculators settled down to become productive and permanent citizens, Dent was primarily interested in the "third class of Settlers" who as "Planters and farmers . . . have migrated for the purpose of securing rich and fresh lands for cultivation, to mend or increase their fortunes by growing large crops." Although this "heterogeneous mass" of people and the "unhinged state" of frontier society troubled him, Dent firmly believed he was among the third group of settlers, which had "the brunt to bare. They have to perform the most difficult part of all who proceed or succeed them."

He catalogued the trials of upper-class settlers who had "to contend with predecessors who are in a semisavage state . . . to open roads, clear the lands, and erect the habitations." There were also laws to form, churches to establish, schools to found, in short, everything to do for the "First stages of redemption from a land of Barbarians to a land of civilization." In fact the frontier's threat of demoralization was so great that "With many it has been the stage of ruin." Trusting that he had escaped savagery, Dent attributed his success to the plantation, believing it the primary means for civilizing the wilderness.[17]

Although he identified with upper-class planters, Dent was very sensitive about borrowing money to buy a plantation. In fact, early indebtedness in Alabama was a status he later preferred to forget. Still, Uncle Dennis probably lent the downpayment for the land purchase. The timing of the trip would indicate this, but the nephew only acknowledged that upon returning to Clayton from Tuscaloosa, "I purchased a plantation on the South Cowikee Creek, ten miles north of Clayton, in the swamp, and in the Wilderness." Nothing "but a small patch had been cleared on it and a small log hut built, but the lands were rich and exceedingly productive. Cotton, corn and what else were planted on them grew nearly spontaneously. And it is said to be one of the best plantations in Barbour, this day, 1880.''[18]

The Cowikee swamp was already known for its blue marl lands of sand loam and lime soils, being on the edge of the famed Black Belt of superior cotton lands, which stretched west northwesterly across Alabama. Hamilton Morrison probably informed Dent of the soil situation before he left South Carolina. In 1837 the South Cowikee Fork was a long way, geographically and culturally, from either Tuscaloosa or Irwinton. Choosing the Cowikee location for its soil productivity, Dent purchased an unimproved woodland tract of 680 acres from A. Holder and legislator L. J. Keener. The price was ten dollars an acre, with credit terms allowing three to four years for total payment. Thus, the young gentleman from Colleton, South Carolina, began planting in Alabama during a depression year with an indebtedness of about $7,000. On the other hand, his forty-five slaves represented a collateral of some $25,000. [19]

More immediately pressing than land debt was Dent's need for a cheap place to live, so that his family could vacate the expensive Clayton shanty. There was a "small log hut" on the new plantation, but it was too decayed for respectable whites' habitation. Furthermore, the plantation itself was temporarily inaccessible. As yet, the only route there was by Indian trail. Therefore, Dent drew upon his Carolina heritage and complemented the swampland plantation with a modest "small pine land place . . . on a public road 8 miles from Clayton and three miles from the plantation." The pioneer explained, "At this pine land abode, afterwards known as Mount Andrew, we had hurriedly knocked up a double pen log cabin, rough as rough could be, but made it sufficiently comfortable to keep out rain and shelter us from the Sun. This was designed as a temporary abode until we could build a comfortable dwelling at the Plantation. At this Pine land abode, my daughter Minna was born March 28th, 1838. A healthier, pleasanter spot could not be selected than this pine land place was." [20]

Sensitive to frontier conditions, Dent referred to Minna's birth to attest to the healthfulness of Mount Andrew. He pointedly ignored the fact that little Robert Morrison had died there of croup in November, 1837. But croup was not Dent's nemesis; that was the swampland's malarial, yellow, and typhoid fevers. Each was prevalent on the Cowikee plantation where he chose to live. Meanwhile, there were priorities other than building a plantation house. These included providing for the slaves, clearing land, and planting a provision crop of corn. In 1838 cotton was not a major item on the Dent plantation, which he named Good Hope. Still the family's permanent residence was not built (and then only crudely) until after "lay-by" time in June and July. Lay-by was the last cultivation of the crop before the final ripening that preceded harvest. Dent's only description of this plantation home was a noncommittal "comfortable," a relative term, especially after a year of living in a double-pen log cabin at Mount Andrew. The journal indicates that the hastily constructed residence was a plain frame structure of sawed plank, which was still unsealed against summer heat and winter cold as late as 1841. Thus, Anne Dent could be hypercritical of this son's Spartan standards in plantation housing.[21]

More silk purse than sow's ear, however, he was aware of the isolation of the place:

> In the fall of 1838 we moved to the plantation, where we were shut out from the world for a season. At night the wolves would come up to the yard fence in numbers and keep up such a howling there was no sleeping for them. The calves had to be kept in the yard for safety. But when one gets use to such they mind it no more than the barking of dogs or hooting of Owls. We lived in the midst of Deer, Wild Turkeys, Wolves, and all other animals and birds belonging to the Country, which made living cheap and abundant so far as game was concerned.

He neglected to add that accessible game was a special dispensation, since wolves reduced the pig population for some time.[22]

No sooner had Dent described the plantation's isolation than he turned to defend the location: "This place was 25 miles from Irwinton, now Eufaula, and 10 from Clayton, near enough to either place for one who had a plenty to do and think about in making a home and plantation." By his reasoning, the plantation civilized the wilderness, and the wilderness, in turn, purified the home and plantation. In fact, Dent's strongest defense of isolation was its moral influence. Thus he argued that newspapers, gossip, scandal, "Rail Roads, Telegraphs, and cheap postage are the great demoralizers." Characteristic of the period's ambivalence toward the "machine" in the American "garden," he thought railroads were a necessary business advantage but a threat to rural lifestyle and moral values. Holding to the belief that plantation civilization and frontier opportunities complemented each other, he concluded, "In a year or two we had this place comfortably settled and doing well."[23]

Doing well included profits, a basic prerequisite for the secure life he wished to lead. Thus, during a period of national economic depression, Dent illustrated the capitalizing effect of close management and a frugal living standard. He held plantation costs, including his family's living expenses, to less than $800 per year, largely by planting as much corn as cotton, and his $8,800 income from cotton during 1839 through 1841 enabled him in three years to reduce his debts by $6,000, leaving a balance of some $800. The economic picture, however, was not always bright. The first year was bleak in more ways than just the gray, dank weather of winter in southeastern Alabama. On January 4, 1838, Anne Dent worried in Charleston: "My dear John: I was quite grieved to hear that you are so straitened in your circumstances. If this really be the case, you may draw upon Messrs. P. & M. for fifteen hundred or two thousand dollars to make the first payment of your purchase of land. I trust that you will apply this sum to that purpose alone, and not upon any new and unadvised speculation, for I really fear that you are too young and friendless in your present situation to venture deeply in that line." [24]

She could not help but so advise. And perhaps John paid heed, for in April, 1839, he went to Mobile and borrowed $2,000 from the Planters and Merchants Bank. If Anne signed the note, her son never acknowledged it, and he was careful to retire it in full by 1841. Nor need she have worried about his youthfulness or friendlessness or "unadvised speculation." John Dent would "get on" with people and business. By November, 1839, Anne could write with obvious relief, "I was very much gratified by yours of the 20th Oct., giving such a favorable account of your prospects, which I sincerely hope may be realized." They were realized and more fully than his mother ever knew. But great wealth from planting during the depression of the 1840s required time, and this strained Dent's patience. For example, while economizing in 1841, he nevertheless felt constrained to buy a closed carriage for his family's use. The frugal planter chose a second-hand one, saved $200, and still grumbled that the $500 cost was a "tax upon the Married." [25]

Throughout the 1840s, his primary concern was the profits he was determined to save from the pitfalls of what his mother called unadvised speculation. Not that young Dent opposed speculation, only losses therefrom. Furthermore, his attitude toward speculation would change between the 1840s and the 1860s. In his youthful drive to become a successful speculator, he expressed keen respect for the vocation itself and fear of the debts and corruption that it could foster. Much later, in middle age, Dent, a highly successful planter-speculator-financier, became so critical of speculation that he almost disassociated his self-concept from his real role as a prosperous money lender. But in 1841 he fused the planter and speculator when he observed that to draw a distinction "between the Regular Farmer who enriches himself from the Value of his Crops And the Speculative Farmer who Speculates with the amount procured from his Crops, hazarding a certainty for an Uncertainty . . . will cause much . . . disagreement . . . as the aims of both are for Wealth, but to be procured in different Ways." [26]

Because Dent planned to become a regular farmer and a speculative planter, he admonished himself in a letter to a "friend," dated May 1, 1841:

> As advice let me forewarn you never to be led again in Error as you were by Men who have been thro constant study habits Speculators. Such Men are dependent on their sharpness for a liveing. It has been their Study from Boyhood. They are well acquainted with human Nature, tricks, & Schemes

of all kinds that will answer their ends. And what is worse, If they make well, . . . good. If they Break, their Creditors Suffer. In short their capital is portable and mysterious, far very far different from yourself a farmer. Consequently let such business alone, unless you make it a regular occupation and Study. But pursue regularly Industriously . . . Judiciously tilling the Ground & Economy & you will grow rich fast enough on a solid foundation.[27]

As a practical agrarian, Dent never failed to "speed the plow." But from this time, he was also a close student of speculative profits.

During 1841 he moralized that the farmer's great object of economic independence required that one "first buy what you only stand in need off; what you bargain for pay cash down; and never want anything unless you have the Money to pay down for it." Yet rhetoric of the work ethic was not enough to preserve him from additional debt. Still owing about $800 on his original land purchase, Dent proceeded to buy a larger plantation, which carried a new debt of $6,000.[28] In January, 1842, he explained, "I have Just become comfortably settled, nay, only tolerably so for a frontier residence, When Speculative motives enter the head [and] rush us on to new objects, for better or for Worse, which time only can decide, altho our Calculations were Sanguine."[29]

These calculations included advertising the first plantation for sale, in terms that revealed the extent of improvements at Good Hope. It was "a Valuable plantation on South Cowikee," he stated, "Well improved in every respect, with a good framed dwelling and necessary out buildings, a Good Gin House and Screw, Cribs Barns &c &c. The plantation contains 680 Acres of Land, five Hundred of which is superior Hammock, And four Hundred cleared and in fine Condition for makeing heavy crops. There is a superior Spring and well of water that has never failed in the greatest droughts we have experienced in 38 & 39. Distance from Irwinton 24 miles, and from Clayton Ten. For further particulars apply to John H Dent on the premises."[30]

One suspects that Dent's skepticism of other planters' advertisements should be applied to his own. Still, he found he could swap Good Hope "Containing Six Hundred & Eighty Acres more or less—Rated at $15 pr Acre equal to $10,200 to Wiley Oliver for his plantation [True Blue] Six Miles below on the Cowikee containing 1080 Acres more or less valued at $15 pr Acre equivalent to = $16,200 Causeing the Boot in favor of W Oliver to be $6,000 payable in three equal Installments of $2,000 the first Installment due on the first Jany 1843."[31] True Blue was at present-day Comer, Alabama.

Dent's calculations for this trade included an estimate that it would require ninety "bags" of seven-cent cotton (at 450 pounds per bag) to fetch some $2,835 per annum. This income would meet the yearly land payment of $2,000, leaving $835 for living and plantation expenses. "The

Credit sheet," the cautious speculator admitted, "is estimated at the lowest Market rates, while the debted Sheet is estimated at the highest rates, merely as an estimate, to be sure that the trade can cause no distress or loss of property. Altho for the next three years we may say we have made nothing clear but afterwards the lands may be considered as yielding a heavy Interest on the Capital employed and vested."[32]

Only now was Dent ready to confirm the trade and give his notes. It was done October 15, 1841. Although a successful planter who was sufficiently solvent to expand during an economic depression, he feared the trade "may be termed one of fancy, as the plantation I exchanged for it was in a fair way for making ready money. But what Induced me to make the exchange was that the Lands on this place [Good Hope] were not enough for my [slave] force or to farm on Judiciously. Lands here would soon demand resting. And no more Lands adjoining could be added on at fair rates. And what could be procured at low rates were too broken and Sandy." It does not seem a dubious proposition to desire enough land to occupy a slave force and have some acres fallowing, provided one could afford it, which Dent could. The really "fanciful" aspect of this exchange was his unspoken willingness to move his wife and children into a more isolated situation, where the family residence was also too small for their needs.[33]

On the eve of leaving Good Hope for Wiley Oliver's True Blue plantation six miles farther down the South Cowikee Creek, Dent wished for foresight, hoping that "pleasure and happiness" would be his family's lot. But it was just as well he could not foresee the weather problems and declining cotton prices of the 1840s, which disrupted his primary plan of producing at least ninety "bags" per year as prerequisite to rapid financial success at True Blue. And just before departing Good Hope in January, 1842, he wisely acknowledged the futility of foreknowledge. "Altho curious and anxious to forsee in hopes of pleasure and happiness being realized, Many they are, who could, but on the Mount of foresight, See and learn what a day may bring forth, would leap down the preceipice, and be buried in oblivion. Let us therefore be as prudent, as our abilities will admit, and be Satisfied with the earnings obtained by Industry and economy and 'Speed the Plough.' "[34]

After the first year at True Blue, the John H. Dents entered a seeming Dark Age, the journals from 1843 to 1850 not being available. The artificial drabness of those years is accentuated by Dent's retrospective negative comments on them. As late as 1880, he recalled making "a bad exchange" for Wiley Oliver's True Blue plantation; "so in 1849 I sold the Oliver place and bought back my first place again" at Good Hope. In 1850, nearer the period in question, he was more sanguine, expressing surprise and joy when "we have repurchased the plantation Good Hope, and moved back again.... It may be asked how could it have happened . . . ? The answer is simple: from the ruleing passion that so often governs man, Interest, or what he conceives to be his interest. Perhaps the exchange'' for True Blue "might have been a bad one at first? The answer is, it was, although we lost no property by it." Still, True Blue "did not suit my purpose." [35]

As noted, Dent's "purpose" was wealth rapidly acquired. He would speculate so long as he lost no property by it. And since property was more than land, Dent lost nothing at True Blue. In fact, he probably realized a tidy profit from selling it and returning to Good Hope (now called Miller's) in 1849. Yet the advance had taken longer than he planned. His purpose also included the lifestyle of a successful planter. This, however, raised a larger problem of definition—when did one have enough wealth to live this way, and where did one propose to live? Surely not on the semi-isolated and malaria-ridden Cowikees. These were the real questions agitating Dent in the early 1850s. And the problem assumed crisis proportion in 1853, when his first wife died at Good Hope of malaria and typhoid fever. The lingering burden of this guilt would in 1880 cast a cloud on his view of the whole period (including the True Blue years). [36]

Financially speaking, the 1840s saw much improvement, M. B. Wellborn's "Dent Sketch" to the contrary. [37] Although True Blue's forest proved more intractable, its soils stiffer, and its climate more unhealthy than Dent had anticipated, he nevertheless emerged from that shadowy decade no longer a debtor. His exact financial status is unknown until 1852, three years after he returned to Good Hope. But his one fragmentary table of cotton yields shows True Blue producing an average of eighty-two bales per year. [38] Even at depressed prices, such a crop would have earned about $3,000 per annum. And this does not include Dent's usual incomes from corn, peas, fodder, ginning tolls, and blacksmith and carpenter services. If his annual plantation and living expenses had run $1,500 (and they were probably less), he would have cleared $1,500 a year. A total net income of $12,000 during his eight years at True Blue would mean that Dent paid his debts and still had at least $4,000 for investment and interest. This hypothetical sketch is compatible with his financial status of 1852, which is known.

Also, in 1849, when Dent sold True Blue and repurchased Good Hope, he added 570 acres to the latter and made no mention of new debts. He was surely the creditor in these transactions, for now he spoke of hedging the perils of this speculation with "long reflection and experience." Furthermore, he believed that if the exchange back "be an error, it is one of the head and not of the heart." Even if the exchange itself was not exceedingly profitable, the next few years were. Dent believed he knew the soils at Good Hope, and he was not disappointed. From 1850 through 1854, his cotton crops averaged more than 120 bales per year. Cotton prices were also rising in this decade. In 1852, his cotton alone grossed $5,000. And within a year he had at least $7,000 on short-term loans, much of it at interest rates as high as 16 percent.[39]

But a measure of wealth from True Blue and Good Hope plantations could not in itself resolve Dent's ambivalent need for both frontier profits and a less isolated existence. The mark of this tension is sketched in two letters of 1852 written within nine days of each other. The first was to his brother, George Columbus Dent, a rice planter near Darien, Georgia, on Anne Dent's plantation. It should be recalled that George was everything that John had not become—well educated in Switzerland, married into the prominent Georgia family of Troup, gentleman rice planter who dutifully managed his mother's estate, poor in his own right, but still one of the local sailing set of planters.[40]

The brothers got along famously, even though John envied George's small yacht and attendance at regattas. But more was at issue than sailing when John wrote disarmingly on November 18, 1852:

> I still feel it a very hard matter to shake off my low spirits, which have been a constant companion with me for a long time. I sometimes try and console myself by reading "Zimmerman on Solitude," a delightful little work, by the by, for the time being it affords me great satisfaction as I am inclined to think I can discover the causes, as set down by himself, which leads to such results. But it is not long before I find myself again wandering in gloom and doubts. I need your Sea Co[a]st Society [as] an alter[n]ative with all its various charms and pleasures, which would act as an invigorating potion to mind and body. I have come to this conclusion, that a Sea Co[a]st man should live and die in his accustomed range. Never stray off to the Interior or back country to settle himself—for his condition there becomes, if thus we can express ourselves, like a sheep that has been lost from the flock and is wandering alone in the Wilderness. You understand me, and can sympathize with me.[41]

In the Cowikee swamp, the transplanted gentleman felt alone and misunderstood—at least momentarily. Did Dent contemplate returning to the rice-planting society of his origins? He must have, many times, if for no other reason than his mother's repeated suggestions that he do so. But she was older now and satisfied with George's management and almost reconciled to John's life in Alabama. Any consideration of returning to the Atlantic seaboard was only half serious. But it was a possibility that Dent felt free to consider because of financial security and the growing need to make a change.

He was, however, pondering more than the gentry of the Carolina low-country. He was also attracted to the West, and he perhaps told George more than he realized when he praised "Prescotts Conquest of Mexico," and admitted being enamored of the "chivalric exploits of

Cortes.''[42] Of course he did not mention (and probably did not realize) that Cortes had become a major symbol of the South's westward movement and the expansion of slavery.

On the other hand, the Alabama Dent had contracted a mild case of ''Texas Fever,'' which he did recognize and discussed a few days later with his Uncle Dennis, who now resided in Mobile:

> Dear Uncle, I am glad to learn from you that you intend moving to Texas. . . . For my own part I shall endeavour to get ready and move out with you. Not that I have any great fancy for Texas for the present. But in time [I] believe it will be a great and most desireable country. As such, it is well enough to move out early, when you can take advantages in selecting a valuable plantation for but little money. From all I can learn of the Country, I deem the Interior most favourable than towards the coast on Eastern Counties. Near the coast you are subject to . . . fevers, also in the Eastern parts . . . other high grades of fever prevail to an alarming extent. As such it would never . . . do to settle down in parts where sickness would be our annual portion, and particularly as your sons and myself have a young family on hand. . . . The most desireable population will concentrate where health and good lands can be combined.[43]

Dent concluded this long, rambling letter with a prescient comment on Texas' future and an unprophetic one concerning his removal there. ''We must plant the tree, our children are to gather its fruits. Its for them that I am promted to move there alone, as it is to be in their day and time that the resources and advantages of Texas are to be realized, and scarcely before, unless Providence in his mercy should grant to us a long and active life. Provided nothing serious occurs to prevent or change my plans, I shall endeavour to sell my Plantation in Alabama, the ensuing Summer and make ready to leave for Texas, early in October 1854.''[44]

Neither John Dent nor his Uncle Dennis ever moved to Texas. But the younger man's preoccupation with sickness and the need for a healthful location tells much about the source of his general indecision and anxiety. Good Hope was still a productive plantation. But it was isolated and increasingly dangerous because of the growing prevalence of fevers. Dent acknowledged, years later, that ''On the Cowikees it was very sickly, and year after year we had to contend with much illness.'' In the three years since the return to Good Hope, Negroes had died at an alarming rate. The master's sense of responsibility dictated a move. Financially, he could afford one, and the burden of choice was on him. The alternatives were not attractive. Rice planting on the Atlantic coast was not especially profitable. A way of life based on virgin land should logically follow virgin land, but he dreaded the troubles of a new frontier in Texas, and Good Hope seemed too productive to exchange it for a healthier, less isolated plantation in Barbour County that, more than likely, was on the verge of being deserted because of depleted soils. [45]

Thus, Dent continued on the South Cowikee. And given the South Carolina heritage of "summering" in safety, his unwillingness to remove the family to sandy pinelands during the dangerous season is remarkable, even inexplicable, unless he judged that he could not afford two households. Whatever the full explanation, he procrastinated and he prospered. The tension between Cowikee profits and responsibility for a healthy lifestyle was enough to produce ennui if not outright terror. Concern for family health would prove to be justified. [46]

By 1880 Dent was able to recall the tragic deaths of 1853 with a calm that belied his earlier despair: "On my . . . Cowikee place my Wife Mary Elizabeth died, Sept. 16th 1853 in her 37th year. This was a great loss, leaving 8 children to my care. The same year some 16 negroes died, all from a malignant fever which assumed an epidemic form. It was what has been called since typhoid malarial fever." This was the hardest blow of his life. Sometime nearer the event, he noted that "September 16th 1853 was a day of sorrow and trouble. That day my beloved wife and companion Mary Elizabeth died, after a sickness of 9 days, which she bore with Christian resignation." [47]

Dent always regretted the loss of Negroes—as laborers, if for no other reason. But Elizabeth's death assumed the character of a judgment. Not that he recognized his response, but the pattern is clear from his sense of guilt and penitential behavior. As a rationalistic Episcopalian descended from French Calvinists, Dent could hold a strong doctrine of Providence as an impersonal force of cause and effect. In the year of Elizabeth's death, he believed, Providence judged him an irresponsible family head and mocked him with the largest crops he ever produced in Barbour County—216 bales of cotton and 4,000 bushels of corn. Now, however, there was but little satisfaction in swampland profits. [48]

Dent's response to Elizabeth's death was one of intense grief and lingering gloom. Because emotional lamentations were neither characteristic of, nor congenial to, the rational Dent, he later concealed those in the 1851-1854 journal by removing some pages and pasting newspaper clippings over others which survive in a mutilated form. On these pages, the strong permanent ink of Dent's comment has withstood extensive soaking and scraping away of pasted materials. Slowly, one finds that his immediate grief became a deadening throb of guilt not easily absolved. Almost twelve months after Elizabeth's death, Anne Dent was still responding to her son's guilt-laden letters:

> It is true that I can do nothing to alleviate your distress but listen to it with the most heartfelt sympathy, and having experienced all your troubles, I

know that it is some relief to be sure that some you love take an interest in all your concerns. Every human being makes great mistakes in their journey thru life, and none more than myself. You have been as much mistaken as others, but as it is useless to repine, it is useless to look back. We must only make the best of our experience to guide us for the future, and with the best resolutions and calculations, you may rest assured that we shall go on making mistakes and regretting them as long as we live.[49]

The letter evoking this response is not available. But Dent identified some of his "mistakes" in the mutilated journal's account of "Settling in Alabama." Now he insisted it was his wife's desire to be near her brother that motivated the move from South Carolina to Alabama. The account also presents his most negative view of frontier savagery. It was here that he distinguished among three types or classes of settlers—first, the hunters and traders; second, the speculators; and third, the upper class, as constructive builders of permanent society and civilization. Dent's inclusion of himself among the third group was perhaps premature, but it was the role he had always defined for himself and the one that he pursued after 1854. Becoming a more responsible member of a less isolated society was in part a penance for previous negligence. On the other hand, it was simply fulfilling the ideal he had always held and lived to a lesser degree.[50]

But any metamorphosis, however elementary, requires some time. And since Mary Elizabeth died late in 1853, there was little Dent could do but remain at Good Hope and plant during 1854. After all, he had a considerable responsibility in some eighty slaves who required occupation and provision of life's necessities. Dent might be emotionally distraught, but he remembered the cost of living. Even though he determined to sell Good Hope, there would have to be one last crop there while he reorganized his life. Preoccupied with the changes before him, he reduced his cotton acreage and paid less attention than usual to planting. That year's small yield reflected unfavorable weather and his negligence.[51]

For the time being, at least, there were problems more pressing than crops and yields. One was whether he should take advantage of this unwelcome disruption to pull up roots and move to Texas' virgin land. The vision of that fever lingered, and Dent was infected enough to put the question. His mother's emphatic "no" was based on her cultured disdain for the uncivilized frontier. "My dear John," she wrote on March 9, 1854,

As you have always expressed a high consideration for my opinion, I feel bound to give it to you freely on a subject of so much importance as another removal.... I must say that I totally disapprove of it.... I feel it a very unwise step. Your gains at present are moderate and your expenses great.

With so large a family, you can never do more than bring them up properly. As to leaving or giving each a large portion, you will admit it to be impossible. To make a fortune by planting requires a lifetime, and a life time spent in privations and annoyances of every description. Civilization is approaching [you] and your railroads and steamers allow you to give your children some education, and in time an intercourse with their relations, of which you now feel the value and regret the loss. Still we are within reach of each other and the younger portion of the family, but if you remove to Texas, you may make a larger income, but your children must grow up perfectly rough and uncultivated. Out of these rough materials have frequently sprung up our greatest men, but I would think seriously before I again plunged into the wilderness.[52]

The frontier might not be all bad, but Anne believed the odds were against its producing a gentleman. It was also in her self-interest to keep John's family in Alabama. But Anne Dent's argument for a cultured life is clear. And when John later declared against removal to Texas, it was largely for the reason she expressed.

If he was to remain in Alabama on a healthy plantation, he had to convince himself of the advantages inherent in replenishing worn soils. Now Dent would declare: "It is high time to abandon this fresh land system of culture. Our jaded plantations can no longer be profitably managed in such a way. Ruin and desolation must be the results. Hard labor unprofitably bestowed and a large capital fruitlessly expended is the result of so injudicious a policy. Our policy is to restore matters, have an eye to readjusting every thing and what is to be done, do it, with an object of permanency and profit."[53] Not that Dent waited until 1854 to begin rebuilding his soils; he was a conservationist from the first. On the other hand, the clear alternative to uncivilized Texas would have to be a more intensive conservation than he had yet practiced.

The further renaissance of this low-country gentleman included the elevation of family health to a higher priority. "The Summer of 1854," Dent recalled, "I rented a house in Clayton to remove my Children to, fearing a recurrence of the sickness we experienced in the Summer of 1853 and Winter of 1854, which sickness continued until the fall of 1854. I also felt bad and miserable on a place I met up with such afflictions and dreadful losses and was anxious to get away from it on any excuse."[54] He could have added, so long as it did not involve any loss of property. But in fairness to Dent's genuine burden of guilt, the pall of his depression persisted.

With all this, however, he managed to reason that eight children, whose ages ranged from one to sixteen years, needed a mother; that a plantation needed a mistress; and that he needed a wife. No satisfactory housekeeper could be had. The reviving family head saw his duty and "spent a pleasant Summer"—a-courting, we may assume. For on

July 26, 1854, in Clayton, Dent "married Miss Fanny A Whipple at the residence of Mr Charles Petty, and was married by Mr Wm B. Neal of the Methodist Church." Since the groom was no churchman, the minister was probably the bride's. Fanny Whipple, a practical, educated woman, was a transplanted Yankee from Richmond, Vermont, who had been teaching school in the county seat of Barbour. Her strong personality and enterprising nature contributed to a happy marriage and family life.[55]

Still Dent's maudlin preoccupation with guilt continued for some time and temporarily increased with marriage and his obvious good fortune and pleasure in the new Mrs. Dent. Surely it was anxiety about the second marriage when he asked himself: "What do you think of dreams, do you dream and soon forget it or do you dream and reflect about them? I do not mean every dream you have dreampt, for too many are frivolous and absurd. I allude only to important dreams such as are calculated to make an impression upon one.... To dream though of the dead one you dearly loved is sometimes pleasant, and sometimes very miserable in it's effects; for instance, to dream you saw your departed wife about to be married to another."[56]

It was this persistent morbidity that two months after the wedding prompted his mother to write with understandable vexation:

> My dear John: I...write you...to express my concern in your great afflictions and to exhort you to strive to keep up your courage.... You have added to your family a young Lady whom you thoroughly approve of, and who I trust deserves the good opinion you have formed of her. It is both your duty and your interest to endeavor to make her happy, which you certainly cannot do if you indulge these morbid reflexions upon the past—that past over which we have no power, but from which we may derive experience to guide our future conduct. I highly approve of the situation you have chosen for your plantation. Your situation has hitherto been too remote and solitary, and when you have finished your house in Eufaula, if I preserve my health and strength, I will visit your family there once more.[57]

While John visited his South Carolina relatives regularly, almost annually, his mother was reluctant to travel west. She had, however, visited her "frontier" son and his "deprived" children in the interval between the death of Mary Elizabeth and the marriage to Fanny Whipple. And as Anne Dent's letter indicates, John had purchased another plantation as well as fourteen acres of land in the city of Eufaula. This was a new departure. Although the recently acquired Jonathan D. Johnson plantation was more healthful and accessible than Good Hope, its location on the Chewalla Creek was several miles from Eufaula and still rather isolated. Furthermore, the new Dent was drawn not to Clayton but to the more populous and accessible Bluff City of Eufaula, where he purchased fashionably located town lots from Eli Shorter for the obvious purpose of providing his family an urban residence.[58]

Surely these transactions were made in a slough of despond, for Dent abided by neither. Perhaps his mother prevailed on him during her trip. At any rate, the Johnson trade was ill advised: the place turned out to be a sore disappointment of dilapidated buildings and hopeless soils. Nor did Dent relish the idea of a townhouse that would keep him away from his plantation. Still, there was the problem of isolation and the need to reduce it, especially for the teen-aged children's education and socializing, needs that a private tutor could no longer meet. Selling Miller's (Good Hope) plantation in November, 1854, the Dents left it in late December with "mingled emotions" and moved to the run-down Johnson's. Perhaps he always meant it to be a temporary location until a more "suitable" plantation could be bought. Dent once wrote that he would sell Johnson's when he could raise its value from $10 to $12.50 per acre. But within two weeks of arriving on the Chewalla Creek, he had traded the Johnson plantation (valued at $10 per acre) for the former William T. DeWitt place and moved to it on the Barbour Creek within five miles of Eufaula.[59] Here he was as close as he ever came to the worn but prestigious estates on the Chattahoochee.

The decision and the second move were so sudden that Dent felt obliged to justify them. Calling the new plantation variously by the names of DeWitt's, Bleak House, Bleak Hill, and Sedgefield, he wrote:

Moved my Negroes to this Plantation from the Johnson Plantation on Monday January 8th 1855. The Johnson plantation I was very much deceived in, the lands were more inferior than I took them to be, and a great deal more broken. So much so I considered they were not worth the labor to put them in cultivation; they would wash away immediately so soon as the roots were out of them. I also found that an immense deal of labor was necessary to put the plantation in order. A large amount of land was to clear. All of the buildings were to be rebuilt, as well as fencing to repair and make new. As Such my prospects were poor for making anything like full crops, hence on consideration, believed it best to exchange it with J. C. Cook for the DeWitt plantation and give him the difference in both, which was $3500. The Johnson place contained 1040 acres, cost $10400, the DeWitt place, 1320 acres— 720 acres cleared (Well and newly settled, excepting the dwelling which needs some repairing)—and cost me $13,900, which is $1400 more than the Miller place [Good Hope] I sold for [$12,500]. Taking into consideration the conveniences of the DeWitt place—it being but 5 miles to Eufaula, the Miller was 25, and many other important considerations as regards health Water and Milking—the boot of $1400 between the two places I considered the relative valuation of each in difference between the two places. The greatest Labor to be done on this place is to put the fences in good repair. Timber is plentiful and convenient, and to bridge the Creek, there is 580 acres level free lands and the hills lay easy to work; the cultivation is by no means hard on hands. Such were my inducements to make the trade.[60]

Yet Dent was ambivalent about the new plantation's proximity to Eufaula. DeWitt's being only five miles from that river town removed the family's need for an urban residence, and plans for the townhouse were summarily dropped. The master must have appreciated this development. One can only wonder whether the new Mrs. Dent was as pleased as her husband. And while John thoroughly enjoyed his and the family's expanding social life, there was reason for pause, as the thrifty planter grumbled, "Living so near Eufaula causes me to make more business there of no profit whatever but considerable expense."[61]

Costs *did* grow apace, and this concerned Dent. But he kept a moderate rein here, even as he concentrated with renewed intensity upon his first vocation as a planter. His major worry was worn soils, which he determined to rebuild with systematic manuring, cotton seeding, marling, leguming, deep plowing, leveling, ditching, draining, rotating, and resting. Always interested in agricultural reform, he was methodical in the late 1850s. Yet he undercut this program at a crucial point, when rising cotton prices led to his increasing that acreage right down to the time of the Civil War.[62]

Dent's major achievement as a conservationist was his resisting the continuing lure of fresh lands. With this sacrifice, his new posture as lord of a "mature" plantation could be condescending. Declining the 1855 invitation of a former associate, H. H. Field, to join him in Texas, Dent was actually rude. Here he appropriated his mother's theme, that the economic advantages of strong soil would not offset Texas' "utter deprivations of Schools and society." In the margin of his copy of the letter to Field, Dent noted smugly at some later date, "Major Field made an utter failure in Texas and died of disappointment."[63]

Yet time and soil exhaustion could momentarily weaken the resolve of even a John H. Dent. By 1858 he was considering advertising Bleak House for sale at $15,000, which was only $1,100 more than he paid for it. He had improved about all he could, given his unwillingness to reduce cotton acreage or buy additional lands for large-scale rotation. Also in January, 1859, he noted that the "repairing on the plantation this year is much less than any previous year, as everything is in good order." Such an observation constituted a logical prelude to visiting Texas.[64]

Two months before traveling west, however, he cautioned himself:

Moving is at all times hazardous under the most favorable circumstances. It is attended with loss of property and time, in short it is a speculation. There are circumstances though, which warrants one to incur the risks and losses attending such a step. To work a force on poor and exhausted lands is a loss of time and capital, an investment poorly made, one in the end sacraficing if not ruinous. As Such, when we cannot procure suitable lands around or convenient to us, to properly employ our forces, a move to a new Country becomes a matter of duty, if not necessity. How then should we act? Why? make a tour of investigation and observation to the West and in so doing bring to bear all the circumstances, pro and con, before definitely deciding on any positive course. For rich lands are not the paramount objects. Health, facilities, civilization and other things are to be classed above rich swamps, more often proving the grave to all your hopes and people, than the benefit in quest of by the move. Give me in preference to the very rich lands constituting Swamps and Lakes, the upland plateau, capable of producing the medium crops, when health and comforts may be enjoyed, and the inundations and disasters of the low lands may be avoided. In exploring the West such considerations shall influence my researches and not the one common idea that rules that Cotton is paramount to all other considerations and objects. [65]

Despite misgivings, from March 9 to April 3, 1859, Dent was absent from Bleak House, examining Texas. His traveling companion was Maximilian B. Wellborn, husband of his oldest daughter, Emma. The detailed memoir of the Texas trip is too long for our purposes, but a close reading of it shows that his "spirit for emigration" included a love of travel and the desire to visit an old pioneering buddy from Colleton, South Carolina, James Hamilton Morrison, brother of the first Mrs. Dent. The Morrisons had been in Grimes County, Texas, since 1847, and were reputedly prosperous and healthy. Dent had been wanting to see them and their "country" since 1852. [66]

He enjoyed visiting the Morrisons, but the locale was not appealing:

Texas so far made an unfavorable impression on me. It was wild, very sparsely settled, and the roughest set of people I ever saw, just that class I met up with in the settlement of the Creek Nation in Alabama. True, they were many good and refined people settled in Texas, but in a territory so large and new, they were found few and far between. But the moore I saw of the Country and its surroundings, the less I fancied it for my future home. I was well satisfied that there was as good lands, and far better advantages to be found in the States of Alabama and Mississippi than Texas then offered, that could be reached with ... [less] expense and trouble, compared to the long overland journey it would take to go to Texas. Again from investigations, I found but few who had moved to Texas were satisfied. At least two thirds were discont[ent]ed and disappointed and heartily wished themselves back to the homes they had left, and would say, if you are doing well where you are now living, best remain quiet and satisfied. I took such advice, and returned to my home in Alabama. [67]

Although Dent had little desire to move west, his capitalistic side required periodic justification for rejecting frontier profits. When he examined the Yazoo delta in Mississippi (August, 1861), he judged the place too unhealthy for his family, not to mention its exposure to Yankee invasion during the war then transpiring.[68] His rejection of Mississippi included the same arguments as those against Texas, but there were other factors he did not enumerate. For example, he still had new ground to clear and plant in Barbour County, and he had become a significant financier and bank investor in southeastern Alabama. From 1852 to 1860, his personal loans rose from $7,000 to $54,000. (The several recipients of personal loans included prominent Barbour County factors, politicians, physicians, and merchants like E. B. Young, Eli Shorter, James L. Pugh, John C. McNeill, and Charles Petty.) After 1858 Dent also owned stock in John McNab's Eastern Bank of Alabama. By 1860 his estate was worth about $200,000. If Dent's slaves were worth $25,000 in 1837 and his assets in 1860 were $200,000, the average annual increase in capital gains was 9.5 percent. Obviously, the rate of increase was much faster in the 1850s.[69]

Such a comfortable member of the Barbour County establishment was understandably in no great hurry to settle a new frontier. Furthermore, short-term loans and bank stock now provided the very financial security that his maturing plantation seemed to threaten. Perhaps Dent viewed his financial business as a type of frontier. He certainly associated it with the West in one statement, which reflected embarrassment at its uncouth demands. As late as January 1, 1858, he complained from Barbour Creek, "When a youth in South Carolina, the New Year was a holiday, celebrated by social parties and amusements. But in the West, now a days, it is a day of Business where creditors and Debtors haul over their papers, ready for the adjustment of their annual contracts."[70]

Believing that moneylending sullied his agrarian image, the later Dent wrote little of this activity, and then in a negative vein, claiming a desire to be free of it. By the 1860s he sometimes refused to identify with speculators.[71] And from the mid 1850s he preferred to discuss scientific farming, not usury, as the means of resolving the tension between the yeoman's uncultured independence and the planter's civilized insolvency. Dent's rhetoric on scientific farming was often idealistic. He sometimes employed the verbal images of the American Garden as the hope of the world.[72]

In 1880 he explained his providential and natural vocation. "Farming," Dent wrote,

> was never my taste or desire; circumstances made me a farmer. My natural taste and desire when growing up was to go to Sea, but in this I was disappointed. Had I my life to go over again, and with the experience I now have, farming would be my choice as a lifetime occupation. Like all other

pursuits it has its trials and troubles, but on the whole, a farmer can manage and controll his affairs, more in accordance to his own likeing and wishes than in any other business. There is an Independence in the life of a farmer, provided he keeps out of debt, that no other occupation affords. A well to do farmer should be the happyest of all men, as his reliance is on God and himself, for his life is engaged in a pursuit that God chose for him to pursue. Its mans natural occupation.[73]

If Dent began planting from a sense of duty to his mother, as he insisted, an early marriage nevertheless made that vocation an immediate source of "pleasure or profit," two aspects of farming he could not separate.[74] Believing that agricultural self-sufficiency and diversification were the means to independence and virtue, he argued that the "first and Great aim" of the

Judicious and economical farmer... is to raise as much of all kinds of Grain and so much of a staple comodity as will not reduce or interfere with his consumption crop, so as not to force him to buy bread abroad or restrict his Labourers or Animals in the least from that plenty, which is the Joy and Happiness of the Farmer. His great object is to live in Independence. Barns Well filled with the fruits of his Labour, Cattle and Brutes of all kinds sleek and fat, and the Husbandman with his household and Labourers recompensed with the bounty of Providence, and the self Government of all that is his not troubled or Harassed with the business of other Men or the frequent Visits of his Creditors. His transactions with Men are punctual and Just, his Word a Bond, and promises punctually performed.[75]

"Laborers" was a euphemism for slaves. And plantation agriculture was farming, provided the plantation produced its own food and escaped ruinous debts. In fact, Dent argued that financial success was merely a matter of management. "It is not the crops made that enhances the Wealth or prosperity of the planter, but it is the care and providence in the management and disposal of the Crop."[76] Dent's method might be scientific farming, but his goal was great wealth. In the prologue to the 1840 journal, he explained, "This Book is intended not only to ascertain the Actual Expenditures and Income of My Estate, But to guide my future Course in Business and farming. By references and Experience, By Referring to dates, Crops &c I can see whether I am backwar[d]s or advanced."[77]

In this same vein, Dent informed his overseer that "System is the only Method to manage a plantation Well." Pursuing the theme, he noted that George "Washington remarked, 'a bad system is better than none.'" Washington's advice to farmers was well known, and Dent's reference to him was fleeting. But it tells much of his concept of farming, since Washington was nineteenth-century America's ideal citizen, who, as a prosperous planter-farmer, rendered the highest possible service to his nation and his fellow citizens.[78]   Many historians prefer to ignore the issue of myths, symbols, and images, but Washington was a major influence.[79]   And, as the product of an age that idealized Washington, Dent's practical agrarianism included a commitment to service as well as to success.   The Alabamian would aid his community as gadfly for scientific farming.

This route of service was not so inviting as it might at first appear, because the antebellum South did not appreciate agricultural reformers. Yet we find Dent on the South Cowikee Creek in 1842, sending a "Letter to the Chairman of the Agricultureal Society of Barbour County, Relative Establishing a Press for the Promotion and Advanceing Experiments and knowledge on Farming & Husbandry."   Herein, Dent said it was "essential to be of much use to the farmers in general or the members of the Society itself that a press should be established . . . on a cheap scale, so as all classes of Farmers can be able to take it.   It can only be by this course that our Society can be of that use and benefit for which it was intended." After suggesting the means for establishing an inexpensive journal, Dent hinted at his willingness to edit such a paper.[80]   There is no evidence that he did, but he claimed in 1886 that he had written for agricultural "Works" for forty years.

As early as 1842, Dent's interest in the "science of farming" was avowedly "to enlighten and improve the manner of Culture, and make the business more profitable in Saving lands and rearing larger crops, by a system of economical husbandry."   Frustration with the Barbour County Agricultural Society seemingly led to some hard feelings, at least temporarily.   But Dent continued to experiment and to present his findings and observations in his own farm journal, if nowhere else.   Many of his manuscript essays were intended for publication and some were printed. Still, in the antebellum period, he did not discuss specific publications or his reading in the agricultural press.[81]   Yet early in the 1850s, he described proper agricultural writing: "if you desire to enter into the field of Agricultural Writers, never suffer your self to be run away with visionary schemes or excited imaginations, but reduce every thing to a matter of fact basis that may be placed in the reach of every man.   Let your experiments, be it One Acre or Fifty, be conducted in a manner as can be carried out in general culture."[82]

It was good advice, but Dent was better at exhorting than he was at objective reporting.   While he refused to identify with other planters whose emphasis on cotton production he both shared and feared, it was they whom he hoped to impress and perhaps even change.   The result was agricultural comment that sometimes sounds judgmental and insincere.   Remarks on the corn crop of 1852 are a case in point.   "My reasons for putting our strongest lands in Corn are for the purpose of making abundant Provisions. I consider it poor policy to make Cotton to buy Provisions with. And again bought Corn fattens stock but little and is dealt out most spareingly. Large, full Cribs enable the Farmer to be prepared to Work with cheerfulness & strength. He feels more satisfied and contented when he knows every thing is well fed, hearty and strong.''

Dent, a long-time hog producer, continued with measured condescension: "Again, heretofore we have entirely neglected the raising of hogs. Tennessee, Kentucky, and New Orleans have supplied us at most exorbitant and ruinous prices, taking from us a large profit of our crops. This I am now endeavouring to remedy, by raising large Corn Crops and other grains, so as I can raise my own pork. We have now a splendid young stock off over 100 head raising, fat and thrifty. Corn with myself is the most important Crop. I pay more attention to it, than anything else I cultivate.'' [83]

Perhaps. But Dent was also an unflagging planter of cotton. Yet for him, scientific farming meant diversification and provisions, primarily corn and hogs. And as early as 1842, he had developed (or borrowed) a complicated system of grain lots that he never fully implemented. Nevertheless, he presented a large design for grain lots that are "too well known and appreciated among farmers, not only for the production and value of the Grain Grown on them, but for the pastureage it affords to stock and the preservation to Lands, when sewn in regular Rotation.'' The plan called for four separate lots of barley, wheat, rye, and oats in conjunction with peach orchards, so that after harvesting the grain and peaches, the remaining stubble, waste grain, and fallen fruit "Serves as a rich and fattening pastures to Hogs. No Farmer can raise or keep a thriveing stock of Hogs until he carries this System in operation on his farm, Unless he uses more Corn for his Hogs than four times their Value. Economy is in its full System with the Grain Lots & Orchards, for the Hogs partake & thrive off that which would be lost.'' [84]

In reality, Dent's fifty to eighty acres of small grains never met the above standards. Nor did he produce more than half the plantation's pork requirement before the Civil War. Yet he persisted in describing the means for improved meat production, even in instructions to young and inexperienced overseers who could not be expected to appreciate his "matter of fact basis'' and close attention to detail. [85]

Surely Dent wanted an audience larger than an overseer when he wrote that in hog production "the Most important and first step is in procureing a Good Boar, and treating him with great attention and kindness. A New Boar should be procured every four Years, unless the change is made in the Sows, and eaven when his get have been selected for breed, it is then necessary for a change of Boar.'' On the other hand, sows "should be selected from the two finest pigs of every litter.... If the boar should be round and heavy built, Sows of Large and long shaped should be selected,

As a cross of such kinds would produce pigs of a medium size and more thrifty and hardy in constitution. The same rule should be applied if the Boar was Large and Long. Select Heavy Sows.''

Proper pens were also important. "Hogs by Nature are rood and crabid, consequently they must be so classed in pens, in order they may be matched in size and strength. Feed them at a regular hour every day, and the most appropriate time is at sun set. Make each class go to its regular pens, feed them, and fasten them for the night and at day light turn them out. By this System they become regular in comeing to quarters every evening; they rest Well at night undisturbed, and are fresh and ready for seeking food in their range when turned out of mornings.''[86]

This plan was for pastured hogs. But Dent, like most of his neighbors, had another kind as well. "Range Hogs should be Never enticed more than twice a Week to the pens if possible, for if they are accustomed to be fed regularly, they would soon be made lazy and dependent on what you would give them and never go in quest of food in their usual Range.''[87] Actually, neither Dent nor the overseer could supervise such intensive care. Thus, by 1852 the master had detailed "one trusty hand to attend to them, and hold him responsible for their treatment, once a Week your seeing yourself that they are properly cared for, and judiciously managed.''[88]

Scientific farming also included sheep "for food and clothing" because a "well disciplined farm here where nature has done so much ... Should purchase only their Iron, Coffee, and Salt; the rest of the consumption should be made thereon." In the matter of sheep, he emphasized "a Good Ram" and "their pens" where they were "made to stay therein of Nights—fed and regularly Salted," being "particular in haveing Green Lots for the Lambs & Ewes when needed. Sheep are an Animal that require some attention for from their timid dispositions, if not Gentled they become Wild, and hard to manage." He cautioned for separate pennings and sheltering "when the Ewes are about haveing their Lamb, for ... in fondness for the Young lamb by the Wether, they are apt to paw them, in token of affection, which the delicate habits of the Young Cannot Stand." Sheep were valued for mutton, wool, and compost, the last of "which is among the richest of Manures for Gardens &c." Dent had thirty sheep in June, 1840, and made regular but disappointing attempts to upgrade his stock with new ewes and rams.[89]

In this same period, he had seventy head of cattle, which were more important than sheep but required less attention. On the subject of beef production, Dent wrote knowingly in 1840, "I am an advocate for a small stock in a Country like this where the Range is inferior ... [and] Cattle dwindle away to be but a shadow of what they really are." He advised his overseer and neighbors,

If your Stock is not of a good and thrifty kind ... dispose of the most inferior beef... and then procure a Good Bull, that will make a good cross and raise his get, with care and good attention. While Young, Allow them a sufficiency of Milk from their mother, and when they become able procure a pasture that will keep them fat, in order to push them forward when Young in Strength and Size. I am opposed to range Bulls, as in General they are inferior from Neglect, and starvation and the Blood may be too nearly connected with the stock he ranges with. Keep Your Bull at home in a pasture, Gentle, Well fed, salted, and frequently handled and turn Your cows to him. In no Instance turn him out, as he may be Injured by others, made cross & stubborn, and... when wanted not to be found. He should be provided for in Winter with a good Shelter, his rack and manger therein, and well fed, his health attended to, So as when spring Season arrives, he should be in readiness to supply as many cows as is required, the Bull being fat, fine life and Spirits, and in appearance a noble looking animal... the main stay for a good stock.[90]

As an experienced herdsman in a frontier situation, Dent deemed

fifteen Cows of a good breed, an ample sufficiency for a plantation consisting of fifty or sixty human beings, provided the Cows are of good quality, and attended to, as I shall now remark. In a New Country like this, where we have no pastures... We must in a great degree depend on the range for their green food or grazeing. But still, when brot to the pen at night for Milk (which... pens should be amply Large, so as to prevent their heming each other... and good salt troughs provided, as well as much tubs, and racks to hold shucks or other forage, and also pens for the calves with necessary equipments for food &c), Each cow should have its food properly prepared in its Tub, altho it be but a small bate, as in Summer, Grazeing is ample with the small bate, consisting of Wash Turnips, Turnip Tops, pea Hulls, Bran; & [when] boilt togeather Tends to gentle the Animal as well as enrich the Milk, and causes their regular return home to their pen in expectation of their Evenings repast. They should be regularly salted and occasionally Sulphur mixed with the salt, which causes the Ticks the[y] get in the Woods to leave them. The above remarks answer for their treatment during the grass season.[91]

Dent also spoke from experience concerning winter months when

your treatment must be more attentive and rigid. The pens in Your Crib Lots should be well supplied with shucks, Pea Hulls, and such damaged fodder as is unfit for Horses, and every day during the Winter Your Cows, Calves and dry cattle should be regularly fed therefrom. And with a little peas in the Hull, pea Hams, and shucks chopped up and Well boilt togeather your milch cows will not be found Wanting in the pail. The Calves while Milked must have the use of a pasture, so as to allow them such chances for growth & size as heretofore alluded to.[92]

Like other frontier planters, Dent practiced much of this advice, in his case with a select fifteen cows and not the full seventy range cattle on record. For on June 14, 1841, he dryly recorded: "Marked and Branded 14 calves . . . 11 head were Bull calves, altered; 3 head heifer calves; total 14." In the 1850s his care of animals improved and their numbers increased when more pasture was available and much "chop food" was prepared for livestock.[93]

Also in February, 1855, he tried again to upgrade his fowls and showed a continuing low opinion of neighbors' methods when he described his eldest daughter's errand and its disappointing result. "Minna went to Eufaula to bring the children from School; directed her to get some hens to mix and change our Stock which has been on hand too long. Succeeded in getting four hens only, p[a]rt shanghis. Will endeavour to get at least a dozen hens and a Mammouth Rooster if possible. Several friends have promised me a Rooster for 12 months past, but I find promises are li[k]e pie crust, nothing like relying on ones own industry and exertions." In spite of this pessimism and recurring fowl diseases, he could boast by March 15, 1858, "Fine broods of chickens are being turned off last few days." By this time, there were also enough turkeys to require separate housing.[94]

For Dent, scientific farming did not exclude cotton. In the final analysis, agricultural reform aimed at larger profits from that staple. But he was sadly persuaded that cotton planting needed no defense; it was already too popular and detrimental to scientific farming. In 1855 he criticized his neighbors' commitment to cotton and probably exaggerated the lack of agricultural diversification, on his own farm at least.

> For the want of foresight in the Cotton planters, these important [grain] crops are entirely overlooked, which causes us to live so hard and stinting. Grain crops are important for two considerations, the first is the benefit to the land in rotating as well as preserving the Soil. Second, to the raising of stock. In these two particulars the Cotton planters are deplorably at fault. We are dependent on the North and West to supply us With flour and meat, for the reason of our neglecting this Grain Crop as we do. We are now scarce of hogs and what few we have are of the most inferior kind. Sheep are also inferior, a dwarfish stock, diseased, and bad constitutions. Cattle are the most common. And how can it be otherwise, when we have no pastures to support or sustain them? Cotton is the most absorbing desideratum, every thing is neglected for it, hence our impoverished condition.[95]

Dent's first concern in scientific farming was provisions. His second interest was retaining and repaying the soil for the purpose of larger and more profitable crops, which included cotton. At Bleak House in January, 1855, he hastily sketched his method for preserving and improving "the broken lands . . . by Guard drains, rotating and manureing, and by the horizontal culture, leaving lands well littered, and stopping every

Wash so soon as discovered." At this time, he explained briefly, "The Level Lands must be rotated, manured, and ditched. To effect the manureing system, litter and straw must be raked up abundantly and our Lots kept well littered. Besides, having so fine a range at hand, a large stock of Cattle should be had who would trample and make a large amount of straw annually into a large supply of manure."[96]

In September, 1855, Dent was more specific on rebuilding worn soils. "My policy is this," he wrote,

> 1st Guard drain the hills thoroughly. 2d drain the flat lands by proper ditches, 3d Manures must be made, saved, and applied. Without manureing, nothing can be done. It needs but attention to have large amounts, as we have the material convenient at hand to make a large amount annually. Litter the Mule Lots, as well as the Cattle pens; have them constantly filled, and the stock penned up every night. 4 The Cow pea must do for us what Clover had done for Maryland and Virginia. Sow our Corn broad cast with it [in] our last plowings, so as it will shade the ground. And when gathered plow in the vine and leaves. By this policy, which needs but attention to do it, fine crops can be made.[97]

Of "Hill Sides or Guard Drains" ditches, Dent explained: "In making these . . . the most important thing . . . is to locate the ditch on . . . the hill where the greatest strain of Water gathers." He advised a normal ditch fall of four inches every sixteen feet and recommended dividing the fall to prevent blow outs and increasing the fall in short curves to prevent overflows.[98] Irrigating swampland rice fields in South Carolina was good preparation for "guard draining" eroding hills of Alabama plantations. In 1855 one of Dent's "most difficult undertakings" was a "long ditch," of 549 yards, to drain a flat of eighty acres. The fall in the ditch was his standard "4 inches in 16 feet," based on "scientific calculations." There were subsequent ditches, reports, and repairs to the general effect that the drainage system was functional except in heavy rains which broke the channels' sandy walls, resulting in further erosion and time-consuming repairs. Along this same line, Dent's concern to conserve resources included water power, on which he wrote pages urging neighbors to abandon the heavy, cumbersome, tub-type of water wheel for the lighter, more easily driven (and thus more efficient), vertical type of undershot wheel.[99]

Closely related to guard drains and their occasional failure was the problem of "handling gullies." Dent wrote:

> Under all circumstances it is impossible to prevent entirely the washings of our rolling lands, but they can be prevented to a great extent by having the gullies filled up with cotton stalks or any litter convenient to find, so soon as they appear, and having placed over them. Where much hauling is done,

ruts are made [and] if not properly attended to will soon gully. As such so soon as our hauling is finished we have the ruts filled up with trash, litter, and properly secured from Washings. It is a good plan to cover such places where we have to haul over first with Corn or Cotton stalks, it will prevent gully or ruts, and at the same time so break up the stalks to make litter and manure. On broken lands, a judicious man will pay strict attention to these matters, and by doing so in time much benefit can be accomplished.[100]

Discussing the problem of manuring, he traced the intimate connection between scientific animal husbandry and the home production of fertilizer for cotton land. "Two things are indispensable for successful management on this plantation," he believed,

the one is to have a large stock of Cattle and Sheep and the other is to make a large supply of manures. Cattle can have a good Summers range, and [be] wintered in the plantation on shucks and fodder, which will be the time for making and saving manures. There is a large Shelter which needs railing in, and by keeping it well littered and tramped, a large supply of the most valuable manures can be had, besides the keeping up the Cattle will add much to their value, and save many a life. Milk for the little negroes will also pay well. Sheep to be cared for in the same way. A ready market can always be found in Eufaula for mutton, and the manufacturers in Columbus need and are anxious for wool.[101]

Despite themes of self-sufficiency, diversification, and urban sales, the cotton planter finally shines through: "I desire very much to turn my attention to these very important matters, for the manures annually made and applied to the crops will pay better than the meats of the cattle and mutton and wool of the sheep are worth. No investment or rutine of duty on the plantation would be found more profitable—in short it [manuring] is absolutely needed to insure fine crops."[102]

Of greater novelty was his brief comment concerning marl at Bleak House. "I am desirious of experimenting on Marl. Shall get up say 1000 Bushels from the Creek Banks, expose it to mellow, and apply it to the land in February next, and plow it in. 1000 Bushels they say will do for 5 Acres. That is 200 Bushels to the Acre." The effect of this almost insoluble phosphate was apparently disappointing. Thus, in February, 1859, his efforts were more conventional. "Hands placing loam soil on our most exhausted beds in the garden, an experiment."[103]

Finally, one of this planter's happiest attempts at rejuvenating soils and simultaneously stopping washes was the careful deployment of portable, temporary cattle lots. In December, 1858, Dent gleefully reported his men "Splitting Rails for Cow pen Manureing. Having a set of light rails split for the purpose of making a Cattle pen to be removed every Week on the poor spots in the Old Quarter flats. My intentions are to have the cattle pend in them every night and fed, and by tramping and manureing on the poorer spots a Week, and then remove them to another, it will be the means of renovating a large portion of lands now dead and unproductive."[104]

Farming, then, was a matter of science, service, lifestyle, and business. More than just profit, it was an end in itself. Even as Dent planned better living arrangements, he criticized his predecessor at Bleak Hill.

> The present fixtures found on this place as arranged by Major DeWitt are entirely unsuited; his Stables are Isolated in the field across the Creek where they are inconvenient for any purposes.... Should a horse get out to run over the crop, or if an accident were to happen to one at night, no one could hear it or discover it until too late to render aid. All must be altered...to be under my eye...where they will benefit...instead of furnishing a snug harbour for thousands of Rats, which are raising such numbers as will take the plantation by storm. There are rats enough in the present isolated stable to eat up the horses, were they disposed and venturesome enough to fancy horse flesh for food. The Major seems to have had no eye to conveniences or economy.... We must alter such injudicious arrangements.[105]

In these and other instances, Dent's practical agrarianism made no clear distinction between yeoman farmer and large planter. This was the case even when he consciously tried to separate the two. For example, he wrote his brother, George, on September 15, 1855, "I am now fully convinced that the most prosperous and happy people on this earth are the poorer classes of Farmers who live at home upon the fruits of their own labors, independent of the caprices and designs of their fellow men." But this was nonsense, and Dent knew it. Having no desire to be poor, he next tried to "Contrast the conditions of agriculturists, the one who raises his own supplies at home, and the one who grows a staple crop for market & purchases all the necessaries of life. I shall designate the one as the farmer, the other as the Planter." So far so good, but still he could not keep them separate because his prosperous farmer produced large quantities of foodstuffs and "some Cotton. Cotton is a second consideration with him."

Finally, then, the only distinction between farmer and planter was a matter of crop emphasis. And when the farmer-planter could find the proper balance between provisions and cotton, "Such a life is to be desired above all others. Its Independence is not equalled by that of Kings and Noblemen."[106] Obviously kings and nobles were far removed from yeomen. And the "poorer classes," with which he began the letter, were completely beside the point. Thus, however much John Dent talked about the farmer, he had no desire to surrender his social position, which rested in large part upon his thirteen hundred acres and one hundred slaves.

The master-slave relationship of Dent's agrarianism included the master-overseer relationship. While many large cotton planters managed their acres and slaves with Negro drivers (dispensing with white overseers), Dent was not one of them.[107] He could not make that sacrifice. Quite dependent on the overseer class, he nevertheless joined most large cotton planters in denouncing that underling. Dent's comments, however, were not all negative. And early in his planting experience, he even saw the need to discipline himself in relation to overseers. In his personal "Rules...in Farming," made in 1841, the first two were general, but three, four, and five dealt with the master's duties to teach the overseer, communicate with him, and finally impress him with one's authority to command. In this last instance, Dent decided, "In Giveing Orders to your Overseers...consider Well the purport an[d] nature of the order. For when Orders are Given and Countermanded in the midst or While executeing Such Orders, It causes not only a loss of time, but is apt to make your Overseer...consider you fickled, or haveing but little Judgement, or Knowledge of what you designed by the Order."[108]

Responsibility for the overseer's temper was another aspect of command. In rule nine, Dent admonished himself,

> Never let passion Get the ascendency of your feeling and Actions; first, because you may do things that afterwards you will be ashamed off and sorry for, Such as makeing a cripple of a Negroe, Horse or any animal of Value. Again, It is setting an improper and bad example to an Overseer, who if passionate will have an excuse for giveing vent to the impulse of feelings. Again, it is encourageing an unfortunate propensity that Habit will soon render natural to one. So much So, in particular and common occasions, Your feelings the least excited will give vent to your feelings.[109]

Obeying his own instructions, Dent wrote long pages of advice and standing rules to overseers. The three extant letters of advice and one set of rules date from 1840, 1841, 1852, and 1855, respectively. Much of this information is used elsewhere in this book. Because the material is repetitious, and because the first two letters have been ably edited and published by W. Stanley Hoole, an interpretive overview of the advice is sufficient here.[110]

These materials and the larger journals show Dent's overseers to have been young, inexperienced men, whom he proposed to teach. In a "Letter to Young Overseer, Unexperienced," Dent wrote, "I shall take this method of giveing to you some admonitory hints, which my experience and as your employer Justifies in my so doing. And I trust the advice I give you may be correct and prudent, Altho by yourself may be considered Binding and unnecessarily rigid. But believe me, In the end, if you are governed by System, discipline, and requisite rigour, and at the same time My Example to you corresponding with such Instructions and discipline as I set forth, You will receive much knowledge."[111]

The major irony of these letters was Dent's combination of condescension with the idealization of an inexperienced overseer into a type of steward, who was supposed to be the most responsible and highest-paid member of the overseeing class. Stewards usually managed the plantations of absentee landlords and sometimes earned $1,500 per year.[112] In his real responsibility and remuneration, Dent's overseer was nearer the actual status of a black driver than that of a steward. And yet the master always listed the overseer's duties as though they were universally inclusive, for example, the care of Negroes, mule lots, corn cribs, other livestock, tools, buildings, fences, and crops. The 1852 letter of advice summarized this ideal: "Care should be bestowed upon every thing belonging to the plantations—to the Negroes, Animals of every description, Provisions, Tools, in a word to every thing, for what is worth having is worth taking care of, it is the secret of Success, the very ground work of prosperity. Your fencing is a part of your field duties hence as important as your crop."[113]

On the other hand, the "Standing Rules" of 1855 epitomized Dent's real domination of this white underling. "1. Negroes," he wrote,

are to be managed with humanity, but at the same time a rigid discipline must be observed. Keep them orderly and no running about without permission.

2. The Quarter to be kept well repaired, in cleanly order, and its fencing neat and substantial.

3. Cribs are to be locked and unlocked by the overseer as well as guarded and cared for. The overseer is to see the allowances shelled out and measured. Economy is to be observed, no wastage or negligence allowed, stock fed and keys always in his possession.

4. Your Horse Lots and fodder lots are also to receive your watchful attention kept locked &c keys in your keeping.

5. Grain, Hogs, Sheep, Cattle and Mules, and manures are the most important matters to be attended to; proper care and attention is to be given to the stock, and the different lots must be kept well filled up with straws and litter, so as to have a large amount of matter being constantly converting into manures.

6. When the above which is the paramount of all other business is attend to, Cotton is there to be attended to.

7. Good fencing is all important; it controls stock, preserves the crop, and makes good neighbors.

8. I reserve full management of every department to myself and am to have the business attended to as I see proper.

9. You are not to leave the plantation without giveing me notice of same; and when business is pressing you must not expect to leave. [114]

The strongest evidence of Dent's domination of overseers was his personal control of crops, the area in which an overseer's reputation was made or broken. Rules six and eight above referred fleetingly to crops, but one letter stated emphatically that "Such as the regular System and mode of Working in prepareing Lands for the Crops designed, or Working the Crop, Harvesting, Houseing it, ... it must be taught you practically ... in the field." [115]

What with high expectations, severe regimentation, and modest pay, it is little wonder that Dent seldom kept an overseer more than a year. In 1841 he claimed to be concerned about this rapid rotation, which he blamed on young men's "vassalateing mind and restless disposition." He also expressed concern for the overseer's reputation, lest so many changes "fit you for no occupation or Business, as men will loose all confidence in your Stability, believeing you to be a 'Jack of all trades and master of none.'" Thus the master advised: "pursue steadily the business you are now engaged in, With Pride, energy, perserverance and determination to obey the orders of Your Employer." [116] But this was sophistry. Had Dent not preferred a rapid rotation of overseers, he would have relaxed the regimen, paid higher wages, and kept some men for longer periods.

With few exceptions, this master trained inexperienced men at minimum wages and then lost them to neighboring planters the following year. William K. Scarborough estimates that overseers' annual salary in the cotton region averaged $450, the maximum ranging up to $1,000 per year. [117] A table of Dent's known overseers would look something like this:

S. C. Watkins, 1840, at $290
John Oliver, 1841, at $200 (stayed two days)
John Brown, 1841, at $180
McIntyre, 1842, at $300
John Brown, 1842-43, at less than $300
Fryer, 1849
McCarroll, 1850 (80 bales)
McIntosh, 1851 (141 bales)
McLoud, 1852 (80 bales)
Sylvester Martin, 1853, at $350 (200 bales)
John Barr, 1854, at $365 (116 bales)
G. B. Bush, 1855, at $250
Joe Summerset, 1856, at $300
H. B. Price, 1856, at $300
Davis, 1856

Turner Howell, 1857-60, at $300
Alex Johnson, 1861
S. Y. McCracken, 1862
Smith, 1865
Howell, 1866[118]

Without presuming to generalize, it is possible to see in Dent the faintest hint (and no more than a hint) of a personal identity problem in relation to overseers.[119] Not that he was emotionally disturbed. In fact his external behavior was typical of his class, who lambasted the same overseers on whom they depended and from whom they profited. Some of this was irrational, and the most obvious explanation for it is the scapegoat syndrome. If Dent was not alone in the practice, he may have been more articulate than many other planters when he freely blamed the overseer for almost every agricultural "backwardness."[120] Because this master managed the crop with single-mindedness, and no man controlled the weather, it was gross injustice and irresponsibility when he averred, "My last years crop was lost entirely to the inexperience of an overseer."[121] There were many statements to this effect.

In 1856 Dent's horse and mule population was rapidly reduced by a mysterious distemper that baffled and defeated his best efforts as veterinarian. On July 3 he noted,

My Fox Horse died last evening of same distemper which broke out amongst the mules and killed two of them. What kind of a distemper it is, I am unable to tell, but it is infectious and fatal. They first take down with sever spasmodic pains in the bowels. After relieving that they look puny and stupid for several days, discharging much bloody matter from the nostrils, with a sivere cough and gradually linger on until death supervenes. I have bled, purged, given Sage tea, turpentine, Whiskey and Laudanum, as well as decoction of tobacco to no effect. The disease was brought up on the plantation by a young mule purchased of a Drover last March. I have seen nothing like it before, and all who have seen it pronounce it a strange and fatal distemper.[122]

These losses continued; four mules were dead by September. And while Dent obviously understood the cause, he could, in a momentary fit of temper, condemn the overseer: "Summersets Mismanagement and inattention to them has been so dreadful as to have almost killed the whole stock."[123] In 1855, at the nadir of Dent's habitually low opinion of overseers, he blamed those men, not planter or slaves, for the exhaustion of Barbour County soils. He blandly informed a South Carolina friend, Lawrence Witsell:

There are an Army of Men among us and in employment known as Overseers, with full powers and involvments as such, but when this is said, all has been said, for their works are different from the calling. Now is the time we want proper Overseers. Now or never. Our lands have lost their fiery edge . . . [and] need such [recuperative] management . . . and without this proper management on the part of an overseer . . . we shall soon be compelled to pull up pegs an[d] go West. Heretofore the policy was to find out the Man that could cut down most timber, tear up most land, and destroy most Soil; the country bears numerous marks of such work. The time has come to alter and commence renovating. . . . In fact the Overseers who have been accustomed to our new lands, where nature has been the husbandman and has enriched the soil and stimulated the plant to rich fruits, have not the patience or inclination to learn to . . . save both Soil and Credit.[124]

This master also blamed his underling for any misbehavior by slaves. In December, 1855, when his overseer, G. B. Bush, left "on his own business, his time being up," Dent complained: "My business at present is in a loose condition. Mr Bush was an indifferent man . . . not energetic or industrious, overlooking many serious faults of the negroes. Hence they became lazy and careless, Thievish, Stealing every thing they could lay their hands upon, and killed at least half the hogs on the plantation. It will require Strict discipline in future to repair the damages caused by such careless management. It is penny wise and pound foolish to hire such Overseers."[125] Here exaggeration verged on falsehood. Dent always had more hogs than he wanted to fatten. And as his own steward, he, too, was responsible for slaves' behavior, an unpleasant fact he preferred to ignore. Finally, he would have retained Bush as a satisfactory overseer, had Bush been willing to work for $300 a year.

Paying Bush a mere $250 in 1855, Dent resented his request for $400 in 1856: "Bush gone up to J. D Johnsons to try [to] get in with him as his Overseer for 1856. Mr Bush leaves me thinking his Services are worth $400 pr annum, which I do not think they are worth. And so will others, who hire him. . . . He has managed a plantation but one year, and now believes he is perfect a No 1. Overseer. Conceit is largely developed in his organization. I feel but little doubts but what I can replace him."[126] Actually, Dent was not sure of this, and he passed through several overseers before he found another "cheap" one so much to his liking.

This planter's preference for an inexpensive overseer was a matter of money, but it was more than that. He believed there was a correlation between an overseer's high salary and his independence of the master, a situation Dent could not bear to imagine, let alone experience. Thus, he sorely resented neighboring planters' willingness to spoil the overseeing class with too-high wages and other laxities. "Overseers this Fall," he fumed in 1855,

are looking up for higher Wages for next year; they are asking from 300 to

500, horse found, Cook furnished, and provisioned in full, in short they are expecting easy times, and good pay. If the planters are willing to pay such, the Overseers are right to take it. But for my own part, I give my whole attention to my business personally, hence cheaper Men or strikers, will suit me best. My experience has been this, I never paid high wages but [that I] made the shortest crops with such men; my largest and best crops ever made were by men who got moderate Wages. These experienced and high famed Overseers are men who will have every thing their own way, right or Wrong; they look upon every thing on the plantation as their own, their Employers as subordinate to themselves, and condecending to ask them their advice or desires in business. Rule or ruin is their motto, and nine times in ten, they ruin their employers more than they benefit them. I have generally found out that these experienced Overseers rely more on hard driving than good management; they are close and pushing in the field and negligent in the quarter and stock departments, Wasteful and extravagant with provisions, careless and regardless of Stock, and cruel to Negroes. Such do not conform to my ideas of a good manager; Give me a careful and economical Man, and one who keeps every thing up and moving without this rush and crushing down of every thing about him. Farmers make more by care than Waste, more by prudence than recklessness.[127]

Because Dent refused to pay high wages, this was an exaggerated description of neighboring overseers who seemed to threaten him. Powerful overseers who aped their social betters reminded Dent of the improvidence of "aristocratic" extravagance in dress, entertainment, and hospitality. "These extra[ordinary] Overseers," he concluded, "are generally the best dressed, best mounted, and most pompos Gentlemen in the Country—requireing more waiting on. And more fastidious in all their habits, they are famous for rideing into Town and a lavishing way of talking, entertaining, and [desiring] to be entertained."[128] It was no accident that the bulk of Dent's verbal attack on this office occurred during 1855 and 1856. These were the years his "outside" loans and investments multiplied rapidly, required much time, and produced profits which occasionally pained his agrarian conscience. Such a trend would soon dictate greater dependence on an experienced overseer. It would also mean increased expenses and less direct control for himself. Observing the so-called "first class" overseers about him, Dent dreaded the change and consequences at Bleak Hill.

On November 6, 1855, when it was certain that Bush would leave his service, Dent wrote his politician friend, Henry D. Clayton, of Clayton, Alabama. The tone of the letter verged on panic:

Dear Sir, I am in want of an Overseer for next year. Can you tell me where I can pick up a man suited for the business? There are hundreds riding round and applying for such situations, and when asked about their qualifications, they first answer by telling you what they must have. The first thing is, they must be paid large wages, a comfortable residence, a good garden spot, a kennel pailed in for their dogs; then comes their horse, which must be well stabled, well fed, and well groomed for his special service and use, to ride over the plantation during the Week, and about the neighborhood on Sunday, as well as an occasional afternoon. A cook must be furnished also, and a young girl for his wife, and a boy required to wait upon himself, another to make up fires, and one three times a day for the horse. Such are the direct wants and expressed conditions of most of the Overseers now in search of business, Who go armed with revolvers, Sticks and large Ox Whips to manage with. You may depend I am in want of no such managers. I want a Sensible, industrious, enterprising and reliable young man, who expects to work for his living and not to ride over and fight every negro in the plantation. [129]

Continuing the plaint to friend Clayton, Dent implied that a strong overseer would end his claim to being a farmer:

I have walked over my plantation every year, and found it necessary for a proper personal attention to my business, having found a horse more in my way when my negroes were at work than of any service whatever, and most frequently requireing a boy to be taken from his work, to hold him from doing injury, or to bring him back after breaking loose and running over fields of Cotton or Corn. As such, I need no Overseer who has to ride to his laborers; it is the result of idleness, more than a duty required. When my plantation is to large to Walk over, I shall consider it too large for one set of hands to work advantageously on, and will divide the force and hire two men to attend to them. [130]

The overseer's horse, which Dent despised, threatened more than stalks of cotton and corn. It would, if it ever appeared on his plantation, demolish his dream of becoming a prosperous, slave-owning farmer who could function without an overseer. Nor was Dent ready to surrender the dream. If he had to have an overseer, let it be a beginner. But why not do without one altogether? A postscript to H. D. Clayton indulged his agrarian fantasy of having no other business than farming and of abolishing the office of overseer in his plantation: "NB. I am well satisfied when a planter resides on his plantation the whole year round and has no other business or engagements to call him from his duties, Our best policy is to take a trusty Sensible Negro and make a driver of him. His services are worth his labor, and by proper training, a mutual confidence and interest will be established, causing him to be invaluable, and causeing us to dispense with this class of Men, now known and hired as Overseers, which in my opinion are of more injury to the planter than benefit." [131]

Abolishing the post of overseer was more easily written than implemented. Meanwhile the able Bush was succeeded by the inept Joe

Summerset, as Dent continued his self-styled "penny wise and pound foolish" policy of employing inexperienced men. Even after allowing for this master's habitual exaggeration of overseer frailties, Summerset *was* pathetically inadequate. The surprise is that Dent knew it from the beginning: "My Overseer Mr Summerset is not only an inexperienced Man but a slow and unenergetic man which will give me much trouble and put a great deal on my hands this year. As such I may anticipate a great deal of trouble and perplexities. The hardest thing to get hold of in Barbour County Alabama is a useful and reliable Overseer." Nor did Summerset improve. Within a month, Dent despaired, "As he possesses neither judgement, Energy or desire to learn, he is inanimate." A few weeks later on April 29, 1856, the master sighed, "On last evening by mutual consent Mr Summerset left me. Settled with him in full, paying him $112.50 for the time he had served. Mr Summerset was entirely incompetent to manage my negroes or plantation, hence he consented to give way. Until I can get a competent man, I have put Vurtur over the gang as driver."[132]

At this juncture, one suspects that Dent chose the inept Summerset in order to force himself to do without an overseer. Whatever the case, all was not settled by the change. Within six days of Summerset's departure, Dent found need to expand the system of black drivers: "Left Vurtur in charge of the Quarter discipline and the hoe department; Bob in charge of mule and lot department and to superintend the plow department; Brown in charge of the Residence and premises."[133]

Predictably, since Dent would not play the steward's full role, the experiment did not work. Summerset left on April 28. A short month later, "Mr. Price set in at $25 per month to Overseeing business." A dejected Dent explained, but only partially: "were it not for having an Overseer at the Quarter of nights to preserve order, and attend to the Mules, [I] Would manage the crop without an Overseers assistance. As I get along better, and more to my Satisfaction than with them."[134] But given Dent's distaste for direct supervision of blacks (even drivers), he had no choice other than to employ a white overseer. Underestimating his dependence on them, he stereotyped all overseers as either domineering or worthless. When the experiment with black drivers failed, Dent employed another inexperienced white; who would not last the year.[135]

By now, however, the master-farmer-financier was in sore need of a better type of manager, so long as he came cheap. Finally in 1857, Dent found what he wanted in Turner Howell. If Howell was an inexperienced overseer, he was nevertheless bright, obedient, and thoroughly trustworthy. Upon his arrival, Dent's comment on the office dwindled to rare, brief, and inconsequential complaints. He was less critical of the overseer than of his own "enforced" absences for financial business in Eufaula and Clayton. Despite four years' service, however, Howell never received the wages of an experienced overseer. Perhaps he could remain at Bleak Hill because he owned property in the community and because his appointment as local supervisor of public roads brought additional remuneration. There was also a "good overseer's house" on the plantation and a warm relationship with the Dent family. The Howell children would spend the day at the Dents', and "Mrs Dent gone with Mrs Howell to her relatives for fruit." When this overseer had a sick child, the master or young Horry Dent would attend his business. [136]

It was a satisfying relationship, one of mutual respect in the last years of Dent's mature plantation system. Of course he continued ordering Howell about, but there was little need to supervise him. It was strong praise in 1860, on the eve of secession and war, when the master wrote, "On 2d day of December, Mr Howell leaves my business his time haveing expired. After four years being in my employment as Overseer, he discharged his duties as well as any Overseer would have done." [137] Yet throughout Howell's tenure, the master had felt constrained to lambaste him periodically. For example, the journal would report of him, "Very wet. Saturated & learn that my overseer was plowing. Such shows what little judgement they have." If nothing else, these asides assured Dent that a master was needed, however much he might be away on financial business. Departing Bleak Hill under amicable circumstances, Howell remained in the community and on good terms with Dent. They visited at a neighboring plantation which Howell managed, and in the fall of 1866, he seemingly returned briefly to assist in the harvest of Dent's first crop made by free black labor. [138]

From 1861 through 1865, the overseers were again transient. Now, however, preoccupation with the Civil War kept journal comment on them to a minimum. Yet the officer continued to be Dent's scapegoat. In reality, the system of management always worked fairly well on his plantations, so far as profits were concerned. No slave or employee could have met the illegitimate demands of this master who was also a farmer. It was irrational to blame the overseer for every ill of slavery and of the plantation system. Such was, however, the prerogative of command. And however much he might deprecate it, "farmer" Dent was also the master of a plantation, which included an overseer, slaves, crops, and his family.

3

SLAVERY

By 1860 John Dent, one of the less than 1 percent of the white southern population owning a hundred slaves, was a bonafide "large planter." [1] Having grown up on his mother's plantation, with its numerous slaves, and having acquired forty-five Morrison blacks by marriage to Mary Elizabeth Morrison, he accepted the institution as being within the nature of things. To a large extent, slavery was the basis of Dent's farming ideal. He admitted his Negroes should "be termed the main Spring of the farm and when that is defective, the rest must go wrong." And he advised the overseer on their management and discipline: "I conceive this to be the most arduous task of all. As by them and through them all is to be done." [2] Slaves also required and received the master's careful attention.

Dent's comments on slavery had largely to do with economics. His greatest interest in blacks was as a system of labor. But he was also a paternalist who expected more than mere obedience from his "hands," the term he preferred over that of slave or even Negro. He never employed the epithet "nigger" until after de facto emancipation in 1865. His evaluation and treatment of slaves was thus an interesting mixture of economics and paternalism.

Addressing his overseer in 1840, Dent was both idealistic and pessimistic in his expectations of blacks. "In the first place," he wrote, "they should be set a fine Example of Sobriety, Industry, a proper knowledge of Business Economy and constant Watchfullness on the part of the Overseer in endeavouring to detect any crime, negligence, or disobedience of Orders or anything that may lead to confusion or derangement of business on the plantation. By so doing it is a visable check on them." [3] Hoping that good example would improve the blacks' characters, he nevertheless prepared for the worst.

Yet the same essay acknowledged Negro wisdom in relation to the overseer: "They are Segacious themselves, watchful and Cunning, and like a good Sailor 'knows what his commander is' in a few hours. Well, as soon as they conceive what your disposition is & your qualities are as a good manager and they believe your System will be put in rigid operation, half the battle is over. Now and then only, some rascal will stray from the path of duty, more for the purpose of Testing your disposition and System, than from any other motive. Never let them know you trust them in doing any thing." [4]

This master's greatest concern for ill-placed trust was in the matter of keys to corn cribs, the granary of the plantation. "When you once trust a negroe with the keys," he told an overseer, "your discipline and just accounts are done, for you cannot vouch for what has been done behind your back. And altho the negroe you trust may be honest himself, he may be careless—or would not inform on a fellow Servants misdemeanor, for two reasons. The first is he would betray his negligence and trust you confided in him. The Second is he would bear the Ill will and censure of all the negroes. Consequently if you violate your duty—they are innocent in a part for their negligence and misdemeanors."[5]

Dent understood much about individual honor and group or community pressures. The Negro was regarded as a complexity of honesty, original sin, and innocence. Although the overseer was "responsible" to the degree that the slave was "innocent," the Negro usually took the stripes for both of them. And Dent knew it. Thus he advised his white underling: "If other business on the farm should call your attention (for your duty is to be with them constantly while at work), on your return the work done in your absence should be over looked and rigidly examined. And if there be any error or Idleness discovered, Correction with the whip is your proper alteration."[6]

In his letters to the direct enforcers of the slave system, Dent was harsh, emphasizing control, first through fear and second through respect, with the last based upon the first: "have your Orders to the Negroes properly & punctually obeyed and executed, making them fear and respect you."[7] Not that he denied all love or "attachment" between whites and blacks. He probably believed his Negroes, or some of them, loved their master, if not the overseer. But Dent refused to expect much of that sentiment and usually reserved his discussion of "attachment" between master and slave for his few sallies against the abolitionists.

A vaguely addressed essay on this matter appeared in the journal sometime between 1852 and 1854. Here, Dent proposed to explain the economic and sympathetic motives for humanity toward his Negroes. "Let me give you as well as I can the relative situation of the master and his slaves. True there are exceptions, but very few in comparison to the number. Slaves are valuable property. That is, a high pecuniary value is set upon the worth of each. Hence one owning them are compelled for self interest to take care of them." So much for economics. "But independent of such, there is an attachment between the master and his slaves, more so than between employers and their hired servants, which prompts humanity and good treatment ninety nine cases in one hundred. And the owner feels more thought about the welfare and comforts of his slaves than the slave does for his master."[8] If for a moment Dent could pose as the wounded paternalist, his real "attachment" to slaves was less a matter of love than of ownership.

Beginning the new year of 1859, his private comment smacks of Old Testament patriarchy:

In commencing the duties of another year, Let us not be unmindful of the Blessings and Bounties of the past year, which God in his mercies has so liberally shown us. Let us as the head of our house hold be just and prudent, firm and discreet, humane and kind to our Slaves, knowing as our Servants we are bound to be just, humane and conscientious towards them. Let us pursue our duties with energy and perseverance, tempered with moderation, not grasping, avaricious, or hard to be pleased, do our parts faithfully and trust in God for our health and his blessings.[9]

However patriarchal Dent might sound in private, his public discussion of slavery was economic, political, and constitutional. He addressed the abolitionists:

You are all the most deceived and mistaken people on the face of this earth as regards to the conditions of the Slaves of the South. They are Slaves by name and law, nothing more. Their situations are by far more enviable than that of their owners, who are in fact the Slaves of Slavery. And a large portion of the Slave owners are aware of this and are disgusted with the institution. But owing to the political aspect you have assumed in this matter, it has caused them to cherish it more and contend for its continuance as a Constitutional right which they intend to preserve at all hazards and sacrafices. Had you at the North not meddled with it..., Slavery would have been gradually given up by the older Slave states and many emancipated by their owners, whilst the rest would have been sold to the people settling the new Western states, and at last it would have been confined to a few states, with hardly the moral force to preserve it. Your fanatical course though has resulted only in fixing more firmly and prolonging more perservereingly Southern Slavery.[10]

The most significant aspect of Dent's pro-slavery arguments was lack of ardor. In a private and moderate comment on the abolitionist Fredrika Bremer in 1856, Dent continued his rationalistic theme of gradual emancipation and carried it to the logical conclusion of colonizing blacks outside the United States. He believed, with some justification, that "The South is more pro Slavery from the interferences of Northern Abolitionists politically than otherwise." But less convincingly, he argued: "Had that question been left to the states to act upon, as it seemed proper with their own views and interest on the subject, colonization would have been more advanced than what it now is." The source and extent of Dent's real concern in this matter is evident in his further observation that slavery "has become a sectional political question, to be settled in all probability by a separation of the North and South. The religious brotherhood have already done it, the people of this Union in time will do the same."[11]

This planter's rationalism was persistent, but not enough to force an environmentalist explanation of Negro slaves' "peculiar traits of character." In response to Bremer's *Homes of the New World*, Dent demurred, "Her sympathies for the Negroes are truly grate, believing them to be endowed with greater gifts than what is their true state. This tho can be easily attributed to her want of knowledge of them. Like all persons unacquainted with the race, they [abolitionists] come to the conclusion that their condition as slaves is the cause of their peculiar traits of character, which experience has taught us to know is natural or belonging to them."[12] As a racist, not a rational environmentalist, Dent believed that slavery was the result of Negro character.

Privately at least, he was kindly disposed toward Bremer's effort, because he respected her religious sensibility and was, therefore, impressed by her philosophy. "Miss B is a fine writer with clear ideas. And on metaphysics, she is very interesting and instructive. Her religious feelings are truly religious, and sympathy for the poorer classes show the benevolent and kind heart which activates her passions."[13]

In an effort to explain the source of Bremer's misinformation, Dent was forced to the inconsistency of withholding his usual appreciation for the business classes of the North. Attributing Bremer's errors "in a great measure to the society in which she fell into," he believed,

> She was too much under the care and guidance of the business classes, who have not had the time or opportunity to inform themselves with that proper knowledge of matters and things which would have been afforded to Miss B. had her association been with the leisure persons in the higher circles of society. When with such, you can observe her ideas and conclusions are more clear and correct than [when she was] with the business classes at the North who are confined only to the business affairs of the Country and not to that general knowledge of so much importance to a stranger in quest of general facts and circumstances.[14]

Here Dent utilized the idea of southern leisure as opposed to Yankee money-grubbing. Yet in this same response to Bremer's book, he could articulate something of Hinton R. Helper's critique of the economic ills of slavery. "Her remarks as to their [slaves] being a drawback to social progress and an enlarged or general [dis]advantage to the prosperity of any State they live in, I agree with her, as she says, 'contrasting the two sections, free and slave, is proof enough of it.' "[15]

For all his materialism, the antebellum Dent must have believed in a divine right of slave owners. In 1867, after emancipation, he perceived a providential development: "Truely the Scriptures sayeth 'No man knoweth what a day bringeth forth.' Nine years ago, who could have predicted such a change. If it is the Will of God, all is right, and will end well." Yet he was flexible and could adjust. By 1880 he had made the change and phrased it in an economic vein: "The Indolence, self Indulgences, and dependence brought about by Slavery was the ruin of the Southern youths and the Southern States. And the greatest boon and inheritance bequeathed to the people of the South was the abolition of Slavery. Thus, the War cost us . . . but it has been well spent, for the good it will do the South in the future. For it will develop the energies and enterprise of the people of the South that before the War was absorbed in Slave labor."[16]

Henry W. Grady, the Atlanta prophet of the New South's capitalistic creed, could not have put it more directly. But in 1880, Dent's business ethic was not new, it was simply readjusted to accommodate history. [17] And this planter-farmer-businessman was correct when he said that antebellum slavery had consumed much of his energy and enterprise. Thus, the vast majority of his comment on blacks dealt not with their character or the peculiar institution but with the economics of their labor as it related to the basic needs of food, clothing, housing, family structure, health, and incentives to work.

Slaves' food was an item important enough to receive a policy statement in the journal. On December 9, 1851, Dent combined economic and humane arguments for adequate feeding under the divine authority of Scripture.

> There is not only humanity exercised in good treatment and plentiful feeding. But in considering it properly there is sound Economy. Half fed laborers and Animals are not only incapable of doing good service, but are not their value as well as existence shortened by this misdirected and inhumane policy? Most surely it is, and the wants of nature, under so parsimonious treatment, must be but a type of torture and subjection. Hence sound Policy and good Judgement, as well as Humanity and a proper sense of duty, would influence us to treat All Well, both Man and Brute, that is under our care and ownership. "The Laborer is worthy of his hire," is a maxmin worthy of consideration, and "do unto others as we would be done by" are rules we should be influenced by.[18]

Such preachment to oneself perhaps hints of some temptation to underfeed. If so, Dent resisted it and could briefly inform the abolitionists that slaves' "food is in general what their owners live upon themselves." While the qualifier "in general" can cover a multitude of exceptions, Dent's assertion was basically correct. His food measures were adequate if not generous. There is only one table of rations in all of the antebellum journals. It is found in the journal of 1842, his first year at True Blue plantation, a time of disappointing crop yields. This particular table shows that fifty-five slaves, comprising thirteen families of about four members each, received a combined weekly allowance of sixty-five pounds of pork, ten bushels of corn meal, and five bushels of sweet potatoes. [19]

Evidently these allowances, especially of meat, increased as the "times" improved. The allocation of food by family raises the question of communal kitchens. One reference in the 1840s indicates communal cooking, especially for Negro children. In addition to the staples of pork, corn meal, and yams, Dent's plantations produced milk for "little Negroes," some rice and wheat, and a variety of vegetables. The master not only planted large gardens, he also encouraged and supervised Negro "patches" of foodstuffs. One may assume these blacks had their own chickens and turkeys, because the master never complained of losing his. Having no hogs of their own, the Negroes sometimes appropriated Dent's. The latter could complain of "gathering up hogs to see if any meat is among them. My hog Man reports that the Negroes have eat a great many of them this fall." But these losses were never enough to enumerate, and Dent always had more pigs than his pastures and corn could fatten. [20]

Surely he perceived the slaves' temptation to eat fresh pork without permission rather than politely waiting to be handed salted meat that had spoiled. Not infrequently the master reported: "Found in giveing out meat allowance to the Negroes this day some of the Shoulders very much tainted owing to the very pernicious season we have had to cure meat." It may be significant that he never recorded destroying rancid meat. [21] In this situation, one can only assume the Negroes were warned to cook such pork carefully before eating it. Negligence here would help explain the slaves' frequent stomach disorders, but Dent never acknowledged a connection between this condition and tainted pork.

The slaves' food might be "in general what their owners live upon themselves," but this planter sometimes provided two qualities of pork, designating one type "Negro meat." [22] Still, the food allowance went smoothly enough to elicit no major concern from the master until the exigencies of the Civil War arose. There is no evidence he used delicacies or holiday meals as incentives for special effort or labor. His hands were fed adequately at all times, but they seldom, if ever, feasted. Yet when a steer was slaughtered and fresh beef distributed among white neighbors, it is difficult to imagine plantation blacks' missing all of the carcass trimmings.

The Negroes' clothing seems to have been of much less concern than their food. The absence of policy statement on dress, appearance, and cleanliness indicates a matter-of-fact approach to these problems, which in large degree resolved themselves. The journals show in barest economic outline that Dent distributed to each slave not more than two "suits" of clothes per year, then usually in the form of cloth to be "made up" on the plantation, probably within the slave family or by designated seamstresses.

The times of distribution were almost always June and during an indefinite period from October through December 25. There is no record of any ritual associated with the distribution. Dent sometimes chose Sundays, but not always, and he never reported these semiannual distributions in a manner portraying himself as having gone beyond the minimal duty as clothier. For example, there is no mention of the white family's hand-me-downs to house servants or of special trinkets to men or ribbons to women.

One suspects that highly efficient slave families were the real source of Dent's nonchalance toward Negro clothing. Only a large degree of self-sufficiency among blacks in making and repairing clothes would explain his distribution by need rather than by schedule. For example, on Sunday, June 21, 1840, he "Gave out Shirts and Shifts to Negroes this day of Cotton Osnaburghs purchased of E&W Young at 10¢ pr Yd." At this distribution of the coarsest and cheapest of cotton cloth, thirty "field hands" received "2½ to 3 yds" each for a total of "87½ yds" at a reasonable cost of $8.75. [23] Since the yardage was for shirts and shifts only, the men must have continued using trousers from the past winter or even the summer before. June was not the season for the adult slave's one pair of shoes per year.

Dent could also distribute winter clothes according to need or reward. On October 25, 1840, a Sunday, he "gave out" to fourteen "Women 2 yards cloth a piece for Jackets." "Also a Jacket to Zack and pants and a full suit to Paul." Two days later, three more men received "full Suits" and two got "Jackets." In this uneven distribution, another two months lapsed before Dent gave each of ten men "5 to 6 yards" of coarse, ribbed wool and cotton "Kerseys . . . at 40¢ pr Yd" for full suits of coat and pants. The four men who previously received some cloth now received proper yardage for "half suits." Also in mid-December, fourteen women each received "3½ yds twilled cotton at 25¢ pr yd," for hard finished shifts, one presumes. [24]

It was not until December 25 of this year that Dent distributed "To Negroe Children Cloth of Mrs Baxleys Weaving." This was probably wool, since he did express concern to dress these youngsters warmly. It was an inexpensive cloth, "Mrs Baxley . . . Weaving Negroe cloth 130 Yds. $7.10." In 1840 the adults' annual pair of shoes was distributed before Christmas but after cold weather: "Bought of E&W Young 31 pr Shoes for Negroes. 28 pr at $1.37 pr, $38.50. 3 pr at 125 cts, $3.75. [total] $42.25. And gave them to the Negroes this 3d of December 1840." This master's major concern for slave cloth and shoes was unit and price. His expenditure for Negro clothing in 1840 was less than $100. [25]

Whether Dent continued using winter kerseys or went to pure wool is unknown. But in December, 1852, he complained, "Our winter clothing is disagreeable warm," a situation that must have arisen frequently in the fickle winters of southeastern Alabama, which can alternate from freezing to summerlike heat. It was trouble with "disagreeable warm" winter apparel which probably explains his purchasing 244 yards of "Cotton Osnaburgs" from Mr. E. B. Young on October 31, 1853. That same order included 120 yards of "Georgia Plains" and eighteen yards of "linseys." The plains were probably for the women. The linseys of cotton and wool were for the "House gang." He was now dressing the house servants differently from field slaves. This bill of goods totaled $69.62. [26]

While this master never commented on the appearance of adult slaves' clothing, the uncharacteristic variety of cloth in 1853 reflected a rising standard of living for them. In the same year, he noted with pride that twenty-five children's "suits" were "cut out" and "made up before given out." These children's clothes of "entirely Woolens" were also sewn on the plantation, but the chore was no longer left to the individual family. [27] By June, 1854, Dent was giving a full summer and a full winter suit to each slave, but he did not liberalize his policy on shoes.

Also in 1854, the year of Dent's second marriage and plans to quit Good Hope's isolation, the master introduced more quality and variety into his Negroes' fabrics. He wrote that winter "Clothing this year has been entirely of woolen goods. The men and women of the Pine knot plains manufactured at the Eagle Factory in Columbus Ga. That for the Men cost 30¢, Women 28¢. The children are of Northern Satinets, cost 25¢. The House Servants Striped domestics." Stripes would at last indicate some little color in the cloth, even though domestic or "ticking" is very hard and durable. But, more important, the children's satinet weave was considerably softer and easier to wear than plain, harsh wool. Once again, all the children's "suits" were "made up" on the plantation before they were "given out this 18th November 1854." [28]

In 1854, Negroes' winter cloth cost $80, and the summer cloth for 1855 was $110. This amount combined with the cost of fifty pairs of brogan shoes at $1.30 each meant that by the mid-1850s the Negroes' clothing and shoes ran about $250 per year, a very moderate amount for clothing almost one hundred human beings. The shoes were probably the cheapest Dent could find, but he did try to fit them. "Went to Eufaula to carry Negro Shoe measures to be fitted to the Shoe, at EB Young & Son." [29] One assumes these rough shoes were necessary for cold weather and working new ground. They were probably shed when moderate weather and lighter tasks permitted. Dent recorded few serious foot injuries.

There is no evidence this master noticed or encouraged individual slave's initiative in dress and appearance. But like most slave owners, he required personal cleanliness, at least on Mondays, when the hands reported to the fields. This rule was disregarded on pain of a warning and then a whipping by the overseer. Thus "Frank ran away" following a whipping he received on Tuesday "because he came into the field dirty, against Overseers orders." Frank subsequently returned. [30] But cleanliness pertained to more than just clothes, and like charity it began in the home, which was also more than the bare cabin or plank house which Dent provided.

The journals' spare comment on slave housing indicates this planter was not in the least defensive about the quality of his "quarter." Almost every year, he had one or two new Negro houses constructed. For example, in 1841 "Sary and Dandy" were "housed up." And in 1852, his men were "making chimneys to new Houses."[31] Utilizing surplus timber and idle hands meant that cost was no great consideration. Dent's earliest quarter on the Alabama frontier probably consisted of log structures with the usual earthen floors, which required periodic removal to clean ground. But by the early 1850s and probably before, his Negro houses were built more permanently of plank, being set upon blocks and provided with wooden floors. The chimneys, one presumes, were also permanent, of stone or brick, as there was no great fear of fire in the quarter, which would have resulted from temporary chimneys of mud and wood.

Upon moving to a new plantation, Dent generally renovated Negro housing. "Between now and the holidays," he wrote at Bleak Hill, I "will put the Quarter buildings in complete repair; new chimneys and under blocks are needing to most of the houses . . . the Quarter is very much out of order."[32] Always one to exaggerate the dilapidated condition of his plantation, Dent was conscientious about repairing physical facilities, including slave quarters. On the other hand, he seems to have assumed no responsibility to "furnish" the Negro houses, not even to the limited extent of providing a quilt or blanket every two or three years. Yet his slaves had these items: "All the women engaged in Cleaning out thoroughly their Houses and bedding."[33] Also he was impressed by the furnishing of some slaves' homes, a matter he apparently left to the individual family. Writing to the abolitionists, Dent explained that "where an Industrious provident Negro is to be found, like the whites, some being more so than others, you will witness an abundance and many comforts in his household." On the other hand, the master found most blacks to be "Careless and Thoughtless of their own things."[34]

Dent's attitude might be one of laissez faire on furnishings for the quarter, but not on cleaning it. He ordered a scouring at least twice a year, at Christmas and during the lay-by season in July. Often the slaves cleaned the quarter three and even four times per year. (Additional cleanings usually occurred from March through April, or from September through October.) Actually any "slack" time in the fields presaged the following entries: "Repairing up Quarters . . . Cleaning up and Washing out the Quarters." And again, "All hands cleaning up their Houses and the Quarter."[35] He saw no need to describe the cleaning methods, but the job was done, and well, to the extent that the master as plantation physician never complained of ill health caused by filth or vermin.

Slave-quarter noise was distasteful to Dent. He seldom discussed the matter, but he did relocate the quarter at one plantation in part to have more quiet at his residence.[36] An ironical effect of this act may have been the blacks' increased freedom to make noise, unless the overseer was oppressive.

The size and number of slave houses is not known. In 1842 Dent listed thirteen Negro families on the plantation. It is almost impossible to conceive of this ambitious frontier planter taking the time to provide immediately thirteen separate cabins. Yet he worked steadily at meeting this need. By 1854 there were twenty-two families among his eighty-five slaves. And in 1858 he listed twelve "new" Negro houses. These were in addition to the several structures left by Major DeWitt, which Dent had had overhauled.[37] One can safely surmise that several, if not all, of the slave families had separate dwellings.

Housing was only one indication of the importance of the slave family, an institution Dent recognized, supported, and disdained. His attitude toward the black family was ambiguous. He could not respect it, but he was forced to acknowledge its practical effect of contentment and inducement to labor. In the journal, however, he preferred to ignore it. His clearest statement on the Negro family was an indirect one—and unfairly negative—addressed to abolitionists, wherein he insisted that slaves were careless and thoughtless "towards their children, as well as to each other. And were they left to their own government and preservation they would soon become the most degraded Savages on the earth . . . vicious and demoralizing."[38]

In broad outline, the racist implication of this statement was the common one among southern whites that the enslaved Negro was a type of permanent child or ward, to be protected and used. Left to his own devices, the free Negro would sink to savagery and extinction. Dent seemingly believed this, for in 1880 he was genuinely surprised that blacks had not only survived emancipation, but had also multiplied.[39] Actually, his disdain for the slave family is most evident in what he did not say. For example, he made no record of slave weddings, if indeed any were openly held. After emancipation, the former master was contemptuous in his attitude toward a freedman's wedding performed on his plantation. He evidently did not attend the ceremony. The antebellum Dent seldom recorded building a house for a slave couple, although it must have occurred. As noted, Dandy and Sary were "housed up" and much later, "Building a House for William at the Quarter."[40]

Some of this attitude was undoubtedly related to slaves' sexual permissiveness. Dent, however, made no obvious effort to reduce promiscuousness among his hands, not even troubling himself to read the Episcopal Service to them, a function he enjoyed with his own family. Listing the parents of black children in 1842, the master noted only eight productive unions: "John & Myrah, Alfred & Betty, June & Sue, June &

Bash, Phillis & unknown, Vurter & Milley, Affey & unknown, Tenah & White.'' Of these eight "families," June was polygamous, while Phillis and Affey maintained households without a regular spouse. Yet Dent made no comment. When he listed thirteen families in the food allowance of 1842, June and Jim were polygamous, and the master expressed no concern. [41]

Nor was he openly disturbed by the "frailties" manifested in the cases of Alfred, Betty, and Peter. Although Dent did not chronicle these liaisons, the development can be reconstructed from the journals. On March 7, 1841, he almost crowed, "Last night Betty was confined with a Son. I called it Peter after the . . . Father, owing to his haveing been a fine faithful and obedient Servant to his Master." This was in 1841. But the next year's food list recorded "Alfred and Betty" as a family unit. And in the 1854 family list, all three—Alfred, Betty, and Peter—were designated heads of separate households. [42]

Dent's acquiescence in his slaves' informal sexual arrangements illustrates his indifference toward the black family and suggests the possibility of the master's vicarious enjoyment of them. Along this same line, he seemingly preferred the "matrifocal" family structure. For example, the 1854 list shows that fifteen of the twenty-two "heads of families" were women. This statement could reflect more of Dent's administrative organization than it does of matriarchal slave families. But this administrative organization probably influenced the patterns of authority in some slave houses. [43]

Another indication of Dent's penchant for this organization was the policy of moving children around from one Negro woman to another. He recorded these acts without explanation. And while the assignments could have applied to children's tasks or chores, they almost certainly related to child-rearing. Thus "Betty took Margaret & Rebecca," and "Violet took Lorene" and "Katie." Also he "gave Toby to Charlotte." As Charlotte's ward, Toby became a house servant. Charlotte, a valued cook and maid from Virginia, one of the few slaves Dent purchased, was an obvious favorite of his, but there is no evidence of an intimate relationship. On the other hand, Fawn Brodie's study of Thomas Jefferson indicates the ease of suppressing this type of historical evidence. At present, however, there is no circumstantial indicator of miscegenation on Dent's plantation. [44] Nor would the master's almost certain continence in this area preclude his vicarious pleasure in slaves' sexual laxity.

But Dent had another motive, however unconscious, for believing and even promoting what he called careless and thoughtless family relationships among his blacks. In summary, this belief gave him a larger sense of freedom to manipulate slaves for his and his family's convenience and profit. Dent did not consciously set out to subvert the black family. He simply used the Negro in a manner not inconsistent with his having a low opinion of that family. The idea of "careless and thoughtless" black families was particularly useful when it seemed advantageous to buy, sell, rent, lend, or otherwise separate the Negroes, either temporarily or permanently. It seems significant that there was more of this activity in the 1850s, the same decade in which Dent stopped making lists of slave families. The last extant one is dated 1854.[45]

Buying slaves was always risky, financially and socially. Purchases in human flesh could raise problems of title, bring social criticism, and create pangs of conscience for dividing families. The expense and social complications probably explain Dent's outright purchase of only five or six slaves. In 1856, this master expressed some pride in having made few such purchases. "Brown, Charlott, Matilda, and Frank were bought; ballance are of the Morrison Estate Negroes. Sam Gantt also bought Negro . . . [he] died August 1854." Frank and Charlotte were Virginia Negroes; Matilda was from Alabama. On February 28, 1855, Dent paid "Cash to Jno C Cook for Boy Frank, $1000." Cook, a substantial citizen, was the local slave trader with whom Dent dealt on more than one occasion.[46]

The uncharacteristic vagueness of these "business" transactions suggests Dent's ambivalence in the matter of slave trading. One entry is particularly intriguing. "To JC Cook, check & Ex for Negro C $755.62."[47] This occurred during the summer after Dent's first wife died when he was trying to find a suitable housekeeper. "C" was surely Charlotte, the Virginia house servant he valued so highly. Also the abbreviation "Ex" suggests an exchange which would mean a sale Dent never acknowledged otherwise. The amount of $755 without an "exchange" would in 1854 have been a bargain price for an accomplished cook and parlor servant who was thirty years old.

Nor was Dent finished with John C. Cook. On "May 28th, 1857," he "Went to Eufaula and sent a draft of $900 to buy me a Negro woman to J. C. Cook."[48] Dent, then, was not above purchasing Negroes who possessed specific skills. And he would acquire them through the sometimes questionable channel of the slave dealer, who could ill afford the niceties of keeping black families together. Nor would this Alabama planter reduce his investment capital in order to purchase all or half of his mother's slaves, even though compliance with her request would have kept intact the families of the "Horry Negroes."

Instead of buying his mother's slaves, Dent hired them out for her in Georgia and awaited her demise in 1856, when he would assist in the division of these Horry-estate Negroes and their families, bringing his and sister Emma's lots back to Alabama. Dent made no reference to any attempt to preserve black families in parceling out seven lots of almost equal value, one to each heir. He received fourteen chattels, Emma got fifteen, and he transported these to Alabama, where his sister's properties rented for an income considerably higher than they would have fetched on the Atlantic seaboard.[49]

Some of Emma's blacks in Dent's care gave him more trouble than he had ever bothered to record of his own hands. There was one Abram who repeatedly stole from his employer, destroyed his property, and ran away. It was not uncommon to read, "Learned that Abram had robbed William Young of Cloths." And again: "Mr. Brunson reports that Abram ran away from him last night." Nor were the new women easily settled. Some of the problems must have related to family division and loneliness. Thus in January, 1860, when "Men hired as high as $250—Women $175," Dent nevertheless "Sold Emmas 5 Negroes as follows: To Sam Jones: Abram $1760, Willowly 1300, Lucy 1300, Babbet 1250. To John Eford: Pendah 900." Total sales were $6,500. [50] The amount per slave totaled more than twice the appraisals of 1856. Such profits justified further division of the "Horry Negroes."

Did Dent, like Pharoah of old, find it easy to harden his heart against the captives? Probably not. He never acknowledged selling his own slaves, and Emma had others whom he had to rent at no personal profit or income. Nor did he, a devoted brother to this oldest and motherly sister, complain of the chore. Dent was, after all, a mere mortal, caught with the threads of more lives at his fingertips than anyone could hope to manipulate honestly or justly.

Being mortal, the paternalist erred, even when trying to do good. After his daughter, Minna, married Maximilian Bethune Wellborn of Eufaula, Dent sent the Negro girl Nancy with them, first to Eufaula and then to distant Arkansas. When his daughter, Lizzie, wed Whitfield Clark of Clayton, three Negro "children" left Bleak Hill to serve the new family in the county seat at a distance of three and one-half hours' steady riding from "home." No wonder Dent and the overseer had to run close checks on mules and horses to know when one had been ridden hard the night before. [51]

Arkansas was even farther away, and Nancy was already there. Then in 1860, Master Dent, being the considerate father, surely brought sorrow to some black subjects when he "Sent out Harriet a girl about 12 years of age to Minna by MB Wellborn to assist her in nursing her children. Obligations taken from MB Wellborn to return Nancy and Harriet when called upon to do so, 13th March 1860." [52] The casual disregard for slaves' feelings speaks for itself. There was more than one way to divide a family. And it must have been comforting for this doting father to believe that the slave family was a careless and thoughtless arrangement.

But Dent was also a capitalist, and his blacks represented considerable investment. While he may have sold very few persons of color (and perhaps only one, or even none, of his own chattels), he studied the slave market too regularly and closely to be unaware of the cash value of his labor force. A counting-house mentality was an integral part of his character. For example, he knew "Price of Negroes January 1854. Men priced and Sold from $1200 to $1400. Women priced and Sold from $950 to $1150. Boys 12 to 15 years of Age $750 to $950. Girls 12 to 15 years of Age $550 to $800. In Charleston a lot of 100 was sold aged from 3 months to 65 years of age at auction for cash, which averaged $600 round."[53] One can almost hear Dent's mind calculating the value of his lot.

Again in January, 1856, "Negroes are rated very high. Men hire from 180 to 200 dollars, Women in proportion. Sales have been effected. Men from 1100 to 1350 dollars, Women from 1100 to 1150; few have been brought into the country by Speculators. In Pike County the Estate of Silers Sold 100 Negroes at an average of $640 round. Smaller Estates have sold at higher sales. Who lives to see another January can compare notes."[54] Two years later, prices had subsided but little, and not at all for girls. "Negro Men Sold for $1250 12 Mo Credit. Women up to $1000. Saw a girl 10 years old sold for $875." And in 1859, he was impressed with "Flourneys Sale" where "Negroes sold very high. Men from $1600 to 1900."[55]

On the eve of Civil War, Dent's one hundred chattels represented a minimal capital of $100,000. It is not surprising, then, that Dent paid meticulous attention to the matter of his Negroes' health. He wrote concerning slaves, "Their owners are watchful of their interest in every respect, in health as well as in sickness." For Dent, this task was the more palatable because of his aspiration to be a physician. The slaves were captive patients. And he thought highly of his medical ability, admitting as much when he boasted, "Some say I would have made a good Doctor."[56]

Dent's pride in his healing prowess is also evident in a comment on Dr. C. J. Pope of Eufaula, a friendly rival for whom he held grudging respect: "Pope has immortalized himself as a Physician. I have seen him raise cases that seemed hopeless, and you know I have had much experience in sickness; he has but one talent, and that is a Doctor of Medicine."[57] By implication, Dent, the universalist, had more than one talent, and the simple life of a country doctor would not have been sufficiently challenging for him. But the planter took his medicine seriously, and carefully explained the few "receipts" or remedies in the journals: "As I have purchased a practical Medical Library, I do not copy many Receipts, except such as are not prescribed therein." The title of the library is unknown, but the paucity of "receipts" in the journals indicates the book was fairly comprehensive.[58]

He must have spent hours with the medical "library," because he treated the slaves almost daily, driven by the complex motivation of necessity, humanity, pleasure, and economy. He also nursed members of his own family, but that is another subject. In the meantime, one finds him studying, recording, and treating numerous ailments among the slaves. A general overview seems the best way to catch the sense of Dent's method. Seemingly without an infirmary, he probably visited the quarter to diagnose, prescribe, and report. If he had any assistants other than a midwife, he never acknowledged it.

Sickness was often rife, especially in the humid heat of summers that invited the mysterious and deadly fevers of the low-lying Cowikee country. It was such a time in July, 1840, when "Sickness makeing its appearance among the Negroes. Tyrah and Nat have been sick for five or Six days. Complaints of the former Billious and Latter Worms and fever. Robert and Phillis down this day; former Billious attack, Latter Cold in her head. Clarinda also down Billious." The liver complaint of biliousness must have covered a multitude of abdominal pains and disorders. Regrettably, Dent seldom described his treatment. But, on the following day, "Just Nat went out to work. Tyrah better but constantly complaining of her Stomach, at present giveing her Elixor Vitriol, as she has taken very active medicines." Two days later, "Tyrah and Robert at present the only sick and they mending."[59]

In the lay-by seasons, which entailed the disagreeable task of "saving" fodder, Dent tolerated no feigned illnesses, but he did pay careful attention to the serious cases. "Robert very sick Indeed, relapsed on morning of the 3d. Constant and very hot fevers. Phillis sick this day, Fever, Billious." The entry for August 5, 1840, shows the constancy of Dent's care. "Robert very Ill, has had a scorching fever since the 3d until about 10 Oclock A M. Now 3 P.M appears free of fever, but under the influence of Medicine. Phillis still sick but little fever." As late as August 14, Robert was "mending but Slowly."[60]

A major source of day-to-day frustration was that Dent the healer was also Dent the planter. In September, 1840, he fretted: "Negroes sickly and every day one or more [comes] up with fevers and bad colds rather the appearance of Influenza. Our County this fall resembles one of affliction and Sorrow. The Harvest is come, and the Labourers are few. Death has visited us and bore away Many unexpectedly from their Sphere of usefulness to their dependent family and their new and needy country." Admitting his dependence was refreshingly honest but not meant for public consumption. On October 1 that year, Dent elaborated: "On Sick List this day, Alfred, Gib, January; Complaints Influenza. All the Negroes have bad colds, their Heads stoped up. It is exceedingly warm for this Season of the Year, this afternoon was as oppressive as in June or July."[61]

Three days later, it was an epidemic. "An Influenza has made its appearance on the plantation. All the Large Negroes have bad colds and very much stopped up. The children are suffering extremely. Doll Jack Sophy—Flora. Dis Anna and Clemon are very sick, especially the three first named that have hot fevers and very much choaked with flim." Nor was flu a respecter of race. "Myself and my two children are in the same situation, Horry very sick indeed. It is a regular Epedemic, the whole country is sick with it. The Weather this day cloudy, very cool, has more the appearance of Snow than rain." But the ailments were not all biliousness, fevers, and influenza. "Myrah . . . sick . . . occasioned by miscarriage of child." Also "Tenah & Alfred laid up, the former bad cold, the latter ground Itch."[62]

After the "sickly" fall of 1840, Dent was cautiously optimistic in September, 1841. "Negroes so far continue healthy here, but a few miles below is exceedingly sickly, many farmers have half their force down with fever." "Below" was down the Cowikee Creek, where Dent would shortly move. Meantime, "On Sick Report, John Brown, Sary, Rachel & Rose. None with fever, merely head aches & Billious." John Brown was the overseer whcm Dent also treated. The master's relief at the absence of fever is obvious.[63]

A malady frequently listed in Dent's catalogue of illness was dysentery, by which he meant minor or simple diarrhea. Thus "Gib sick Dysentery." It was not unusual for dysentery to incapacitate five or six hands on a given day, "retarding work" considerably. The old and young were particularly susceptible. "Sick Report, Old Judy and infant Sue, Dysinterys."[64]

Dent recognized that some stomach disorders were related to diet. "John, very sick indeed came very near dying to day with cramp in the Stomach, from overeating Buttermilk While in a low State of health." This "doctor" blamed some dysentery on careless habits of eating wild fruits and berries. In June, 1856: "Sick report, Tamar. The Sickness now on the plantation proceeds from the quantity of plumbs and berrys the Negroes are eating on Sundays." Two years later, in May, Dent noted "more tendency to sickness than we have had this year. It must be owing to the quantity of green Berries." There was also intemperance in drinking. "Sick report, Hannah, Violet, effects of drinking too much water." Except for one accidental death, however, he identified no chronic problems with alcoholic beverages.[65] References to slaves' unwise eating and drinking were few. And, as noted, he never associated dysentery with the consumption of tainted pork.

In April, 1842, Phillis was "laid up with Tooth Ache." While Dent's family used dentists in Clayton and Eufaula in the 1850s, the slaves probably removed their own unhealthy teeth.[66]

It was not unusual for this master to go for days with no sickness to report, especially in the mild weather of springtime cultivation and autumn harvesting of the crop. Thus he frequently wrote, "All hands in field" or "none on Sick report." There are no allusions to special measures taken against hypochondria and malingering. Dent's personal supervision of sickness and knowledge of each black was probably enough to deter most temptations to exploit the sick report for purposes of leisure. That he never recorded any problem of this nature suggests that his power of command was intimidation enough, for tacitly or otherwise it promised some harsh doses for would-be fakers.[67]

The most lethal ailment on this place was "typhoid malarial" fever. Throughout the Cowikee period from 1837 to 1855, it was not unusual to have "chills and fever prevailing to some extent on the plantation. 3 cases among

the Whites and 3 among the black." Numerous Negroes were victims of
these fevers.[68]

Dent's preoccupation with typhoid fever led him in the early 1850s to a
rare and extended comment on treatment, which also serves to illustrate his
systematic approach to illness. "The Typhoid Fever," he wrote,

> is one among the most insidious, protracted and dangerous complaints I have
> ever met up with. It comes on slowly, progresses slowly, but deep and danger-
> ously are the vital organs diseased—the Brain, Liver, Lungs, and Bowels are
> all involved, each in their turn, presenting most dangerous symptoms. Hence
> in the treatment of this dreadful complaint, a Sound Judgement is necessary,
> penetration is requisite, and caution indispensable. In a word guard against a
> rash or forceing treatment. Patience you must have, and prudence must be
> exercised in all your course, for it runs a long course and varied in its symptoms.
>
> In the first instance, I purge out the bowels with a small dose of Oil and tur-
> pentine, and restrain their actions after one or two operations. After this it is
> necessary to pay particular attention to the Bowels, as they are generally the
> first organs seriously affected. Keep strong pepper poultices over them, and
> if the irritation seems to run high, place over them flannel cloths saturated with
> turpentine, keeping the patient on this preparation, *12 drops Turpentine,
> 6 drops Laudanum, a teaspoon of Gum Arabic, dissolved in 4 oz. of water,*
> giving a table spoon full of the mixture every hour or two hours, as the case may
> Require. The tongue will be red and dry, all Secretions apparently suspended.
>
> So soon as you see the Patient restless, unable to sleep, and eyes very sharp,
> you may know that the Brain is involved, hence it is necessary to attend to that
> organ. Keep cold water to the head and cup the temples and warm rocks to the
> feet. You may give a full dose of Dovers powders in a half cup of Flax seed tea.
> Should delirium ensue, pour cold water over the head, put mustard plasters to
> the thighs, warm socks to the feet. I have found Mercurials in its smallest use
> to act as an irritant. And so long as the tongue continues red rely entirely on
> the Turpentine preparation above named and nothing else as internal
> remedies.[69]

Dent wrote with the authority of one who had saved typhoid patients. He
did not, however, save his wife in 1853. If his medical self-confidence led to
a questionable independence of professional physicians (and there is no
proof it did), it is well to remember that regular doctors also lost typhoid
patients—and in large numbers.[70]

One also observes that Dent carefully distinguished between simple
dysentery and a more serious diarrhea that he called flux or bloody flux.
"Fed down with loose bowels, passing some blood, which I fear are
symptoms of flux." In 1853 when typhoid was threatening, perhaps before
Dent fully recognized its symptoms, he wrote dejectedly that bloody flux had
"been rageing in different sections of this Country since last spring, Fatal in
many instances and in many Localities. In May we had one case of it, Affy,

who was confined down with it some 4 weeks, prostrating her very much. The case proved a stubborn and tedious one [and] Recovered slowly."[71]

Although Dent practiced too little prenatal care, he tended infants as he did children and adults.

> Straffon, Infant son of Affy, Was taken down with flux in June, he was teething at the time; he lingered some five weeks with it. Every time a tooth appearing [he] was relapsed and prostrated; he died in July. Lucy, Infant of Myrahs, Teething, was very much reduced and prostrated; her case is cured, but returns with the appearance of each tooth. Considered subject to relapse at any peri[o]d. Dave, Infant of Rose, Up and down with same complaint. Liable at any moment to relapse have had much trouble with him. Nancy, 4 years old, has been very Ill of same complaint; discharged after 10 days treatment.[72]

Later Dent realized this flux was related to the typhoid epidemic of 1853 and 1854. Meanwhile, there were simpler infections more rewarding to treat. "Sick Report, Grandison, riseing on his foot." On another occasion, Frank was "laid up with a large boil under his arm," but Dent never mentioned the lance.[73]

The master also enjoyed naming less obvious symptoms of more complicated ailments. In July, 1858, he "found all well except Violets child Kate, which appears to be dropsical." The abnormal collection of bodily fluids must have been obvious, for later that month he reported "John . . . neuralgia," "Violet . . . Flooding," "Phillis . . . Rheumatic," and "Kate . . . Dropsy."[74] His treatment is not recorded. The distinction between neuralgia as nerve pain, and rheumatism as swelling and stiffening of joints is both careful and revealing of the man's attention to medical detail.

But Dent was not above summoning C. J. Pope or some other physician to attend his family and slaves. Matilda was a valuable house servant whom the master purchased for that service. She was only one of many he finally drove to the doctor. "Went to Eufaula and carried Matilda for Dr Pope to examine her condition, as she is in a bad state of health, soars breaking out about her ears and jaws." Perhaps it was scrofula; Dent did not report.[75]

The master also used Pope's hospital when his sister Emma's slave, Lucy, was returned by the purchaser because of syphilis. "On Friday 30th March, Mr Sam Jones sent the girl Lucy (belonging to Miss Emma Dent, whom he bought from me, as agent of Emma Dent, in January last) home. Sent her by his son Sammie with a letter dated March 30th 1860, in which he says, 'I send the girl back to you, for I cannot pay for her.' Sent a message back to Mr Jones by said son Samuel that I would meet him in Eufaula on Wednesday next, and see about it. Mr. Jones says a Physician pronounces the girl constitutionally unsound." Subsequently, "Dr Pope examined Lucy, pronounced it an old case of Syphilis. Left Lucy at his hospital for treatment. Terms, Thirty ($30) dollars for the case, and Ten ($10) dollars pr month board." She remained two months before "Dr Pope sent Lucy home on yesterday." Her condition is not recorded. This occurred in 1860. Dent acknowledged only one other case of syphilis, which killed a young Negro man in 1856.[76]

Of greater threat than syphilis was pneumonia. "Amy has been quite ill for last two days of Pneumonia." It could persist for months. "The Pneumonia in a most agrivated form has assumed an Epedemic form on the plantation." This was usually complicated by pleurisy, an inflammation of the membrane covering the lungs, which causes acute pain. Dent frequently wrote to the effect: "Israel still quite sick, case of severe Pleurisy. Trying the Botanic system of practice in his case."[77]

Less dangerous but more constant were colds, which could be "very prevalent among whites and blacks." Dent tried to regulate clothing, jobs, and exposure, to minimize colds. "Backward in picking out Cotton. The Last week has been unfavorable for work, it being rainy and the country so sickly could not expose the Negroes."[78]

One of the slaves' more exotic disorders was "fits." In January, 1860, "Rebecca still has fits at intervals." Dent could not relieve them. When "Rebecca still continues with fits," he "sent for Dr Pope to see her." It appears the Eufaula physician was no more successful, and Rebecca's convulsions continued.[79] It was seldom that Dent could not use a more specific term than "fits."

In April, 1860, he described symptoms which sound like mumps. "Soar throats and large Swellings under the jaw seem to be a common epidemic throughout the country." Shortly there was a more serious threat. "A case of Small Pox is reported in Eufaula ... will hear to morrow the truth of it." He subsequently learned: "In Eufaula there is much alarm and talk about the Small Pox. Several families are leaving the City, moving out to the country." The Dents took no precaution except to stay at home. And the panic soon ran its course.[80]

Accidents among his Negroes seem to have been infrequent. In spite of much going barefoot, there was little snakebite. But in 1858, "Ben was bit by a snake—on the foot, very much swollen and painful." And in 1866, "A grub rattle bit Katy on the outer side of the heel last evening; it is badly swollen up to the knee and very painful." While there is no evidence of a fatal snakebite, going barefoot could result in cut feet. "Brown cut his foot by stepping on a glass bottle. Jane cut her foot by stepping on an ax." The upper extremities were less liable to injury but not immune. "Casualty. Paul is laid up with a very bad hand having had it mashed at the Screw raising at Adams, last tuesday."[81]

Dent apparently saved the hand and set other broken bones. "Gibs mule threw him down on yesterday, and put one of his fingers out of Joint by trodding on it." More serious than a "trod" finger was the "Accident" whereby "A mule threw Jacky this morning and broke his leg below the knee." Pranking was also dangerous. "Jack was playing with Peter to day and broke his arm.'' Dent not only set these fractures, he also attended Toby, who was ''shot through the thigh by a pistol, makeing a narrow escape of Severing the artery or breaking the thigh bone, by Alfred and Herberts carelessly handling a pistol.''[82] The evidence of these daily reports shows knife and gunshot wounds among Dent's blacks to have been almost nonexistent before emancipation.

Finally, in the matter of health care, the pregnancy of slave women was a major item. In the 1850s Dent wrote of the economic importance of raising little Negroes, but actual practice shows that the mother's work was more important than her offspring. Women worked as near to delivery as possible; nor did Dent allow a long ''lay up'' period. And there is no mention of light work for nursing mothers. On June 26, 1841, he noted: ''Bash laid up in confinement & will not be out before the 1st of July.''[83]

This does not mean that the master totally ignored problems peculiar to females and their pregnancies. ''Sick Report, Jane who has been confined some time with painful menstruation, brought out last evening some medicines from Dr [William H.] Thornton for her.'' On the next day, ''Jane does not seem to be relieved by Dr Thorntons prescription. Continuing the medicines.'' Three days later, ''Jane still continues down with pains in lower part of belly. Mendah ailing, pregnancy advanced.''[84]

Dent recorded the slaves' pregnancies, and accompanying problems, much more freely than he described similar conditions in his wife. He reported a slave's every complication down to ''Celia's Prolapsus Uteri,'' and probably enjoyed the challenge of a displaced uterus. But the reader of the journals never knows of Dent's wife's delicate condition until after her confinement (and then from the briefest notation), except when a longer entry was necessary to relate a delightful joke on Dr. Pope: ''Mrs Dent confined this morning ¾ hr past 8, with a Son; her labor was so rapid that the Child was born before the Doctor arrived.'' The planter apparently delivered his child, but dared not treat the Eufaula physician who ''took sick'' and ''went to bed,'' whereupon Dent ''sent Dr [Carlisle] Terry to see him who remained all night.''[85]

Because of numerous entries on Negro ''miscarriages'' and ''abortions,'' one wonders whether the latter resulted from choice. Probably not. Still, ''Tenah very sick this morning . . . miscarried at 11 O clock AM.'' This was in 1841. The following year ''Tenah confined 12 to day with a Son.'' But in 1858, ''Tyrah, a case of miscarriage.'' There were numerous miscarriages and fewer abortions, but in 1853 ''Phillis threatened Abortion.'' And in January, 1860, ''Helen abortioned last night.'' Aside from the miscarriages and abortions, which Dent did not summarize, the infant mortality rate was very high. One cannot be sure that he recorded all such instances. At least six Negro infants and children died in 1857 alone. A few scattered examples show an appalling frequency of death from premature birth that probably indicates overworked mothers. In May, 1852, ''Bashes infant died to day.

Also Philis infant by premature birth.'' In February, 1858, "Tamar Confined to day with a Boy, the child seems premature from its extreme smallness, hardly think it can live.''[86]

In 1852 the master blamed some infant mortality on "mismanagement . . . by the midwife'' whom he did not identify. Perhaps it was he. In 1858 there was a cryptic reference, "I am still sick, . . . My nurse is Death, she has killed more little Negroes than any other person living.'' But Dent continued to document the primacy of cotton culture over Negroes' prenatal care. In May, 1860, amid financial security, he could only resent the fact that "Our force is much weakened by Pregnancy among the Women and sickness among others; in working over Cottons this time, we have been short on an averge at least 8 hands daily.''[87]

In 1860, one-half of Dent's slaves were under twenty years of age, and almost a third of them were ten years old or younger. These percentages had not changed significantly since the early 1840s. In the twenty-year period from 1836 to 1856, his slave force increased from forty-five to eighty-five persons, a real increase of only two persons per year. During these twenty years, he recorded thirty-six deaths, excluding some stillbirths and other types of infant mortality. Eighteen, or one-half, of the recorded deaths were of children ten years and younger. There were four deaths among the teen-aged, two in their twenties, two in their thirties, three in their forties, none in the fifties, two in their sixties, one in his seventies, none in the eighties, and five in their nineties. The causes and numbers of death were: dysentery, seven; typhoid, five; old age, four; pneumonia, three; accidents, three; whooping cough, two; teething, two; and unknown, two. The following caused one death each: worms, convulsions, apoplexy, dropsy, child bed fever, venereal disease, croup, and scarlet fever.[88]

The master's fatalistic attitude toward Negro deaths is evident in his account of a tragic drowning, which was one of the accidents listed above.

> This day Wednesday 26th January 1842, John with his wagon and Team of Six Mules In hauling a Load of Corn from my old place here, procured Some liquor from Morrisons Teamster Green whereby he was intoxicated. When he arrived at the Creek, Instead of leaving his wagon on the side he was, Rushes the Mules in, Wagon & two Small Boys who were along to help load the Wagon. The Creek very high indeed. The Result was The Mules six in number perished. And one of the Small Boys Met a Watery grave owing to the Teamster being DRUNK, the other escaped by a miracle.[89]

Perhaps in this instance, Dent was most concerned by the loss of six valuable mules. But he noticed Negro deaths, especially when "Old Sillar plantation nurse died. Severe dysentery occasioned by Cold from nursing the sick of nights. Sick about fifteen days.'' He also reported the loss when "Sue our Children's nurse'' died of typhoid during the epidemic of 1853-1854. And he followed closely the case of the house servant Charlotte, in April and May, 1856. On May 15, "Charlotte has another back set and is now dangerously ill. Throwing up a great quantity of green viciated stuff." Three days later, "Charlotte died at 6 PM, abscess of the Lungs." Reports of men's deaths were noticeably less frequent, but he did observe that "January died May 13th 1862 of consumption aged about 42. He was an excellent Negro faithful and reliable," and therefore qualified for a brief memorial. [90]

Yet Dent eulogized few slaves and no other as he did Aunt Jinny, whose obituary is a sterling exception, not to be confused with the master's matter-of-fact regard for the average hand. "These few lines," he wrote, "are in Memory of one whose Life was a long scene of the most devoted servitude of the most examplary Moral worth and constant devotion to her God, her Masters and Mistresses, and to her fellow Creatures."

"Jinny, a Slave, better known as old Aunt Jinny," he continued,

> died this 4th day of June, A. D. 1852, at 15 minutes past Two P. M., Aged about 100 years.
>
> In the death of this old and faithful Servant, we can record with truthfulness, and unmeaning praise, her high and elevated Character, her many Virtues, and her fidelity. Through a long and eventful life, which won the affection and esteem of her owners and the Kindest regards and admiration from all who knew her, She faithfully served four Generations as body Servant and Nurse. And each has handed down to their Posterity her character as one most faithful and in whom all reliance and confidence could be placed. Her memory will long last by those who knew her, and her surviving owners can never forget her. To the last, so long as her strength endured, she proved faithful to her Trust and duties. For many many Years, she was a member of the Baptist Church. Her Religion was manifested by her works, her faith steadfast, and she looked forward to death to bring about that great and everlasting reward of eternal Happiness, which was the efforts of her long, dutiful pilgrimage in this World. [91]

Comments on the dead, or the lack of any comments, show Dent distinguishing between house servants and field hands. Here, as in all matters, he judged Negroes according to the work ethic and was exceptionally warm in his praise of Jinny's religion precisely because it manifested itself in the good works of obedient servanthood. This master was consistently silent on the matter of the slaves' funerals and was reticent on the entire subject of their religion. The few exceptions to this rule were usually less positive than his comments on Aunt Jinny's Baptist Christianity. Addressing the abolitionists regarding slaves' religion, Dent affirmed:

> They have all access to religious privileges, and they join as they deem proper either the Baptist or Methodist Churches. And like our own [white] people some are true christians, whilst others are only so by pretense. On Sabbath

the day is their own, their owners calling on them to do no manner of Work, except on the house servants, whose tasks and duties are light all the year round. And by turns they are allowed the privileges of a Sabbath on the plantations, whilst in towns and cities they enjoy every one.[92]

Religion was work and vice versa. This planter might not drive the blacks on Sundays, but he frequently wanted to. The extent of this sentiment is most clearly revealed in his recurring Sunday entry, "Nothing . . . worth noting" today. Yet the tradition for a free Sunday was so strong that Dent had to "give" two slaves a Sabbath on Saturday, probably to ensure their working on Sundays. Thus on Saturday, June 9, 1841, "Jim and Dandy takeing their usual holy day."[93]

As a nominal Episcopalian, the antebellum Dent found it difficult to respect evangelical Methodists and Baptists of either color. His disdain for emotional Christianity might explain his ignoring black funerals. On another occasion, with Fed "extremely Ill with Pneumonia" and "Dr Pope . . . to see him last evening and . . . again this morning," the master was no less incensed that Fed in his delirium was "a maniac about religion, wild, and talks of nothing but going to heaven." Unwilling to surrender Fed to the next world, Dent "Put a blister on the back of his neck" one day and on the next "had his head shaved . . . to apply cold water to it all day," eventually breaking the fever and saving the slave for usefulness in this world.[94]

In the response to Aunt Jinny and Fed, this planter showed his assumption that a slave's true religion was obedience. Hard work was Christianity enough for blacks. But his Negroes were not as "religious" as he wished. Dent articulated some of this when he wrote the abolitionists regarding slaves: "Their labor is not as hard or as protracted as that of the white man. Nor are they worked in the rain or extreme cold or after sun set." He helpfully explained which white man he meant when he continued, "In short so far as hard and exposing work is concerned, a New England Man does more in one month than a negro does in two."[95]

The designation New England man was general. At various times, this antebellum planter expressed respect for the Yankee farmer, manufacturer, and mechanic. Which did he have in mind at this point? Probably the farmer, as the white man whose work most nearly paralleled that of the Negro slave. It is true that Dent's blacks were not New Englanders, but they worked enough, whether from force or choice, to satisfy their querulous master. He was not given to praising anyone, let alone slaves. But he expressed satisfaction with their labor in numerous subtle ways during this period. And after emancipation, he consistently praised slave over free labor.[96]

Master Dent also knew that his slaves' work was harder, colder, and generally more demanding than he would admit to the abolitionists. Numerous winter mornings were "very cold, the ground thoroughly frozen."

Yet the plows were running, "ridgeing up in the Cox fields" while other "Hands burning off." A recurring wintertime entry reads, "Weather has been continued cold, freezing every night. All hands engaged this Week in spring flat New ground—rolling, piling, cleaning up, and burning, which has been a slow and heavy Job." Dent realized that clearing virgin forests with an axe and human sinew was no light undertaking. There was also the constant danger of overexertion and too much exposure, if the overseer's judgment was poor. Amid sudden cold, wet weather, when the overseer was too distant to be advised, this master could fret, "If the overseer is considerate, all hands are housed." [97]

While it was rare, even in a December, Dent could covet some rest for the hands. Thus on December 3, 1852, his plantation "business" was "very much retarded," but "it is well enough that our Negroes should slack off, having been pushed up to the mark last year. Next year I shall push them up" again. He probably sounds harsher than he was in practice. For example, one occasionally reads, "So rainy and cold all work Suspended." But this Monday, November 15, 1858, entry was unusual. There was almost always something to do in wet weather—preparing manures under the cattle shelter, if nothing else. This particular leniency was almost certainly related to the visit of Episcopal Bishop N. Hamner Cobb on this date. "The Bishop came out to our Residence on the Plantation and Christened Mrs Dent, Anne, Charlie, Sallie, Kate and Fanny. Dined with us, and accompanied by E. C. Bullock." Thus when the bishop came on a Monday, the hands were lolling about the quarter in uncharacteristic ease. So much for the guise of relaxation that an otherwise hard-working slave force could assume when special guests arrived. [98]

An occasional day's rest, however, was a rhythmical part of a larger scheme of incentives to labor, a scheme which was simultaneously more subtle, complex, and effective than mere whippings. On the other hand, the whip was the most obvious item among the slave's incentives or controls. Dent wrote of whipping the blacks on several occasions but never with enough clarity to define his policy regarding the practice. For example, he told his overseer in 1840, "if there be any error or Idleness discovered, Correction with the whip is your proper alteration. Any offence behind your back should cause severer punishment." [99] Yet Dent would not tolerate an overseer who depended too heavily on the whip. Thus the master could later discourage its use.

In 1852 he urged his overseer to substitute personal attention and encouragement in place of physical punishment:

Severity to Negroes I do not believe in. It is injurious and wrong. Your personal attention and due encouragement will entirely do away with Severity. Wherever you see Severe Overseers, it is occasioned by their own bad conduct. They neglect their duties by running about to see others, or are Idle. Hence they rely upon the whip to make up what their own inattentiveness has brought about. This is criminal in two respects—first in the misdemeanors of the Overseer himself and Secondly in punishing the Innocent for the guilty.[100]

Although Dent recognized the invitations to injustice implicit in the practice of whipping slaves, he did not categorically prohibit the policy. As late as July 21, 1859, he could write with maddening brevity, "Whipped some 13 women and girls for Stealing water melons."[101] The overseer usually gave the whippings, and for offenses much more serious than this. Did the master in this instance wield the lash himself? He only implies that he did. If so, were his motives other than the mere loss of melons? He wrote of no whippings in relation to theft of hogs and corn by Negro men. On the other hand, there could have been more whippings than the few he recorded. The unevenness of this reporting reflects his seeming misgivings concerning the practice.

A more characteristic entry on whipping preserves Dent's image of the aloof patriarch who heard the plaintiff slave and upheld overseer Turner Howell's action and authority. On July 7, 1859, Dent wrote that "Johns Jack run away last night. Mr Howell went to whip him for wasting fodder against his directions. He became stubborn and insolent, and would not submit. Mr Howell gave him a good flogging, and after comeing to me to complain, he, receiving no comfort from my self, walked off. Jack is not blessed with much sense, dodgeing off is no new thing with Jack."[102]

In the case of Jack, as in that of Frank, who was whipped for having dirty clothes, Dent implied that physical punishment came after specific directions, warnings, and even insubordination. A flogging, however, might be interpreted as more than a mild whipping. At any rate, each punishment was severe enough to provoke a running-away. When Jack returned after only a night and day's absence, Dent acknowledged, "I expect Howell whipped him most too severely, feverish." There was a similar case with Israel, who "had a difficulty with the Overseer on yesterday and run away." But Israel was gone five days before he "came home this morning of his own accord." Frank's "vacation" also lasted five days before he "came home last evening of his own accord."[103]

This, then, seems to have been the pattern—disobedience, whipping, running away, and voluntary return. The high incidence of running away in relation to the few recorded whippings suggests one of two things. Either these punishments were unusually severe, or whippings were rare enough to spark the rebellion of temporary leaves. The latter was probably the case, for the sense of the journals is that whippings *were* rare, and Dent's regret of them made him tolerant of running away, an act he seemingly did not punish.

It is significant that this slave owner did not mention pursuing runaways with hounds until 1865, after the animosities arising from emancipation had set in. Master Dent's understanding of the violence possible in the chase of a runaway is captured in a note from 1855 that communicates this "genteel" businessman's disgust with that drama: "Mr Varner was in no business mood, having the evening before had a valuable Negro man killed by Daniel Stanley his overseer and John Lewis who was running him with hounds. The Negro was badly beaten and Stabbed in several places by Stanley." [104] Dent must have sensed that his whipped slaves' running away and peaceful return was as important a control as the flogging itself.

Certainly an incentive more important than whipping was the seeming omnipresence of the master and overseer in their inspection of blacks' work and attention to the master's possessions. A case in point was the slave's use and care of mules, an item of large expense and necessity. In February, 1860, an acceptable mule could cost as much as $175. "Bought two mules from Hughs for $350.00. Gave him a check on Eastern Bank of Ala. for $350.00 through Turner Howell." The expense and importance of mules and horses could move Dent to purple prose: "it is by the Aid of the Noble and Segacious animal that our most arduous, as well as Lucrative, Interest is performed." [105]

He firmly believed that his and the overseer's inspection of mules and gear (and everything else for that matter) was sufficient to prevent the worst of slaves' negligence and abuse. The mules would suffer "Unless you see such [good] treatment given him," because "Negroes . . . possess but little humanity and feeling to attend to the wants and comforts of the fatigued and hard worked animal." The best means for order was not the whip but inspection: "Again Your Horses should be put up perfectly clean and dry, So if one should be rode or used by a Negroe at night contrary to orders, it can be detected." [106]

On the one hand, a system of inspection and detection by whites should foster responsibility among blacks. "Never let them change a Mule with each other, unless it be done for some necessary reason given by yourself. . . . Each ploughing and attending to his own constantly can be made responsible for the condition of his animal." The key to this order through individual responsibility was personal attention. "All such is not to be performed thro your orders, but by constant & personal attention on your part." Paradoxically, however, the outcome of such intensive supervision was limited responsibility. The master admitted, "I would not trust them to hoe and thin down Pond field Corn without the Overseer was present to superintend." [107]

The ill-defined role of the whip and the great emphasis upon inspection, detection, and reporting suggests that one of Dent's major means of controlling blacks was a slave's knowing that the master would know of any shirking or carelessness. But it is impossible to measure the strength and universality of this sanction. One can only report it in relation to another powerful incentive, the matter of how much time a slave could expect to be free from the master's work.

Dent's Negroes could expect to labor in bearable weather from daylight to dark, six days a week, with an occasional half day free on Saturday afternoon and a few free days on Saturday—or even on a Monday, when the bishop was expected. Free time was rare during the work week, even in inclement weather. Keeping the slaves busy was one of the motives for building livestock shelters for the "making" of manures in rainy weather. There was also cleaning and sewing to be done in the quarter. But nights and Sundays (or the equivalent of a Sabbath rest) belonged to the slaves. Night work was tiring, and it was unpopular with blacks and with Dent. Yet overseers must have wanted it occasionally, probably in fall and winter harvest, when daylight shrank out of proportion to need. But Dent, following a tradition too strong to be broken lightly, insisted, "Night work should be avoided as much as possible. The days are long enough if properly made use of to turn to advantage."[108]

No doubt, the careful observance of these strictures in ordinary times made the blacks more willing to work nights and Sundays in extraordinary times. Sunday, March 11, 1855, was such an unusual period. It was "An unfavourable day for fires. All hands out guarding against a fresh outbreak of fire at the Oat Field fencing." Despite the extra work, slave morale was high, and the woods fire was contained. Five years later to the day, on Sunday, March 11, 1860, "Hands up all night fighting fire, the woods being on fire between us and Bighams." Owing to his slaves' diligence, Dent's loss from woods fires (which were a recurring threat) never exceeded a few hundred "panels" of rail fencing. While the loss could run into thousands of rails, these were of concern more as a matter of time than money. They were always quickly replaced, which indicates a stockpile of rails from new ground clearings for the immediate refencing of valuable crops against loose and foraging livestock.[109]

These blacks' readiness to safeguard their master's property may be considered admirable, but their motive was not completely selfless. In the first place, such threats diverted the "hands" from tasks that were routine, if not downright monotonous. When "Fires broke out," it generally "stopped all hands from work" and gave them a fresh, if harder, task.[110] It is an unusual soul who fails to find invigorating challenge or release in danger and even in tragedy. Also, uncontrolled fires would have threatened the slaves' homes and food supplies, as well as the master's.

On March 9, 1855, Dent reported a "Great Fire" in an entry that illustrates his loss of fences, the threat of further losses, and the slaves' motivation to save the quarter. "The woods on the North as well as the South side of the Plantation is on fire, and everything is so dry with our March winds they are making devouring progress. We lost some 200 pannels of fencing on the North string this afternoon and some pannels on the South. The fire is not checked but progressing rapidly. On tomorrow will be a trying day for us to save our Oat field fencing, and the Quarter will be in some danger. Will suspend all work and attend to the fire. My overseer is also absent having gone to Millers for the Hogs.''[111] Dent and the hands were equal to the task without the overseer, preventing further damage except to fences. The slaves' interest in stopping woods fires is only one evidence of their good morale.

Another matter that engendered some contentment was Dent's consistent effort to ''undercrop.'' For him, undercropping meant cultivating less than twenty acres of corn and cotton combined for each adult or ''full'' laborer. He explained to the overseer in 1840:

> I am no advocate for over planting to the hands. I deem fifteen acres to the hand an ample crop. More can be made from that quantity of Ground than Twenty acres, for the 20 acre business is merely run over, half tended. Consequently your ground cannot yield as well by One third as crops that are kept clean of Grass [and] Weeds and properly worked when needed. The Twenty acre system in my opinion is hard on hands, Injurious to Lands, and a Loss in the crop at the end. Two acres of corn, Cotton, or any other product, properly prepared, planted and managed will yield more than four acres planted [in] the manner in which they farm in this Country.[112]

Thus Dent regularly calculated the total number of full hands, adding half-hands and third-hands to make a whole. Then he planned his acreage (which was still large for ''scientific'' farming). In 1842, with twenty-four full hands (eight were ''plows'') his corn and cotton acreage when combined averaged fourteen acres per hand. There were forty-two acres to the plow. And in 1855, on ''older'' soils, he planted seventeen acres for each ''full'' hand.[113] Such care increased productivity, and any ''undercropping'' meant easier control of grass and made it the more likely that the slave would enjoy his traditional free time of nights, Sundays, and the holidays of July Fourth and Christmas.

Neither Saturday nor Saturday afternoon was a regular holiday on Dent's plantations. In fact, his blacks probably worked more Saturday afternoons than not. ''Giving'' the slaves Saturday ''PM'' was this master's most obvious way of inspiring them to greater effort. Saturday holidays were either earned by the slaves or given from Dent's magnanimity. For example, such a gift could encourage completing a job before the new week began. On Saturday, March 13, 1858, hands were''manureing with Cotton Seed. Wagons hauling out Lot Manures. Will get through to day, PM. Will knock off work, giving Negroes this afternoon.'' Other short, dirty, even muddy tasks were best left to Saturday because of the end of the week washing of clothes and persons. One of these was setting sweet potato shoots directly behind a good, wetting rain. On Saturday, March 20, 1852,

Dent noted that "Until 12 M, planting potatoes. PM, Gave negroes ballance of the day." [114]

Another device was to rest Saturday afternoon in anticipation of a hard and important week ahead. It was such a time in March, 1856, that Dent, "After building a Cow pen, gave the Negroes the ballance of the day. Trusting on Monday next we may be able to proceed in planting corn." And the blacks understood this expectation of extra effort. At peace with his plans, the master "Went to Eufaula." [115]

Often, however, a half-holiday on Saturday was no holiday at all. Dent frequently "gave" such a "PM" for "Negroes to work their own crops." Slaves' crops were not clearly defined, but they included cotton and vegetables and were often called "patches." He seldom allowed the blacks an entire day for their vegetables and cotton until he was satisfied with their cultivation of his own crops. It was, then, an unusual entry on two counts on Saturday, July 24, 1852, when the planter "gave Negroes to day to work their own crops, having our crop in pretty fair order." [116] Such praise was not characteristic. Furthermore, the overseer must have supervised such mass cultivation of Negro patches, because the blacks used Dent's equipment and seemingly employed the gang system. Such regimentation showed on a June Saturday in 1853, when "Plows and all hands Working out Negroes crop to day." [117]

July Fourth and Christmas were the only holidays regularly observed on this plantation. Before the southern states' acts of secession in 1861, the nation's Independence Day was too important to be ignored. The antebellum Dent even counted the years of freedom, noting on the appropriate day in 1858, "82 Year of American Independence." When July Fourth occurred on Sunday, he was forced to make Saturday a holiday. This was bearable, since he preferred that any break in routine occur at the end of the week. He usually resented Monday holidays, however, and any other interruption of the work-week schedule. Thus on Monday, July 4, 1859, he was, for whatever reason, somewhat testy. "Finished plowing out DeWitts flats at 8 AM and knocked off, and gave Negroes ballance of the day." [118] At work since dawn, the slaves had labored at least three hours and probably more.

Christmas holidays were also erratic in number and point of beginning, depending on the weather, the state of the harvest, and Dent's plans for the new year. Not infrequently the hands were "Jobbing, cleaning up, Inspecting fences, and brushing some Washes" right down through December 24, especially when it occurred at the end of the week. Dent seldom allowed more than four days for Christmas, occasionally even less. There is no mention of special food, dinners, liquor, or any other bonus at this time. In this season, however, the master could tolerate some additional noise at the quarter and the slaves' attendance at the circus. [119]

Planting, like any other human endeavor, requires good timing, but especially is this true of the harvest. Because there was no income until the crop was gathered, processed, transported, and sold, the planter Dent was obsessed with time. And he used the formula "time is money" to motivate a rapid harvest and sale of his cash crop, cotton. The plan was simple and it worked. The slaves could not attend to *their* cash cotton crop until the master's was carried through a particular stage of production. Thus "Plowing Negroes Cottons" meant that Dent's crop was clear of grass. And Negroes "picking their own cotton" meant the master's crop was housed. [120]

It was a strong motive for early harvests, and Dent's cotton seldom remained in the field until the new year. In fact the Negroes usually picked their own cotton in November and December. This meant that Christmas week was a good time for "Gining Negro Cottons. Packed it this afternoon." Sometimes this process waited until January, which was still comparatively early in the marketing year. And then, between late December and early February, after Dent's cotton had been transported to market, some teamster "hauled down Negro Cottons to Eufaula." We are not told the yield of the slaves' crop. Apparently it totaled from two to four bales per year and was immediately sold in Eufaula by Dent or the overseer as the representative of the heads of Negro families. On December 29, 1858, "Mr Howell carried Negro Cottons and sold it. The heads of families went to make purchases." [121] The economic incentive is obvious, and Negroes' cotton income was a major source of those extra comforts which Dent admired in the homes of provident slaves.

Aside from the incentives of the whip, close supervision, the certainty of free time, and profitable family patches, Dent also used certain duties as a type of reward and punishment, listing special officers by name. In February, 1841, he noted: "Sary, Cook for the field Hands; Sophy, Cook for Children; John, Black Smith; Alfred, Carpenter; Cudjoe, Shepherd." None of these duties were given to household slaves, who served as nurse, cooks, maids, and butler in the Dents' home. The cooks were young women who served while their behavior was good. An altercation with Mrs. Dent could draw swift sentence to the field. In 1856 there were four cooks and maids in the master's home. The teen-aged butler named Brown doubled as a driver and trusted errand boy in the early 1850s, until he reached the age and size of a prime field hand. When Brown left the house service, he was replaced by ten-year-old Toby and the sixty-six-year-old Dandy. The position of family nurse was reserved for an older, highly responsible Negro woman. Dent's esteem for Aunt Jinny was based on her service as nurse to his wife and children. When Jinny died, she was succeeded by the respected "Old Sillar," who later succumbed to typhoid fever. Subsequently, Sue and Betty, both in their forties, were nurses and later, Amy, who was almost sixty years of age. [122]

At any given time, only about half of the Negroes were classed as regular field hands. For example, in 1858 Dent listed forty-nine blacks in the gang and forty-one "not in the field." Obviously, many of the latter were children who worked irregularly or not at all. At times, however, "Four small hands, Zack Nat Bash & Tyrah," could be "Employed Burning of[f] a part of New Ground Cleared this Winter." In addition to house servants and children, the nonfield force included carpenters, blacksmiths, seamstresses, communal cooks, keepers of nurseries, cleaning gangs, livestock minders, and wagoners. [123]

Wagoning must have been an attractive duty. Who else, except the skilled laborers, could, with the master's permission, see so much of the outside world? In 1840, Dent's major teamster was thirty-five-year-old June who hauled everything from plank to corn meal. But Dent had also trained eighteen-year-old Bob to drive. And in 1841 with "June still sick," the master could send Bob "up with the Cart to Aaron Burlisons for Some peach trees he gave me." Shortly thereafter, Bob virtually replaced June as wagoner. Dent regularly rotated hands into and out of this task. [124]

Road work was another duty that gave some respite from plantation regularity, and the hands worked with willing spirit and ready strength. Several entries from September, 1841, illustrate: "Men working on road, opening a New Road from Greys to Clayton. . . . Men still working on the road. . . . Men on Road." And four days after they began, Dent "Stopped the Hands from going on the road this day as they had cut it out and opened it as well as all other roads in the County." Another task in which the blacks joined willingly was helping neighbors. "Boys went to assist Adams raise his screw." Admitting he had favorites among the Negroes, the master would have chosen these for the more agreeable duties. [125]

Now the discussion of Dent's incentives for slave productivity moves to the more subjective realm of psychological inspiration. He wrote of "Vurtur's gang" so frequently and in such positive terms that one senses Dent's faith was a major source of these slaves' responsibility. Vurtur, a fifty-year-old driver, and his special gang of prime hands could be trusted with any duty except skilled labor, and they frequently assisted the carpenters and blacksmiths. "Vurtur's gang" appears in the journals almost as regularly as matters of health. They were "hoes," "axes," ditchers, pickers, grubbers, litterers, general trouble shooters. [126] Dent's pride in this force was quiet but strong, indicating the subtle power of a significant authority figure to mold a subordinate.

A similar psychological spur is suggested by the care with which the master listed prime hands and half-hands, not just by number, but also by name. He knew the strong and weak as individuals, and his journal distinctions surely carried into personal relationships. The "plows" were his strongest, most dexterous slaves. In 1841 four of the nine "Regular Plough Hands" were women. Zack, January, Bob, Gib, and Sam were men. But Tenah, Hannah, Violet, and Affy were female "Plows." That same year only four of the eleven "Effective Hoe Hands" were men. He pointedly listed the names of "Non Effective Hoe Hands, or half hands."[127]

Along this same line, a less subtle and very public judgment was giving the most "Effective Hands" new tools and passing the older worn ones down to "half hands." "Gave four new Axes to wit June Vurter Sam Gib, ballance hands kept axes formerly in use." Rather surprisingly, Dent never complained of slaves' treatment of tools, and usually carried most implements over to the next year's use. On March 21, 1841, he wrote: "Hoes given out to Hands as follows this day. All have been in use, as I shall not give new hoes until in May. Plough Hands received none, as yet, until I purchase, and about that period the plough force will be diminished and Hoes increased." He purchased the best quality of tools available for the slaves, believing southern-made ones, when they could be had, were superior to northern brands marketed in the South.[128]

Dent's satisfaction with slaves' care of tools stemmed from each black's personal responsibility for his implement. No slave was free to lose or abuse his hoe or axe or other equipment, on pain of public exposure and, one suspects, humiliation. For example, there were three grades of hoes: "Old hoes in good order," "ordinary hoes," and "new hoes." Old hoes were returned, classified, and reassigned. An "ordinary hoe" was good enough for a "half" or "one-third" hand. Such a person knew his place, being marked by more than just slave status. The strong, productive black received new tools, not to be abused but to be used, preserved, and passed on the next year. There was much peer pressure implicit in the system.[129]

Dent never replaced more than half the slaves' tools in a given year, and he usually replaced much less than half. One reason for this was his careful distinction between heavy grubbing hoes for new ground and light weeding hoes for crops. He provided both types of tool, and the slaves knew when to use which. In 1842, only nine of eighteen hoes were new, and Dent methodically listed the names of slaves receiving them. In 1856, there were twenty "good" and "ordinary" old hoes, which supplied half of the weeding force. And in 1862, during the Civil War, he only exchanged four new hoes for old ones out of a total of fifteen.[130]

Nor did he complain of the treatment of other tools for plowing, carpentering, and smithing. Rather, he was more apt to write, "2 set carpenter tools, a complete set smith's tools, all in satisfactory order." The carpenters and blacksmith were Alfred, Hardtimes, and John, respectively. We shall come to them momentarily. Meanwhile, there was something of this same psychology of exposing each individual to the group's inspection in Dent's record of a slave's weights of cotton picked. He also figured averages of the individual black's pounds per day. It would have been in character had he announced the individual's performance in relation to the average amount of cotton picked, which could run as high as 165 pounds on a good day's harvest.[131]

This master had similar opportunity for instilling incentive in the necessary function of sending someone to right another fellow's wrong. Much of this could have been unconscious, but that would not lessen its effectiveness. Surely grown Negro men sensed the message when Dent sent his teen-aged son, Horry, "up to Fryers to see about the 10 Sheep lost by John & Hardtimes." Horry came home with the sheep; nothing had to be said. The criticism was made. [132] But the same process could work in reverse. Dent's second son, Herbert, was less responsible than Horry. And, if horsemanship was a significant measure of a man among blacks and whites of that time, Dent communicated much to the Negroes and Herbert when he sent two blacks to "hunt Brooks that got away from Herbert at the academy X Roads school on yesterday, with bridle and saddle on." The slaves, Brown and Grandison, brought the cantankerous and aptly named Preston Brooks back home. [133]

Such occurrences would indicate room for pride in small victories among the servant race in the Old and New South. In this instance, black pride, ironically, worked to the master's interest in producing a more valuable servant. On the other hand, Dent may have suffered more insubordination from his slaves than he cared to admit. For example, plantation tools could have been more abused than he acknowledged. Furthermore, he never interpreted running away as an act of rebellion. Nor could he conceive of fires and slow-downs as being deliberately contrived. The success of his command depended upon some self-deception, and it is difficult to say how much there may have been.

In Dent's case, the complexity of the dual accommodation between master and slave is best seen in his relationship with the skilled laborers John, Alfred, and Hardtimes. John, the blacksmith, and Alfred, a carpenter, were Morrison estate Negroes whom Dent moved to Alabama in 1837. Hardtimes, another carpenter, was a Horry estate Negro whom Dent inherited from his mother in 1856. The work of these skilled hands indicates the white family's general dependence on every level of slave labor. In May, 1841, the master noted "Work alloted for John & Alfred to do until Cotton is ready to pick. Commenceing on 7th Inst. Get out posts and paleings for the Yard, and thus fence it in, and make proper Gates. 2nd Get out a frame for Carriage House and Stables. 3d Put Good Blocks under the dwelling House. 4th Get out the timber and put up a wood and Smith Shop. 5th Put new Axle trees to the Road wagons. 6th Ceil the House as far as Lumber will go." [134]

These tasks were probably more than John and Alfred could hope to complete before cotton-picking time. At any rate, they began them with no great alacrity. On May 14, 1841, "John & Alfred hauling up the pailing posts and slats for the Yard fence, which they finished geting out the 13th." And on May 27 they had taken some short cuts. "John & Alfred pulling down Keeners Smoke house to erect for a Shop." [135]

Amid the numerous blacksmith jobs associated with planting and cultivating the crop of 1841, John and Alfred had not completed the above tasks before Dent sent them on August 20 to the place of his brother-in-law, Hamilton Morrison, near Spring Hill. Here the skilled blacks would undertake "a Job as follows of three Log Houses. One Kitchen 12 X 14 feet, Rafter roof, floored, One door One Window And a chimney. One Smoke House, 16 X 16 feet, Rafter roof & not floored. One House 16 X 18, rafter roof, floored, one door. Boards to be three feet in Length. Morison furnishing Nails, flooring plank, Sheeting and plank to Weather board Gable ends. For Which he pays me Sixty Dollars."[136]   Cash income took precedence over improving Dent's own plantation, or he was accommodating his wife's brother. If the third house Dent described was a slave cabin, it would tell us something of Morrison's Negro quarter and perhaps of Dent's.

Since John and Alfred earned from a dollar to a dollar and a half per day, the project at Morrison's required about a month. Collecting from seventy-five to eighty percent of their income, Dent naturally encouraged John's and Alfred's "foreign employment." He also trusted them to find work on their own, complete it, and idle back home in their own good time, whereupon they settled financial accounts and either set out in search of more work or labored at their master's tasks, either skilled or unskilled. Thus in April, 1842, "Men in New Ground, except John & Alfred who were taken out to work in the [blacksmith] shop for Miller." Providing blacksmith services for neighbors was another source of several dollars' income each year.[137]

Every time the master changed plantations, he breezily reported, "John and Alfred fixing up black smiths shop." While John's major contribution was making, repairing, and resetting plow points, Alfred was the better carpenter of the two. Alfred made and repaired the wooden stocks of plows. A recurring phrase throughout the journal is "John repairing up plows ready for planting corn" or cotton, or for cultivating them. Such repairs must have seemed endless, as Dent could decide at a moment's notice that the "angle" on an entire set of "iron" plow points needed adjusting. The wooden stocks required much less attention. When "Alfred remained home for want of foreign employment," the master might "put him to make a gate at the end of the lane" while John worked plows.[138]

When Dent inherited slaves from his mother's estate in 1856, Hardtimes, a carpenter, joined the traveling team of Alfred and John. "Alfred and Hardtimes Stopped at home this Week to rebuild a wagon wheel, make some new plow stocks, and repair foot bridges across the Creek." In fact, Alfred and Hardtimes were often the traveling team, leaving John at home "Working in Shop." Dent was always the ultimate scheduler, as on March 24, 1860, he "Kept Alfred home to repair up school house."[139]

Nevertheless, these skilled laborers enjoyed some immunities in the slave system. If anyone took advantage of the sick report for malingering, it was

John and Alfred, with never a complaint from Dent. Although John's forbidden intoxication resulted in drowning six mules and a small Negro boy, there is no evidence Dent imposed severe punishment. And a work slow-down in the blacksmith shop could bring the resourceful master as close to whining as he ever came: "John has disappointed us, in not having all our plows in order." [140] Such passive aggression revealed a dependent side of paternalism. But Dent's ultimate defense of John had to do with a fire that the blacksmith may have allowed, a possibility the master never even considered.

The fire occurred in April, 1841, during one of those hectic plowing seasons when Dent would, without notice, decide upon the immediate adjustment of the plow points of the entire force. The contemporary account of the occurrence does not present John's carelessness as an act of retaliation. If Dent suspected arson, he may have sensed that John was justified. Notice the master's haste to accept full responsibility for the "accident."

> This afternoon Commenced Working the Old field Cotton, When I received intelligence that the Black Smith Shop was on fire. Originated as follows. John Had been fixing some ploughs for Siding cotton With, and I sent for him in great haste to fix them on the Stocks in the Cotton field where they were waiting on him. In his hurry to obey the order, his fire in the forge was not properly outed. The High Wind blowing at the time communicated by a spark blowing from the forge to Some Shavens, and before the hands could get from the old lot to the Shop, it was entirely enwrapped in flames. [141]

The destruction was considerable. "My loss Sustained is about $150; besides the Smiths tools were a full set of Carpenters tools, parts of Wagons running Gear, Wagon Harness for Six Horses, and the finest and a complete set of the best Chisels, about 30 in number I had selected in Charleston from 1/8 of Inch to 6 Inch Chisels and furrers." The building and equipment were replaced with as much speed and cheer as one could expect. [142]

Despite Dent's distrust of Negro character, his faith in John and his affection for him were very strong. On December 22, 1884, he wrote revealingly of John's origins and of their relationship.

> I learn from Col M. B. Wellborn that one of my old Slaves John OBryan, who was a favorite with me and was my Black Smith, died on Sunday the 14th. John at the time of his death was 76 years of age. Johns father was an Irishman named Johnny OBryan, who was hired as a ditcher on the Morrison plantation in South Carolina. His mother was a Slave, a black comely woman named Patty, who died a Slave of Hamilton Morrison in Barbour County Alabama about the year 1846, her age was about 80 when she died.... After he was emancipated by the Government and ... when I left Alabama, I gave John a full set of Black Smiths tools as a present for his kindness and attention to me when

a slave and after freedom. And had he continued a Black Smith instead of a Doctor, it would have been better for him. [143]

Dent further explained that after emancipation, John "gave up his trade as a Black Smith and took to practicing medicine among the negroes as a root Doctor. He made nothing by his practice and lived and died in poverty." [144] John, the freedman, probably identified blacksmithing with his former condition of servitude. One wonders if his interest in medicine stemmed from close association with Dent, and perhaps his having given assistance to Dent in medical treatments.

Yet the master's blindness to the possibility of slaves' retaliation is not explained solely in terms of his affection for the mulatto John. There was a similar instance after the Civil War involving female house servants, at a time when Dent was in open conflict with freedmen. He claimed he had not the slightest idea who could have set his house on fire. This time, however, there was no damage except to the feelings of the whites who lived there. [145]

In the meantime, the antebellum Dent was far more committed to the myth of the good master than to that of the happy slave. For him, the latter theme came after emancipation. Meanwhile, it was the watchful and kind master who was supposed to deter crime among the Negroes. He informed the abolitionists that "Crime amongst the slave population is like the whites, confined to certain classes amongst them, but owing to the watchful care of their" kind master, he seems to be saying, there was less crime than one might expect. [146]

In March, 1856, four years after this note to the abolitionists, Dent indicated that Negro crime was worse near Eufaula than it had been on the more isolated Cowikees. "Last night my boy Brown with our watch dog Bull chased off a robber; in his haste to make his escape good, left his horse hitched in the lane, which is yet in my possession. On Saturday night Bighams Boy Ben and Harwells John stole two Turkes from us. They were detected by dropping their knife where they jumped over the fence, which led to their conviction. Living so near Eufaula in these scarce times leads to such scenes and crimes. In the Summer they induce our Negroes to Steal Corn." [147] But these crude attempts were the exception, not the rule, nor were the times all that "scarce." And "they" were surely whites, whom Dent knew to be responsible for much Negro crime. With his cribs locked and his fields watched, this master lost a minimum of corn, or of anything else, for that matter. Still it was slave crime that led him and many of his neighbors to Clayton on May 27, 1859.

In the journal, he described

The Execution at Clayton: Went up to Clayton to witness the Execution of Mat and Dabney, slaves, Mat for the murder of his Master Mr Orr, and Dabney for an Assault with intent to kill Mr Garland. Carried Herbert with me, returned home same afternoon. The crowd in Clayton was large some 2000 to 3000 persons. At 2 PM, the Culprits were brought to the Gallows, under escort of the Clayton Guards. And after the prisoners mounted the Gallows, a solemn and fervent prayer was offered up to the Throne of Grace in behalf of the unfortunate victims, by the Rev Mr Golson of the Methodist Church.[148]

Dent was intrigued, and no doubt gratified, by the verbal testimony of the condemned.

Mat made a confession to the audience to this effect, that he was induced into the crime as a participant by a white man, by the name of John Houston. He did not shoot his Master, but furnished the balls to load the Gun, which was once owned by himself. At the shooting (at night) he was not present, but near by, some 60 yds distant in charge of a horse. He believed that John Houston shot Mr Orr. He regretted very much the circumstances, was sorry for the trouble brought upon the family, and was perfectly reconciled to his fate, wishing all his colored bretheren to take warning from his example and be obedient to their Masters.[149]

This was hardly the theme of the happy and loyal slave, except for the lesson that a loyal Mat could have lived and been happier for it. Dent also recounted a similar testimony of the second condemned man, Dabney, who

made but few remarks, he seemed to be more troubled in mind than Mat, but perfectly resigned to his fate. He spoke cheerfully to those who spoke with him, with a pleasing smile on his countenance. His crime was in assaulting Mr. Garland with a knife in his hand, and biteing off a piece of Garlands ear; he did not use the knife. Dabney's last confession was that disobedience had brot him to the Gallows, and adviscd his colored bretheren to take warning by his case and be obedient.[150]

In each instance Dent perceived the conventional lesson of whites to blacks: slaves, be obedient and live. And as though to seal the ritual quality of the act, he observed:

Mat and Dabney then bowed down in secret prayer on the platform of the Gallows for a few minutes, and when concluded, the ropes were adjusted round their necks, the caps brot down over their faces, and the ropes made fast to the beam, [and] (whilst in prayer) the sheriff Mr Thomas Robinson severed the Cord with a hatchet that held up the drop, and they were launched into another world with but little struggling or apparent suffering. The whole was conducted in a very solemn and proper manner.[151]

In the English tradition, Dent believed that crime, especially slave crime, could never pay, either in this world or in the next. Leaving Clayton for

Bleak Hill on this day, he probably considered how an attentive master would have prevented the carryings on of a Mat or a Dabney. That, at least, was Dent's hope and faith for his own plantation. He saw his slaves as children, not brutes, and he tried to be responsible. There is every reason to believe that he arrived home from this execution satisfied with his own security, and that he slept peacefully, free of dreams of Nat Turners or John Browns.

If he dreamed at all on this May night in 1859, it was surely of crops and hoes and plows. And if the dream was an anxious one, it probably related to some "arrearage" or backwardness in the agricultural year, which Dent directed with all the art of a master planter.

4

THE PLANTATION YEAR

As a serious planter, John Dent knew that land was the center of his universe. Similarly, the agricultural year was somehow cosmic, sacred, a type of absolute, a ritual to be observed with the highest recognition, one's daily life. For all of Dent's thoughtfulness, he was first and last a planter-farmer, manifesting the scholastic strengths and anti-intellectual limitations of that vocation.[1] Thus he bore the marks of nature and its recurring seasons. For him the environment was a given to be accepted on its own terms and manipulated for food, staples, and profits, but ultimately to be accepted. With a subtle, but certain, fatalism, he was acutely conscious of an ultimate dependence upon an Other, which manifested itself impersonally through nature. He was religious, but not theological, prudish but not pious. He was a rationalist of sorts, and something of a Christian, though seldom a churchman. His philosophy centered in a Providence he expressed in both personal and impersonal terms.

Dent pondered the ways of Providence, especially at the beginning of a new year and on his birthday. On August 5, 1855, he wrote of God in personal terms.

This day is my 40th birth day, Which in the common period of Man's life has carried me over the half way stage of my journey—40 years has been passed in health and with many blessings, although having encountered deep and sorrowful afflictions. Those afflictions were in common with the dispensations of an all wise and Merciful God to his creatures on this earth. And tho hard and painful to endure, We should have submitted with humble resignation to his Will, for what he doeth is his pleasure and is done for some wise purpose, unknown to ourselves. In Providential afflictions, We should bear up under them with an humble resignation, for He who has made the Wound is able to heal it. The most blind, most wicked and most dangerous course is not to put our Trust in God and implore for help and relief, but to trust in one's own strength and will to releave himself from the visitations of the Most High and powerful ruler of All. Such a course has turned Sorrow into Misery, and misery into wretchedness, and all has been occasioned "by vanity and vexation of Spirit." My future now is dark and gloomy, surrounded with doubts, with neither chart nor rudder to guide me on. How long will be the journeys end no man knoweth, but let us trust in a Merciful Providence to help us on.[2]

More characteristically, Dent expressed a less personal idea of Providence and a more optimistic outlook for himself during the new year of 1852: "Before commencing the duties of another year we should be mindful of the Providence of the last, which was a year of peculiar favours to the Planter, remarkable healthy and peculiarly favourable for fine and bountiful crops."[3]

In keeping with a fatalistic view of Providence, Dent refused to believe the easy, commonsense fusion of moral and material progress, whereby a just, hardworking man was "supposed" to succeed. On the contrary, one could be moral and hardworking and still fail in business:

> Man in a great measure is the architect of his own fortunes. Such is the opinion of some, but observation and experience causes many to doubt the correctness of the proposition. In a moral point of view we readily assent to such facts, but in the common duties of life pertaining to the business pursuits of our several callings, We differ in the opinion of the assertion. We have seen too many instances where the energies Industry and incessant aim of Man have been zealously directed to his business with signal failure, whilst on the other hand Men have blundered into fortunes in a careless manner of business and habits, astonishing the most scrutinizing observers. [4]

Lacking a satisfactory explanation for this, Dent returned to the problem in 1880: "The lot of men in this world has certainly been very different, some hard, some easy, and some dreadful. Is it to be imputed to luck or fate? From what we have seen and noticed, it looks like luck has had much to do with man's fortunes in this life. But be it what it may, it seemed to be inevitable." [5]

His was no clear distinction between luck and fate. And whatever his momentary doubts, he nevertheless believed in work, lived its ethic, and kept his agricultural journal of works righteousness, a southern counterpart to New England Puritans' diaries of confession for regeneration. [6] Although Dent denied a necessary connection between morality and material progress, his practice of the agricultural year fused the sacred, secular, and profane into a meaningful life. And, as a scientific farmer, he was no simple fatalist. Man should manage as best he could to outdo the weather at its own destructive games. Thus Dent watched his adversary, recorded it daily, summarized its past patterns, planned ahead, gauged his tasks accordingly, and usually gained an encouraging yield.

There were, however, moments of dark despair, when he could exaggerate with the most pessimistic southern doom sayer. Such pessimism almost always related to the weather, a matter he obviously could not control: "In Seventeen years planting, I have had Fifteen crops Injured by rains. As such we may almost despair of good luck.... The rains are beyond our control, as [to] the destroying we therefore submit in spite of our exertions: hereafter, I have not the heart or will to hope. I shall plant but with all confidence of destructive rains. My Journal terminates, after Seventeen years labours." Despite the pessimism, 1853 was one of his best crop years. Nor did the journal terminate. It continued with the passing years. [7]

In tracing the plantation year, one finds that Dent, like Ecclesiastes, believed each planting duty had its appointed time. He would synchronize time, duty, and slave gang to create something of the interdependence, interaction, and creative pressure of an assembly-line system such as that described by Robert William Fogel and Stanley L. Engerman.[8] Instead of a factory, however, Dent's managerial symbol was that of a ship and its crew. He was the commander who tried to "save" the vessel, weather the "storm," and land the "cargo." Such metaphorical crises usually occurred in midyear, but also applied to every month, and especially January, when the real problem was getting the plantation year under way.[9] Dent was determined to leave the leisure of Christmas week in quest of meeting "arrearages" and pursuit of new beginnings. To assure a brief Christmas holiday and a fast-paced new year, he planned ahead, devised more projects than the hands could complete, and announced each intention, forewarning the blacks and perhaps giving them some room for later satisfaction in jobs not begun for want of time.

This planter feared Christmas lethargy and dreaded the energy it required to move his business off dead-stop in order to start the plantation year. By November, 1855, the tasks were falling over themselves inside his head. He enumerated

Work to be done so soon as finish picking Cotton and preparatory to planting crop of 1856.

1. Finish 2 negro houses on hand
2. Repair thorough Oat field fencing
3. Build a cow lot for wintering cattle and makeing manures
4. Clearing New Ground, 80 acres
5. Build a kitchen at residence
6. Outer fencing thoroughly overhauled
7. A fence to build on Creek bank Cox fields
8. Chimneys of quarter to overhaul
9. Two Branches to ditch and reclaim in Cox fields
10. Some hill sides ditches needed in Gin House & old mans hills
11. 2 Ditches to make in old quarter field
12. 1 [ditch] in 50 Acre cut in Cox fields
13. Bigham flats and Wigham hills some ditching.[10]

Here Dent was less organized than usual. His concerns can be summarized as construction work, new ground tasks, fencing, and ditching. The master was temporarily overcome by the numerous "needs" of his new plantation at Bleak Hill. By December 25 of that year he was more composed and gave succinct directions: "1. Kill all the hogs that are fat first cold day. 2. Complete grubbing new ground, cut and roll it, burn off and start plows breaking up. 3. Put men splitting rails to fence it, and fence it first suitable chance." There were additional directions on fencing the new plantation, but the priorities were clear: pork, new ground, and fences—preparatory for plowing.[11]

If this sounds simple, it was so only on paper, and then because Dent here neglected to note how each new year required some attention to the last year's crop. In another context, he noted his more usual sense of January "backwardness": "Our start will be late. The crop of 1851 being large has occupied much time in housing it and preparing for market. And having had a slow and inferior Gin and but one Wagon to do the work for want of more mule power, we have been seriously put back which only a favourable Winter and Spring can enable us to catch up."[12]

Ideally, crops of the previous year were harvested before Christmas. Housing corn, bedding sweet potatoes, and saving other foodstuffs were usually completed before December 25. Cotton—with its various processes of picking, ginning, packing, and hauling—was another matter. Thus January 8, 1858, was not untypical. "PM packing cottons. 102 Bales Cotton packed in all, up to date." Later that week, the "Wagon carried 4 Bales Cotton to Eufaula." And shortly one learns that "Up to date have 110 Bales Cotton packed. 79 in Eufaula." At four bales a trip, "wagoning" consumed much time and energy, leaving Dent fearful that the teams of mules would be too "jaded" to complete winter and spring plowings on schedule. It was an unwelcome rest, however, when he wrote amid hindering rains, "Roads too rotten to haul off cotton" and concluded, "This weather will put us back very much in plowing."[13]

January hauling was primarily cotton and manures. Corn, generally housed in the fall, required no hauling in January, except when Dent moved from one plantation to another and was forced to take that product with him. To preserve his mules, he preferred a complicated trade in corn even though it meant exchanging superior grain for an inferior lot. Upon making such a move, he studied and practiced several methods for measuring bulk corn in the crib, traded on lenient terms, sacrificed some of the surplus corn he liked to keep, and even then was forced on occasion to haul the commodity to a new plantation. In 1855 he hired wagons and drivers to complete this task at expensive rates in order to save his own man and mule force.[14]

Killing hogs was another January "arrearage" from the previous year. This process of slaughtering and "saving" pork generally began with the first cold days in December, often well into the month. In the absence of refrigeration, cool weather was a necessity to get the bulk of the meat "curing" in layers of salt before warming weather could speed the decomposition process. Dent watched the weather for fair days (which indicated cold nights), and noted on New Year's Day 1859: "Saturday 1st.

Fair and pleasant, first fair day we have had in many. The Sun looks cheerful. Killed 12 hogs.'' The following day was ''Fair and Pleasant,'' and Monday must have dawned the same, for Dent's hands ''Killed 6 hogs,'' despite an ominous note: ''PM, turning warm.'' Yet the next day came fair and cool enough, for he arose calmly and proceeded to ''Eufaula to buy Cans for holding lard.'' He explained the process: ''Trying up lard, stuffing saussages, salting away meat.'' Later the salt-cured meat would be hung in smokehouses. [15]

Dent, however, disliked the task of killing hogs. An unwilling participant, he preferred to supervise or delegate the responsibility. ''Directed Mr Howell to kill ballance of Hogs.'' This planter's distaste for the job probably explains his few references to the process and tells something of his need to worry. He could be ''very uneasy about the meat killed on yesterday. The weather is so damp and warm will be compelled to put the Joints in pickle.'' Too-warm weather was the real hazard: ''The weather for the last four days has been pleasant and fair, but nights very cool. Meat hung up on 15th I feel some fear off owing to the days being too warm.'' His small pleasure in this item of self-sufficiency, the danger of decomposition, and the high cost of corn to fatten hogs help explain Dent's policy of ordering about half of his pork from New Orleans. Hog-killing was also a frustrating time because of his January absences from the plantation on financial business. [16]

Thus on January 3, 1859, Dent ''Went to Eufaula and Settled my annual accounts.'' The entry, however, is misleading, because accounts were never settled at once. Throughout that month he was frequently absent, sometimes several days at a time. He also oversimplified when he wrote, ''Went to Eufaula. . . . Plantation business entirely under . . . Mr Howell.'' Although tasks were under Howell's direction, Dent knew of the smallest job. He would go to Eufaula on a January day while ''At Plantation men splitting rails. Woman gang repairing and filling up washes.'' [17]

Still he fretted, ''I am now so much engaged with outside business that I do not know what is going on in the Plantation.'' In reality he knew, and he missed it, but not enough to dispense with banker's profits and the urban camaraderie he hesitated to acknowledge. If he felt guilty at being away from the ''natural'' occupation of farming, it was at least comforting to know and record, ''Men splitting rails, part women gang mending road through plantation, part repairing washes.'' [18]

There were numerous small tasks in cold and disagreeable January, and Dent tried to name each one. ''With two plows, sowing Oats at Dwelling lots but find it a very slow business.'' Experience gradually led him to change oat-sowing from fall to January and February. Explaining the procedure, he criticized the northern turning plows, which he nevertheless continued to use: ''Sowed down our Oats at the dwelling lots with the Northern turn plow which turned over the land in flat fleaks and shallow furrows, which I attribute our loss of stand to. Had they been plowed in with the half shovel which was my usual custom, the ground would have been deeper broke, and better pulverised, and secured a full stand, and have stood the very cold winter."[19] The points of turning plows were longer, narrower, and flatter than those of the shovels, which ran wider and deeper.

It was a special January joy when "The weather is mild enough to commence gardening." Roads and bridges were also improved during this month and, as always, provisions and supplies were hauled from Eufaula. These included "fish, molasses, salt, iron," and a "corn sheller." Animals were tended, especially sheep, which were easily scattered in severe weather to lose their lambs and their own lives. Trees and shrubs were set: "Mrs Dent set out 62 peach trees. Went to Mrs Fields" for china trees. Also, "Mrs Dent setting out shrubbery and trees."[20]

Just as planting trees and shrubs was an annual affair, the children's schoolhouse required yearly attention before the January term. Sometimes there was a new building when a neighbor shared the tutor. In 1852 Dent's "Carpenters and 3 hands putting up a School house with Major Fields hands on the road between our Residences." There was other construction work in January: "Men started to get out logs to build a Kitchen; women jobbing about the plantation. . . . Alfred working at home, can find no jobs abroad." Dent had some logs sawed for part of the planking he used, a task which involved more jobbing. Littering stock lots with straw, cobs, and shucks was another interminable duty. He described the procedure, which had to be reorganized at each new plantation: "Pens should be made, and the litter and contents of the Stables and Lots, and the waste shucks, cobs and everything that will make manure, after haveing been well trod should be put away in their proper pens—to be carried in the fields when needed." Not even a "Freshet" stopped all the raking, piling, and littering, which was partially protected from the elements by laboriously constructed "shelters."[21]

Directly and indirectly, every January job pointed toward the large item of plowing. Land preparation was the primary task of January and February. Clearing new ground was the most prominent evidence of this concern. The journal phrase, "Burning off and cleaning up . . . lands," could appear any time from July of one year into the following May. Still, January and February were the critical months for this task, due to the necessity of planting new-ground corn in March. Journal references to new ground are too general to tell exactly the number of acres cleared yearly. Also, there were various stages in the evolution of new-ground culture. In 1856 Dent reported fifty-five acres cleared during the past year. He usually attempted thirty to fifty acres per year, without describing the stage of clearing completed. As late as 1859-1860, his slave force took the first step of "deadening" no less than one hundred acres of timbered lands.[22]

Clearing new ground was so important that Dent developed a procedure, in theory, at least, for the most efficient process. His presentation of it was a bit pompous.

> The fault or error I should have said with most planters in their taking in New ground is they make it a late Job, instead of an early one.... In the fall of the year when too wet to pick cottons, I am at work at my clearings, and endeavor to have them cut down, rolled and burnt off, ready for the plow as early in January as practicable. So soon as I can plow, I start my plows with Skooters and break up the ground thoroughly. The earlier this can be done, so much the better as the frost and freeze may have its beneficial [loosening] influence upon the land. I have invariably noticed when New Grounds have been thus early broken up and pulverized by frost, then crops are materially increased, and their culture rendered more easy. I plant them early in March.[23]

So much for armchair advice. In actual practice, deadening, shrubbing, trashing, cutting, rolling, and burning were not so summarily accomplished. Completing all of these steps required several years.

The first step of "deadening timbers," that is, girdling or stripping trees of their bark in order to kill them, could begin in any season and frequently occurred years before the tree trunks were actually removed from the soil. Meanwhile, corn was planted among the roots of leafless trees. On any given January, there were acres of thoroughly deadened timber to be cut, rolled, piled, and burned. Dent explained: "Weather has been continued cold, freezing every night. All hands engaged this week in spring flat New ground—rolling, pileing, cleaning up, and burning, which has been a slow and heavy Job." And again, "Men cutting up Logs in New Ground, Women burning brush." On a typical January day with "Cloudy and raw AM, PM moderating," the hands were "Burning logs in Cox fields. Men rolling logs," while others were "working on school house." Not all logs were burned; some were saved for lumber and others were split for rails. Building and repairing fences was a natural corollary of clearing work. Fencing, like new-ground jobs, continued on and off throughout the entire year. "Part Boys splitting rails in Cox fields to divide it off for planting Corn.... Vurturs gang trimming down branches in Cox fields."[24]

Regular clearing of water courses was essential for drainage: "Particular attention is also needed in keeping the ditches in fine order and constantly cleansed out.... Great labour and immediate attention is required in keeping the main Creek cleared off rafts and Logs, otherwise great Sand bars are formed, which retards the passage of the waters from running off rapidly in times of freshets." With free drainage, freshets could also assist in new-ground work by floating troublesome logs down creek, there to harass any neighbor who happened to be less attentive to clear water courses.[25]

There was also the related matter of ditching to reduce erosion of fields.

"Vurtur and four girls cleaning up a skirt of brush wood and making guard drains at Dwelling lots." Dent supervised: "I am going to try and lay off a large guard ditch where the flats join the hill lands." He also explained, "The new ground will require two ditches also the Faison Hammock one all large and long. These ditches are or can be conveniently layed off so as to take up no land of value, and all will intersect each other at the mouth of a pond which is the natural vent of the waters."[26]

As time neared for full-scale plowing, last year's crop stalks and sedge loomed large to be "thrashed" down: "Day cloudy and very cold, all appearances of hard weather. Men cutting up Logs. Women thrashing down Cotton Stalks; ordered Mr Bush to burn off sedge lands to day if they would burn." When winter weather eased occasionally, as it can, even in January, in southeastern Alabama, the jobs increased proportionately: "Day cloudy and Warm. Light rains last night. Making guard drains at the dwelling lots and sowing Oats with two plows. Men cutting up Logs. Women and children cutting down Corn stalks."[27]

The rhythm of the year neutralized some of Dent's intensity. As a time of endings and beginnings, January was a more relaxed month than later ones. Cold, wet weather reassigned some new-ground days to light work or leisure, and the master was more relaxed than he would be later. The weather was fickle and vexing. One should not expect too much. Thus "proceeding with my clearing but slow." By late January or early February the planter hoped to "quit the New Ground. About 3 days rolling yet necessary to complete it, with about 7000 rails to make. Put the hands to cutting up Logs in Macks field, Women thrashing down Cotton stalks." Even with a change of emphasis to plowing, part-time clearing would continue, at least into March and April. It was seldom he did not lament, "My backwardness this year is owing to my endeavoring to take in too large a new Ground."[28]

A recurring concern that influenced Dent's January crop planning was "That my provision crop will be short and the Cotton crop also shortened. My present opinions are for the next year . . . to shorten my Cotton Crop, put my Lands in good order, and put a heavy crop of provisions in Corn, potatoes, and oats." Such an emphasis was not new. He generally planted a minimum of two hundred acres of corn, with cotton acreage nearing five hundred by the late 1850s. Plans for the crop of 1858 will illustrate: "Corn . . . 205, Cotton . . . 465, Oats 70, Rye 15, Potatoes 15." Dent's acres were not loose estimates, but of careful measure based on poles twenty-one feet long. Invariably after each move and careful measure, he found the number of cleared acres fewer than had been advertised.[29]

Allocating his acreage to specific crops was essential for "undercropping" hands and for an efficient program of manuring. From the early 1840s, the laborious process of manuring lands was very important on Dent's Alabama plantations. Except for the first year on a new place, he could always write, "We shall have a very large amount of manures to haul out, Lot [compost] as well as Cotton Seed . . . it will take at least six weeks to haul it out." A large amount of manure meant that he had as much as he could afford the time and labor to spread. In January he usually reported, "Our heaviest job from this period before planting is the hauling out manures, having a large amount of Cotton Seed, as well as lot manures, to haul out." Once last year's corn and cotton stalks were "thrashed" down, wagoners and spreaders began the slow process of hauling and distributing manures on the poorest lands. Oxen pulled the heavier loads of lot compost, while mules moved the lighter wagons of decomposing cottonseed. [30]

Dent did not describe the actual distribution, only his large design for rotating and enriching the soil. In 1854, he explained: "As for example, say we had a plantation of which there was 650 acres cleared lands, in cotton 300 acres, Corn 150, Oats 80, Wheat 50, Rye 50 and potatoes 20. The lands selected for cottons should be in regular rotation after the grain Crops, and the amount exceeding the grain crops should be manured with Manures made from trampled decomposed litter and straw. My Corn should be planted on lands after Cottons, and manured with Cotton Seed." Although his grain acreage was never large enough for a significant rotation of cotton lands with them, in 1856 Dent manured a third of the 720 acres in cultivation. He was satisfied that the hands had done their utmost. Of course, manures were also spread on vegetable gardens. [31]

With old stalks coming down and manures falling upon the land, it was time to "start" the plows. He sometimes had the plow stocks and points prepared in November. Usually however, he had to wait for this until the new year. Early in one January, he "Directed Mr Howell to have cole burnt, shop repaired, in order our plows may be repaired and started as soon as possible." Perhaps there was a charcoal kiln supplied by hands: "John & Alfred getting out timber for coal kiln." A few days after ordering these preparations, the master "Went to Eufaula. . . . Bought Bellows for the shop and Iron for plows." Also "John commenced working at home in my Service." Whereupon "John and Fedrick" began "fixing up new Shop." The next step was "Preparing our plows for starting." [32]

The muddy task of breaking and ridging land for planting corn usually began about mid-January. Dent's terms for this endeavor were "break-ing," "listing," "bedding," and "ridgeing." Hardly anything deterred the hardy "plows," which term meant person, mule, stock, and iron point moving as one across the miry earth. For example, on a January 16, "AM, light Snow, weather bitter cold. Men splitting rails. Gang fencing New Ground. Plows breaking up." [33] Breaking up was simply the turning up and over of all the earth with half shovel or turning plows, preparatory to the ridging, bedding, or listing into separate rows for subsqent planting, of which, more later. Meanwhile, as January waned and February began, the pace of plantation work quickened. Former jobs continued, especially on new ground, but plowing was the paramount concern. There was one short month before it was time to plant corn.

A prerequisite for land preparation was cooperative weather. Thus Dent was relieved when "February has been a favourable Month for work, was not so cold or wet as January." Warmer weather, however, had the side effect of hurrying the "season" along and moving the master to impatience with laborers' cold-weather lethargy hanging over from Christmas. Although Dent sometimes rested during January, owing to minor aches and pains that he could afford to nurse in that month, February was no time for the "slows." And he could rant irrationally against temporary idleness, phrasing the attack in the idiom of a subsistence farmer facing hunger. He emphasized food, not profits, that February day when he complained that his "hands were Idleing about, and the overseer well satisfied at such a state of things. This is certainly a flattering prospect towards starvation for another year, and no crop made to defray expenses."[34]

The continuity of work from January is striking. In February, 1852, Dent reported, "Our cutters are reduced but to 7. [4] splitting Rails. 1 working in shop and 2 hauling. . . . Sent to Clayton for Iron from McAndrews." On the following day: "Burners burning off before the plows. 7 axes cutting up logs in the Norman field, 4 splitting rails, Wagon hauling out Seed" for manuring. Not every February was warm. Dent described that of 1852: "This is said to be the coldest Winter known in America North and South." Despite the freeze, there were "4 men deadning in New Ground."[35]

Such deadening, or girdling, of trees was fast work, and these hands could be "taken off in the afternoon to attend to Log heaps." On this same day, while "Plows in North field listing up," Dent "Started Bob to lay off for Cotton in Rusty Field." And ahead of some plows, there were "Women pileing up and burning brush that has been cut down in Branches in the Rusty and Ridge fields."[36] Obviously each plot of cleared land needed a name for easy identification, planning, and direction.

In breaking land, the plows ran as deeply as possible, but usually no more than four or five inches, even in sandy soils. Laying off was plowing furrows in parallel lines at distances that ranged from three and one-half feet up to five feet apart. These laid-off furrows designated the rows to be planted. Evenly spaced rows required a good eye and much skill. Dent used the terms listing, ridging, and bedding indiscriminately to indicate the throwing of dirt in straight furrows toward the laid-off, or row, furrow, until all of the middles or alleys between rows had been thrown up into a ridge or bed ready for future planting.[37] Cotton was planted on the ridge or bed. Corn was planted in the new water furrow, or hollow created by ridging out the original middles.

Such soil preparation was fairly routine on old lands free of dead trees and some stumps. In new ground, however, the forest giants were too numerous to be removed at once. And while one could plant around deadened trees, these whitening ghosts refused to drop their debris all at once, as Dent knew only too well. Thus hands rolled and rerolled new grounds ahead of the plows: "Will finish rolling Logs in Norman field, which completes the regular rolling of the plantation. There are so many fresh fields, we may expect a rerolling before planting." This entry continued, "Also finished breaking up New Ground. Will start on tomorrow to List up for Cotton. Burning logs progressing slowly."[38]

Fresh lands with decaying trees also threatened man and beast: "Wind boisterously high from SW. PM, suspended plowing in the Norman field for fear of falling timber." Until each tree was down, even minor winds required trash gangs to remove debris from the rows. Nor was plowing in new ground inspiring when stubborn roots set plow points hanging or sent them shooting out of the ground. Any new-ground plowing was "very rough and straining on the Mules." Such was, however, a good time and place to "gentle" half-trained animals. In February, 1856, Dent wrote of buying two unbroken "mules from Mr Black of Teenn" at a cost of $245. Yet they must have been partially trained, as they came around quickly and satisfactorily, and were soon working "gently and kind."[39]

Negro John's care of the plows was thorough enough that Dent seldom bothered to list these implements. In 1846, however, he reported "12 Skooters, 6 Northern turn plows, 6 half shovels, Round shovels, Sweeps, and 1 Sub soil." Skooters were small vertical points used for breaking rough new ground and for opening and covering planted rows. Turning and shovel plows had long sharp points and flared mould boards for breaking and listing soils. Sweeps (both solid and flat) had blunt shallow points flaring on each side to form a V for cleaning the middles and throwing loose dirt around young plants. The sub-soiler was for deep breaking, though rarely used because of the time and mule power it consumed. Additional plow "gear" included "Hames and Collars, Traces, Single trees, hock chains," etc. [40]

Dent was rarely satisfied with his land's preparation, for reasons he enumerated in 1852: "Our plowings this year have not been as thorough and as deep as I could have desired. One reason is we have had a large amount of New and very rough lands to contend with. The season has also been dry, which has baked and hardened the ground very much, and our plows altogether do not suit. Before bedding up our old lands I contemplate having them [plow points] reset, so as to throw up and turn over the land more effectually." A lapse of nine years brought no significant improvement that Dent could see, and a so-called crop "failure was not entirely owing to the drought but to the careless manner in which our land were prepared by shallow and hurried plowings and tardy and indifferent cultivation."[41]

It was always his intention to "see that the ground is deeply plowed at an early period." Yet invariably, he reported, "Our fall and winter plowings heretofore have been entirely too light and shallow, no lands on this place has ever been broken over four to five inches deep. We need an 8 inch depth to do any good." It is understandable, then, that new grounds, an overworked mule force, and numerous other projects consistently absorbed the time that would have been required for deep plowing. It was more comfortable, however, to blame northern plows for this failure than to accept one's existential use of time. Already by February, each task was "forward" or "backward" according to Dent's mental calculation of the agricultural year. In 1853, February saw 255 acres listed for cotton, with "120 yet to list," and the comment, "would have been forward had not our burning retarded us very much." [42] Any sickness among the hands was another hindrance.

February also brought the usual tasks of "repairing up," killing hogs, saving shucks for feed and litter, gardening, and planting fruit trees. In the gardens, it was time for starting Irish potatoes, green peas, cabbages, and lettuce. Fruit trees were a regular affair for February as well as January: "Mr Howell with part of the Men building a new fence around the garden, trimming up fruit trees, and set out some fig sprouts." And again in February, Dent had "Set out fifty apple trees. Last week, Mrs Dent set out some 68 peach trees as well as apples. A snug little orchard, the trees though are very small." [43]

As February ran into March, Dent understandably intensified all preparations for planting corn. In the meantime, however, more moderate weather invited other earth-moving projects. On March 3, 1856, he "Went to Clayton to petition the Commissioners Court to make public the road running by the Quarter to Eufaula." Although Dent was temporarily thwarted in this goal, March was a good time for constructing and repairing bridges, which were essential on a low-lying plantation. In March, 1859, his men built a "Bridge across ravine in New Ground." In fact, at Bleak Hill small footbridges were necessary for travel and communication from "the Residence to the Quarter, or from the South side of the plantation to the North." [44]

While March "manureings" proceeded apace, sprouting rye and growing gardens were items of keen interest. As the tender tips of rye tinted the land soft green, garden seed came up either thickly or "scattered," to gladden or sadden the heart. Dent's thought was also drawn to "peas, beets, and cabbages," and other provisions as well. The hands barely finished killing hogs in February before the next year's needs dictated a March "Assorting the Hogs. Small sized will be kept in Lot during the Season until Grain fields are opened. The Large hogs will be turned into the woods and fed every day." [45]

Completing the manuring about mid-March, the master saw that plows continued to run. The ground could freeze and the teams could tire, but the plows kept listing up for planting corn and cotton. Despite the strain on himself and others, Dent relished the race to be the first in his community to plant corn. Not every black could plow, but almost any one could assist the preparations for planting, as "new ground" work wore on. One March, Dent reported, "Women taking . . . Grubs & tussacks out of New Ground slip in the Cox fields"; "Clarinda and children to pick up roots and brush in Bluff Spring flats"; and the "Ditchers have been engaged in making a large Venting ditch through the Bluff Spring flat."[46]

Through ditching for drainage, Dent hoped to plant the high and low grounds evenly at the same time, rendering cultivation less complicated. But rainy weather often hindered this and other March tasks. As "Men splitting Rails to fence in old Cotton field, Women attempted to burn logs at the Holder place, but found it impossible owing to the wet weather." Thus Dent brought them "home" and put them "resetting Small orchard patch fence adjoining the Yard."[47]

In Barbour County, Alabama, there are more rainy springs than dry ones. During periodic freshets, Dent was painfully reminded that he farmed in a swamp: "Saturated, Sobby, boggy, and Watery is the Ground. What a time to plant, and how little confidence is there in what is done. We are now backwards and will be made more so by these everlasting rains. . . . We have hoped against hope, Until 'hope defereth maketh the heart sick.'" The frustration of excess rain might turn him to Scripture, but not to church. Thus it is understandable that in 1855, his one notable dry spring (when, having moved to a new plantation, he had no manures), he had the land broken and rebroken and chopped for the best prepared soil he ever planted: "Plows rebreaking Sedge lands intended for corn, the turf being too cloddy for good planting"; and "Hands chopping up sedge sods that have not pulverized . . . preparatory to planting."[48]

Most importantly, however, early March meant planting corn. In a statement which was probably intended for the local agricultural society, Dent argued: "I consider it Judicious to plant New Grounds [in corn] early . . . [because] our soil is strong and vigorous, Our Summers hot and long. . . . Corn requires a climate moderately cool to produce a heavy solid grain. As such, to remedy these deleterious consequences, Early planting must be resorted to. . . . It may be said that planting too early it may be cut down by frost; bear this in mind your standing timber is a shelter and protects it."[49]

With his farmer's sense of the mysterious, Dent preferred, perhaps superstitiously, to begin large, important jobs like planting corn on Mondays rather than in mid week. On Wednesday, March 7, 1855, he admitted, "It was my intention to have commenced planting Corn to day, but have put it off until Monday next. Plows listing up the Whigham hills for Cotton. Hands cleaning up cleared patches &c." This was a significant postponement—it left him behind his neighbors' planting schedule. That backwardness troubled Dent enough to seek a rationalization for waiting. He found it the following day: "Fine weather at present for planting Corn. Hear of several planting. Vegetation is very backwards." Ergo, his neighbors were rushing their planting and John H. Dent was still the wisest of them all. It was, nevertheless, a difficult wait. He even put the hands to "Grubbing up and cleaning off around the Dwelling" as the ultimate in make-work before the fateful Monday for planting corn. [50]

Dent seemingly saved his own seed corn and used it or swapped with neighbors. He advised, "*Select Seed Corn* . . . in the field. All Stalks that have two full Ears, Select the largest Ear on such stalks and have them placed separate and from such procure your Seed for the next crop." His reputation in this matter was such that "H P Adams sent over to exchange Seed Corn." [51]

Explaining his corn-planting process in relation to the larger problem of soil preparation as sketched above, Dent wrote:

> I plant them early in March, that is when I plant it in Corn. I lay of[f] the rows for drill five feet distance, and with half shovels break them out thorough, deep and well lapped. The last or water furrow is laid off or plowed out with care, as in it the corn is planted, dropping the seed every Thirty inches, and covering by running a skooter furrow on each side of the last or water furrow. When this done, although it will be said by many that it requires a vast amount of plowing and labor to accomplish it, I will candidly say to such that the ground is in fine order. The seed well put in comes up strong and vigorous, grows off stout and strong. And with but ordinary seasons, a full crop will be gathered of stout heavy Corn.

The main emphasis was on "breaking out thorough," or "bedding out flush," which left no "balk" of unbroken land in the middles. The only way to speed this process was to leave an unplowed balk or alley for subsequent breaking and cleaning. [52]

The major difference in preparing new ground and old land for planting corn was the use of cottonseed manuring and deeper plowing on worn soils. Yet the young, rough lands were the slowest and most exacting to plant. In 1853 Dent explained: "planting New Ground Corn, ground rough, heavy and Wet; it will be a long tedious Job, which will draw down our Mules very much. I calculate that it will take us some 8 days to plant it." This new ground was less than one hundred acres. By 1858 when the fields were older and new grounds fewer, Dent's Negroes planted more than two hundred acres of corn in less than eight working days. [53] The methods and laborers were efficient. The basic keys were year-round work in new ground and early plowing.

In spite of great efforts at ditching, wet weather often prevented the simultaneous planting of high and low portions of a field. For example, Dent would "put Vurture and Magwood to ditch several broad branches in New Ground in order we can plant them in Corn." Yet when the time came for

"Planting New Ground in Corn," the "Branches are so wet, we will have to skip them for the present." In many of these instances, rice was the only solution: "The dryest part of said branch lands will be put in ... [corn], and the wet parts must be gradually reclaimed by rice, the proper mode of reclaiming all branch lands, and paying best in cultivation." And even then, "Some quarter draining will be necessary to reclaim it thoroughly." Rice was so important he was not above ordering it from Charleston or Savannah.[54] It was probably a low-country variety.

While February's weather was fickle, March's was treacherous. On March 22, 1853, with the corn crop recently planted, Dent lamented, "Tremendous Rains, Flood ... A general destruction, Washes terrible, Much Timber blown down, fences washed away, and the height of the Corn Crop to be plowed up and replanted. In short the Plantation torn up, thrown us back fully 3 weeks." In the midst of March winds, Dent was again "fearful that much timber will be blown down in our fresh lands." Such was usually the case, which meant "Hands employed in cutting up Timber fallen.... Women picking up Brush." Then there was the dread March freeze: "The change of Weather since 5 PM of yesterday has been that from Summer to Winter. Day cold, dark flying clouds from the North appearances of Snow. The fruit trees are now in full bloom. Should a freeze occur, fruit will be destroyed, about half of our Corn crop is in the ground. Steady cold rain all the afternoon, as cold a rain as we had this year." Amid these and other uncertainties, corn was planted and replanted until the tender shoots broke the earth in acceptable stands. Finally, a bit of Dent's anxiety was allayed when he could write, "The first plantings of Corn Bigham flats are comeing up very well." No sooner did the plant appear, however, than another problem arose: "The birds are destructive, have minders at them." Evidently these minders were the young and the aged.[55]

It required strong men and women with much determination to stop the "Great Fires" that could rage and threaten for days and nights during March's drying wind. Dent reported several of these fires, always with the highest regard for the blacks' efforts and general success in stopping each threat. Such emergencies meant extra work and loss of sleep, but the major damage to the plantation was destruction of fencing, which burned readily, especially when cut from the resinous "heart" pine called lightwood. During one March fire, Dent noted lackadaisically, "Day fair and mild, and fortunately it is so, or we would loose much more fencing. All hands attending to the fires. Bob hauling rails to replace those burnt from the cross fence in the Cox fields."[56]

No sooner were fires stopped, fences rebuilt, and corn planted or replanted, as the need might be, than Dent was speeding the plows in cotton lands. In fact, since early March, he had frequently "Started ... ploughs ... in the field intended for Cotton," while "ballance hands finishing cleaning off Hammock field for planting Corn.'' But his compulsiveness occasionally proved too much for his general health. By his own testimony, Dent was quite ill in late March, 1855. His acute concern for crops that year manifested itself in signs of ''nervous'' disorder. A few journal entries will illustrate: first, ''Bowels very much disordered''; later he was ''confined to the house sick.''[57] This particular problem carried into April: ''My health is so bad cannot go into the plantation . . . my disease is Nervous with a thorough derangement of the digestive organs, my system feels completely shattered, like a break up.'' And again: ''John H Dent sick in mind and body''; finally, ''Myself sick, riseings on my right hand. Billious derangements of the system, chill and fever, mind distracted, body wrecked, every thing out of gear.'' In this year, he did not recover until well into the season for planting cotton.[58]

The month of April normally (with the possible exception of 1855) riveted Dent's attention on final preparations for planting cotton. Following his own advice, he had been collecting seed since the previous fall. For the most part, he planted his own seed, selected according to his personal directions: ''This task should be Commenced in the field when picking Cotton, And Seed designed for planting should be selected from the Cotton picked . . . [from] the second opening. The Cotton gathered with the seed for planting ought to be picked from Twelve Oclock until evening, when the Cotton is perfectly dry, rid of dews &c. Such placed to itself and undergo one of two Sunnings.''[59]

Dent liked the Pomegranate cotton, but he was also aware of experiments with the Banana, Sugar loaf, and Petit Gulf varieties. On at least one occasion, he planted Boyds Prolific seed in the ''chop,'' with only three seeds per hole, in order to make them go further. At another time, he experimented with a small amount of ''Buckley Cotton Seed,'' which, he explained, ''was given to me in Texas by Gwin Morrison who states it was introduced into Texas from Central America by Judge Buckley; it is represented to be a prolific Cotton, it is a great favorite with the planters of Texas.'' To improve germination, he rubbed or soaked the seed whenever time allowed. Dent's experience, however, was that seed made less difference than land preparation and the weather.[60]

In the matter of planting cotton, he again described ''proper'' methods, using a judgmental tone: ''Just before you are ready to plant allowing yourself sufficient time,'' he wrote,

> the Lands should be deeply and well broken with the [half shovel] plough, and then [after laying off rows] ridge up with the plough say five or three furrows, the last I deem sufficient when the lands have been well broke. Open the ridge then with a very short and narrow Skooter, and after the seed have been rubbed, Sow them thinly in the drill and cover them by hand with a rake on the end of helve, similar to the Hoe. This method is tedious and slow, but en-

sures a regular and good stand of cotton, comeing up the same time; if the seed
are good, and if seasons are good, it grows of[f] rapidly. It being sowed thin and
regular in the drill and covered the same depth, You have but little trouble in
chopping it to a stand and can observe or get that regular distance in the drill
that should be aimed at, so as not to loose ground or crowd cotton, one or the
other is generally the result when cotton is planted too thick or careless. By
this method of planting your cotton will be all of one age and easily managed. [61]

To increase the time for soil preparation and to preserve tender cotton
plants from March's treacherous cold, Dent advocated a late planting, that
is, during the first two weeks of April. An April freeze was possible but rare,
a chance the southeastern Alabama cotton planter had to take. He wrote a
long paper on the subject, in which he promised to argue the advantages of
both early and late planting, to Bertram Hoole of the Barbour County
Agricultural Society. In reality, Dent found no significant advantages for
the earlier date and concluded his case: "Late planting . . . from the first to
the tenth of April . . . will not only put your Seed in the Ground in good order,
but is very certain to come up regularly and quickly, Grow off rapidly,
continue healthy, overtake the forward planting in Size, not subject in
particular to the many dangers and diseases early Cotton is liable, And in the
end like all healthy pe[r]sons, animals or plants to be more productive in the
end." Dent found that when "early" cotton did survive March cold, it was
susceptible to summer rust and other problems. [62]

As a former rice planter who succeeded with cotton culture, Dent
experimented with the Sea Island "dibble" and found it entirely
unsatisfactory for his rough frontier lands. His goal was to plant

> Cotton in the Chop . . . at a distance of two feet in the drill. To do this properly
> chops must be made by the Hoe on the Ridge at the regular distance. Or the
> hole be made on the ridge by what has been termed by the Sea Island planters
> in South Carolina the dibble, made of a straight piece of wood with a marker
> or pointer attached therefrom. So as the person punching the Hole for the seed
> places the punch again in the mark made by the pointer, consequently keeping
> and shewing the regular distance to be observed by this method.

Not surprisingly he found the dibble "too slow and tedious a method to
undertake." [63]

In order to bring "the plant to the proper and desired stand as soon as
planted" in rough lands, Dent preferred "The system of planting in the chop
with the Hoe . . . provided the distance be observed on the ridge, which must
require Hands of great exactness and Judgement, in keeping up the
regularity and niceness in a large Crop, without looseing the proper
distance, crowding or looseing ground." Finally, for greater speed he was
forced to open "the Ridge with a small skooter plough, Sowing the seed after
as thin as practicable in the furrow, and covering it with a small harrow made

for the purpose, and must rely on my attention, perserverance, and Judgement in haveing it properly chopped out with the Hoe to a stand averageing about one foot nine Inches or two feet in the drill. This plan I adopted for the best in making headway in the farm."[64]

Dent tried to begin planting cotton during the first week of April, but there were frequent delays. One was the continued planting and replanting of corn. In April, 1852, he reported of it: "The Stand is so badly destroyed by Birds and Squirrels that I am apprehensive that it will be to plow up and replant in toto. I never saw a stand so thoroughly destroyed." Even if he exaggerated in this instance, corn culture did hinder cotton planting. On April 7, 1853, he worried, "We are very much behind with our plows; we should now be planting Cotton instead of which we have 100 acres Cotton lands yet to bed, and 20 acres Corn land to bed out and plant. We calculate to Commence planting Cotton on Monday next."[65]

When cotton planting finally began on April 11, 1853, Dent described the complicated process of synchronizing tasks: "Commenced planting Cotton in Old Quarter field with 4 plows, 2 opening and 2 Covering. In a day or two hence will increase the planting to 8 plows." Meanwhile, corn was still demanding attention: "10 Plows rebedding and replanting the destroyed Corn in Pond field. So Soon as through will plant the Keener Hammock in Corn; it was laid off for Cotton, but the Corn crop promises so unfavourable that I think it best to curtail the Cotton 10 acres, and increase the Corn that amount." Cultivating corn could also hinder cotton. "We have as yet 25 acres of Swamp Lands to bed up for Cottons, but must procrastinate it until we can work out our Rusty field and Pond field corns, which are suffering on account of the Baked condition of the Land."[66]

In well-prepared corn lands of even stands, the April "culture" was supposed to be "light and to the purpose. As in throwing back the bed to the corn, the earth is loose and gathers around the plant level and sufficient, the hoes having but to level the dirt around the young plant." In practice, however, corn cultivation was seldom so easy. More frequently, by mid-April Dent was forced to report that in "All the fields Corn and Cotton are exceedingly fould and want working out very much indeed." Fould meant grassy, a threatening condition of wet years, in which rows had to be hoed clean as well as plowed. On the other hand, April droughts brought their own problems. "Most of our Cottons have been in the ground two weeks and is comeing up very badly, so much so, we feel great apprehensions of not procureing stands. We are skelping off the top of the beds with the hoe (being baked) in hopes of its comeing through immediately."[67]

When skelping proved insufficient to secure a stand, there was nothing else to do but "Ploughing up and reridgeing with 5 furrows Cotton West ½ of Middle Hammock, as the Stand was not sufficient to Warrent any dependence on it for a crop." Dent "Ordered it replanted by sowing the

John Horry Dent (1815-1892)
(From an oil painting owned by John Horry Beury and
used with his permission)

John Herbert Dent (1782-1823), father of John Horry Dent
(From an engraving by Charles B.J.F. de Saint-Memin,
reproduced courtesy of Mrs. Lillie W. Rapp)

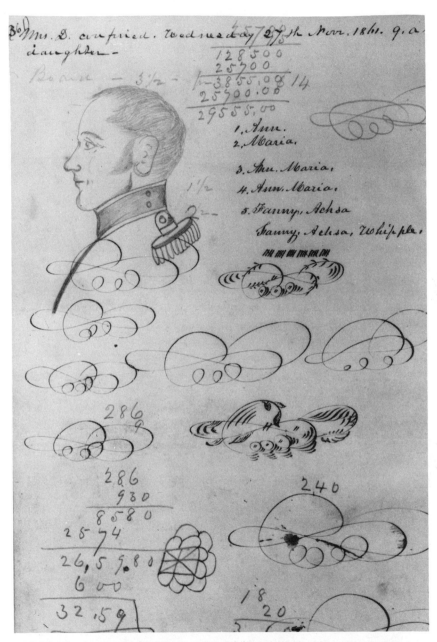

Profile of a young naval officer, probably John Horry Dent (1840-1864), the son of John Horry Dent (1815-1892). The father apparently sketched his son in his *Journal* (V, 361).

The world is but a scene of strife
Which meets each one, in life,
They who have gained, what all are seeking
are abused by they, who mispuiy.
This great first object, of mankind

"The Money Chest and the Banker" is the caption of this pencil sketch in the *Dent Journal* (III, 266). This seems to be Dent's sketch of himself seated before his mysterious money box.

"Declining Life" is, no doubt, a self portrait; it appears in the *Dent Journal* (II, 343).

Memorandum   1

Copy of Notes and Drafts due John H Dent A.D. 1854 & 1855.

Date of Notes	Drawers	When Due		
1854				
Feby 24	Edwd B Young	Pd	Iany 1. 1855	$1259 71 —	Pd
March 3	Charles Petty & B F Petty		Iany 1. 1855	683 43	
Feby 25	B I Hoole of captor I Hart Sons		Feby 25. 1855	580 00	
Feby 24	Batt Peterson of captor E B Young		Iany 15. 1855	1392 00	Pd
Feby 6	Robt Dill & B F Petty 6 notes $45 each		Iany 1. 1855	270 00	
Feby 7	D L Miller & T S Tullis		Iany 1. 1855	580 00	
Aprl 8	E B Young	Pd	Aprl 9 1854	493 67 —	
Feby 6	James Clark. prob Clark & B F Petty		Iany 1. 1855	652 50	
Feby 6	Robt Dill Lem Hargrove & B F Petty		Iany 1. 1855	652 50	6563 81
Iany 14	T I Roquemore	Pd	Iany 1 1855	325 00 —	Pd
Iany 3	Benjn Marley		Iany 1. 1855	593 64	
Feby 1	G W Whipple		Feby 1. 1855	858 66	
Iany 9	Alpheus Baker Jr	Pd	Iany 1. 1855	972 00 —	Pd
Decr 21	Zach Roquemore		Iany 1. 1855	1190 68	
Iany 2	C M Couric		Iany 1. 1855	864 00	
Decr 28	H D Clayton	Pd	Iany 1. 1855	702 00	Pd
Iany 7	I B Glover pd $90 00		Iany 1. 1855	268 00	5773 98
Iune 19	M B Wellborn		Iany 1. 1855	80 00	
Iune 21	Robert Dill		Iany 1. 1855	75 00	
Iune 20	Benjn F Petty		Iany 1. 1855	215 00	
Aprl 27	John Colby of captor E B Young		Feby 1. 1855	575 00	
Iune 6	Wm Varner. 2 notes of $625 0 each Pd		Iany 1. 1855	1250 00 —	Pd
Aprl 18	B Williams & C Petty 13 notes		Iany 1. 1855	562 50	Pd
Iany 20 1853	Thos Robinson H N Freed		Iany 1. 1854	862 93	
1851	Ino L Roberts. H N Freed M Oliver		Iany 1 1854	1290 56	
Iany 6 1850	Andrew Lee Geo W Fryar		Iany 1 1852	44 75	
Iany 28	I S West Ias D Slaughter		Iany 1. 1854	112 50	
1853	Ino Bledsoe 5 notes		1854	93 00	
Novr 7	Ias A Stringer		Iany 1. 1854	178 00	16591 24

An account page by Dent from *Dent Journal* (III, 1).

A page from the *Dent Journal* (V, 224) with news of the impending civil conflict, and expressing "apprehension" about being unable to communicate with his son "owing to all communications being stopped by Lincoln."

Pencil drawing of a sea battle between two small ships,
from the *Dent Journal* (II, 330).

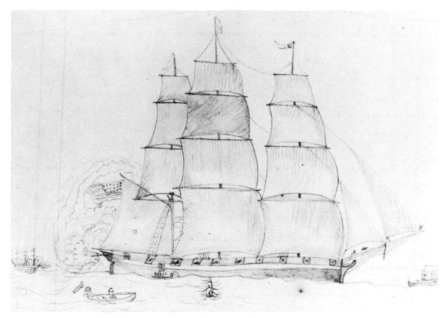

Pencil drawing of a frigate in a sea battle,
from the *Dent Journal* (II, 339).

Seed thicker and Covered by the hand." When the stands were weak but too nearly adequate to destroy, he had them nursed by hand with an intensive hoe culture that sometimes continued into May. "Owing to the very bad stand of Cotton we have this Spring," Dent could write,

> I am makeing the Hoes working it very careful, and thinning it as nearly as possible to one stalk distanced in the drill of an average of Six Inches. I have used this care and precaution As the Cotton looks puny and Sickly, and a great deal may yet die. And if the working and thinning it is now undergoing should here after with favourable Seasons prove beneficial, I will then work it again, so soon after I discover it growing and thriveing and bring it to the proper Stand. By this care my hopes are that I can be able to nurse the crop so as the pernicious season it has encountered with will not materially affect it in its growth and production here after. A good Shower now would be very beneficial to Cotton and especially the Corn we have worked.[68]

The "backwardness" described above was unusual. Generally speaking, there were good stands, April showers, and grass. Much grass sometimes required the practice of "barring off," which meant that the plows temporarily "threw" the grass-infested dirt away from the cotton plant in order to facilitate the hoes' cleaning and thinning. Dent described the procedure: "Owing to the very Grassy condition, Shall put all ploughs to immediately Baring the Cotton, running very lightly and throwing the grass and durt from the Cotton. Clean the Cotton with the Hoes, immediately turn back with the ploughs and break out the middles, and rework the Cotton over again as soon as possible, throwing the durt to it."[69]

If April was the month for replanting corn, planting cotton, and giving each crop its "first working," May was more diversified. Cultivating crops remained paramount, but there was more variety of duties in that month, during which John and Alfred could be given time to "get out" heavy timbers as "sills" for repairing the family dwelling which was "rotten underneath." Rarely did a tardy frost cause replanting in May, but one occurred in 1859, necessitating the "4th replanting of some corn."[70]

May was ordinarily the month of luxuriant gardens, when any remaining cabbages were set. It was also the time Dent began watching for the rain that would prepare the ground for setting out his twenty acres of sweet potato plants called slips or "drawers." The slips would be transplanted from a plantbed into the fields only after a soaking rain. Thus it was a matter for concern when once, as late as May 24, Dent had to report, "Potatoes, None set out as yet"; or again, "had not a sufficient season on yesterday to set out drawers." Nevertheless, he usually could record sometime within this month: "good showers, set drawers"; and "Hoeing our Root [Irish] Potatoes, and setting out potatoe drawers." Beginning in May, this process could last into June and even July.[71]

Also in May, Dent noticed when "Rice Is completely smothered up in

Grass weeds and bushes." Such comment was prelude to careful cleaning. Another matter of provisioning was fattening the hogs that consumed crib corn at an alarming rate. It was great relief for Dent when the swine "tender" could turn "100 hogs on corn" out to "pasture" in the small-grain stubble and waste seed after the hands had "saved" the rye. An adequate crop of rye was stacked, dried, shocked, and stored for later thrashing. Inferior crops of grain were fed immediately as silage: "feeding Rye to horses in chop." Dent was a great believer in "chop food" for animals, and numerous green things salvageable from garden and field were fed in this manner. While there was, apparently, no means for preserving silage, additional grain pasture was available for hogs in May, when Dent "put John and Brown to cutting Oats." The quality of this grain was uncertain, and when "Oats Has suffered from want of Rains, light and Inferior," they were probably fed as chop food, even as inferior rye had been. [72]

Saving small grains required cutting, "taking up, tying, and shocking," all of which was costly in time and manpower. The final product had to pay for the energy taken from cultivating corn and cotton. Sensitive to this balance, Dent wrote, "Our hoe force at present is very much weakened and irregular as much time is taken up to tye up the Oats and Rye." A related concern was his constant fear of a "short" plow force. The latter threat materialized only once in an acute form. That was in 1856, when distemper was dropping his mules one by one. On May 21 of that year, he noted, "2 of our mules having died last week which to a plow force too short at first has made it now inadequate." Despite fewer plows, Dent managed. A major compensation in such situations was the Negroes' general healthiness during May, that is, with the glaring exception of the typhoid epidemic in 1853. [73]

Also in May the weather usually cooperated for successful cultivation. It was seldom too wet or too dry, though each condition could occur. Generally, the month began with the "hoes blocking out Cottons," which meant chopping or thinning it to a proper stand. In dry weather, the grass was easily controlled, but this kind of season was dusty and that reduced hands' efficiency: "Chopping Cotton in the old quarter flats. Very dusty to do good work. Negroes are in a cloud of dust when working. Shall start 4 plows sideing the Cotton after the hoes at noon." Ideally the plows would follow the hoes, but not too far behind: "Plows in the old stable flat *doing bad work,* being so far behind the hoes (the grass has grown very rapidly for the last week). They *throw the grass upon the beds, and this showery weather is setting it out among the Cottons....* half the day engaged in taking up, tying, and shocking Oats." The last sentence helps explain the cotton planters' aversion to raising very many foodstuffs. [74]

Even with hindrances, May cultivation was relatively easy. Notice Dent's relaxed tone during this period: "4 plows (Northern) sideing and lightly dirting cottons after the Hoes"; "merely running round the Cottons with solid Sweeps''; "12 ploughs running round the Wellborn Cottons, sideing very close, so as to stifle up a coat of small grass just up''; "very little grass and ground in splendid order to work''; "Stirred 400 acres land this week." In these favorable working conditions, complaints could even sound a positive note: "Our backwardness in a great measure is owing to the very great pains the Overseer takes in cleaning it. He cleans it thoroughly as he goes''; also "They have thoroughly cleaned the crop as they have gone over which will render their work in future much lighter." Too-clean cotton, however, could indicate drought and a retarded plant. For example in 1858, there was "very little grass," but cotton was "small and puny."[75]

Another significant problem was the crop pests that were evident this month and remained a nuisance throughout summer and fall. By early May the bud worm could be "bad in corn." Gardens were often unpromising because of "Cut Worm. In the Garden the cut worm is ruinous. It is impossible to get a stand of cabbages; so soon as we reset out they are again cut down." Summer cotton was threatened by rust, lice, "soar shin," boll worm, and "pierce bug." A cold spring brought lice and rust, which "weakened stands" and retarded growth. Sometimes Dent reported with misleading finality: "For the last few days Cottons are becoming Lousy, have not grown any, assuming a diseased appearance. Stands dying out." Actually these "depredations" were always spotty, yet he would write alarmist-like, "Our Cottons are dying out to a fearful extent with the Soar Shin," which was a type of fungus. A bit later he would dread the "pierce bug ... piercing many forms." Locusts appeared on two separate occasions. In May, 1855, he noted, "The Woods are covered with what is called the Bell Locust, which keep up an incessant ringing sound. We had them here before in 1842." Such brief comment would seem to indicate no significant damage from locusts.[76]

Circumstances in May occasionally turned previous cottonseed manuring to an unexpected disadvantage. "Our old land Corns in growing order [but] much of it is frenching; that is the blade is in a rotting condition which is said to be owing to the Cotton seed manure." Apparently too much had been used. On these rare occasions, the unmanured corn was stronger.[77]

During the second "working" of corn in mid-May, Dent noticed the stalk and ran comparisons: "Last year at this date commenced giveing Corn 2d plowing. Corn was hip high. This year our best Corn is hardly knee high." To promote height and large ears, the hands "suckered" corn, pulling unwanted shoots that would detract strength from stalk and fruit. Thus early in the month, Dent would observe, "Rusty Field in fair Order, wants Suckering''; and perhaps later, "Corn is in good order, freshly plowed over, and suckered."[78]

On one occasion, he described an ideal second working of corn as though it would be the last or "lay-by" cultivation. "The Second plowing need be but light, merely sufficient to dirt the corn a little deeper, and plow in the pea crop. The hoes leveling off perfecting it in splendid order. With these two workings after planting, the crop is laid aside to mature, and at an early period, giving one a fair sweep for the Cotton crop."[79]

Such an ideal corn culture would be completed by June 1. In fact, however, Dent seldom resisted the temptation of a third plowing of corn in late June or even in July. Whenever the laying by occurred, seed peas that had been carefully saved from last year's crop would be sowed among all the corn. Corn was almost always laid by during the month of June, thereby receiving three plowings instead of two. The June 9, 1858, entry was typical: "Having had no sweeps that run flat enough, Sided our Corn lightly with half Shovels and Northern plows and broke out middles with Solid Sweeps, taking 5 furrows to the row. In all, our corn has been given 18 furrows to the row in working out, Viz. 7 furrows 1st plowing, 6 do 2d plowing, 5 do 3d & last plowing."[80]

With so many furrows or trips to make for each row, the plows could lag behind the hoes, but the observant Dent was equal to the situation: "Plows in Smarts field Corn will get through it PM, and proceed in the old Sedge Hills Corn. The hoes were about over running the Plows, So drew them off, and put them to hoeing out a very grassy piece of Cotton adjoining the Cattle Shelter. Will resume hoeing the Corn on to morrow." It was also possible to counterbalance the hoes' speed by requiring other duties of them: "The force is very much reduced as a part are dropping peas before the Plows and a part are tying up Oats." At various times, he wrote of cow peas and speckled peas, but by whatever name, peas were food for man and beast. Dent also believed they replenished the soil.[81]

The third working of corn almost always occurred in weather so predictably dry that Dent drew rain maps to illustrate the axis on which clouds regularly by-passed his plantation during June. He also claimed, "I am the only Sufferer for want of Rain in the County. The rains have passed round me, again and again, and fallen plentifully even at my adjoining neighbors." Again he wrote in June, "Rains have been superabundant all round me. My adjoining neighbors, Adams, Field, Threat, Bigham, Harvels, and Smarts, have not Suffered a day for want of Rains. With us, our grounds have not been wet Since April, a few light Showers have been our portion."[82]

At such times, Dent believed, "as long as the Weather is dry the solid sweeps are our best plows to clean with." He knew, as well, the value of substituting hoe culture for plowing in a drought: "I have heretofore when the ground was very dry not plowed the Corn the third working, merely hoeing it = which I find the best." Yet he could seldom resist the temptation to plow crops the third time, even in a drought. On more than one occasion, he had to admit, "Our Corn seems to have fired up very much of late. I can account for it in no other way but having been plowed and hoed in the very hottest and dryest weather we had. It is tasseling out well but backwards in shooting. The lateral roots of the Corn being cut that very dry weather did not recover in time to supply the shoots. Will never plow Corn again at that age unless there is a full season in the ground.''[83]

The vow was meaningless. He took the same risk again and again. In 1858 he plowed corn deeply in a drought and brazenly dared fate, ''Rain or Ruin to my Corn.'' It rained. Dent's jeremiads to the contrary, the larger crops were almost always saved by tardy but adequate rains. A temporary drought, however, would ruin some spots of corn on the higher, thinner soils: ''The drought is so severe on us that our Corn has failed. The Old mans hill and Gin house Hill has let down; half of the . . . [stalks] have no shoots and the other half nubbins.''[84]

These losses notwithstanding, stormy rains in late June often brought miraculous recoveries in the wake of destruction. In 1852 June rains washed up peas and other plants, but on balance Dent appreciated ''This rain of infinite service to the Corn Crop.'' He believed it would also ''start off Cotton to grow.'' Some summer storms were severe enough to require the righting of stalks and the covering of roots by hand. Gentle June rains were ideal, but they were very few and far between. Hard rains also complicated cotton culture. On a June 25, Dent observed that ''from extreme drought, we are now experience extreme Wet. It is now to wet to plow or Work Cottons to any advantage. Directed that the Cottons be hoed as lightly as possible, picking out the grass and deposite it in the Alleys.'' Such wet respites, however, gave the hands another opportunity to set sweet potato ''drawers.''[85]

Meanwhile, the master watched for his first cotton bloom. After moving to Bleak Hill on the Barbour Creek, it pained him considerably that Cowikee cotton bloomed earlier than his. On June 23, 1840, he summarized four months of planting developments that illustrate annual plantation concerns from March through June.

March 3d commenced planting Corn
April 6th commenced planting Cotton finished 16th
April 30th planted out first potatoe Sprouts
April 16th commenced working Corn
April 16th finished planting our full crop Cotton
May 2d Commenced choping out Cotton and
May 11th observed first forms on Cotton
May 14th Finished choping out whole crop of Cotton
May 21st Finished planting Corn for this Season
May 16th planted first peas
June 7th observed two blossoms in old field cotton.[86]

June was apparently the regular month for killing and quartering beef with neighbors. Perhaps each family provided the beef on a rotating basis. Apparently Dent was in charge of slaughter. On June 3, 1841, he recorded a costly and embarrassing experience: "On Yesterday Morning shot a young three Year old Heifer at Seborn Burlisons pen for Beef. Made a bad shot that merely wounded her. She run off, and since cannot be found, presume she died. At the time could not get any dogs what would catch or follow her. Hunted the Range very closely for her, but could not find it."[87] Between a large, open range and beef-hungry neighbors, it is understandable that Dent never recovered the wounded animal.

Not to be deterred, he acted five days later and "Killed a three Year old Steer of the Hays stock for Beef. Shared it as follows:

1 hind qrtr to Morrison	weighing	78	lbs
1 fore qrtr to Stringer	''	73	''
½ fore qrtr to Seborn Burlison	''	43	''
Kept hnd qrtr for self	''	77	''
and the Rack '' ''	''	32	''
	total	303	lbs."[88]

The rack was the remaining portion of Burlison's one-half quarter. The total dressed weight of 303 pounds was about half the live weight, which can be estimated at 600 pounds, a very small animal for three years of age. No wonder Dent complained of his region's inferior livestock.

Another provision entry of June, 1861, notes that his laborers "Sunned and packed away 234 large Western shoulders. Meat enough to last 9 months or up to 1st March, 1862." Pork previously salted, hung, and smoked could also require summertime attention. On July 1, 1859, Dent reported a problem, "Our Hams and Shoulders have been unusually preyed upon by Bugs and Skippers this Season, owing no doubt to the very wet winter and spring. For the last two days have had them well Sunned, then dipped into boiling water, and after being dried, rubbed over thickly with powdered Charcoal, and laid away in a tight barrel."[89]

Provisioning meat was important enough to interrupt work on cotton. But ideally by July the drill rows of cotton stalks would be free enough of grass to let the plows go first, having the hoes follow to complete the laying by. But if cotton was grassy before the third plowing, the hoes would have to pass through the crop twice on the last working. This was the meaning of the following problem, which Dent, disregarding the rainy weather, blamed entirely on the overseer: "Our Plows and Hoes are too far Separated and the hoes should be immediately after the Plows, but instead of this, they are ahead of the plows, cleaning our drills which have been foul all the year, a mismanaged affair of McLeods which has been in this condition all the year. I will try and arrange it so soon as I can get the drills in order."[90]

To his credit, Dent rightfully assumed blame for over-plowing corn and cotton. In 1854 he observed:

For the last three years, I have noticed that the Cotton crop has a most promising and flattering appearance until July, when it receives its last plowing and
a broad cast shedding Seems to take place, which cuts off the crop materially.
I am of opinion this state of things is brought about by plowing our lands too
late. The lands in this part of the Country are Sandy and have been cultivated
for a number of years; hence their productive powers are very much lessened,
or in other words, they do not brace up a crop as long through the Seasons as
when fresh.[91]

In this situation, he saw the value of substituting hoe culture for the last
plowing: "Picking grass out of Cottons with the hoes." Yet he had little
success at trying to leave cotton alone, probably because the "jobs" were
fewer in July and slaves' leisure pained him. To "busy" hands, he would
even put the "Hoes In Peas" that were growing in laid-by corn.[92]

While June was commonly dry, July was usually wet, but not in 1859.
During this drought, when it was again raining all around his plantation,
Dent was hard put to resist the conclusion of divine retribution. He drew
elaborate weather charts, showing how the rains by-passed him, and even
though he knew "it has rained on every side of me for the last four days," he
made no special effort to attend divine service. He did, however, have the
Reverend and Mrs. William L. Steele for frequent and extended visits.
When they returned home to Eufaula on July 30, Dent must have resolved to
attend worship at St. James Episcopal Church, because on the following day
he felt constrained to contrive a (thoroughly unbelievable) rationalization for
staying home: "Mrs Dent and all the family gone to Eufaula to Church. I
feel quite unwell, and no room in carriage or Buggie for myself as the
children going to Sunday School." One wonders what Dent thought that
same afternoon when he "barely missed" another good rain.[93]

The customary wetting rains of July were not always entirely beneficial.
They sometimes had the negative effect on cotton of increasing rust,
shedding, and worms. Dent would "Notice the grass worm in our flats and
Norman field Cottons, completely cutting the tender branches and young
forms."[94] Yet a certain amount of water was required, and Dent usually got
it—if not quite as soon as needed, then later.

After laying-by cotton in July, there was less-pressing plantation work
until the fodder was ready to "save." Dent waited until August to pull or
strip these corn stalk leaves in order to assure a mature ear of corn and dry
blades of fodder. Meantime, multifarious jobs reappeared in the journal,
not that these tasks had ever completely stopped. Now, with the crops abandoned until they should mature, Dent had time to record the smaller regular chores. He tried to keep the slaves as busy as ever. Thus one reads
again of "All hands" littering lots, which meant saving manures and hauling new straw for more littering. With so many laborers, this daily task
could not have required very much time. There was also the entry, "4 hands

thrashing out Oats,'' which earlier had been stored in shocks. Now following a hard rain, there was plenty of time for numerous hands to pass leisurely through the fields ''Setting up Washed Cottons.'' In this interim, most of the slaves were ''promiscuously engaged'' at jobbing, weeding, ditching, and even cleaning fence corners. With rail fences laid in a zig-zag pattern, cleaning corners could have been a gargantuan task. Jobbing also included new ground, even in July: ''Will clean up some skirts of land in Oats field and strip between New ground and potatoe patch''; also ''deadning timber.''[95]

Because each period of relaxation invited construction projects, July was a time for ''Building a crib for peas''; also ''Men have been employed last week in geting out boards and other timbers for Corn Crib.'' In the summer of 1855, Dent devised enough construction projects to last four years. July work in new grounds provided timbers for framing, for riving shingles, for sawing plank, and for splitting fence rails. This last repair was necessary every month of the year, but especially in July, when fat, sassy hogs were ripe for breaking out of small grain pastures into the fields of maturing corn.[96]

Finally, August neared, and hands began stripping corn stalks of their blades, for fodder. Dent's attitude was consistently glum about this task. Perhaps it was the wait for harvest that soured his mood. Or maybe the blacks were as uninterested in the project as he always insisted they were. The unrewarding work was steamy hot, stinging, and monotonous. Perhaps the master resented the necessity for it. A July 29 entry reads, ''Fair, commenced pulling fodder ... it is such burnt up stuff, it will turn out poorly.''[97]

This work lasted far into August, and ''foddering'' hands seldom pulled ears of corn as they went, which meant once again ''going over'' these fields. An exception was the year 1841, when Dent's blacks ''Commenced pulling fodder.... Stripping the Stalk Clean as We go, as the Corn is sufficiently matured.'' Pulled from the stalk, blades were left on the ground to cure while hands attended to other tasks: ''A quantity of Fodder down not cured. Hands Working and drawing the slips last planted in the Orchard. Breaking up Turnip Ground for Sowing the first Rain. Observed Cotton opening.''[98]

From August until the last crop item was gathered and housed, excessive rain was Dent's nemesis. This was especially true for curing fodder. On an August 12, he wrote, ''Morning Cloudy and Afternoon a Steady Cold Rain, the Holder field fodder being down and not cured, Will be lost if the Sun does not shine on it to morrow.'' Following his maxim of ''waste not,'' Dent saw that damaged fodder was summarily used. Nor could a little rain stop new-ground work in August: ''A Greater portion of the fodder down ... is materially dammaged. Ordered it took home and fed to the Mules. All hands in New Ground Grubbing and chopping.'' Once cured, the fodder could be housed or stacked for preservation against the rain.[99]

As noted above, new-ground and construction work went along with foddering: "In a few days shall start them to deadning land, some to getting out shingles." In August, 1859, Dent's force began girdling one hundred acres of trees. [100]   Large new-ground projects were feasible in the 1850s, after tired lands and improved strains produced smaller cotton stalks, which did not require the time-consuming August duty of "topping" that Dent had sometimes practiced in the 1840s.

The purpose of topping cotton on strong, rich lands was to stunt the stalk and channel the plant's strength into the pods of developing fibers. Thus Dent topped in August after the plant was sufficiently hardened to retard or preclude troublesome suckers. In 1840 he wrote a lengthy exposition on the subject to his friend, Bertram J. Hoole, of the Barbour County Agricultural Society. Later, in a brief aside, Dent synthesized the detailed argument. The abridged version reads: "On the first of August We topped Cotton about half of the Crop, and there is no comparrison; that untopped has run up to Weed, and scarce any fruit on the upper part, While the Topped has branched well and crowded with bolls." [101]

Watching the cotton mature through August, Dent was again susceptible to minor nervous illness, as he fretted over rain, rust, grass worms, and boll worms. Summarizing his anxieties, he wrote on August 9, 1856: "Cottons are failing very fast, top fruit shedding on account of the drought. Rust in spots about, and notice an army of grass worms making their appearance in the plantation. It is reported below this that they have swept every thing." [102]   Needless to say, pests and other problems would reduce the yield, but Dent's habitual bogey, total crop failure, never materialized.

Nor did he really expect disaster. Realist that he was, his preparations for picking cotton always proceeded on schedule. One annual preparation was machinery repairs. In August, 1855, his hands "Brought down Gin from the Johnson place on yesterday, requires new bristles in the Brush, the rats having destroyed" the old ones. Dent's gin was always housed either crudely or handily, depending on the length of time he had lived on a given plantation. The cotton press, called the "screw," also required regular attention. Thus one frequently reads of "repairing up screw" or "raising" a new screw. [103]

The screw, or baling press, consisted of a wooden box more than twice as large as a compressed bale. The box was appropriately hinged to release the bale, which had been bound after the sliding lid, or top, had been forced down against the cotton by a great wooden screw turning through a sturdy mortised frame above the box. The heavy screw was turned down against the lid by two mules pulling fifty-foot levers attached to it. This arrangement was capable of compressing a 500-pound bale. Binding the bales before their release from the press required bagging and rope which had to be purchased in Eufaula and hauled to the plantation. [104]

By the last week of August some hands would begin picking cotton.

Meanwhile, there were the small jobs like "hauling up" sweet potatoes. This was also the time to dig and expose marl to be conditioned for next year's use, but Dent never made a regular practice of it. There was also miscellaneous hauling, such as transporting up to Clayton in 1856 the handsome monument for Mary Elizabeth's grave. But when hands finally began picking cotton in earnest, Dent relaxed. Surely the overseer could direct this task, leaving the master more time to ride about the country on pretext of buying land, a good excuse for visiting and comparing crops, pastimes Dent genuinely enjoyed.[105]

Still the master checked his plantation almost every day to know exactly what was transpiring. During these times, hands picked steadily except when it rained, and then they "jobbed" until it was "dry enough to resume picking Cotton." An elementary, yet cardinal, rule of planting was to work outside so long as weather permitted, saving indoor or sheltered work for inclement weather. Overseer Bush surely knew this, but anyone can miscalculate, especially when beginning a task not done for a full year. Whatever rough parallels might be drawn, planting was not as repetitious as assembly-line production. In one instance, Dent's ire, born of aggravation at relaxing his own vigilance, was unfairly, but understandably, heaped upon the underling Bush, when the master sneered sarcastically: "New mode of picking Cotton. Introduced by my Overseer Mr Greenberry Bush. This morning clear and fine for picking cotton. Mr Bush takes *all* hands and spends until 8 Oclock to clean up Gin House. Afternoon rains hard, takes all hands to pick Cotton. Is it any wonder with such Wisdom in manageing a Short Crop is made?"[106]

Actually neither Bush nor slave was inept, and Dent must have known it, when, in a matter of a few days' work he could report: "Cotton Picked out up to 1st September . . . 39255 pounds." These weights for green seed cotton were quite good. In fact, Dent's cotton picking usually went so well that by early September he actually mellowed, remembering some good times, not just the bad ones—August usually looked best in retrospect. In 1840 he observed, "The Latter part of August was more seasonable and favourable to the Crops than we have had since the early part of June. Cotton opened very fast. . . . Hands averaged 120 lbs at picking the last Week in August. Negroes also have been healthy." By the late 1850s his hands sometimes averaged 165 pounds per day.[107]

In such situations, Dent could become surprisingly optimistic about fodder and even caterpillars: "Weather at present very favourable for . . . the New Ground fodder." And, laconically, he "Observed a few Caterpillars in the Cotton" as hands had "saved and stacked from the Corn fields . . . 16 Stacks" of fodder. The size of a stack is unknown, but by now Dent was satisfied with the results, even when "Most of the fodder Saved was in a damaged State." September was also encouraging when "The prospects of a Pea crop is exceedingly abundant."[108]

With these satisfactions, journal entries decreased in number and length. Not surprisingly, most of them dealt with picking cotton and jobbing. A sampling of September, 1855, reads:

> Mo 3 Fair and Warm, hand[s] picking heavy weights of Cotton
> Tu 4 Fair and Warm picking Cotton
> Wn 5 Fair and very warm, went to Clayton. PM heavy Rains
> Th 6 12 M. heavy rains. PM. picking Cotton
> Fr 7 AM cloudy and cool. Wind fresh from SE—until 9 Oclock
>   AM hands cleaning out fence way round old Oats field to
>   repair fencing.
> Sa 8 Fair and pleasant—picking Cotton
> Su 9 Fair and pleasant.
> Mo 10 Fair and warm, picking Cotton.[109]

Dent kept daily tallies of cotton picked and had several small jobs pending to assure the hands a sufficiency of wet-weather work. One of these was roads: "Men Working on road opening a new Road from Greys to Clayton." He described the larger work substitution. "From 12 M all the afternoon had hard rains and a great quantity of Water fallen. Had to stop picking Cotton, and put the hands repairing my private road." It rarely rained enough in any month to force this master to admit that his "hands were unable to do any thing." While this occurred on September 3, 1841, the very next day Dent could report, "Picking Cotton with all hands. Stopped the Hands from going on the road this day." Weather hindrances were temporary.[110]

Regardless of earlier repairs, machinery often required September tunings: "As soon as Alfred is able I design putting the Gin in order and commence Gining. As the Cotton now picked is too damp to be covered with other pickings." In Barbour County's humid climate, there was no need to let cotton sweat before ginning. In fact it sometimes required drying before it could be processed. September was almost too late in the season to be receiving a new gin, but on September 19, 1840, he reported: "This day Received from the shop of Atwood in Gerard Ala One friction roller Gin 50 Saws. Accompanied with a letter from L G Beckwith rel the Same." Beckwith probably delivered later than Dent had expected, for in May, 1852, he "Received from E T Taylor of Columbus Factory a 50 Saw Gin" which had been "ordered last Winter." In September, 1859, Dent had a Clemons Brown Gin from Columbus, Georgia. At that time, it was malfunctioning too seriously for his men to repair it. Awaiting a special mechanic from Columbus, Dent grumbled his conviction that Daniel Pratt in Prattville, Alabama, made the best gin around.[111]

Repairing and rebuilding the screw was less frustrating than were broken-down gins. A local carpenter could construct one with care in a matter of days. On September 1, 1852, "Turner Williams set in to build a

Screw. He and Alfred in search of a pin." Fifteen days later, they "Raised the Screw built by Turner Williams. Got her up with ease, and apparently a good Screw." These September repairs occurred while the majority of the hands continued "picking the fields in rotation so as to Save the Cotton next [to] the ground as soon as practicable." The lower fibers were most exposed to dirt and rot. Bolls on foliaged cotton opened erratically, usually on the middle of the stalk, then at the bottom, and finally in the top.[112]

Meanwhile, construction jobs proceeded in good order, though slower than scheduled. All of this building involved numerous trips to Beauchamp's mill or to Gerke's and Whipple's mill for planks and for "Windows and doors stuff," usually selected by Alfred. September was also the time to curse the Yankee-made wagons while purchasing poplar and pine boards for repairing and rebuilding the "bodies" of these conveyances, which were soon to be in great demand. Wagons were already hauling provisions, such as "meat and molasses" from McNab's store. It was also the time to replenish the stock of sheep and to finish "thrashing out" any remaining oats or rye. In September, the hot, sultry weather also moderated, but usually not so much as on the thirteenth day of that month in 1840 when Dent found "fires very comfortable. Morning and Evening and nights very much like a frost."[113]

October brought more consistently cool weather and a more complicated harvest because of provision crops to be "saved" and "housed." Because the division of labor became more intricate and continued so into December, the tasks of October and November are best discussed as an entity. By mid-October Dent usually wrote to the effect: "Will commence gathering Corn. There is half of the DeWitt flat and all the South Western Cottons (about 100 acres) pretty White yet to pick. A part of the hands under Vurture will continue picking, Whilst some will be drawn off to gather Corn. About 40 acres of the Cox fields are also white." Separating ears of corn from the stalks was called breaking: "Commenced gathering Corn, breaking in the Cox fields."[114]

Another division of labor was "Part hands picking Peas." Here, blacks gathered the crop for food and seed, unless time was especially short: "Pea Crop may be Considered a fair One. Will only pick a sufficiency for Seed next Year, Owing to my hurry." However, there was still to be no waste; the hogs would consume the peas left in the fields. Picking peas was women's work, as distinct from men's heavier jobs. These latter included building a road bridge. Starting this arduous task during the harvest season seems odd, perhaps, but such construction requires very favorable weather. Also a strategic bridge could simplify heavy hauling. Dent explained the complications and the anticipated advantages of building such a bridge. "Day fair and pleasant, put both Wagons to hauling Corn, hauling out Smarts field. 6 Boys assisted with 4 from Mrs Snipes are getting out timber to put up a Bridge on our rout to Eufaula, a heavy Job for private

CORN YIELDS

Year	Plantation	Corn Acreage	Wagons	Bushels Per Wagon	Total Bushels	Bushels Per Acre
1838	Good Hope					
1839						
1840			67	30	2,010	
1841		135	61	30	1,830	13.5
1842	True Blue	150	34	30	1,020	6.8

(In 1842, the plantation required about 1,250 bushels corn)

Year	Plantation	Corn Acreage	Wagons	Bushels Per Wagon	Total Bushels	Bushels Per Acre
1850	Miller's Good Hope					
1851						
1852		215				
1853					4,000	
1854		160	108	30	3,240	20.3
1855	DeWitt's Bleak House	195	115	30	3,450	17.7
1856		240	110	40	4,400	18.3
1857						
1858		205	115	30 (40)	3,450 (4,600)	16.8 (22.4)
1859						

(In 1860s, the plantation required about 2,800 bushels corn)

Year	Plantation	Corn Acreage	Wagons	Bushels Per Wagon	Total Bushels	Bushels Per Acre
1860						
1861		287			4,879	17
1862		535				
1863		490				
1864		490			3,120	6.4
1865		490			4,224	8.6
1866		150 (free labor)			1,575	10.5

undertaking; but a few Children picking Cotton; shall continue to haul in Corn until the crop is harvested, as it is loosing and wasting in the fields. This building the Bridge is a heavy tax upon us, and a draw back to our plantation business, but it is on our direct road to town." [115]

With his attention divided among corn, peas, the bridge, and cotton, Dent could become uneasy about his money crop. In October when "Children picking Cotton only," or when "Vurter and children picking Cotton," he concluded, "We are loosing a most glorious Season for picking Cotton." Thus with as little as one day's notice, he might "stop harvesting Corn for the present and pick out the Bigham flats Cotton, Which never have been picked in as yet. The Sedge Hills and Cotton Corns are yet to Gather. Men still at the Bridge. Alfred values not time. PM Repairing the Screw with John & 4 Boys." When the weather was right, Dent simply could not resist "picking Cotton." He would postpone gathering corn until less favorable weather.

Ordinarily, the corn crop was housed in October and November, whereupon Dent immediately measured the yield, which was usually between 3,000 and 4,500 bushels. He compared each crop with that of previous years. For example in 1856, there were 110 wagons of corn. At forty bushels per wagon this was about eighteen bushels per acre, somewhat above Dent's usual production. Yet he deprecated the large yield, insisting in 1856, "Corn is remarkably light. It will take 3 bushels this year to equal 1 bushel of last years. The drought was blasting on it." Even this situation was not a disaster—the plantation consumed about 2,500 bushels per year and he usually had a surplus of 500 bushels or more. While the consumption figure is a loose estimate based on information from 1842 and 1866, the corn yields listed on page 141 are more nearly exact. They rest on data from Dent's annual summaries.

As soon as corn and peas were housed in October or November, pastured hogs were released on these fields, provided the hands had completed the "cross fences" that were a priority on each new plantation. Cross-fencing was necessary for taking maximum advantage of field grazing. Still these fences required watching, as they were easily knocked down by "fat wild & unmanageable" hogs. [116]

Meanwhile cotton picking continued, and the gin was in full operation, except in 1858, when Dent was awaiting the Columbus mechanic. Believing this delay to be unpardonable, he busied the gin hands in building a new crib. When the mechanic, a Negro man, appeared on October 29, Dent indicated displeasure by an uncharacteristic use of the term *boy*: "Yesterday Clemons Brown & Co. sent a Mulatto Boy Ned to repair Gin. Defect was in the wearing of the Ribs; put in 13 new Ribs, and started her off, apparently performing well." [117]

A simple machine, the gin consisted of saws with teeth that pulled the fibers free of seed between the narrow ribs, which were too close for the seed to pass. The brushes cleaned the saws of lint, and fans, in turn, cleaned the brushes. By early November in the mid-1850s, it was not unusual for Dent to have "Up to date 120 Bales Cotton packed out. 36 hauled to town & 84 at the Screw." Ginning cotton meant a growing pile of seed. Dent provided pens for containing them in banks. There were also seed shelters for controlled decomposition, preparatory to spreading the fertilizer on corn lands ahead of breaking plows. [118]

The very important provision crop of sweet potatoes was harvested in September, October, or November. Dent's fifteen-to-twenty acres of this root crop produced between eight and twenty-four banks of potatoes each year, depending on the "seasons." A bank of sweet potatoes contained approximately thirty-five bushels. Dent described the process of harvesting and storing them: "In diging Sweet Potatoes," he advised,

> Let them remain in the field exposed to the Sun, and stop digging ample time befor[e] sun set, So as the potatoes can be piled and covered with Straw before the dews fall on them. Making the Bank as follows: Five feet in diameter at the bottom, well littered with Straw So as to prevent the dampness of the Ground from ever affecting the potatoes, the potatoes then piled up regularly until they come to a point, makeing a regular Circle, and tapering regularly to a point. Then Cover them with litter or straw next [to the] potatoes, then procure Wide Bark as long as the pile, and Cover the potatoes and Straw similar to Shingleing, then cover the Bark with dirt, about four inches deep, leaveing a hole on top for Air, and have the hole covered with Bark and dirted, so as to prevent Water getting in, But air must not be stopped from Circulating. [119]

No sooner were sweet potatoes bedded than hands "put our meat hogs in the potato patch" to fatten on roots, vines, potato scraps and other leavings. In November, after these animals had passed successively through pastures of small grains, corn, peas, and potatoes, Dent would "Put up 5 hogs in floord pens for early killing, the ballance are still in the potatoe field, will not put them up until the potatoes are eaten up." [120]

Cotton picking continued into December or January, until every boll had opened or had been pulled for "scrap" at the last "going over." As these green-white fields gradually browned out one by one, ordinary tasks reappeared in the journal. On one rainy November day, the hands were "Packing Cotton Raking up Lots and pileing away manures," while others "Built Cow pen for making manures at quarter." Also Dent was already planning next year's crops, designating fields, and measuring the manures in anticipation of spreading the compost as quickly as possible. On another unfavorable November day, he reported the hands "raking up Straw and littering lots" while "Boys splitting rails for repairing Oat field fencing" and

"One plow breaking up House lot preparatory to sowing down Rye for Winter pasturage for Ewes and Lambs." There were similar preparations for sowing oats.[121]

By December the hands were "Picking Scattering Cottons," which were inferior and dirty. Dent described the aggravating process: "Our last pickings of Cottons as well as those put up in pens have been so heated and injured by the heavy rains we had, as to occasion much trouble in keeping them cool. We are obliged to scatter it on bagging laid out on the ground and keep it sunned and stired the whole time. . . . It is also very troublesome to Gin, it being so dirty and rotten, as to keep the saws constantly gumed up." Such work went on often into the new year. Meanwhile another late-December job was "Thrashing out Rice with Eight hands."[122]

By now hauling was constant work, a need which must have bent Dent's prohibition of night labor. It was often hazardous, especially on trips to Clayton and Eufaula. In December, 1852, he pondered the risks and indirectly praised his men's ability: "It is hard weather and dangerous roads, but what are we to do? The Cotton is exposed at home, and our hauling is very much behind hand. As such we must make the risk, and trust to the Teamsters caution and Judgement." He was almost always fortunate in having able wagoners.[123]

Having been at new-ground work intermittently since July, the hands experienced no novelty in one December when Dent wrote of putting "men cutting up Logs in New Ground, Vurture with Women stopping up Washes in old Lands." At any point in the last quarter of the year, it is common to read, "Hands in new ground." Less common was the December task whereby they took "down smoke house, removing it further off from the house." New-ground work again led to rail making and the annual task of "culling" weak rails or portions of the fences to be replaced with stronger materials.[124]

Like farmers before and after him, Dent loved the phrase "crop up," especially when he sensed the threat of snow, which does fall occasionally in southeastern Alabama winters. Still it was a rare December when "The ground is completely covered with Snow, every thing." He rejoiced when its sojourn was brief, because "Cattle must suffer very much" in it. In spite of snow, however, "All hands in New Ground." December was also the regular time for overseers' contracts and removals. On December 31, 1852, Dent "Sent both Wagons with Bob and Paul to move Mr Martin to his quarters as Overseer." With or without an overseer for next year, the master did not wait to buy "iron." He did not have to have an overseer to "start plows immediately" in January, if not in December. Nor did John, the blacksmith, have to be reminded of this December duty.[125]

Despite this multiplicity of tasks and the nearness of Christmas, the work force was also set in to clean the quarter thoroughly and to kill as many hogs

COTTON PRODUCTION

Year	Plantation	Cotton Acreage	Total Bales	Bales Per Acre	Price	Cotton Income	Loans
1838	Good Hope		24 (?)			$ 800 (?)	
1839			57		7-9¢	$ 2,000	
1840			73		9-10¢	$ 3,500	$ 1,800
1841		175	70	.40	8¢	$ 2,500	
1842	True Blue	180-197	75	.40		$ 3,000	
1842-49			660			$23,115	
an. avg.			82.5		$35 bale	$ 2,900	
1850	Miller's Good Hope		80			$ 3,600 (?)	
1851			141 (156)			$ 5,000	
1852		330	80	.24	8-9¢	$ 5,000	
1853		370	200 (216)	.58		$ 9,000	$ 7,000 (+)
1854		300	100 (116)	.38		$ 4,000	
1855	DeWitt's Bleak Hs.	380	151	.39		$ 6,000	$20,000 (+)
1856		400 (430)	155	.36		$ 7,000	
1857			124		10-11¢	$ 6,000	
1858		465 (470)	186	.40	10¢	$ 9,600	$37,500 (+)
1859		470	125	.26		$ 6,500 (?)	$49,000
1860		480	87	.18		$ 4,500	$54,000
1861		440	103 (sold 71)	.23	16¢	$ 6,000	
1862		72					$64,000
1863		110					
1864		60					
1865			65		20¢	$ 7,000	
1865			26 seized & returned		19¢	$ 2,600	
1866		350	75 (by free labor)	.21		$ 7,500 ($5,000 net)	$14,000

as the cool weather would allow. Cleaning the quarter, killing hogs, and Negroes' attending their own cotton were tasks that often shortened the blacks' Christmas holiday. In 1859 the plantation force killed and saved no fewer than twenty-seven hogs in the period from December 8 through December 23. This meant hands were "working meat" on Christmas Eve. On December 29, 1852, Dent's hands killed "8 hogs." He was "afraid to kill any more the weather has been so changeable." In this instance, he acknowledged, "Brown and Sam tending to meat." [126]

In 1855 hands repaired chimneys, rebuilt lot fences, and cleaned the quarter on December 24. Only brief mention was made of "merry making" on Christmas day of this year, but the hands killed and saved fourteen hogs on December 26. On December 27, 1858, Dent "allowed" the Negroes to gin their own cotton, preparatory to receiving the cash from the sale of it. Apparently, however, some were more taken with the spirit of Christmas than with Dent's work ethic, because he mulled, "would that all were thus employed to day." [127] In spite of his best efforts, there was a good deal of relaxation during Christmas week and later in the cold, rainy days of January and February. Even as the plantation tempo slowed at the end of the year, Dent's mind was already anticipating the hindrances and challenges to a successful management of time, task, and gang for profits in the next year.

His annual direction of this sizeable labor force and synchronizing of its work at so many different jobs is difficult to convey. He enjoyed the challenge, believed his gangs were efficient, and was happiest during the harvest season, when his journal entries were less regular and less detailed. As if to atone for such neglect, he occasionally compiled a summary of the beginning and ending of important projects. A good example of these tables is the one from 1842. It also illustrates his general satisfaction with his slaves' efficiency:

Oct 8th to 10th Gathering Wheeler Field Corn.

Oct 11 Dismissed D McIntyre as Overseer.

Oct 26 & 27th Harvesting & Banking Potatoe Crop.

Oct 27th Afternoon Started Ginning.

Oct 28th Harvesting Young Corn planted in Oliver Hammock,
      did not Mature. Stacking Stalk fodder & Corn for forage.

3d 4th & 5th November hauling Home Wheeler field fodder.

Nov 8th Commenced breaking in New Ground Corn.

Nov 9th Commenced packing Cotton, packed until noon of the
      8th and had to discontinue owing to the Screw being
      out of order, Cannot put up good Bales.

Nov 14 Jno Brown set in as Overseer from this date to the 1st
      January 1844.

Nov 15 hauled home from Stanleys 2½ stacks fodder. One Stack
      still remaining.

Nov 16th up to this date packed out 26 Bales Cotton. Ginned
      out 30 Bales and very cold Weather for picking Cotton.
      Freezing.
Nov 21 put up 26 Hogs to Bacon, Weather very Cold, Ice &c.
Nov 25 Started first load Cotton to Irwinton [Eufaula]. [128]

Dent preferred to sell his cotton in Irwinton-Eufaula, when the market
there was lively enough to assure the maximum price. A slightly higher
price on the "bay" at Appalachicola did not, to his mind, offset the cost of
freight, wharfage, weighing, and other charges, not to mention inconven-
ience. E. B. Young, a close friend and business associate in Eufaula,
bought much of Dent's cotton. The planter usually sold it as quickly as he
could transport a "lot" to Eufaula. This process began in late autumn and
sometimes continued into the following February. When necessary, Young
would temporarily store these bales for Dent at little or no cost. The
planter-financier reciprocated with short-term loans at minimal interest.
He also dealt with other cotton factors such as R. R. Murphy, A. Roberts,
and T. J. Cannon. [129]

Dent seldom produced as much as one-half bale of cotton per acre. Usually, he expected no more than a third of a bale per acre. A table of his cotton
yields, cotton income, and loans (in which dollars have been rounded to the
nearest hundred and thousand) is given on page 145.

Despite his financial success, Dent was so much the planter that he often
resented the commercial arrearages of selling cotton, collecting interest on
money lent, and renegotiating these arrangements, each of which bridged
and obscured the natural and rhythmical break between one agricultural
year and the next. Yet for him, the plantation year was a matter both of
nature and of business. The plantation itself was complex and inclusive.
In addition to being an agricultural system based on slave labor, it was also
the place of his family and home, two words for the same reality as Dent conceived it, perhaps the most basic aspect of this planter's existence.

5

FAMILY

Like other Americans, antebellum southerners (especially upper-class males), supposedly subscribed to the ideal of a patriarchal family structure. According to this ideal, the plantation or home was ruled by a powerful father whose authority came directly from God and nature, for the benevolent control of subject slaves, children, wives, and other family members. Anne Firor Scott defines this "patriarchal dream" as a "'domestic metaphor,' the image of a beautifully articulated, patriarchal society in which every Southerner, black or white, male or female, rich or poor, had an appropriate place and was happy in it." Such an organic society would have made the master's immediate family as much a part of his autocratic domain as the slaves themselves. The "metaphor" was one of white-male "domination" in the extreme.[1]

While Anne Scott questions the historical validity of the nineteenth-century "patriarchal dream," Bertram Wyatt-Brown believes the patriarchy was real, although not so autocratic as the image would indicate. Whether or not the patriarchy was functionally dead by the end of the Civil War, there were forces at work in the Old South that did dilute the power and authority of the family head. The experience of John H. Dent in relation to his "nuclear" and "extended" family illustrates some of the practical limitations on the real dimensions of the Old South's patriarch.[2]

In broad outline, Dent's need for women to assume domestic responsibility, and his genuine love for mother, wives, and children, restricted his authority and delegated a great deal of power to the women and children. Although he never discussed the patriarchy as such, he often claimed that he loved his home above all else. In these affirmations, he made no distinction between home and family. On more than one occasion, this farmer-businessman insisted, "No diversion, or excitement, or scenes or associations could detach my thoughts from home. Home has been my comfort, my enjoyment and my pleasure all my life." He also denied any need for the political or public arena: "I never had any aspirations or ambition for a political or public life. Home and quietude has always been my pleasure, and I have always been self reliant for my amusements and pleasures which I have always found at home."[3]

These several protestations, his basic commitment to business success, and numerous journal sketches pertaining to naval and military glory do, however, raise some question about Dent's comfort with the role of patriarch. A cursory examination of his journals shows that he was "supposed" to be a responsible and happy family man. His mother, Anne Dent, liked to remind the mature John of her "dear children's" happiness when they "used to laugh and sing so merrily around the fireplace at

Fenwick.'' Yet when John dutifully acknowledged his youthful happiness at Fenwick, he added another dimension, recalling: ''When a boy and was sent off to School I never left home without a bitter cry. And for days before I had to leave, I became sad, gloomy, and unhappy. . . . I always loved my home.'' Home was happiness and pain, much of the latter stemming from a sense of responsibility rooted in the education he had initially spurned. Education, especially good education, meant separation from family, an internal conflict for John H. Dent that persisted when it came to educating his own children.[4]

If John's father, the captain, had been as irresponsible a family man as the able Anne Dent suggested, she was determined to rear his son as his opposite. Part of this program meant denying young John a sea-going career. Another factor was the image of young John's maternal grandfather, the drab Jonah Horry, who was extremely devoted to his daughters, wife, and wife's family. Any part of the foregoing was enough to give a young man pause, especially when he was confronted by a strong mother who was determined that he should grow up to manage her own affairs wisely and profitably. To a large extent, Anne Dent had her way. John became much the kind of family man she wanted, except that she could not control him. Earlier we saw how he matured, tired of his dependent life, determined to set up for himself, chose a girl his mother approved, married her, and shortly moved to Alabama to rear his family beyond the reach of his mother's direct manipulations. Yet the mother's influence continued for years, through letters that condemned John's abandoning her, thereby dividing her family circle.[5]

As late as 1854, Anne Dent was at one with most nineteenth-century defenders of the American family in naming competition, profits, and avarice as the basic enemies of community and family unity. More specifically, she attacked John's devotion to business—and he knew it, a fact that helps explain his several affirmations of being a ''home'' person. ''Competition,'' Anne insisted, ''that necessary impetus to trade and manufacturers, is the destruction of plain neighborly intercourse.'' She also believed, ''We are all justly punished for our avarice. Had we been contented with moderate gains, we might yet have been enjoying family union, instead of being so widely scattered and unavailingly lamenting our mistake.''[6]

This implied criticism of John and conveyed her understanding of the family's vulnerability to economic forces. The lesson was not lost on her son, but he took it to the more positive conclusion that profits, surplus wealth, indeed a fortune, were requisite for a family's social position and stability. Again, to use pieces of his experience as partial background for his views, he must have learned quite early that whereas grandfather Jonah, the patriarch, had ''provided,'' Captain Dent had died leaving Anne ''disappointments and disgrace . . . great debts'' and ''a very small income.''[7]

And while our Dent never set down an analysis of the meaning of South Carolina's economic depression in the 1820s, he was shaped by its effects and understood more of it than he bothered to explain.

His clearest statement on the patriarchy was a definition in financial terms that attempted to reconcile business and family interests. He titled the postwar paragraph "Half a Century." It was August 5, 1865:

> This day I am 50 years of age, at a period of life when our Civil War has left us without property or the means of comfort excepting what nature has given us to labor with, our head, hands, and strength. I had made a large fortune, and calculated the evening of my days were to be spent at ease and comforts, with the means at hand to raise and educate my large family. But our hopes, prospects and calculations have been suddenly cut down by our conquerors, leaving us poor and dependent on our own exertions, which we must exert to our best abilities, and try and labor diligently to do a fathers part. [8]

Dent exaggerated his straitened condition, but for him a father's part was the mundane one of assuming financial responsibility. Debt, not business, was the real threat to family stability. He always resented and exaggerated his mother's outstanding accounts, attributing them to her expensive summer vacations in Walterboro, Charleston, Flat Rock (North Carolina), New York City, and Montpelier. This resentment helps explain his irrational criticism of vacations and watering places. Such views also clarify his unwillingness to have a summer home away from the sickly Good Hope. The larger problem included his ambivalent attitude toward travel—an experience of both pleasure and anxiety. He obviously enjoyed his journeys; he devoured published travel accounts and he wrote pleasantly of his trips. Yet in all seriousness, he would insist, "After I became a farmer I never had any desire to travel about, home was my choice, but not withstanding, I have made several trips and seen a large portion of the United States." [9]

There were stronger disclaimers: "If there is any thing on earth that I dislike and is attended with more pain and melancholy and sadness, it is in leaving home for an absence of a week or more. . . . And I never in my life enjoyed a visit when from home." [10] Yet this seeming falsehood is more accurately termed a half-truth. For while Dent found a certain pleasure in travel, he also experienced it as a burden of pain, melancholy, and sadness. Perhaps he associated travel with the debts that accompanied his mother's vacations. Seated in the human predicament and his conditioning, the tension led him to justify each trip in terms of meeting some specific family need, an act that would also allay any guilt at enjoying the journey.

The conflict between a father's part and a devoted son's duty was evident when Dent's mother complained of his missing his brother by "eight hours in Savannah, and all owing to your naming your own day for coming, instead of consulting us before-hand and allowing me to fix the time.''[11]   In this instance, Dent was ostensibly traveling to the Atlantic coast to accommodate his mother's design for a more genteel education of her granddaughters, who had been deprived of such things on the Alabama frontier. For the most part, John combined the elements of family duty and individual pleasure in a thoroughly enjoyable trip, as in November, 1854, when he escorted daughter Minna to Charleston at her grandmother's behest, and brought his Lizzie home to Alabama.

The account of the trip says little of family needs: "Novr 22d being Wednesday,'' Dent wrote,

> I started for Charleston So Ca. taking my daughter Minna with me. Left home in the carriage that morning [with] Brown our coachman and waiter. Went to Eufaula by the way of the Johnson plantation to see John [O'Bryan] who had a few hands in charge to build some negro houses, gave him a few directions and proceeded on. We reached Eufaula about 2 PM. After making some preparations, Leaving the carriage at Mr [E. B.] Youngs and sending the horses home with directions to meet us in Eufaula on Friday the 1st December, at 5 PM took our Seats in the stage coach for Columbus, Ga, passage $5 a piece. The night was fair and very cold, 4 other passengers our fellow travellers, men from Florida visiting their old homes in the old States.[12]

Preoccupied with the details of the journey, Dent nevertheless returned to the theme of family responsibility as a man's motive for travel, identifying his behavior with that of Eufaula grandee John Linguard Hunter, who was also escorting his daughter:

> At 5 am, reached Columbus where we remained until 10½ am and took the Cars for Macon, many persons on board, among whom was Genl Hunter carry- ing on his youngest daughter to Montpelier. Reached Macon at 5 o clock PM and took the Cars for Augusta via the 79 mile Station, Wainsboro &c. Night cloudy and some rain, reached Augusta at 4 am, and remained until 6 o clock when we took the Charleston cars on the South Carolina railroad. Cars were very much crowded, reached Charleston at 2½ PM on Friday 24th . . . making the time from Eufaula in 46½ hours, distance, 461 miles.[13]

Arriving in Charleston before he was expected allowed Dent some independence. Once there, he organized the womenfolk's time and enjoyed the area's economic improvement:

> Put up at the Charleston Hotel, in two hours found that Mother was in the city. Emma [his sister] and Liz had just left in the steamer Calhoun for Savannah, immediately telegraphed to McKenzie of the Pulaski House in Savannah to stop them on their arrival and let them await my coming in the next steamer; this was done. I remained in Charleston until Monday afternoon 27th,

spending my time very pleasantly with Mother, Mrs Roper and Mrs Rhett
[his sisters] and other friends. From all accounts I could gather the planters
in Carolina are in a very prosperous condition, more so than in our New States.
The city was full of life and bustle, much business seemed to be doing, and a
general improvement going on.[14]

Charleston and company were pleasant, but Alabama beckoned, and Dent
planned a rapid exchange of daughters for a quick return to Barbour. Notice
the night travel, the brief Savannah visit, and the implication that Minna
freed him for an immediate journey home. "Monday 4 PM. with Minna,"
Dent

left [Charleston] in the steamer Calhoun for Savannah taking the outside passage by sea. Had a fast run and smooth sea. Among the passengers, found
my old friends, Col John S Ashe, P Deveaux, H L Toomer and McMillan King.
We reached Savannah at 1 a m. and met Emma and Lizzie at the Pulaski House.
Minna here determined on going on to Darien with her Aunt Emma. So Liz and
myself took the cars at 8 a m. [Tuesday] for Macon, Ga. Weather extremely
cold, reached Macon at 6 PM, remained there all night, was disturbed about
midnight by the cry of fire, a large carpenters establishment was in flames.
Having no interest at stake and night being cold, turned in comfortably to
bed.[15]

Fires were frightening but commonplace, as Dent's experience the
following day would show. "At 6 am (Wednesday)," he

took the cars by South Western R. Road for Columbus, weather very cold indeed. Cars very much crowded, this is a slow road as the company make it a
rout of business accomodation rather than one of express, reached Columbus at
1½ PM, found the city in the greatest confusion as Mr Motts dwelling was
on fire. Every body seemed to have deserted their business, the Banks had
closed, and it was said that a Jury in court had rushed out precipitately to
the scene of conflagration leaving his Honor on the Bench and a worthy
counselor in the midst of his harrangue, amazed and confused alone in the
bar at so sudden and general a panic. The house was soon consumed which
brought men back to their vocations, Among whom was the stage agent,
which afforded us the chance of procuring our seats for Eufaula.[16]

His single-mindedness made Dent short on sympathy and strong on
gaining home. Dreading the Eufaula stage, he completed the trip a day
ahead of schedule. With no one to meet him and Liz in Eufaula, he
rented transport to their Cowikee home.

At 3 PM. [Wednesday] after eating a hearty dinner, got in the Stage [at Colum-
bus] with seven other passengers and started for Eufaula, distance 45 miles
which was performed in 14 hours at the rate of 3 miles pr hour, bringing us up

at Mr Youngs door at 5 am, Thursday 30th . . . [November]. All safe and sound but cold and wearied out with so monotonous and tiresome a night ride. Remained in Eufaula until 10½ am, hired a buggie and an old hacked stage from the Livery stables to take me up home. The day was cool and bracing, roads Sandy and heavy, and the old horse stiff and jaded from a long life spent in the public use. So we courted patience and reached home at 5 P M, found all well and the children very glad to see us indeed.[17]

He summed up on personal pleasure, not daughters' education or other family duties: "Thus ended my trip to Charleston and back again . . . one which afforded many pleasures in being once more among my relatives and friends, amidst the scenes of my early youth. Charleston has very much improved, particularly the newly built part of the City. A large commercial business is done there in the import and export line. Her wharves are filled with ships of all classes. . . . From all appearances nothing is wanting but the energy and enterprise of her own citizens to make her a large commercial city."[18]

From Dent's point of view, the distinction between his nuclear and extended family, although real enough, was not always clear-cut. Still, he saw no need for duty to outweigh self-interest. In May, 1855, he was summoned "to Charleston on business of Mothers, in relation to the selling of her plantation on the Altamaha river in Georgia." He resented the timing, as on his plantation, "Grass sprouting broadcast. Cotton not over the second working, and Corn backwards. I must hurry on and back as my Overseer is unexperienced and needs my presence and instructions." Yet he went, because Anne Dent, aged sixty-five, had, with her children's assistance, managed her own slaves until this last year of her life. Now in failing health, she wanted John to buy or manage her slaves, either way removing them to Alabama for humane supervision. Having no intention of investing his surplus capital in Negroes, the Alabama son presented financial estimates to argue that moving E. A. Dent's slaves to his locale would entail a new debt of $17,000, which when added to the existing one of $14,000 would exceed the value of her Cedar Hill plantation. In this way, John carried his point without having to refuse the burden of managerial responsibility that he was determined to avoid.[19]

Almost single-handedly, he reorganized his mother's plans and directed the rental of her slaves in the Darien area. Still, he complained in December, 1855, when it was time to return to Georgia to complete these arrangements. "Have been summoned to Darien," he wrote, "to attend to Mothers business, leaving my business under the charge of Summerset a new hand. Such trips are very much against my interest, but the duties of a Son to a Mother demands it."[20]

In the next few days, this dutiful son became so engrossed in the details of the tiring trip that he barely mentioned his mother's deteriorating condition:

Left Eufaula on night 27th in stage for Silver run [Seale, Alabama], dark and rainy, roads nearly impassable with 6 Horses to a coach and passengers walking ankle deep in mud, reached Silver run 6 AM of 28th in hard rain, where we took the Cars for Columbus; in 7 miles of Columbus, the track had sunk, so we walked a quarter of a mile in mud in a hard rain to another train and proceeded on to Girard [Phenix City, Alabama]; arrived at 8 AM, in torrents of rain; got into an Omnibus and proceeded to the Perry house in Columbus; rained hard all day, the country being completely flooded with water; did not go out in the city.[21]

Travel conditions on Friday, December 28, continued uncertain. "At 2 PM, Started on train of the Muscogee Rail Road for Macon, raining down a deluge. The road so saturated and in some places washed over with sand that the train was run very slowly and with the utmost care to keep it on the road; reached Macon at 8 PM where we embarked in the Central RR for Savannah; rained hard all night; reached Savannah 8 AM of 29th. At 10 AM, embarked in Steamer St Johns Capt Freeborn for Darien, day rainy, fogs heavy; reached Darien 9 PM of 29th. Met George at the wharf, found Mother quite sick in bed."[22]

He arrived on Saturday night. Although Sunday was cloudy and disagreeable, seaman John Dent had to take "a short sail in Georges Steam Yacht called 'the Idle Hours.' " And on Monday in the rain, John "Hired Mothers [best seventeen] Men to Mr Bryant to work at the Turpentine business. Women and children are to go to . . . [the James Troups'] Court House place to plant provisions and Cotton." There was no mention of visiting privileges for separated blacks, but Dent expected the arrangement to net his ailing mother $5,000 per year. On the same day, "At 11 AM, Mr Rhett, family and negroes reached Cedar Hill in Steamer TG Haight." It seems that Rhett assumed responsibility for Cedar Hill.[23]

On the following day, Dent the businessman completed his arrangements, and with but brief reference to his mother began the trip to Alabama.

Tuesday January 1st, 1856. Raining, could not move Negroes to day to Court house on account of the inclemency of the weather. Mother quite unwell; left with George the removal of the Negroes, and taking the note of Bryant for the Negroes. At 2 AM of 2d, in the hardest rain I ever saw fall, embarked in the Steamer St Johns on her return trip from Palatka Fla to Savannah; day cloudy cool and some rain. We arrived at Savannah at 1 PM, rained all the evening steadily. That night carried Herbert to the Theatre; he was very much amused, thin house, acting miserable.[24]

For a family man, this was small notice of his second son, who accompanied him to Darien and back.

Homeward bound, Dent's main concern was a rapid, safe journey. "At 5 AM of 3d, took the Cars for Macon, raining hard, reached Macon at 2 PM.

At 3 PM, took train on SWRR for Columbus, track very much out of order from rain, reached Columbus at 11 PM. Friday 4th, laid over in Columbus until 3 PM (first Sun shone since 24th Decr), and embarked in Steamer DJ Day Capt Wingate for Eufaula; laid by most of the night being dark and cloudy; reached Eufaula 8 AM of 5th January. Met Minna & Liz there, found my Cotton sold at 8 cents. Hired a horse and buggie and reached home at 12 M, found all well."[25]

His mother's death was imminent. She died February 16, 1856, and the estate was settled the following month. Dent was again called to Darien, this time on a business trip that involved more socializing than physical hardship. Nevertheless, on March 26, he protested the interruption with characteristic want of persuasiveness:

I have been summoned by George C Dent and Miss Emma Dent to meet them at Darien and see to the division of the Est of Mrs EA Dent. It takes me off at the most important juncture of my affairs, in the midst of Planting, where all is left to the charge of an incompetent manager and Overseer. Again so far as the affairs at Darien are concerned, all is conjecture, as nothing in a Legal form has yet reached me from Mr Petigru who is the Estates Atty, [as to] who are the Executors or what is to be done.[26]

Again he left without delay. This time the excitement was not the trip, but developments that would transpire at Darien.

Wn 26 Started for Darien in Steamer DJ Day from Eufaula, reached Columbus Thursday morning 8 O clock, left in train of Cars for Macon 1½ O clock, reached Macon 7 O clock PM. Left for Savannah at 9½ O clock, reached Savannah Friday Morning 28th at 7 O clock, At 10 o clock left for Darien in Steamer Thos G Haight, arrived at Darien 8 O clock PM, met George on the wharf, went up to Mr Rhetts [Cedar Hill] where I met Emma in deep grief. Remained with her one hour, and with George in a row boat at 10 O clock at night, started for [the James Troups'] Broadfield where we arrived at 12 O clock, all the family had retired for the night. Went to bed and slept soundly.[27]

After a whirlwind trip, the visit was more leisurely, with some of the holiday mood that accompanies a realistic family's adjustments to death. Among extant sources, this is Dent's only description of socializing with his siblings. Perhaps there was freedom in his mother's demise? "Saturday 29th," he wrote, I

rose early, spent the morning with the Troup family, lunched at noon. Soon after, with Dr Troup & his lady & 2 children and parson Brown and George & Jack, embarked in his Steam Yacht for Cedar Hill, had a pleasant sail, day calm and pleasant, reached Cedar Hill to dinner, found Emma more cheerful, Mr Rhett and Kate very agreeable. Spent the night at Cedar Hill, George returning alone with Jack after night to Broadfield.[28]

On the Altamaha, Sunday was also a time for family visiting, even when it meant crossing wide water. Nor was Dent more pious here than in Barbour. "Rained heavily in the Morning, which was a sad disappointment to the parish, as Bishop [Stephen] Elliott preached and confirmed 8 persons at the Darien church, did not attend service, remained with Emma & Kate conversing on the illness and death of Mother. In the afternoon George returned from Broadfield accompanied with Thos Forman, spent the afternoon with Mr Rhett." [29] Dent was reserved with Rhett, but the latter would take refuge with Dent during the Civil War.

Because Anne Dent's debts consumed much of her land, the major item in settling the estate was dividing the Jonah Horry Negroes, a matter which John had come from Alabama to assist. Without qualm in the matter, he simply fulfilled his mother's belief that "The death of . . . all Parents who leave Property is considered more a gain than a loss." She did, however, expect "all the decencies of life . . . a most decorous funeral" and "a handsome monument." After that she asked, "What more can they do?" Anne believed, "No thinking person would wish those they loved to be made unhappy by their death." [30] John professed no grief, made no mention of attending her February funeral or assisting with the monument that marks her grave beside the captain's in Bethel Presbyterian Cemetery, Colleton County, South Carolina.

Continuing in his practical vein, Dent described the division of Negroes. "Monday March 31st. Thos Forman, Richard Morris and Brailsford Troup, as appraisors, with George & myself, went to the Court House plantation of the Troups to appraise and partition off the Negroes of the Est of Jonah Horry among the Heirs, reached the Court House at 12 Oclock when it came up a heavy rain and storm with sharp lightning and thunder, proceeded to appraise and allot off the Negroes." There were seven lots of thirteen to fifteen persons in each, valued at the conservative estimate of just over $7,000 per group. Once divided, the lots were "drawn," Emma receiving number one and John number three. [31]

Dent gave the next few days to rest, relaxation, and paper work. "Tuesday 1st April, PM," John wrote, "went to Broadfield with George in Capt Keenes yawl, cold and windy. Wednesday 2d, AM, went gunning at Broadfield with parson Pinkerton and Jimmy, shot two birds, dined at Broadfield with Orphy [Ophelia Troup Dent, George's wife] and her two sisters, Mr & Mrs Pinkerton, at 6 PM, got a canoe and with boy Harrington went to Cedar [Hill], had a long and tedious paddle, reached Cedar Hill 8 pm. Thursday, preparing papers for the Heirs of the division." [32]

With business completed, Dent immediately returned home. Assuming responsibility for sister Emma's Negroes, he transported them to Alabama and rented them out for her. The return trip required five days owing to Dent's economizing by making the last fifty miles on foot. "Friday preparing to start off Negroes for Alabama," he explained, and at 8 pm. Left Darien in the Steamer Welaka, Capt King, for Savannah with Emma & George who were on their way to Charleston. Myself with Emma's and my own negroes consisting of Lots No 1 & 3 bound for Alabama. Reached Savannah 11 O clock Saturday 5th, and embarked on the cars at 12 O clock for Macon, reached Macon 2 O clock am of 6th, and at 3 took the cars for Columbus, where we arrived at 7 AM. Sunday 6th, Hired a Wagon from Pitts & Hatcher to haul luggage and children to Eufaula, left at 12 O clock, walking myself a journey performed on foot of 50 miles for the first [time] in my life, reached Eufaula Tuesday 8th 9 AM, fatigued and rejoiced the Journey being over with. Ben was sick with Dysentery on the road. Reached home at 11 O clock and found all well. [33]

Because of Dent's obvious affection for sisters, wives, and daughters— not to mention the same for his brother, sons, in-laws, and friends—it is safe to conclude that he was closer to his mother than his language of "duty" would indicate. Actually, this medium-sized man of wiry frame, penetrating eye, and strongly set jaw was really very likeable, partially, perhaps, because he vented so much of his hostility in the privacy of his beloved journal. While Anne Dent could criticize him pointedly, she nevertheless made him, in 1855, the titular head of her affairs. Her strength of character probably limited the tenderness he showed her, but there was much respect between them. She wrote John in 1855: "I was amused by the knowledge displayed in your letter of the character of my sons-in-laws, and your discrimination of character generally. This, I think, you have inherited from your mother." Later that year she confided, "I think we understand each other. I rely upon you and shall always call upon you in time of need and you may rest assured of all my statements, as far as I know." [34] With such a mother, Dent was not unaware of the real and potential power of woman in antebellum southern society. Yet he was not defensive about it, a fact that probably reflects his ultimate sense of security as a type of "patriarch."

Dent's early and advantageous marriage also contributed much to his self-confidence as family head. The first wife's property and unassuming nature gave him economic opportunity and personal freedom. Surely it is significant that his first wife was much less self-assertive than Anne Dent. Somewhat critical of his mother, he romanticized Mary Elizabeth Morrison, not just after her death in 1853, but also in the early 1840s, when he described her as she was in 1835, "at that period a lovely beautiful girl of 18 Summers, Modest and unassuming, yet fascinating in her manners, her expression bore more, those lovely marks for admiration that entices so many bashful youths to become the daddys of Spoilt children." [35]

Did Dent romanticize Mary Elizabeth's youthful beauty because it faded on the Alabama frontier? Drabness was a characteristic of young married women in nineteenth-century America. [36] Perhaps he had her in mind when he criticized his peers for exposing their wives to frontier hardships that spoiled their charms.

I have seen many a fine woman whose lot in early life was cast among the refined, whose husband had embarked in this mode of speculation, and the
change that had come over "the spirit of her dream" was sad to behold, exiled
we may say, from all pleasures and comforts of early enjoyments, and now to
be settled down in the woods, and sheltered from the elements merely by a few
logs and oak board coverings, no comforts, churches or society to change the
monotony of so dreary a life. They become domestic Industrious housewives,
and how can it be otherwise, when labor alone is the only employment to cheer
up life in this dreary solitude. "What can't be helped, must be endured."[37]

If this was an indirect comment on Mary Elizabeth, Dent would have
appreciated her industrious nature and regretted her fading beauty,
romance, and other enticements. Aside from these hints, one knows
virtually nothing of her, but there is every indication that she was a
supportive wife, a willing mother, and an admirable homemaker, who left
major decisions to her mate, including the one to move to Alabama. She also
had the unquestioning approval of mother Dent. Mary Elizabeth bore her
portion of plantation responsibility so efficiently and quietly that her
husband, taking it for granted, had no cause to mention her particular
duties.[38]

As one would expect, her realm was the home in general, and
child-bearing and rearing in particular. The Dents' first child arrived
exactly nine and one-half months after the wedding, whereupon Mary
Elizabeth settled into the dutiful routine of a new baby every two years, a
pattern that continued until her death. By 1842, when Dent penned the
romantic recollection of this beauty enticing him to become a father, the
children were Robert Morrison (dead of croup the first winter in Alabama),
Emma Julia (Minna), John Horry, and Mary Elizabeth (Lizzie). Only Robert
Morrison, the first-born, did not have a Dent family name. After 1842 these
offspring were followed by John Herbert, Anne Horry, Charles Baring,
Sarah Lining, and Kate Constance. The last was six months old when her
mother died of typhoid fever in September, 1853. John meted out praise to
this wife for suffering in silence. Although she lingered for days, she met
death with calm Christian resignation. Another indication of Mary
Elizabeth's "worth" was Dent's later admission of his having taken her for
granted. He was also genuinely embarrassed by the various needs dictating
that he remarry so soon.[39]

The family, of course, means children, and Dent sincerely believed he
spoiled his. He accepted them as the natural fruit of marriage, who were to
be loved, protected, enjoyed, and prepared for adult life. All stages of
fatherhood came easily for him with the possible exception of formal
education, wherein he lacked either self-confidence or commitment. It was
in this context in 1855 that momentarily he believed a "person . . . fortunate
. . . to have but one or two children." Yet in 1858 he was more ambivalent on
offspring, as he rhymed:

When men have the money, something else will stop,
Too many little children, or an if or what not.
For here in the South, children are the rage
Every man that marries soon fills a cage.[40]

Dent's commitment to family included an intimate involvement with their health, clothing, and pleasures. If he initially became plantation nurse from necessity, he nevertheless learned to enjoy the practice. Dent treated his wife and children as readily as he doctored slaves and livestock. He was very successful in this role, as all of the children except Robert Morrison survived their youthful illnesses. Still he did utilize the services of local physicians like Pope and Thornton of Eufaula and John C. McNeill of Clayton.[41]

As a self-confident health officer whom the typhoid epidemic of 1853-1854 did not deter, Dent would treat a problem himself until it was necessary to obtain more professional help. In March, 1858, for example, he wrote, "Our infant Fanny has an attack of cholera Infantum." Three days later he was treating whites and blacks. "Fanny, Herbert, Charlie and Nellys Infant Bell all are taken with Vomiting and purgeing, our Babe has been quite Sick." Four days later, needing assistance, he "Went to Eufaula for medicine for little Fanny from Dr. Thronton." She recovered along with the others, who apparently were not as seriously ill.[42]

When Dent's children were ill, he was often sick right along with them. Perhaps some of this was sympathetic. When little Fanny was ill in 1858, he reported himself having "chills of a light character, a deranged state of the Liver." As Fanny improved, he worsened and wrote an interesting case history. "I was taken down very sick last night with acute pains in the Liver and Cramps in the Stomach; from 1846 to 1853 was subject to such attacks, but have had none until now since 1853." If the children had colds, he contracted one, too. Manifesting more than one eccentricity, he could "feel quite unwell" and convince himself he had "taken a very bad cold" from "having had my hair cut very short last afternoon."[43]

Dent's personal aches and pains included "dreadful sick head aches," a "Soar throat," and "chilly sensations" due to a "billious" condition. For the last ailment, he often took "Cooks pills," even though they occasionally "operated badly." His worst bouts, however, were with a "deranged liver and stomach and feverish symptoms." He described it in 1861: "I am quite unwell today, deranged state of liver, suffering from pains in the back, hips and over the eyes, medicated but does not relieve me." He could be bedridden with this condition for days at a time, usually in the most relaxed or most pressing seasons of the year.[44] In later years, a serious kidney ailment was diagnosed.

Being sensitive to his own health probably made Dent more empathetic with others. This was, however, more the case with his family than with the slaves. For example, he could diagnose Mrs. Dent as "quite unwell. Neuralgic affection." He also knew when she was "not mending as fast as she ought to do." His wives' ill health was often associated with pregnancy. Asking no quarter from the most serious illnesses, this father also watched when "Our little Charlie is extremely sick. Pneumonia." These few examples are enough to illustrate the centrality of family health for Dent, especially when "Lizzie seems no better, feverish all night." In this case, he remained with her several days and nights, making the ultimate sacrifice to gain a full recovery: "Owing to my attendance on Lizzie am not able to go over the plantation."[45]

In the matter of personal sacrifice for health's sake, Dent took much satisfaction in having surrendered the productive Cowikee plantation of Good Hope-Miller's in order to safeguard his family from summer chills and fevers. It was a proud man who wrote, "Went to Clayton with Mrs Dent. A great deal of Sickness in the Vicinity of Clayton as well as on the Cowikee Creeks. Chill and fever as well as Typhoid fevers."[46] After 1855 his family was free of these worst threats.

As soon as it was feasible, he "referred" the family's dental problems to urban professionals. Thus in March, 1858, he "Went to Clayton and Carried up Mrs. Dent" where she "had her teeth worked on by Dr. Wellborn." The following September he "Went to Eufaula with Mrs. Dent to have two teeth extracted. Extracted by Dr H Clarke, under electric influence; the operation was quick and very little pain." His nonchalance on the subject of pain indicated that Mrs. Dent was the patient. On another occasion, he "Carried Liz to Eufaula, had two of her teeth pluged and one extracted."[47]

Concerning the family's need for clothing, Dent believed in meeting it promptly, though modestly. While living on the Cowikee, he made many of these purchases outright. Later living near Eufaula, he willingly assisted Mrs. Dent's shopping. From the Bleak House plantation, trips to town for "shopping" were numerous enough to appear contrived. In this he probably justified much harmless, albeit "nonproductive," socializing. In any event, the mail did have to be fetched from Eufaula. When Dent was not free to get it, he sent Brown, his coachman, or one of the children. A recurring entry on shopping reads, "Went to Eufaula today to buy clothing and shoes for the children."[48] This was a regular spring and autumn affair for the entire brood, with similar, but smaller, purchases in between.

Special occasions meant special purchases. In 1860, before his second son departed for school in Greenville, Tennessee, Dent "Went to see Herbert before starting; in addition to his prepared wardrobe, bought him a Hat, pr shoes, waistcoat, neck tie." Most shopping, however, was commonplace. Dent was not exactly stingy, but he was close with money. Still he believed in gifts for the children: "Mrs Dent and I went to Eufaula in carriage to buy some things to send out to Minna as presents." Minna was married to Maximilian B. Wellborn of Eufaula in 1857. Prior to daughter Lizzie's marriage to Whitfield Clark in 1861, Dent "Went to Eufaula with Mrs Dent to shop for Liz."[49]

It was a simple matter to combine business and family purchases. On February 9, 1858, he "Went to Eufaula to day with Mrs. Dent to shop for the family. Business rather brisk. Cotton . . . at 10¼¢. Foreign news favourble." Some shopping trips, however, brought disappointment. In April, 1858, he "Went to Eufaula with Mrs. Dent to see Minna and purchase summer clothing for the children. Business dull. Most of the male population were at Clayton attending court." Family purchases also meshed with social calls and meals. "Went to Eufaula with Mrs Dent to purchase supplies for herself, dined with Mrs. [E.B.] Young." And by fall of the year, frequently in October, the cycle was completed as he again "Went to Eufaula with Mrs. Dent shopping, to purchase clothing for children." A moderate provider, Dent recorded each penny expended but without full itemization, making it impossible to know exactly what was spent for the family's health, clothes, and so on. In the late 1850s, however, he usually held all plantation expenses to $3,500 per year or less.[50]

John Dent also promoted and enjoyed the "young folk's" amusements. Accompanied by Harriet Camp, his favorite of the tutors, Dent could go to Eufaula and purchase "a little wagon for my son Columbus." Referring to his favorite overseer and older sons, he wrote approvingly, "Howell, Horry, and Herbert gone to a Barbecue." On almost every July Fourth, Dent "Went with the Boys to town to witness the celebrations of the 4th, grand military parade, an oration, and excitement." By 1858 the new year sometimes brought the young folk "Gay times in Town with the party goers, as Balls and parties are the go," and "Eufaula Guards parade." When it came to circuses, Dent could hardly contain himself: "What with Christmas holidays at home and the circus in Eufaula, the Boys and the Negroes are almost to the exploding point. How many are gone to the circus I cannot say, but all to be presumed who can muster 25 cents." Nor was this father above going "with the Children to the Circus."[51]

To be involved with children's pleasures, however, was to invite sadness. For example, Christmas, 1858, was "A dull day for our House as Mrs Dent is quite unwell. Children gone to spend the day at Mrs Fields. Miss Camp and Liz gone to Church. Myself, a dreadful head ache. No Christmas dinner or jollification, not one drop of spirits." On Christmas Day, 1855, the father regretted that "The inclement weather mars the merry making of the young folks." The arrival of circuses was so unpredictable that Dent studied the prospects each year and once forewarned the children it might not be in Eufaula as scheduled, because "as the company got into a fracus at Locopocha last week and killed a man of that place, a part of the company were arrested for the alleged murder.'' Yet this preparation lessened no one's pain when the "Children returned PM, no circus. Disappointment very great."[52]

Happily for everyone, the pleasures of visiting and churchgoing were more constant and dependable than the transient circuses. From Bleak House, Dent watched approvingly as the older children scurried about the neighborhood, drove the younger ones to their activities, and generally enjoyed the proximity to Eufaula. Not all visiting, however, awaited the move to Barbour Creek. On the Cowikee as early as 1841, and in rainy weather, Dent would leave "home with the family for Clayton."[53] And by the late 1850s socializing was rife. Some of it was with family, much of it was with friends. And while Dent tried to report it all, he never bothered to spell names consistently.

A few examples of the children's visiting will suffice: "Minna came out last evening to spend some days with us"; "Horry & Lizzie gone to Clayton in Buggie to see Carrie"; "Ammy and Effy came from Clayton last evening in the Stage. Horry gone to Eufaula for the mail. Lizzie and Carry gone to Mrs. Smarts"; "Marion Snipes, Maria Danforth and their 2 Brothers came out to spend the day with Lizzy"; "Horry gone up to Cowikee to see Holiday Hodges." Church attendance served for socializing as well as worship: "Mrs. Dent, Miss Camp, and Children gone to Church. Horry went in for Minna to see Lizzie by her request"; "Mrs. Dent and children gone to Church. Minna and Mack [Wellborn] came out and spent the night with us"; "Horry and Carrie McNeill went to Church."[54]

While Dent usually appreciated the children's guests, he could complain good naturedly of a *"Casuality"* when "Bullock, Marion Snipes and Lizzie DeWitt spent the day with us." Enjoying the ballyhoo of children's special occasions, the father nevertheless felt constrained to deny it. By way of example, on May 31, 1855, he explained the "Start for Eufaula this morning with my family to the great dedication ceremony of the Union female College. . . . Every thing in great bustle and confusion in the house, dressing and fixing for the day, with excited imaginations of the wanders of the day. As in the programe there is to be a Balloon ascension this afternoon." His excitement is unmistakable. He even arranged an out-of-town trip so that he could view the spectacle. Yet in the same context, as though he feared for dignity as well as his solvency, he demurred, "The quiet business life at last suits me best. None of this sudden outburst of confusion and excitement." In the final analysis, this repressed personality was ultra-serious about family responsibility.[55]

Dent could not restrain himself when his two eldest daughters married "well" and at home. Of Liz's preparations to marry Whitfield Clark, a widower and Clayton merchant, Dent exclaimed on May 2, 1861, "Confusion reigns for order. Such as fixing of House, Cooking, Barbacueing, Dressing. Excitement and moving hither and thither as Lizzie

Marries to day Whitfield Clark.'' Clark, a wealthy financier, was equally impressed with his wife's family. When Lizzie died in 1870, he married her younger sister, Annie, the following year. (A daughter of this last marriage, Mary Clark, became the wife of Thomas E. Kilby, future Governor of Alabama.) Whitfield Clark was fifteen years older than Lizzie. Living in Clayton, the Clarks visited Bleak House regularly: "Whit and Lizzie came down to dinner yesterday''; "Lizzie came down and spent the day with us, bringing Jenny and Effy McNeill with her. Carried Amy and Sally back to Clayton with her.''[56]

Dent and Clark had a close friendship, based on mutual respect. There were some business dealings between them, and they frequently exchanged expensive gifts. The father-in-law was no less fond of Maximilian Bethune Wellborn, Mack or Max for short. A prominent Eufaula lawyer and land owner, Mack was thirteen years his wife's senior. His parents were Dr. Levi Thomas and Roxana Bethune Wellborn of Eufaula. Dent managed some of Max's investments, lent him money at no interest, and showered the family with gifts, especially when they moved to Lewisville, Arkansas, in 1859 and when the Wellborns' children began arriving. A child of this marriage, M. B. Wellborn, Jr., became the first board chairman of the Federal Reserve Bank in Atlanta, Georgia.[57]

Pained by Mack's decision to move west in 1859, Dent nevertheless determined to support him. Thus he noted amiably, "Minna and Mack came out last evening, and spent the day with us, prior to their starting West." The following day the father "Went to Eufaula to tell Minna and Mack good by, they expect to start to night in stage.''[58] Now a pattern of his own history had recurred, though without exact repetition. Dent no doubt recalled his own move west and his mother's hatred of it. Among other deprivations, Anne Dent had dreaded the frontier's lack of civilizing effects for her grandchildren. Somewhat true to her prediction, Minna's clear, practical prose was less accomplished than the grandmother's polished letter style. But there is more to life than polish, especially for the John Dents of this world. And he could not have been more pleased than when, in 1859, he "heard from M. B. Wellborn that Minna had a daughter on 20th Sept." It was the following March when "Grandpère" Dent sent with Wellborn the twelve-year-old Negro Harriet (in addition to the former loan of Nancy) to assist Minna "in nursing her children.''[59] This, too, was a departure from Anne Dent's practice of controlling every slave until the year of her death.

Dent's sending a helper does not imply that Minna was spoiled. In fact, this father never complained of his daughters' education for womanhood as he did of his younger sons' preparation to be men. In addition to their domestic duties in the home, Dent had depended upon the older girls (before marriage) to drive the younger children to school and to church, and to perform business errands for him. Although he never expected any child to produce in the laboring sense of the word, the girls and boys in adolescence were assigned specific responsibilities, especially Horry, the oldest son. As we have seen, Dent would send "Horry . . . up to Fryers to see about the 10 Sheep lost by John & Hardtimes." The son also fetched the preacher. "Sent Horry down in Buggie to bring Mr Steele out to spend the day with us, arrived at 10½ AM."[60]

Using the same tone he applied to slaves, the father would start "Horry at 2 A.M. to Clayton with Horse and Buggie for Liz. Told him to leave Clayton for home late this afternoon, so as to avoid the intense heat of the day." Desiring supplies, he would send "Horry to town for Lamp oil, Tea and ginger," and for "Coffee, stationary, Black pepper and the mail." Given this dependability, Dent could tour Texas in 1859 in consideration of moving the family there, bringing Horry home from school in Virginia to "assist" overseer Howell and to keep the farm journal.[61]

Like his mother before him, Dent expected the most of his oldest son. Perhaps the influence of primogeniture lingered in his behavior; he apparently spoiled or neglected the younger boys. Herbert, the second son, was only four years Horry's junior, but the father seldom depended on him. It was a rare entry that read: "Sent Herbert to Eufaula to mail letters &c." This was minimal responsibility for a fourteen-year-old. As we saw in the trip to Darien, the father could travel with Herbert for days at a time, mentioning him but once and then only in passing. For whatever complexity of reasons, Dent, like many other American parents, was slow to discipline children. Herbert was involved in killing one horse, losing another, and accidentally shooting a slave in the thigh. Yet the journals mention no disciplinary measures. Later, the outcome, with regard to the younger sons, was a sore disappointment to the father. The promising (by his father's standards) Horry died of yellow fever while in the Confederate Navy. Herbert survived his soldiering in that war to clerk in Whit Clark's store. Charlie, the next son, became a traveling adventurer who periodically came home to work for his father.[62]

It was, then, hindsight that led Dent in 1880 to pen descriptions of two types of preparation for manhood. Now he believed it was "Best for Boys . . . when young and raising that they are brought up and educated to know that they had to . . . depend on their own exertions, for all our distinquished and successful men were raised to rely on their own exertions. Hence as soon as educated, many educating themselves, they went to work and made men of themselves and rose to respectability and influence." If this had been the case with Horry, it was not Dent's experience with the sons then living. Thus he concluded, "The great error made with our Southern Boys, especially those that had parents well off, they were brought up dependent, relying on their parents for even their pleasures and amusements, and were so to live until their parents done something for them or died and left them just enough to keep them from working, hence made worthless men of them, miserable tramps and dead beats, perfect nuisances in action as well as by example." In 1880, Dent refused to accept full responsibility for his sons' economic dependence, blaming much of it on slavery and the South's lack of free education.[63]

The church was another authority this father was slow to impose on his children. Perhaps he saw it as a threat to his control. In February, 1855, after moving to Bleak House, he hoped "by now living so near to town that the children may be benefited by Religious opportunities," because "Heretofore no such privileges have been enjoyed." Even with this statement, Dent was no churchman. For him, worship services were for women and children and then perhaps only because the second wife insisted on attending. Despite much comment on Providence, Dent was something of a rationalistic skeptic and anticleric.[64]

In 1880 he summarized his skepticism with regard to the Christian church if not the faith:

I have seen the Churches made up of members of men known to be corrupt...but they are good Christians in the eyes of the Church.... Hence Christianity in the churches is more in name than in reality. The result of such our best men and women are becoming skeptical and are trying to work out their own salvation through the convictions of their own hearts and minds. True, this is a dangerous expedient. But if we are true in our feelings and actions and conduct ourselves uprightly, it is better than this outward show of religion.

In 1858 he indicated the same sentiment in two proverbs: first, "There are some Christians that pray upon their knees on Sunday, and pray before their neighbors all the Week"; and second, "Honor and shame from all conditions rise. Act well your part, and their the honor lies."[65]

Dent's antebellum disdain for evangelical Christianity was consistent. His every mention of revivalism was in a context of contempt. Some of this was defensiveness, because his second wife, a churchly person, leaned toward the Methodist denomination. The first Mrs. Dent, isolated on the Cowikee, had remained home on Sundays, allowing her husband to read the Episcopal service, despite her own background, which was either Presbyterian or Methodist. Within easy driving distance of Eufaula churches after 1855 and with the second wife's determination to attend worship, Dent was forced to act to save his family from the evangelicals with whom Fanny Dent, a New England Congregationalist, was perfectly comfortable.[66]

The story is implicit but clearly evident in the journals as Dent, in mild desperation, forced himself to the Saint James Episcopal services and guided his wife to be baptized in the more acceptable faith. With this accomplished, he planned a special occasion and on Sunday, November 14, 1858, "Went to Eufaula to attend Divine Service at the Episcopal Church, Bishop Cobb officiating." On the following day, "The Bishop came out to our residence on the Plantation and christened Mrs. Dent, Anne, Charlie, Sallie, Kate and Fanny." The other children were either already baptised or too old to manipulate. Mrs. Dent's cooperation did not soften the husband's resistance to church attendance, except during the year preceding her confirmation. Even then he generally refused to accompany her to a Methodist, Baptist, or Presbyterian church in Eufaula on those Sundays when the Reverend Steele had to preach in Clayton. When Steele was away or the weather unfavorable, Dent preferred to keep his family home, where he would read the service "to the children." Mrs. Dent did not always comply, and the master, at home alone, often lacked an audience. Even as John Dent left the slaves to their own religious devices, his children's religious training fell largely to their mother. [67]

As one might expect, Dent, the rationalist, was more concerned with his children's education than their church attendance. Sometime during the 1840s, while living on the Cowikee, the family began employing a female tutor who was probably from South Carolina. She lived in their home and taught the children in a separate schoolhouse, which the father provided on the plantation. The lack of journals from that decade obscures the details. By 1847, however, the tutor was Miss Elizabeth Gilbert of Colleton County, South Carolina. Her Cowikee tenure was due to the intercession of Anne Dent.

Having been to Colleton in 1848, Anne wrote her son in September,

> I saw Mrs. Gilbert yesterday, who seemed to wish her daughter to continue with you another year, provided it was agreeable with her to do so, but she said that she wished me to be answerable for the payment of her salary, which I am willing to do, but cannot afford to advance it. So, when due, you are to give Elizabeth G[ilbert] what she requires to purchase such articles of clothing as she stands in need of—particularly a new bonnet, fashionable dress, shoes, etc. The residue must be transmitted . . . subject to my order for her mother's use. [68]

Tutor Gilbert remained in the Dents' service at an annual salary of $100 until 1853, the year of the disrupting typhoid epidemic and deaths. By that time Grandmother Dent was having the older girls, Minna and Lizzie, to live with her so that their aunts might tutor them gratis and smooth away some of the roughness that resulted from a frontier environment. Minna spent 1852-1853 at Darien and Charleston, and wherever else her grandmother chose. In 1853 Lizzie went east and Minna returned to Alabama. Traveling from aunt to aunt and vacationing with Grandmother Dent cost over $200 per annum. Of this, John paid $125, leaving the balance as his mother's responsibility. In February, 1854, Anne gamely defended the expenditures: "I am happy to say that everyone thinks Lizzie is improving. She is fatter and clearer, and begins to feel a desire to learn. We all love her very much for her sweet temper. Her greatest fault is her disregard to truth, a habit if once acquired [is] the most difficult to overcome, and attended with many dangerous things, as well as disgraceful results."[69]

By her grandmother's standard, Lizzie, aged eleven, made satisfactory progress. Yet when Anne Dent rotated the girls again in November, 1854, the experiment had run its course. Two months later in January, 1855, Minna returned to Alabama in "distress." She was homesick and ready to join her brothers and sisters in the local boarding schools of Clayton and Eufaula, which had temporarily taken the place of the plantation's tutorial system. More specifically, the Union Female College of Eufaula was dedicated in May, 1855, and the Dent girls enrolled. Since October of the previous year, Horry and Annie had boarded in Clayton to attend R. B. Yarrington's academy. And at Bleak House on April 16, 1855, Dent was glad to have "Started the children daily to school from home."[70] The seeming revolution in educational procedure was due to the grandmother's intervention, the death of Mary Elizabeth, the second marriage (to a school teacher), and the exchange of residences.

Anne Dent's criticism of her son's plantation school is revealing of children's daily life and education on a frontier plantation. In February, 1854, after visiting the isolated Good Hope, she chided John,

> You do indeed require some one to compel you to act wisely with regard to your children, for it is nothing but self-indulgence which prevents you from sending those boys to a N[orth] Eastern School. You love to look at them, and therefore can't bear to part with them, tho you know it will greatly benefit them and relieve the house from the torment of two great idle boys, who are at one moment associating as companions with a sett of poor degraded slaves, and the next tyrannizing over them, as I witnessed with my own eyes, and could not reprove the boys as they had no other companions. Now, my dear John, you know how this will end, pollution of all kinds.[71]

At this point, Anne digressed, in order to praise her own sacrificial example of sending her son, George, to Switzerland for a good education. Returning to the immediate problem, she admitted that John's sons would now "find the confinement intolerable after the free roaming about a plantation they have been accustomed to, but you are duty bound to turn a deaf ear to their regrets." She believed the youths' momentary suffering and the father's pain would be better than having the boys grow up resembling Dent's overseer "Crewe." This statement was perhaps her harshest verbal attack on John Dent. The mother not only suggested that he was like her steward, Bunting; she also likened John's sons to the lowest type of white man he could conceive, an Alabama overseer. Whether this was the prime spur to a boarding-school education is not known, but Horry was soon off the plantation, living in Clayton, and attending Yarrington's school.[72] It was a long way from the Harvard Yard, but it was better than tyrannizing over slaves in the Cowikee swamp. Despite his mother's preference for northern education, John Dent was not prepared emotionally or financially to send his sons to a distant school. Reflecting the American bias for local education, he kept the children in Clayton and Eufaula academies for a few more years.

After Minna left South Carolina in January, 1855, the grandmother questioned Barbour County education enough to evoke John's response entitled, "Letter to My Mother in relation to the Education of My Children." Dated September 2, 1855, the letter criticized the Union Female College, attacked democracy, advocated a practical, nonaristocratic education for girls, and pled a questionable condition of poverty that was supposed to excuse not sending the children to a northeastern school.

Beleaguered by his mother's importunities, Dent opened defensively, and unconvincingly: "Your letters in relation to this most important matter, I thank you for, and I can assure you it causes me more concern than all the rest of my affairs do. They have but a certain time in which to perform this task, and I frankly admit that by far the greater part of such time has been wretchedly misused, in having them at our Miserable schools, such as we have in this country."[73]

Rather than consider an eastern education for them, he attacked local indifference to developing good schools:

> Would we but pay one tenth the attention to establishing a School and procureing the Services of competent instructors as we do the Election of a town council, we would be acting wisely. But unfortunately for the children, their parents are acting the parts of fools, and their greatest inheritance are being kept from them. In no Country on which the Sun Shines is education so much neglected as in this part of Alabama. And at the same time no people possess [more of] the means and the opportunity of having established among us good Schools, would we but turn our minds to the subject as we should, feeling it an imperative duty most sacred in trust.[74]

Condemning the finishing-school ideal of the Union Female College, he blamed this aristocratic and impractical education upon frontier democracy. The seeming contradiction was probably not so ambiguous in practice. "They have recently established a female College in Eufaula," he explained:

> Its construction and appearances in the Mechanics Art are praiseworthy; if the arts and sciences are as well executed within, by its teachers, into the heads of its pupils, all will be well. But I have my misgivings, and I base them on what I can see and hear. Its a grand scheme to make an impression, nothing more, for in passing one is at once struck with the jingling of pianos the shrieking of voices, a perfect bedlam of discordant sounds. This in Modern Science is termed the first accomplishment for a Young Lady to take her seat at the piano and astonish the assembled admirers with such airs as "Old Zip Coon," "Dan Tucker," "Suzanna," and "Old Uncle Ned." What a farce, what a farce indeed it is. But as Alison says, in all Democratic governments, "the public will or opinion is omnipotent, it is despotic." We are in every sense of the word Democrats here, hence—what is, is right.[75]

Attacking piano playing as a symbol of decadent woman placed Dent in the mainstream of the agricultural press of his period, which praised the energetic, hardworking, productive farm wife, as against the abhorrent idea of an idle, urban woman of fashion, spending time reading novels and playing the piano.[76] Nor was he through on impractical female education.

Condemning the school's lengthy vacations, Dent indirectly judged his mother's expensive summering habits, another of the so-called fashionable, urban woman's dangerous ways, so threatening to rural-minded men.

> Here is another feature of improvements and provident wisdom among its Faculty. The Summers vacation is so arranged as to be long and peculiarly convenient to wit, June July August and September which to a child is an age, and a very important one indeed. They unlearn or learn more bad habits in these four months of long days than is made up in useful instruction in the rest of the eight months. But this is modern improvement, modern custom, backed by public opinion and approval hence right and proper. The whole secret is this, the teachers now a days of such institutions are not as in days gone by, Matrons, but a set of young Adventurers—Missess, Mdm's de, who have come forth on a venture—the gay to train up the gay. As such, after Eight months of fashionable teaching, and displays in the Institution heading and leading the Society in Town, these four months vacations are intended for special rounds to the watering places and fashionable summer resorts. Such is the course of these Modern Female Colleges which are now filling the world with a class of young women, as competent to fill the duties of domestic housewife, as a Jew

would be to fill the chair of the Pope; in this progressive age though, things not taught in college, presume will be by all "who run may read."[77]

Dent also claimed to despise the courtly sycophancy implicit in this educational system. Believing "There is one thing so disgusting in all this as to appear and show how base is the ground work of the whole proceedings," he insisted,

> it is all a Humbug. The rates of tuition are high but no higher than they ought to be, with proper instructions; the policy though in addition to tuition is this—sycophancy must become a part—that is, the mothers must be as kind as courteous as attentive to these Lady teachers as the Ladies of one Court are expected to be to the Ladies of another. Such ensures to their daughters peculiar attentions and instructions and above all, most distinguished honors at examinations, making true the old saying, "Kissing goes by favours."[78]

Finally he got down to what were the basic reasons, one suspects, for educating the children in Barbour, the matters of cost and distance. "A person so fortunate as to have but one or two children, with the means, should send them of[f] to the older states, where the practical advantages of a sound education may be had, something real and substantial. But we who have been so prolific, with our eights and tens of children, may consider ourselves truly fortunate if we can give them a fair education near our home, as it would require the ample means of a Banker to send of[f] and educate such a host."[79] There was some self-deception in this, but when Dent's economic status did improve markedly in the late 1850s, he sent the children to distant boarding schools. After the Civil War, he showed even more interest in educating his offspring.

In the meantime, after his mother's death in 1856, John's sons, Horry and Herbert, stopped boarding in town and simply went "to school daily from home." In January, 1857, the father reestablished the plantation's old field school under Miss Mary H. Randal, who was from Canada West. This Yankee tutor reflected Dent's mother's appreciation of northern education *and* his second wife's New England origins. In February, 1858, Randal was replaced by Miss Harriet H. Camp, daughter of Lyman G. Camp of Montpelier, Vermont, Fanny Dent's native state. Camp's annual salary of $300 above room and board was as much as Dent paid his overseer, who, admittedly, came cheaper than most. Camp gave satisfactory service and left of her own accord in 1860. Being more than a teacher, the tutor was also a type of family member, baby sitter, companion, and supervisor of servants. Addressing her formally as Miss Camp, Dent treated her much as he did his daughters. He accompanied her on errands, especially when buying the children's books. He also saw that she had holidays and visits with friends in Eufaula. Regrettably for posterity, recording the tutors' social calls was more important to Dent than reporting the subjects they taught and the books they used.[80]

In 1860, Camp was succeeded by Martha Lynde, also from Vermont. Lynde remained until April, 1861, when the exigencies of war sent her scurrying home. Dent was not uninterested in education, it was simply of a lesser priority than other concerns. While he gave the matter less time and thought than he claimed, as his financial status improved (he invested in John McNab's bank in 1858), he sent Horry to Brook Hill Academy near Charlottesville, Virginia. Dent's checks to Dr. Charles Minor were for large amounts, more than $500 per year. Horry was there from 1857 until February, 1859, spending summer vacations at Bleak House in Barbour. In August, 1859, Dent arranged for Horry to go to Philadelphia "as an apprentice to Norris to learn to be a machinist" at the Richards and Norris locomotive works. Here the son's expenses were minimal, about $8 per month for board. Horry remained in Philadelphia until April, 1861, when he, too, returned home because of the civil conflict.[81]

With an eye for cost, in 1860, after Horry's Brook Hill expenses had ceased, Dent sent Lizzie and Herbert to schools in Tennessee. One contact for this program was the Episcopal minister. In January of that year, Dent reported, "Mrs Dent went down with me this morning carrying Liz" to Eufaula "to start to Columbia Tenn to school. Mr. Steel takes her on." Herbert left a month later under the care of Harriet Camp, who now sought her fortune elsewhere. Dent's sense of inadequacy in educating his children found its clearest expression here. It was February 19, 1860, when "Miss Camp left to day for Eufaula, to take the first boat for Columbus, on her rout for Greenville, Tennessee. Concluded to send Herbert with her to be placed at a School of her choosing near Greenville, as I know of no schools here for Boys worth patronizing. I must trust to Providence in my childrens education, in part. I have my part to perform, but in God we trust for his direction and aid."[82] Dent's dependence on Providence was not new, but such a laissez-faire spirit was unusual.

Perhaps he intended these boarding school ventures to be short-lived. It was a half-hearted effort. A skeptical interpretation is that he arranged or "misarranged" the whole affair to justify a trip into Tennessee. At any rate, both children returned home the following June. When on the twenty-fourth of the month, Dent planned to "leave in the morning for Nashville Tenn. to bring Liz from Columbia," Herbert had already arrived from Greenville. This probably concluded Liz's formal education, as she married Whit Clark the following year. Herbert subsequently enrolled in the local Riverdale Academy, remaining there till 1861, when he went to preparatory school in Tuscaloosa.[83] The Civil War soon disrupted his study as well as the intermediate education of the middle group of children. Dent's postwar policy of schooling was more efficient and expensive. While this antebellum father was interested in education, the plantation and business were more pressing. He could not attend to everything.

Not that he really tried to decide everything himself. Actually, Dent was very dependent on his mother and his wives, especially Fanny Whipple. The capable Fanny was a practical check on her husband's authority in several areas, and he accepted that fact. As we shall see, Fanny required more consideration than Mary Elizabeth had.[84] When John and Fanny were married in 1854, he was thirty-nine years old, she twenty-five. Fanny, who was teaching school in Clayton at the time, was one of those nineteenth-century American women who had had much freedom in youth. When she married, she became a dutiful wife and mother, but she refused to be "laid on the shelf," or confined to the home, as so many young American wives were reported to be. Dent would have one believe that from Mary Elizabeth to Fanny he passed from romantic love to naturalistic realism or utilitarianism in his attitude toward wives.[85] Actually, the first marriage was not devoid of practical considerations. And conforming to the period's "pattern" for second marriages, he wed Fanny in a dark mood of despondency but soon developed a deep affection for her, which would not be obscured.

Dent's devotion to the second wife rested on respect for her initiative and business acumen, which she possessed in greater degree than had Mary Elizabeth. If Fanny was in the least attractive, he never acknowledged it. In fact he probably had her plainness and energy in mind in 1880 when he advised young men in

> choosing a wife, let the gay Butterflies alone, and choose the plain un-affected girl who shows wisdom by her actions, a girl who is willing to adapt herself to circumstances, and who is not haughty and conceited, and is kind and social with all she meets. But for the Good Lord's sake, keep away from the girl who stands on family Aristocracy, family blood, and all such stuff, and get the blood that stands upon its own merits and shows its worth by its actions—in a word, avoid a conceited girl and marry the girl of hard common sense that can talk about business and show business qualifications and when you pick such a girl you will have gotten a prize and a companion that will be a help to you, a friend to you, a true wife.

He gave the same advice to young women, though more succinctly.[86]

It was a measure of Dent's maturity, self-confidence, and security that Fanny's strong personality was more like his mother's than Mary Elizabeth's had been. While Fanny was not necessarily a better mother than Mary Elizabeth, Fanny had broader interests and more obvious influence on her husband. Nevertheless, her first responsibility was the home. If we may trust the journals, the older children and their stepmother got along well. Five years after his second marriage, Dent wrote of being "surrounded with many comforts and blessings in my domestic relations." These rendered his home "life desirable and pleasant," for which he gave thanks. [87]

A competent manager, Fanny ran the household staff of three to five slaves with no evident intervention by her husband. When a disturbance occurred, she handled the problem, leaving John to note an "Exchange of Cooks. Mrs Dent sent Nelly in the field and took Violet in her place." Fanny also did her own shopping, purchasing for the entire plantation when necessary. She enjoyed the task and frequently shopped alone. The master felt no need to accompany or assist her on these trips, though he frequently did so in times of leisure and relaxation. [88]

Fanny was also a stronger influence for repairing the family residence than Mary Elizabeth had been. No sooner was the family moved to Bleak House in 1855 than Dent began a major remodeling of the plain dwelling, a process that continued for several years. After rotting sills had been replaced, a special concern was the kitchen and dining area, which Fanny was determined to raise to her standards. The first new kitchen at Bleak House was a hurried affair. On a February day in 1856 Dent had "3 Boys getting out logs for a Kitchen." A mere ten days later, he reported a "New finished Kitchen." When time permitted two years hence, the hands were again "Working at Kitchen Stuff." Perhaps Fanny was already considering the cooking stove she would select in New York City during her trip north in August, 1858. Of this proposed revolution, John Dent wrote in October of that year, "Mrs Dents Cooking Stove reached home on 14th, in good order and sound." A few days later there was more remodeling and much misgiving. "John and Alfred building a cooking room adjoining the eating room for the stove, an experiment, for I doubt if ever a Negro will cook on it properly, they are made for the Yankees who manage them properly." A short week later, however, Dent had to admit that the Negro women "Cooked supper for the first [time] on Fannys stove, done admirably well, a great convenience." [89] Apparently Fanny and the cooks were more communicative, capable, and compatible than the master realized.

Yet the urge to progress is never sated, and on December 12, 1859, Dent had his favorite "John rebuilding chimney to eating hall, owing to it smoking so badly." Nor did all of Fanny's innovations transcend criticism. The master declared that her new sewing machine was "a complete Humbug. Can't get it to sow a stitch, a perfect Humbug." The machine's performance probably improved, but he also tired of having to sell old pianos to make room for new ones from New York, and he was literally stupefied when it took a man named Carter seven full hours to tune an instrument. With a melodian from New York at $75, tuning bills, and the difficulty of selling old instruments, it was little wonder to Dent that his "Family & Plantation Expenses" ran $2,551.62 in 1859. [90]

Despite Dent's criticism of music in the female college, a piano in the home did not threaten this family head. Pianos were for the children and tutors, not just Mrs. Dent. And Fanny *was* a producer. Having the corn meal and wheat flour ground at Keener's inefficient mill was an endless aggravation at which this wife assisted and sometimes supervised. "Mrs. Dent made up 5 new mill sacks out of stout Cotton osnaburgs, and gave them to Tom on yesterday, and are under his special charge." While the husband oversaw the planting and cultivation of vegetable gardens in plots near the residence, Fanny attended to the gathering and preserving processes. She also worked toward ample provision of fresh fruits, planting trees and vines and availing herself of neighbors' surplus fruits. Since hog killing was particularly demanding, Fanny usually did her share of this work. When minor illness temporarily precluded her helping, Dent recognized her worth and wrote, with hyperbolic bent, "As Mrs Dent is an Invalid and Miss Camp in School, had to attend to the trying up Lard and making Sausages myself, a most tedious occupation for John H. Dent, put up some sausages in lard for Summer." [91] Infrequent complaint of an unfair division of labor is the best indicator of both wives' energy and hard work.

Fanny's interest in gardening extended to landscaping as well as nutrition. In addition to planting water oaks and "shrubbery," she sent to a neighbor "Mrs Fields to get some China trees." These were quick-growing and would provide shade. Her ability as a gardener was considerable enough to challenge the master's prowess and vanity. Writing to daughter Minna of Fanny's successful gardening, he took refuge in the defensive and petulant satisfaction that "your ma gets tired of such things very soon." Here, as always, the father and the children referred to Fanny as the children's "ma." It is an interesting title in light of Dent's care to address Anne Dent as "mother." With his own children and grandchildren, he was the more formal *papâ* and *grandpère*. [92] While one should not make too much of this, modes of address do indicate hierarchy and control. Yet Fanny Dent was far from powerless.

As the daughter of a Yankee farmer, she could have demanded her own small cotton patch. And why not, when each slave family was free to have the same? Yet Dent was not averse to the idea, and he wrote on a June morning in 1859 that the hands had "hoed over Mrs Dents patch and Cotton." Income from her own crop gave Fanny a measure of economic independence that Dent could accept. Perhaps he was a source of the practice. On June 16, 1859, he approved, when "On yesterday Mrs Dent employed Alfred to build a sleeping room on the South end of the house." Here the implication is that Fanny paid wages for his skilled Negro carpenter. Her personal financing of remodeling would explain the master's ready support of her several reconstruction programs, which directly affected man, beast, and fowl on the plantation. It was probably her New Englander's passion for neatness (which Dent admired) that led him to move the Negro quarter, livestock lots, and smokehouse farther from the family residence. And when young fowls required close supervision, there was a job "Building a Turkey house for Mrs Dent at residence."[93]

While they enjoyed mutual pleasures in plantation projects, the Dents' marriage was not idyllic. Again we have only his side of it, but Fanny must have tired of his closeness with money. She also enjoyed visiting and managed her numerous tasks to allow a maximum of it. Having guests and going visiting on a regular basis, Fanny was no stay-at-home. Without recourse to harsh words, Dent's tone criticized her riding about the countryside. Personally, he was as ambivalent on local socializing as he was on long-distance travel. Hardly an introvert or recluse, he nevertheless insisted, somewhat defensively: "I like company and association but it must be with those where there is a congeniality of taste and feelings, some persons are an annoyance to be with, others I like and I like a few more than many, in fact, I enjoy myself with one person, more than with two, three or four."[94]

Yet when convinced that duty called, Dent could calmly depart for days at a time to serve on grand juries or as a witness in court at Clayton. On business in town, he regularly dined with gentleman friends like E. B. Young, James L. Pugh, Henry D. Clayton, M. B. Wellborn, and others. Still, that was the extent of his comment on it. Dent was uncharacteristically verbose about H. D. Clayton and still told little, when on January 3, 1858, he wrote: "Started to Clayton, met H. D. Clayton on his way down to my house to see about Mabry and McCalls Drafts, returned to my house with Clayton. PM, went to Clayton with H. D. Clayton and spent the night with him." Although he traveled regularly to Eufaula and Clayton, Dent seldom described developments in town unless they were catastrophic events relating to the loss of property, as in March, 1860: "On Thursday night 8th the Block on Broad St Eufaula was burnt up opposite the Hotel square, loss considerable on owners, their being no Insurance."[95]

In keeping with his reservations about socializing, Dent's journals project the illusion of an intellectually self-sufficient plantation. The children's field school was one example of this. A further reflection of the pastoral view of mental independence was Dent's insistence that "Reading, writing drawing gardening and occupation on the farm has always been my pleasures." Books, newspapers, correspondence, the journals, and account books did occupy much of his time. We have already seen how this family man appreciated Fredrika Bremer's *Homes of the New World*. He also enjoyed the children's tutors for their informed conversation; and he corresponded with one during her scheduled absence for summer vacation. These simple interests, however, reflected neither feminism nor infatuation.[96]

In keeping with his love and fear of trips, Dent liked to read published travel accounts. He also kept copies of a large correspondence until its sheer volume compelled him to destroy it upon his removal to north Georgia in 1866. History was another favorite. In April, 1858, he "Went to Eufaula. Received 2 Mantillas and Abbots Histories from Stage office, sent by W. Clark from Clayton, who bought said articles in New York for me." He appreciated Whit's New York trips for the books and bound, legal-sized diaries that this son-in-law brought him.[97]

Being unselfconscious about his reading, Dent failed to keep a systematic record of books bought and used. Instead, one finds fragments like "Cash to McCoy for Books for selling hide 1525." Some of these books were for the children's school. Although Dent's newspapers are more in evidence, an incomplete record of them makes it impossible to say exactly what he read at a given time. In 1854 he received J. Black's *Spirit of the South*, which was published in Eufaula. That year he also subscribed to the *New Orleans Delta* and the *National Enterprise*. In 1859 he received the *New York Herald*; and during the early 1860s he supported Rhett's *Charleston Mercury* and took the Macon *Telegraph*, Columbus *Daily Sun*, and Richmond *Dispatch*. As previously noted, the antebellum Dent obscured any direct dependence on the agricultural press, which, however, he must have read with regularity.[98]

Drawing was another plantation amusement. Sketches provided in fantasy a romantic life of conflict, such as naval battles between graceful ships and land skirmishes against noble savages. Dent's range of subjects was broad and included battles, profiles of himself, designs for bridge superstructures, caricatures, road maps, and rain patterns. Some of this escapism can be related to his mother's censorship. Yet not all was fantasy. Bridges were useful, and garden designs helped beautify the drab plantation. Dent's attitude toward the residence was not totally utilitarian. For example, in February, 1861, he wrote to Minna with pride: "Before the door I have laid out two flour gardens, most tastefully laid off and enclosed by a low neat fence to keep the horses out, a plan of which I will draw you so you can see the arrangements and serve you as a garden should you have one."[99]

Yet guilt and repression persisted. Planting and gardening, man's natural occupations, needed no justification. Other diversions, however, being less natural, required rationalization. The only surprising thing in this is that such minor items invited comment at all. In 1859, he dutifully recorded buying "a small double barrel gun from Bray & Bro. to amuse myself with on the plantation price $20.00." Although he believed himself a good mechanic, it was not until 1858 that he "Bought set of tools for own using.'' Even then he deprecated himself, concluding it was ''rather a freak than otherwise.'' Nor did this creative person explain what he meant by sending ''Fed to get me out a block of cedar to make a model with.''[100]

It is easy to see how a person of such restraint could be somewhat unnerved by Fanny's zest for visiting and churchgoing. From Dent's perspective, it was the sorest point in their relationship. Thus, the journals force the second wife to bear the image of socializer whom Dent merely accompanied or supported. He probably presented another public front. Living at Bleak House on the stage road from Eufaula to Clayton, the Dents were easily accessible, had their share of guests, and made their share of calls. Most visits involved the children and Mrs. Dent, but the master had his callers in E. B. Young, H. D. Clayton, Mack Wellborn, Whit Clark, Reverend Steele, Dr. McNeill, and others. There was no clear distinction between visits by family and friends.[101]

Nor did Dent see any need to describe these associations. Examples of his terse notices are: ''Mrs Dent went to Eufaula to see Sarah Green and do some shopping''; and ''Mrs Charles Petty came down last evening in the stage to see Mrs Dent. '' Mrs. Petty was an old friend from Fanny's teaching days in Clayton. Two days after her arrival, ''Mrs Petty went up in stage to Clayton this morning. Mrs. McNeill came down afternoon.'' At the end of three more days, ''Dr McNeill came down from Clayton and spent the night with us. This morning he returned to Clayton with his wife, Carry and Lizzy.'' When the Dents returned these visits, sometimes staying several days with friends, Horry would keep the journal, explaining, ''Papa & ma went up to Clayton in the buggy.''[102]

Although Master Dent was neighborly, he preferred to phrase it in business terms. For example, he would work more than his share of the public road, keep an eye on plantations for absentee owners, share a schoolhouse and tutor with the Fields family, assist neighbor Adams in raising a new cotton press, and even divide an estate of Negroes. Performing this last service for the heirs of the neighboring Snipes family was a significant measure of Dent's status in the community. There was also the regular division of beef among neighbors. Dent supervised the butchering and quartering. For him, a business relationship seemed safer than a social one.[103]

Although he clearly disapproved some of the family's visiting and church attendance, Dent aspired to do a father's part, which meant providing a sufficiency of buggies, carriages, and horses. He might grumble about someone's gadding about, but he generally assisted it. Thus on November 2, 1858, he ''Went to Eufaula with Mrs Dent, shopping. Bought a Buggie from Corry & B, $135.00, gave my old Buggie in part payment at $20, which made the note for the new buggie

$115, payable 1st January 1859.'' Obviously the old one was worn out. And while the plantation had a smith in John O'Bryan, Dent had his best horses shod in town. [104]

In 1860 the old carriage had to be replaced. A new one required new horses. Thus in April of that year, Dent "Went to Eufaula with Mr Whitcomb and Fanny to try the horses, performed well.'' Fanny must have approved them, for on the following day, "Silas Whitcomb left this morning for Columbus, left the match horses with us price $850.00.'' With growing responsibility, Dent complained, "Fine Carriages and Horses Require care, attention and fine keeping. One who invests a large amount of money in such outfits should first have a coachman and hostler fully competent to take care and charge of both carriage and horses.'' [105]

Interlacing pride with this lament, Dent was still too much a farmer to acquire this last trapping of a decadent aristocrat. Continuing to attend such needs himself, he "Went to Eufaula and had carriage axle trees set, they were sprung and did not track.'' He not only saw to the transportation of his immediate family, he also sent carriages and buggies hither and yon, fetching visitors and returning them home. He did this at least once when it meant stopping a plow in the field to provide power for conveying visitors to their home. Perhaps the temporary removal offset any sacrifice in cultivation. [106]

Dent probably came closest to a row with Fanny over his attendance at church services. Yet she had her sanctions and could occasionally prod him into attending the Methodist meeting with her. One assumes this wife's power sprang from the husband's high respect, affection, and need. Perhaps she was so much like Dent's mother that natural behavior stimulated cooperative responses. While the last is conjecture, his devotion to Fanny is fact, and on January 29, 1860, he "Went to the Methodist Church in Eufaula with Mrs Dent.'' [107]

Another example of his devotion to wife and family is given in the journal account of Fanny's trip to her Vermont home in 1858. The episode illustrates the master's self-concept and some of the gaps between his beliefs and behavior. The lengthy travel account also exudes a romantic view of New England. Although the journal does not explain Fanny's early plans for the trip, Dent was favorably disposed, and on July 9, 1858, he "Went to Eufaula to see about Mrs Dents procuring a passage in steamer of 17th that sails from Savanah for New York, wrote to Thomas Holcombe on the subject.'' Holcombe was at Savannah. Four days later, Dent again "Went to Eufaula to make arrangements for Mrs. Dent starting, drew $400 Deposit money from EB Young to defray her expenses.'' He planned on the fourteenth "to start for Columbus in the morning with Mrs Dent, who starts north to see her family in Vermont.'' [108]

The journey began in easy stages, taking an entire day from Bleak

House to Eufaula and on to Silver Run (Seale) where they would board the train for Columbus, Georgia. It was Friday, July 16, when the Dents "Left Silver Run by Cars at 7 AM. Over crowded with passengers. So much so the gentlemen had to stand on feet in the Baggage Cars. Reached Columbus at 8½. Put up at the Perry House.... Procured by check from Bank Columbus $400.... Mrs Dent left for Macon in train 3¾ PM. Very much crowded. Placed her under charge of Wilson Bates to Millen. In Savannah Mr Holcombe was to meet her and see her on board of the steamer for N.Y." [109]

Dent's uncharacteristic attentiveness was due to his wife's taking their eighteen-month-old daughter with her, even though the mother was four months pregnant with George Columbus. As a Yankee "school marm" who came South and married well, the determined Fanny would no longer wait to share her joys with northern kin. In his journal of July, 1858, Dent neglected to mention his wife's pregnancy or her decision to take little Fanny. He obviously thought Mrs. Dent capable of the journey. After all, his mother had ventured to Newport when his own birth was imminent. John's assisting Fanny to Columbus and planning ahead for her was not expansive chivalry. In fact the chivalrous thing would have been to accompany wife and child to Vermont, since he soon went there anyway. But it was lay-by time on the plantation, and Dent's self-image as both hard-working farmer and conscientious father would not let him go, not yet. Perhaps Fanny thought it best to precede him, to prepare the way among abolitionist kin. [110]

The complexities of Dent's decision to remain at home and his later Victorianism are evident in the 1880 misrecollection that he actually joined Fanny on the northern trip to assist "carrying along . . . her first born infant, Fanny Whipple." Later conscience to the contrary, however, Dent put Fanny and daughter on the train in Columbus, visited with William Young, toured the Eagle textile factory (whose Yankee ethic he approved), and returned home on Sunday in roasting heat. Awaiting the foddering in Barbour, he simmered physically and psychologically until he could justify his own journey north. Almost beside himself with desire either to join Fanny or simply to travel, Dent became more irritable by the day. One entry put it, "My dear Wife is at the North on a visit to her family, hence I feel lonesome and dejected." [111]

Wanderlust and sexual lust were upon him so strongly that he turned to poetry, an uncommon but not unique medium for J. H. Dent. Here, with characteristic fatalism he vowed,

> Was it in my power, how speedily I'd go!
> On a journey Northward in quest of Ice or Snow.
> For here! in the South, the Sun is burning hot
> Melting one to death, oh! what a dreadful lot. [112]

Disclaimer notwithstanding, Dent had been free to go. And the sexual aspect of the heat imagery was real, making the abstinence implicit in these four lines the strongest corroboration of circumstantial evidence that Dent practiced the sexual continence of the single standard.

The poem's second and third stanzas confirm the initial interpretation of sexual frustration. From southern heat, Dent's mind moved to the theme of "Too many little children" which was noted in an earlier context. Although the poem revealed a sensitivity to Fanny's second pregnancy in less than four years, he refused total responsibility for her delicate condition:

> They say that Northern gals are reasonable wives
> The[y] never have so many, valueing their lives.
> All such is perfect stuff, they breed just as fast
> And have as many young ones, as any other lass.

The theme of Yankee girls' greater contraceptive powers is almost supernaturalistic, but Fanny, a fast breeder to date, was no wonder woman. Whether Dent was bragging or complaining is an interesting question. Despite that ambivalence, he, Fanny, or both spaced subsequent children further apart. While Mary Elizabeth had nine babies in less than eighteen years, Fanny's six children in twenty-one years of marriage were spaced at intervals of two, three, four, and seven years.[113] Dent's professed interest in birth control was probably genuine, although the spacing could have been the natural result of increasing age and declining fertility.

Meanwhile in July and August of 1858, this husband was preparing to justify the northern trip that he had probably intended to take all along. Never connecting his loneliness or love of travel with current plans, he preferred to write of Fanny, "If nothing serious turns up to prevent [I] expect to start on 12th for Richmond, Vermont, to assist her on her journey homewards." Without procrastinating, he sent the next day "to Mr Holcombe to engage me a passage in the Steamer that sails from Savannah on 14th for New York, as I am going on to Vermont for Mrs Dent." By August 10 his repetitious "selflessness" wears thin: "I have determined on going to Vermont to assist my wife back to her Southern home." He left Thursday, August 12, affirming again his duty in the trip: "My intentions are to start this evening in the stage from Eufaula for Richmond Vermont, to assist my Wife home. I do so as a duty I owe her."[114]

On the eve of departure, the old anxiety set in, whereby he could only "trust that God in his mercy and goodness will protect me in my Journey, Save me from the dangers of the Land and Sea, preserve my health and Strenth, and permit me to join my Wife at her fathers home in safety, and all may be Well." Thinking of the children, Dent's anxiety deepened; they explain much of his unwillingness to accompany Fanny on her northern journey. Now in leaving the children, he dutifully prayed that God "may protect and preserve their lives, and let us after a few Weeks absence be rejoined in the family circle, all well and happy. May God in his mercy vouch safe unto me a Safe and prosperous journey." [115] Yet Dent's prayers were meaningful. Once they were completed, he left, took the journal with him, thoroughly enjoyed this three-week trip, and apparently dismissed all concern for children and home. Nor did Fanny's health trouble him significantly.

Still, the speed of his travel bespoke anxiety. Waiting until the last moment to leave, he rode two nights and a day to make ship connection in Savannah. Leaving home Thursday evening, he was in Columbus during Friday midday, where he again met friend Young and attended to financial needs before hastily departing for Macon and Savannah. The details of travel, as usual, consumed him.

> Reached Columbus Ga, 9 AM, day very warm. Saw Wm H Young, procured 3 checks on Bank of the Republic NY, 1 for $300, 1 for $200 and One hundred dollars in Gold, also borrowed a check on Bank of Republic of NY from W H. Young for One hundred dollars for 60 days. The $100 check borrowed from W H Young on Bank Republic NY, let EB Young have it, as a loan, the Said EB Young paying Same to the Bank of Columbus when due. 4¼ PM, Started on Muscogee train Cars for Macon, Ransom Godwin and Wm Simpson being my traveling companions. Reached Macon 9 PM. 9½ PM, started in Savannah train for Savannah, cars very much crowded, reached Savannah 7½ am of 14th. [116]

In the port city on Saturday, August 14, Dent made straight for his agent and tickets, boarding the ship within two hours of his arrival, exhilarated with anticipation of sea travel. Insatiably curious, he prowled the deck for hours:

> Savannah. 7½ am, reached the city. Morning cloudy & Sultry, procured tickets pr Steamer Florida for New York at the Agents, Paddleford Fay & Co, price $15.00. Went on board the Florida at 9½ am, as advertised to Sail at 10 am. The crowd of passengers were immense comeing on board, which detained the Ship to 12 m, when we cast loose from the Wharf and proceeded down the river to Sea under an ordinary head of Steam. The propeller Montgomery bound for NY, just in our wake, passengers on board Florida 169. At 2 PM, crossed the bar and Shaped our course for Cape Hateras, Wind fresh and braceing in our teeth. The Florida is a fine Sea Boat, making good head way against a head Sea and Wind, at 9 PM, off Charleston light. [117]

Although his Sabbatarian journals left no space for a Sunday entry,

Dent irreverently made space for it, as he always did, showing he spent the day on deck. It was a "fine clear day, head Sea and Wind. Sea Sickness confined pretty much to the Ladies and a few Gentlemen, made a good run. Saw Several Sail PM, bound South, nothing unusual occured. At 8½ PM, off Cape Hateras a heavy Sea on, exchanged Signals with Steamer Nashville bound for Charleston." [118]

Monday, the third day at sea, was still exciting, although Dent joined other passengers in declaring the trip monotonous. The question of detainment for quarantine by health officials was an immediate disappointment. "At Sea," he wrote,

> Morning clear and mild, much warmer than South of the Cape, a heavy ground Swell on, Wind light from East, Saw many Sail. Some Sea Ward others in shore, Saw two Whales spouting water on our Starboard bow, had a fine run to day, the Steamer though rolling more than on the voyage South of the Cape. Our time was monotonously spent as we were becoming tired of the ship and weary at looking at the wide expanse of Waters. PM, Saw many Sails, whilst nearing the coast of New Jersey. 8 PM, in sight of the Light houses. Pleasant night, the steamer making rapid head way. At One AM, reached the Quarantine Station on Staten Island, was boarded by the health officer, and brought to Anchor, owing to a Sick Man on board. At this disappointment the countenances of all the passengers were elongated, our speedy arrival in New York was made a matter of doubtful suspense, and loud and uncharitable were the imprecations on the poor Sick Man by all, for being made to Stop at Quarantine. [119]

On Tuesday, August 17, disappointment became impatience before the passengers were released to dock at New York:

> This was a morning of agonizing Suspense, the health officer appointing 8 AM. to revisit the Ship, and decide upon the Sick mans case. At 8 am, he boarded us again, and pronounced the case a bad one, perhaps the yellow fever, ordered the Sick man to be carried on Shore to the Hospital, the ship to remain at Anchor, until the case developed itself further. Our passengers to a man became provoked and despondent, but imprisoned we were to await the orders of the Health officers. The morning was spent in watching every movement at the Quarantine buildings, in hopes of a discharge, and most yearningly gazing on the Ferry Steamers passing every ½ hour at our Stern, filled with merry passengers, free as the air, whilst the Florida and her passengers were fast anchored down, our fate Seemed hard, our destination being in sight but immovable was our situation. At 2 PM, the joyful news was received from our Captain (Crowell) just from the Quarantine buildings that we were discharged. Anchor was soon up, and away we steamed for the Dock in NY, where we reached at 3½ PM. [120]

After Tuesday night in the city, which he did not recount, Dent took the trains for New Haven and Hartford, Connecticut, and then for Northfield, Vermont. On the cars in New England mountains, the slave owner could not resist idealizing the "happy" land of Yankeedom. In a moment's melancholy, he knew he was one apart from these people, but he believed Fanny was a sufficient bond for community. It was "8 AM" Wednesday when Dent left New York City

in the New Haven Cars for Richmond Vermont, the point of destination my heart was set upon...reaching. The Cars were overflowing in passengers, crowded and hot, and at every depot more came on. At New Haven the throng was intense, every body seemed to be on the move. After leaving Hartford and going up the Connecticut River R R, the Scenery was grand and beautiful in extreme, the towns so neat and prettily situated, the waters of the river so blue and clear, the farms so neatly cultivated, every thing looking so rich and productive, truly it may be said, we were in happy New England, every thing wore that aspect. The Scenery from Holyoke became more grand and Sublime until we reached Bellows falls where it was grand in extreme, this RR skirts the margin of the River and the mountains, crossing the river high up frequently and the speed they make is at least 30 miles pr hour. I felt alone in this far distant country, a stranger alone, but my spirits were cheerful as I was rapidly approaching the spot where my Wife was and where I wanted to get. At 9 PM, reached Northfield Vermont, where the train laid over for the night.[121]

The theme of neat, prosperous, happy New England implied the South was deficient on all counts. On Thursday, August 19, one week after departing Bleak House, Dent left Northfield, Vermont, for Richmond, where he was delighted to see Fanny. Touching her appearance lightly, almost too lightly, he was captivated by New England scenery and Yankee hospitality. "At 7½ AM," Dent recorded,

resumed my Seat in the Cars for Richmond, day cloudy and Wintry cold, reached Richmond at 9 AM, where I met my Wife at the Depot anxiously awaiting my arrival, our meeting was a happy one. Left immediately for her Fathers residence, where I needed rest and repose after so long and tiresome a Journey. Mrs Dent was much improved in her looks, that pure bracing air of those Green Mountains having restored the New England color to her cheeks. The whole family gave me a hearty greeting, their hospitality was unbounded. I soon felt as one of them. The Scenery around was beautiful, the Camels hump near on our left and Mansfield in our rear, the rich meadow with its rich and verdant crops in our front the Onion River meandering throughout it, skirted by the R Road. Monotony was no part in the view, every thing Seemed beautifully variagated, cheerfulness was on the countenance of all. No where in the United States have I seen better living in the greatest abundance, finer cooking or a more hospitable people.[122]

In 1880, after Civil War and Reconstruction and Fanny's death, Dent would insist that northern and southern peoples were "different in all their ideas, customs and habits." He did not, however, feel that way during the visit of 1858. The contemporary journal shows him at ease among kindred spirits whom he genuinely admired. To his mind, these New Englanders were true farmers. On Friday, August 20, he

> Spent the day in examining a New England farm. Mrs Dent Father being a farmer, had every opportunity of seeing the management of their farms. It was haying Season, hence all were busy in saving Hay. Horse power and Machinery were used, which economised labor and expedited their work. The Corn I saw on the farm was estimated in product from 75 to 100 bushels pr Acre, it looked rich and promising, the grass crop was luxuriant in extreme, also potatoes and Oats. Nothing though, have I ever seen, or could have imagined to equal their Cattle and dairies. Cheese was the Staple crop. Their Cows were large and fine, average 4 gallons of Milk pr day. The tables of the farmers were loaded down with rich and plentiful fare, their Beef was of the finest and richest qualities I ever saw or eat. So was the Milk, butter, bread and potatoes. Sociability in extreme seemed to assist among the people for constant visitors was at the house.[123]

Dent implied his host was more hospitable than he. Family ties were also strong among these Vermont farmers. On Saturday, "By promise and appointment," he explained,

> the family Spent the day with an Uncle of Mrs Dents, a Mr Rufus Stevens. I hired a horse & buggie to take her down, with a view of making a long circuit to their residence, in order we could look at the Country and neighborhood. Neatness comfort and thrift was apparent on every hand, and the village of Jonesville was a neat and pretty place, much more so, than the village of Richmond. At Mr Stevens we spent a most pleasant day indeed, for he was the most prosperous farmer I had Seen, and had every thing about him in the very best of order, surrounded by Comforts of all kinds, and a most pleasant and interesting family, the day was most agreeably Spent.[124]

On very good behavior, Dent even went to church on Sunday, where he was unprepared for a small attendance. Yet by afternoon he was tiring of so many people. "Went to Richmond to church, attended the Congregationalist Church, the Sermon was on Christian duties, delivered by a young man of fine address and fluent in his Style. The Congregation was much Smaller than I expected to See. The afternoon was spent in receiving numerous visitors."[125]

Dent was also preoccupied with the return trip home, which began on August 23. Notice the lack of consideration for Mrs. Dent's condition.

The following Monday "As we were to commence our journey for home this afternoon," he wrote, "the morning was spent in packing up and making preparations. At 5½ PM, took the Cars at Richmond depot for Burlington on Lake Champlain. At 6 PM, reached Burlington and put up at the American Hotel. Buren Whipple accompanied us to Burlington and as far as Whitehall. The Hotel was well kept, very attentive and accomodating to their guests." Once he departed, Dent added, "In leaving Richmond, I felt as though I was leaving friends, although the time was short in forming a friendship, it was strong and sincere, for life impressions were made, which will be reverted to with mingled feelings of pleasure and sadness." [126] Some of the sadness that related to the abolitionist movement is treated below.

The trip home was to be a tour. Tuesday on Lake Champlain was strenuous, but Fanny was up to it. Here Dent revealed a military bent and perception of a correlation between expense and aristocratic taste. "Early after breakfast," he

went with Mrs Dent Shopping. At 10½ embarked in Steamer for Whitehall. Boat not crowded. The Lake was quite rough, a Strong Southerly Wind prevailing. Saw Mr Converse on the Wharf and spoke about Miss [Mary] Randal [tutor at Bleak House in 1857]. The trip down the lake was very pleasant, Scenery very fine. Old fort Ticonderoga was the great attraction, nothing now remains of it but a part of two walls, which is in a most dilapidated Condition. The Site chosen was a fine position for a Fort, commanding the Lake from its Southern approach as well as the channel passing northward. This is the point where the passengers for Lake George embark. At 5 PM, reached Whitehall, and took the Cars for Albany via Saratoga, Cars crowded, Schedul rapid, reached Albany 8 PM, and put up at the Delivan House, a house very fine, Aristocratic and Expensive. [127]

After a river trip from Albany to crowded, noisy New York City where the Dents settled in the Astor House, he made the first contemporary reference to little Fanny. Also Dent's response to New York was typically agrarian. It was Wednesday, August 25, in Albany when

At 8 AM embarked in Steamer Metamora for New York, boat crowded, day fair and Warm, had a splendid view of the Scenery on the North River. Reached New York 4½ PM, crowd and Jam at the Wharf as usual. Went to the Astor House, given a very fine room. Hired a girl to take charge of Fanny. After tea went to Barnums Museum. More entertained at the Panorama than the Museum. In the Museum the only interesting sight was that of the Happy Family, which consisted of Animals and Birds, by nature at variance and enemies, now living togeather in perfect peace and harmony. Cats and mice were loving friends, Hawks and Doves, Fox and fowls. The noise and confusion in New York completely confused and confounded me.

There was no Sleeping owing to the noise in the Streets as Omnibuses, carriages and people Seemed to be going all night. Night and day Seem necessary to the wants of these busy and numerous people.[128]

The next day was similiar except for his wife's plans. "Procured a nurse for Fanny this morning," Dent wrote,

which allowed Mrs Dent and myself to go about. After breakfast we went down to No 230 Water Street to see Edward Hildreth an old school companion of Mrs Dent. Hildreth was a Clerk in a Stove Establishment. Mrs Dent bought a cooking stove, had it shipped South, in hopes of Cooking like the Yankees. Afterwards sauntered about the City, had our Deguareotypes taken, done some shopping. PM, went up Broadway, looking at the stores and fine buildings. At night went to see Woods Ministrels perform, was very much amused by their performances. Returned home weary and willing to leave this noisy and bustling city. Sleep though was at intervals, as the noise in the streets was incessant.[129]

The third day in New York City, Friday, August 27, proved more bearable because it was the last one and because Dent toured a naval frigate and visited with E. B. Young from Eufaula.

Showery this morning. After breakfast went down to see Hildreth again. Afterwards went to the Dusseldorf Gallery, and remained an hour or two, in it was Power's Greek Slave, to my judgement they were only 3 or 4 fine paintings. After dinner went over to the Navy yard to see the Steam Frigate the Niagara. Went all over her, her model was Superior, but her finish within was very plain and Substantial. She was dirty and confusion, the cable being delivering to a Schooner at her Side, and crowds of visitors upon her decks. At night Mr EB Young and three Sisters called to see us and spent an hour with us. After their departure, packed trunks and prepared to Start in the morning for the South, by the Philadelphia train of Cars.[130]

Dent would come to regret taking the land route home from New York. On Saturday "8 am," the family "left in the Cars from Jersey City for Philadelphia, Morning rainy. Cars very much crowded. Scenery through New Jersey uninteresting. At 12, reached Philadelphia, the crowd on board the ferry boat being intense, at 1, left for Baltimore, cars crowded. Scenery much more interesting and pretty, than in New Jersey, reached Baltimore at 4½ PM. 5½ PM, left in cars for Washington City, scenery pleasing, reached Washington at 7½, put up at Browns Hotel."[131]

Touring the city on Sunday during its hottest, most dismal season, Dent found the district enervating. "Washington is a disgrace to the Government, Were it not for the Government buildings, it would be but an ordinary Village. The City seemed abandoned, dirty and desolated. Browns Hotel is a dirty place, poor meals, badly kept, and Rats and mice were running over the rooms. PM, hired a carriage, rode over the City, had an external view of the Public Buildings, admired the public grounds, and Statuary. So tired of the place left it on monday morning.''[132]

One day from New York to Washington and one day in the nation's capital were enough to send Dent into uninspiring Virginia, where he despaired of the overland route. Silent on his wife's and daughter's condition, he probably preferred traveling alone, which would reduce the baggage and the pressures of crowds he dreaded. He began on Monday, August 30, "Washington to Burkeville," and continued,

> 7 AM, went to the Ferry boat and crossed over to Alexandria, had a fine breakfast on board the boat. Took the Alexandria and Orange R Road for Richmond, reached Richmond to dinner, cars very Crowded, day warm, dust and dirt prevailing, Scenery between Alexandria and Washington very uninteresting. PM, took Cars at Richmond for Burkville, when we reached at 8 PM, and laid over all night, had comfortable lodgings, a good nights rest, and pleasant company. The Scenery from Richmond to Burkville was very interesting and variagated, Much more so than north of Richmond, the Country has a barren appearance, and the crops Seemed to have suffered much from drought. I regretted very much not having taken the Steamer from New York to Savannah, as the land rout is So dusty, fatigueing and attended with troubles in the crowds encountered and baggage to See after. If I ever make the trip again the Sea rout for ever for me, where the journey is made Short and easy.[133]

From Burkeville, the mountain scenery was interesting, but Dent could hardly enjoy it for the crowds, delays, missed connections, and the general burden of time. Inadequate accommodations at Bristol, Tennessee, forced the family to press on in a freight train. Meantime, on Tuesday morning in Burkeville, they

> took the Cars for Bristol via Lynchburg. Cars densely crowded, hot and dusty, reached Lynchburg at 12M, and continued on merely changeing cars. Scenery to day was beautiful, the Alleghany mountains on our right and left, passing the Stations of the far famed Virginia Springs, where the crowds Seemed to be congregated. At every Station, crowds would get off the Cars, and Crowds get on again, making its confusion greater, the detension was such, caused us to miss the Connexion at Bristol, 3 hours after time, which threw us back 24 hours. Reached the Central Depot at Sunset, where we got another Engine which proved defective. Stood on the road at a halt three hours to repair damages, after starting made all speed possible, reached Bristol at 4 am, 3 hours after the departure of the Cars for Knoxville. The Passengers were so numerous, could not find entertainment for all at Bristol, so about 100 of us were sent on by a freight train for Knoxville, leaving Bristol at 6 am, and reaching Knoxville at 6 Pm, where we laid by until 11 am of 2d, to await again the regular through train.[134]

The freight-train trip on Wednesday must have been in a passenger car. It was one of the happiest aspects of the homeward journey. "The trip by the freight train from Bristol to Knoxville though slow was very pleasant," Dent reported,

> as we had more room, and ample time was allowed the passengers to get their meals which is not the case on the passenger trains. The Scenery we could view at leisure. (This was the day Spent travelling on the Freight train between Bristol and Knoxville.) The Crops through Virginia and Tenessee were very much injured by drought, not a half crop of Corn was made. We reached Knoxville a[t] 6 Pm, put up at the Humphrey House, which is near the Depot, found excellent accomodations, a good table, and most attentive and obliging host, and free of that hateful crowds. [135]

On Thursday, September 2, however, travel conditions from Knoxville to Atlanta, again worsened.

> At 11 Am, the regular train reached Knoxville, cramed and jamed with passengers, as it had the passengers left by the preceeding train at Bristol, besides the passengers of this train. Some 500 passengers and 600 trunks had to be transfered from the train just in, to the train just starting, which delayed us ¾ths of an hour behind time in the start. The Cars were too crowded to be pleasant, the Scenery though was interesting; by not stopping for dinner, or delaying unnecessarily at the Depots, we reached Dalton in Georgia in due time. Here was Confusion, three trains on the spot, and the time required to deliver 600 trunks and then to recheck 600 trunks for the two Starting trains caused bustle and confusion in extreme. I never was so worried out with Rail Road travel in my life. At 6 we started off in the train for Atlanta, Georgia, where we reached at 11½ Pm, tired and worried out, put up at the Trout House, a poor and dirty affair, another Browns Hotel at Washington City, enjoyed our nights rest very much. [136]

By now one suspects the largest source of Dent's irritation was his wife's presence, plans, and appointments. In Atlanta on Friday,

> By appointment, we were to spend this day with Mrs Cyrene Stone a Schoolmate of Mrs Dent which she had not seen for some 8 years. So early in the morning, I dispatched a note of Mrs Dent to Mrs Stone by a Boy. Mr Stone resided two miles out in the Country. After breakfast Mr & Mrs Stone called on us at the Trout House, requesting us to spend the day with them. Sent in their Carriage for us, Went out and spent most agreeably day with them, at their neat and comfortable mansion which was nearly in a state of completion. Found Mr Stone a most agreeable and refined gentleman, Mrs Stone a nice and elegant woman, living in comforts with all around to make life pleasant and happy. At 8 PM, Sent us back to the Trout House, as we were to leave in the Cars at 11½ PM, for Columbus Ga via Lagrange, West

Point and Opelika. I was disappointed in my expectations of Atlanta, expected to see a compact well built City, something like Augusta, but it would not compare with Macon, it is scattered and irregularly built up.[137]

Disappointed by Atlanta and three weeks away from home, John Dent left that city on Saturday night, traveling straight through to Eufaula. His insensitivity to wife and daughter could have made him more critical of others' lack of chivalry. Having just come from New England's cleanliness also made southern filth the more repulsive. "At 11½ PM of 3d, in the midst of a heavy rain and thunderstorm," the family

left in Cars from Atlanta. Crowd not so great as heretofore, reached Lagrange at Day light, West Point at 7 am, where we had a most excellent breakfast. At Opelika, changed Cars for Columbus, where we reached at 11½ am, found it hot, and the Perry House as characteristic. At 2 PM, took the Omnibus for the Girard R R Depot, hot and dusty. Cars Crowded with hooziers, the Gentlemen or Men Selected all the Shady Seats in the Cars, the Ladies placed in the broiling Sun, so we had it to Silver Run, when at 3 PM, we were Seated in the Stage for Eufaula, 5 passengers, and as luck would have it, a cloudy afternoon, had a pleasant ride to Eufaula where we reached 12 at night, all passing aggreeable excepting the most dirty Supper at Glennville to which ever man set to.[138]

On Sunday, September 5, the Dents left Eufaula at "6 AM...in Clayton Stage for home, arrived 7½ o clock where we found all well and our journey terminated. Praise be to God for same. Amen."[139] Being able to travel from Atlanta with hardly a break for two nights and a day, the pregnant Fanny Dent was perhaps a more resilient traveler than her forty-three-year-old husband.

Before a final word on the tour of 1858, one might ask in summary, what kind of "patriarch" was John H. Dent? These pages have described him as a responsible family man who strove to be independent of, and dutiful to, a strong-willed mother. Perhaps Anne Dent influenced some of his concern for limiting the number of children, commitment to the single sexual standard, nursing the sick, and responsibility for gardening. There was, however, a clear division of labor between Dent and his wives; women were homemakers, keepers of children, preservers and preparers of food, etc. From his point of view, family life was harmonious, which meant that the women and children saw their duty and did it. But he was no tyrant. The wife had much practical power in matters of the home such as repairing the family residence; controlling domestic servants; shopping for clothes, supplies, a cooking stove, sewing machine, and piano; managing visitors and visits; and making her own plans for attending church.

The children also had much freedom from this father's control in matters of religion, discipline, education, and marriage. Dent did not emphasize advanced education, and his penchant to attend to everything himself probably stifled independence and ambition in his sons, with the possible exception of Horry, the eldest. This planter's self-concept was that of a secure, prosperous provider, a dutiful son, a helpful brother, a spoiling father, a doting and even romantic spouse, a cooperative neighbor, a respecter of in-laws, and a responsible traveler. He assumed his upper-class heritage, wealth, and farmer's rootedness in the soil would shield him from the excesses and debts of an effete, slave-owning aristocracy. Dent's criticism of female education showed some anxiety about the new type of woman that seemed to be emerging.

Finally, the 1858 trip to New England illustrates much of his concept of self and of the South on the eve of secession and war. His negative attitude during the return trip from New England was characteristic. He liked to travel but was always anxious to get home, even when he was not needed. Although fond of Fanny, he desired her at home, not as a traveling companion who would make plans he would rather have devised himself. Uneasy about trips in general, he preferred traveling alone, without the burden of dependents. He also liked water transportation better than railroads. Another problem for him could have been the Whipples' abolitionism. Dent did not mention it during the trip, but he had debated the subject with Fanny's relatives since 1856. In 1880, five years after this wife's death, he described Vermonters bluntly: "Politically they are one people. Radical in all their ideas they were the most fanatical abolitionists, and even in their own State Government a Radical policy prevails, extreme in all their notions—the result of their Puritanical sanctions."[140]

Even as the Whipples' abolitionism was not new, Dent's sense of the South's inferiority to the North had a history. Throughout the journey in 1858, he passed subtle judgment against southern crops, cattle, labor, hospitality, railroads, hotels, and food preparation. Nor was this simply the result of having a northern wife. His mother, Anne Dent, who was fond of northern vacations, was a long-time admirer of the Yankees. John had been reared on the concept she summarized in 1848: "when you see the difference in health and strength between Northern and Southern children it is enough to make one regret that one's lot was not cast in those much forward non-slave-holding states."[141]

Dent's respecting the Whipples and admiring their lifestyle may also have had its negative undertone of jealousy and resentment. One cannot say for sure. But in June, 1859, when he "Went to Eufaula with Mrs Dent to have her childrens Deguarreotypes taken to send to her Mother," he did not join the sitting, which included the children, their nurse, Amy, and Fanny Dent.

Still, this amiable family man did not court complete alienation from his wife's relatives. In May, 1860, some months after the generally divisive effects of John Brown's raid on Harper's Ferry, Dent lavished praise on things northern, in this case two Vermont horses that were selected especially for him by Fanny's brother. The southerner was delighted with their Yankee training.

> I am more pleased with my Morgan Horses the more I use them; in comparison with them, I never saw a Southern broke horse yet, they are like a Locomotive, you can travel them as slow or as fast as you please. They look as if they would tare every thing to pieces, and still as gentle and tractable as lambs—it shows how well broke and well managed they have been under their Yankee education and training; they can make their ten miles an hour, as easy as Prince can three; they are roadsters I tell you, and show blood every inch of them. Mrs Dents brother says they are the best blooded Morgans in Vermont and were selected for us with great care and trouble.[142]

Dent's old appreciation for northern efficiency and his affection for a Vermont wife of abolitionist background would combine with his conservative business interest to make him a reluctant Confederate, despite his roots in the state of John C. Calhoun and secession. From his complex, conservative stance as a slave-owning farmer-capitalist, Dent viewed both abolitionists and secessionists as revolutionaries, to be feared almost equally—but not quite.

6

REVOLUTION

In the 1850s and 1860s, while the slavery controversy, the sectional crisis, secession, war, and emancipation were transpiring, John Dent's responses to them were basically conservative.[1] He could sound Whiggish, but he was actually a South Carolina Democrat who declared on July 4, 1841, "Our Union is in danger, as at present political Zeal is under false and Speculative pretentions, Whighism of '41, Corrupt and deceptive." Yet the Democratic Dent, not a straightforward Jacksonian, harbored a mugwump's disdain for professional politicians and politics. He boasted in 1880 that he "never had any aspirations or ambition for a political or public life."[2] And while questioning religious extremism, he voiced a suspicion in March, 1858, that politicians were not even religious. "Great Revivals of Religion are going on in New York, Boston, Albany, Philadelphia, Charleston S. Ca., and Mobile, in fact all over the United States, except at Washington City."[3]

Despite his conservatism, he was also a southern-rights man. During 1854, the year of the explosive Kansas-Nebraska Act, Dent criticized southern politicians for their moderate response to the antislavery forces.[4] Two years later, he approved Alabama Democrats' abortive attempt to nominate Franklin Pierce for a second term as president. In March, 1856, when it appeared Pierce might not receive the nomination, Dent perceptively but narrowly attributed this to professional politicians who were after the corrupting spoils of office:

> The South endorses the course of President Pierce as sound, Constitutional, and patriotic—Fearless and honest, doing what a President should do, being governed by the Constitution of the United States. His party South, which is the Democratic party, gives him credit for such and shouts hozannas to the acts of Mr Pierce. But mark, with one voice they Exclaim, it won't do to re-elect such a Man President, another must be chosen, and why—because if Mr Pierce is re-elected he will retain in office men that are now in office. Such will not do. They are many of us wanting office, and the only chance for us is to turn the Constitutional and patriotic Mr Pierce out of Office. Elect Mr Buchanan or some other Man President, and the faithful wire workers will be rewarded. Such are the schemes of the Convention Men, who are loudest in the cry for Rights and the Constitution. Oh Shame where is thy blush, oh Politicians where is thy patriotism? Echo answers, thine own personal aggrandizement and not the good of thy country. Talk no more of Southern Rights or Constitutional measures; neither is aimed at, but office, office, as my portion of the spoils.[5]

Also in March, 1856, the planter blamed the Kansas imbroglio on opportunistic politicians. "There is a great commotion in the County among some persons, chiefly Politicians, aspirants and Office seekers about Kansas territory,'' Dent wrote.

> This commotion has been set on foot [in Barbour] by Major [Jefferson] B[uford] with the intention of carrying Men to Kansas as settlers in hopes of making the territory a Slave State. He goes by contributions so as to defray the expenses of his party as well as to settle them on homesteads in the territory. This move has been undertaken to counteract a similar movement in Massachusetts to make it a free state. As such, there is an effort South and North, on opposite motives, to make the State of Kansas Slave or Free. How it will result time alone will decide. Two such opposite elements meeting with opposite aims will apt to result in bitter strife and contentions which will create in the two sections of this union a bitter sectional animosity among at least the politicians.[6]

Fearing politicians' stupidity, Dent nevertheless aided Buford's cause. After all, Buford was a neighbor, and the business community would surely act to save the Union.

> The business Men North and South are steadily pursuing their business, paying but little attention to this [Kansas] strife. It is in the hands of Men whose business is politics, hence with such let the future be what it May they are answerable. But no doubt when they have brought matters to the exploding point, Business men of the country will have been aroused from their pursuits to a sense of the impending danger and by united actions and counsels [will] Quiet matters to a natural course, which destiny has marked out for our country. As such, the storm may arise and threaten to overwhelm us but means will be found to avert its fury.[7]

Dent's easy optimism of March, 1856, was shaken by the unsettling events of the next few months, such as the struggle for Kansas, the Sumner-Brooks incident, and the presidential candidacy of John C. Frémont, a "Black Republican" who opposed the extension of slavery into the territories. Largely in response to this last development, Dent wrote his wife's relative, Joseph Whipple, on July 17, 1856:

> Your letter I read with astonishment at your remarking that "no state dare leave this Union." Are you of the North our Masters that you speak thus? Has the South sunk to that degradation and Servility that she dare not exercise a freemans right? Nonsense, away with such folly and presumption on your part, for the South before long must Secede from a Union with the North, or give up all pretensions to honour and self respect. Why, it is as essential for her to do so as for a man of spirit to resist a robber or to quit the company of a set of blackguards. You but little understand the Southern Character if you think they will remain in a Union with a people who wish to treat them as inferiors. No Sir, we will quit the Union so soon as you elect a

Black Republican President, cost what it may in blood or treasure. You may attempt to overrun us and whip us back into a Union again, but when such is undertaken by the North, you will then find that you have made the separation more complete and permanent, the South a free and independent people. We have made many blunders, but the most fatal was in not disrupting this Union when John Adams was allowed to introduce his Abolition petitions in Congress and they were received and treated with respect. Such forbearance . . . [by] the South encouraged the North to the point she has reached in her present arrogance and usurpation. You are right in your opinions that the South has submitted so long She [apparently] will never resist. But sir, let me assure you those opinions must some day be changed when you see the South act and act as she should.[8]

Although he overreacted in this instance, Dent knew the firebrand secessionists' argument. He grew up in South Carolina; Barnwell Rhett, the so-called father of secession, was his brother-in-law. And Dent's Alabama friends included prominent southern-rights men of the Eufaula "Regency" like Lewis L. Cato, Edward C. Bullock, and Henry D. Clayton. As a staunch Democrat, Dent's mugwumpery and conservative business interests did not divert him toward the American or "Know Nothing" Party, which succeeded the defunct Whigs and ran Millard Fillmore for president in 1856. On August 15 of that year, Dent reported going "to Eufaula to witness a Fillmore Ratification Meeting. But not to participate as I am a Buchanan man."[9]

Despite his Democratic politics and the July outburst to Whipple, Dent actually preferred a calm approach to the sectional crisis over slavery. For example, in the privacy of the journal that same year, he was amazingly generous to Fredrika Bremer, the Swedish abolitionist whom he thought to be misled by the uninformed classes of northern society.[10] Also Dent's dispassionate reading of reopening the foreign slave trade sprang from what might be called conditional Unionism or financial concern or both. Whichever, his comment of June, 1859, was that of an upper-class conservative: "The African Slave trade is begining to interest the Citizens of the South and is becoming a political question. So far as public opinion is concerned there will be two large parties pro and Con. Those for the reopening of the trade will be in favor of a Dissolution of the Union; those against the reopening will become Union Men."[11] For Dent, the issue was not worth disunion.

Even more interesting along this line is the absence of any significant journal comment on John Brown's private revolution at Harper's Ferry, Virginia. Brown's frontal attack upon the southern "slaveocracy" occurred in October, 1859. His early capture, trial, conviction, and execution evoked strong emotional response from both sides of the Mason and Dixon Line. But Dent's only extant notice of these events was on December 16: "Green and Copeland hanged in Virginia as accomplices of John Brown."[12] Dent obviously chose silence in this instance. Surely his appreciations of a New England wife, a northern tutor, and respect for Yankee efficiency combined to show him the exceptional nature of John Brown's raid as well as the personal disadvantage of an emotional response. He coveted family harmony; the children's school was important; and his own Unionism persisted and even increased as national ties continued snapping one by one.

In a letter of August 28, 1860, during the presidential campaign in which southern Democrats for John C. Breckenridge had broken away from the national or northern Democratic Party of the compromising Stephen A. Douglas, Dent admitted to his son-in-law, Max Wellborn: "I think Breckinridge is daily loosing ground, and the fatal mistake with the Democratic party was in ever making war with Douglas, who was the *great breakwater between us and the Abolition tide.* He kept back its surges as no other man could and in losing him, onwards and rapid will be its flow upon us."[13] This letter also shows that Dent understood and accepted Senator Douglas' Freeport Doctrine, which admitted that squatter sovereignty could in practice nullify the Dred Scott Decision. Evidently for Dent, the "Abolition tide" meant Abraham Lincoln, the "Black Republican" candidate for president. For this southerner, Lincoln's political strength threatened slavery, money matters, and health. Dent's investments and digestive tract were both subject to nervous disorders.[14]

When Lincoln won the presidency in November, 1860, and South Carolina seceded, Dent's immediate concern was business stability: "Since the Secession Movements have been contemplated by the Southern States and South Carolina Seceded from the Union, Business matters are completely depressed and deranged. The Banks North and South, with few exceptions, have suspended specie payments. Cotton dull and little or none selling. Troubles and hard times are anticipated in every part of the once United States. And no man can predict what is to come to pass. Every person is absorbed in political matters and [has] left business to take care of itself."[15]

In these days, Dent was first a businessman, then a southern nationalist. Thus on January 1, 1861, he grieved over "troubles," "discord," and the "house divided" before advancing a dispirited justification for southern independence: "The South Secedes from the Union owing to Northern aggression and a determination to interfere with our Negro property. A Southern Confederacy is our only honorable and safe course."[16] While somber in private, this Douglas Democrat with a Yankee wife had to keep up appearances. Some influential Barbour countians were already celebrating Alabama's preparations to secede. The Lewis L. Catos were among these. The family was Eufaula "society"; he was a leader of the fire-eating Eufaula Regency. And on

January 3, Dent admitted, "Mrs D Liz and self went to Eufaula to a party given by Mr & Mrs Cato. Staid at night with Mrs [E.B.] Young." Amid sectional crisis, Fanny Dent the New Englander was socially acceptable.[17]

Yet no diversion relieved the sober events of that time, which Dent reported succinctly and without joy. On January 5, "Florida convention in session for Secession." Two days later, "Alabama holds her Convention to day." On February 2, "The Clayton & Pioneer Guards left for Montgomery to day." Two days later, "The Delegates of the Seceeding States are to meet in Convention at Montgomery Ala to day to form a Provisional Government." Even so Dent hoped for compromise, adding: "Delegates from the Federal United States are to meet in Washington City to try and adjust some measures to prevent other States from Seceding."[18]

By now, however, the drift apart was accelerating. On February 12, "The Eufaula Rifles started for Pensacola this afternoon." Here the Federal Fort Pickens was the object of interest. Sometime before February 25, Dent accepted the probability of armed conflict and predicted the place and cause of its initiation. He wrote his daughter, Minna Wellborn, in Lewisville, Arkansas, that

> Matters are at present in a very quiet state in this county as so many persons have left for Pensacola to await what may turn up under Lincolns administration, which seems to indicate war like measures. The dreadful conflict though must take place in Charleston harbor in the storming of fort Sumpter. If persistently retained by the United States Government [it is] as a menace to the people of that state, and a failure to recognize the Independence of this Confederacy. Early in March we shall know for certain what will take place.[19]

Also in this letter, the conservative Dent accepted southern "Independence" as a "settled fact." But he feared social revolution in the South and therefore welcomed "a most excellent choice made in our President, Genl Davis of Mississippi, who being a Statesman, Soldier, and Patriot will carry us through our difficulties if any man can." The last phrase is a revealing one. And Dent's approval of the Confederate constitution as a necessary "reconstruction and reunion" against radicalism was an acceptance of governmental centralization far to the right of Barnwell Rhett's opposition to the Davis regime.[20]

Dent manifested more Unionism in February, 1861, when he wrote Minna of his South Carolina family's response to the secession crisis. "Emma is now in Charleston," he sighed, "during Mr Rhetts absence to the Congress in Mongomery." Emma, his oldest sibling, was with Kate Rhett, assisting in nursing, as all the children have the Scarlet fever. Emma I think will be out this spring to see me, as she thinks of carrying back her monies to Carolina during the troubles, fearing Alabama debtors and stay laws. Sarah [Lining] is in Walterborough grieving over [her sons] Charlie and George's having had to resign their commissions in the U. S. Navy. Constance [Baring] is at Pon Pon [in Colleton], abusing the Secessionists for having destroyed, as she thinks, the finest Government on earth. Anne [Roper] I know but very little off... and George is the Captain of a fierce troop ready to charge so soon as an enemy invades the lower parts of Georgia. [21]

The ready approval of two sisters' Unionism is obvious. As described, brother George appears ridiculous, and Dent cared little for the Ropers. On the other hand, poor Kate Rhett, subject to her single-minded husband, was allowed in all charity to nurse children without regard to political opinions. Most important, however, sister Emma's views on Alabama economics were Dent's own. He literally bristled with hostility toward the Alabama stay law, which prevented his annual collection of "bills receivable" and interest. "Business dull... collections suspended" was a recurring complaint these months. Late in March, 1861, he explained much of his demoralization: "Money seems abundant, owing to the Banks suspending Specia payments. And [because] the Stay laws are in effect the tight times are for the future, as these injudicious laws make the people indifferent as to paying their debts and reckless in their money matters. Cotton brought a good price, and every man could have paid his debts if it had been required of him." [22]

Dent believed that stay laws exemplified the social revolution that secession was encouraging. Thus he loathed the ardent secessionist politician who owed him money and used the stay law to postpone payment. "John Cochran," Dent explained heatedly,

has taken advantage of the Stay Law on the Judgement we had in the Court of Chancery for the Peterson notes, notwithstanding the liberality we granted him. So that matter is laid over, unless he accepts of a proposition made, to turn over so much of his Cotton crop to be made this year.... And what is worse, the Stay law is most favourable to all such who have enlisted in Companies subject to be ordered in service, and Cochran has enrolled his name in the Eufaula Rifles, merely to take the benefit in full of the Stay law, and the Rifles are gone to Pensacola and Mr Cochran is basking around the flesh pots in Montgomery—*hound like*, awaiting the chances of a mouthful from the emptyings of the Scullions Swill barrel. When his attorney informed me of his course, I was so indignant, that I sat down and wrote him a very severe letter, which I am reproved for so doing by some of his friends, but his acts were so ungentlemanly and so dishonorable, I may say so rascally, I felt bound to notice them, as in part they were a breach of faith toward myself. Some intimate he will be bound to call me to an account for my letter; if he does I shall respond, for I done nothing more than what his acts justified my doing.[23]

Dent probably exaggerated his willingness to duel, but the frustrations of the 1860s might have led him to bend an earlier pledge against dueling, which he based on prior responsibility to his family. He believed he had nothing to fear from Cochran, but Dent was no less committed to his family's needs in war than in peace.[24]

Responsibility to family began with provisions, particularly foodstuffs. These were already scarce in Eufaula. In March, 1861, he wrote of the "Results of Drought of 1860," observing: "Provisions of all description are so scarce that most of the merchants in Eufaula have dispensed with dry goods and become dealers in provisions. A vast amount of Corn, Oats, Flour and Bacon has been imported. And the demand is active and steady and large. The provisions hauled out in the Country is immense. Every wagon goes out loaded down, and the supply is far from being sufficient."[25]

In this comment, Dent was not describing his own adequate supply. But on April 12, he "Suspended planting 35 acre cut until Monday, to determine whether I will plant it in Corn or Cotton." One week later, he "Went to Eufaula and bought 100 Bu Corn at $1.00." He explained, "I think I have enough to make out on. But fearing it may be a shrinking allowance [I] purchased to be sure of enough." Finally after studying the situation carefully, Dent concluded on April 28, "War must produce changes. As our Country is at War, we must plant more for provisions than for Cotton. As such, I am going to X [out] more cottons and put it in Corn." War, however, does not alter everything, and Dent continued complaining, "Plows in . . . corn getting along slowly; hands seem Sulky. Overseer incompetent." His exaggerations notwithstanding, these laborers in 1861 produced 4,800 bushels of corn and 103 bales of cotton.[26]

Family responsibility might begin with provisions, crops, and profits, but there were other concerns, and each was complicated by war. When the Confederates opened fire against Fort Sumter on the morning of April 12, Dent acted that same day to bring his son, Horry, home from the apprenticeship in Philadelphia: "Went to Eufaula to day and made arrangements with [the banker] Mr [John] McNab to send on $50 to Horry to come home with, as the Charleston Batteries have opened on Fort Sumpter, War." While anxiously awaiting news from Horry, the father finally made visible sign of supporting the Confederacy: "Went to Eufaula and took Five thousand dollars of the Confederate loan to assist our Confederacy in maintaining its Independence."[27]

By April 22 Dent was understandably worried, because "The people of the north are exasperated at the news of the Surrender of fort Sumpter and are volunteering by thousands to subjugate the South; a bloody war may be anticipated. Horry has been sent for on 12th to return and has not arrived or been heard from. I feel some what uneasy about him, apprehensive he may have fallen into the hands of an exasperated mob, and... unable to get a dispatch through by telegraph owing to all communications being stopped by Lincoln at Washington City between the North and the South.'' Two days after expressing this concern, Dent sighed with relief that "Horry Reached home on yesterday.''[28]

Meanwhile, other family plans proceeded apace, in spite of impending war. One of these was Lizzie's marriage to Whitfield Clark. On April 26, "Mrs Dent and Liz and Self went to Eufaula to day to shop for the 2d May.'' A few days later, "Kliffmuller came out to fix up and tune the old piano. Horry sent to town with orders to buy Negro cloths, rice, potatoes, hoes &c. Sent John to buy a Mutton and Kid.''[29]

Sectional crisis might not hinder a wedding, but it temporarily disrupted the plantation school. It was June 1 when Dent "Went to Eufaula this morning with Mrs Dent, to arrange some business for Miss Lynde,'' the teacher. On the following day, a Sunday, "Miss Martha Lynde left this morning for Wilmington, Illinois, owing to the War existing between the North and the South which has left our Children without a School.''[30] But the resourceful Dent was not easily thwarted, and he seems to have replaced Lynde rather quickly. By 1864 the family was pleased to have regained the services of the same Elizabeth Gilbert of South Carolina who had taught the Dent children in the 1840s. At the war's end, a local person, Eliza Sternes, was tutoring on the plantation.[31]

In June, 1861, however, educational inconveniences were trivial compared to the family's anxiety about Horry's imminent departure. On June 6, when Dent "Went to Eufaula to day to see the Barbour Greys start for Virginia,'' he was reminded of the inevitable separation, which occurred June 12: "Horry Dent [has been] Ordered by Secty [Stephen R.] Mallory to report at New Orleans to Captn Rosseau for duty on board steamer MacRea as 3d assistant Engineer C. S. Navy. [He] Started off today from Eufaula for New Orleans.'' On July 3, it was a proud and emotional father who "Went to Eufaula and sent my Navy revolver by Hardens Express to Horry at New Orleans La.''[32] Horry fulfilled his father's life-long fantasy of a sea-going career. Yet Dent feared for the son's safety running the blockade or whatever else his duties might bring as he served on the *McRea, Charleston, Chattahoochee, Juno,* and *Coquette.*

On August 22, 1861, the older Dent wrote anxiously: "Having not heard from Horry for some time, I expect his ship has gone to Sea, if not captured in the attempt. So God only knows when we shall hear from him again. I hope they will make a lucky cruise and in time return safely back to their homes, although it is a hazardous and dangerous expedition they have gone on." Despite capture, imprisonment, exchange, shipwreck, and battles, Horry survived until July, 1864, when he died of yellow fever on board the *Coquette* near Smithville, North Carolina. [33]

Meanwhile in July, 1861, Dent's second son, the sixteen-year-old Herbert, was sent to preparatory school in Tuscaloosa, where he remained for several months. Shortly, however, "Private J. Herbert Dent" joined the "Eufaula Light Artillery" and saw three full years of hard fighting. Herbert survived the war, settled in Clayton, Alabama, and married Anna Virginia Petty. Yet we know little of this son, mainly because the father's heart belonged to the "loving and gentle" Horry. [34] In 1861, with all sons alive and well, Dent was busy planting, building county bridges, nursing the sick, securing a tutor, visiting friends, and writing observations on the large comet of July, 1861. In September he even inspected the Mississippi Delta for a possible relocation, which did not occur. The "seasons" that year were unusually wet, but the corn produced seventeen bushels per acre, for a good crop. [35]

Now provisions were more certain, but Dent could still grieve, for the Union if nothing else. This emotion was implicit in his ambiguous essay on Independence Day, 1861: "This 4th of July, the Natal day of the American Union of 1776," he wrote,

> finds this once Memorable day with the Union dissolved and a War wageing between the Northern and Southern States of America. Two Governments destruct. Thus has ended the Works of our Patriotic fathers of 1776 . . . destroyed by the fanaticism, avariciousness, and aggressions of the Northern States, which violated the Constitution and all compacts existing, in trying to make the Southern States their dependents and inferiors. And as the South could not maintain her Equality in the Union she sets up for Independence out of it. That independence is now being contended for by our brave people at any and every cost and Sacrafice. The Union of 1776 was dear to every Southern man, but the Union of 1850 to 1860 became hateful, as it was used only to oppress and disgrace us. Hence in 1861 Eleven States withdrew from such a Union and proclaimed to the world their Independence.

This idealization of the American Revolution and use of it to justify secession smacks of William Gilmore Simms, the South Carolina novelist and low-country planter. [36]

A scant four days later, as Confederate armies of the "best blood of the South" gathered in Virginia to "meet the rapscallions of the North," Dent rationalized: "Honour and manhood requires that we should meet the odds against us and rely on Providence for our success. If we are conquered, serfdom is our doom, for the North wars to subjugate us and make us her vassals. Hence fight we must at all cost and sacrafices. Defeat would be our ruin."[37]

Despite the threat of vassalage, however, Dent articulated enough reservations about this war to evoke a cry of disloyalty from his devoted daughter Minna. Against this charge, his defense was a shallow use of secessionist rhetoric; it was August, 1861, when he answered her:

> Yours of the 1st came duly to hand. And why you should allege such a charge against me, as you do, I cannot divine. You say, "I expect we would quarrel if we were to meet, Your sympathies seeming to be so much with the North." Such is certainly a grave charge. And my defense is, Can you revert to one word or line in any of my letters to that effect, since the Secession of South Carolina? Before the South Seceded or acted in her defence, I did admire the North, and why—because she had shown her superio[ri]ty at the expense of Southern Submission and degradation. But since the South has acted, Seceded, and declared her Independence, I now appreciate, honor, and love her for assuming a position in character with her former renown.[38]

The response is not convincing. His dominant concern was economic stability. He was at best a doubting Confederate. In the autobiography of 1880, he would recall the prescience of his pessimism: "Whilst at Carrollton [Mississippi, in September, 1861] I remarked that if the War continued long, there was a probability of the Yankees coming to this Country as well as to Alabama and Georgia. The people seemed amazed at my saying so and said 'that no Yankee Soldiers would ever pass South ward of Tennessee and Virginia.' Alas for our prophesying."[39]

Already by July, 1861, Dent was pondering the Union blockade, forseeing that "Coffee, Salt, Bagging, Rope, Tea and many other articles will be cut off." Studying battles, he saw gore, not glory. On July 22, 1861, he "Received telegrams of the great Battle fought at Manasas Va. Between the Confederates and Fedrals" and perceived "terrible slaughter on both sides." Later in December he empathized: "How many Widdows and orphans and broken up establishments has this war brought about? See what destruction and ruin has taken place at the seat of war in Virginia. To us, who have not witnessed it, it is incomprehensible." Whatever his neighbors were thinking, Dent could imagine the horror and wonder where it would stop.[40]

By November, 1861, he believed "Business Matters" were ruined: "The war has suspended business. Trade is confined only to necessities and economy is the order of the day. Markets: Salt from $10 to 12 pr sack. Bacon 28¢. Bagging 30¢. Rope 28¢. Coffee none. Rice 6¢. Shot & powder none. Cotton 5¢." It was "Hardtimes" already because "The country is destitute of clothing, meat, Coffee and but little Salt. Suffering will be inevitable for a time to come.... Heaven knows what I am to do for Negro clothing and meat this year, all having been bought up for the Army."[41] Dent exaggerated, of course, and provided much better than this passage would indicate.

Yet his pessimism increased. In December, he as much as admitted that the Confederacy was lost. He believed that without a navy there was no way to raise the blockade or dislodge the Federals from Port Royal, South Carolina. England was more apt to aid the Union than the Confederacy. Cotton would never again be so profitable as it had, and slavery was doomed, even if the Confederacy survived, which seemed very unlikely.[42]

The letter to Max Wellborn that bore these admissions also showed Dent valuing family and socioeconomic stability over southern independence. In fact, one's family and business should take precedence over the Confederate army. Dent criticized a son-in-law to a son-in-law: "Whit Clark is in command of a horse company, and will leave shortly for the coast. Liz writes heart broken. I think it was an uncalled for and precipitate step in Whits volunteering and a complete sacrafice for all his business." At this point, Dent was hoping to invest his $5,000 of Confederate Bonds in cheap western lands. In the same context, he imagined wartime developments that would "bring about a revolution in the affairs of all mankind and governments. Changes which no man as yet can predict will take place, and wrought changes in commerce, agriculture and politics—everywhere." He expected "much losses and distress broadcast" because: "I have always said from the beginning we had more to fear from some [of] our own people than from the people of the North."[43]

In January, 1862, he identified "our own people" whom he feared:

> There is a general disposition with most persons not to pay their debts, not from the want of means, But owing to the Stay laws. The Stay laws passed by our Legislature will in the end bring about more losses and troubles than the War will have done.... The Stay law has been inaugurated by our Legislators, not so much as a matter of necessity, as an act of popularity with ... a certain class of people, whose votes are secured by such legislation. The result will be the injury of a large class of worthy and enterprising men for the sake of a worthless and unprincipled set whose only sense of rectitude was through the fear of the law. There is no doubt but such laws are unconstitutional, as unjust, and will create more distrust and losses than a ten years war with Yankeedom.[44]

Despite his protest, however, Dent eventually invested a total of $44,000 in Confederate and state bonds. He also served two years on the unpopular conscription board.[45] Now as a frustrated financier and cotton producer, his only intellectual solace was yeoman agrarianism. It was this idealism that led him to exaggerate the importance of crops to the South's war effort. "Our [crop] loss," he insisted, "is more to be dreaded, As our Country is at War for her Independence, and the loss of a provision crop will effect her more than all the Armies of the North combined against her."[46]

Another comforting ideal was the agrarian panacea of self-sufficiency. On November 15, 1861, he outlined the one positive effect of the terrible revolution:

As our Ports are blockaded by the Enemy and Exports and Imports cut off leaving the whole Country in a scarce and deplorable condition as to supplies of every kind, The Planters must resort to home productions. . . . Heretofore, we have planted Cotton to purchase all our necessaries and supplies. Hence in the way of clothing, meats, comforts and luxuries, our dependence has been on the North and Northwest. The War has now put an end to all such, and we trust forever, in order necessity may now make us a self reliant people, and plant and make what we need for our own use and benefit.[47]

Shortly he would report his family's contribution to the "reformation" of the South:

I am now writeing by a candle of our own moulding, and I have made a loom, spinning wheels &c to embark at once in domestic manfacturers. The Socks I daily ware is of Mrs Dents knitting, and she says she will not stop until we are clothed in part out of our looms. Such is the right spirit; reformation was needed, for before the war we had become an indecent arrogant people, who were living off vanity and reckless extravagance. Our daughters now must go to the looms instead of piano forts and our young men instead of fast clerks to something more useful and practical. With this great evil, a large amount of good must also come from this war. Even Annie and Sallie have knit their own stockings for their winter use.[48]

It was a proud and somewhat hysterical man who could theorize that simple agrarian self-sufficiency would offset his losses from stay laws, the blockade, and a Union victory. He was simply whistling against the gathering dusk of defeat and ruin, nothing more. Furthermore, he almost acknowledged the catastrophic possibility that slavery could be abolished. Why else would he have considered placing his family on a small Tennessee farm separate from his large slave force? As early as August, 1861, he pondered the possibility of escaping history by means of yeoman agrarianism. The farm, as he called it, was no new dream. But the urgency for it was new. Dent explained: "If I can possibly get a fine plantation in Mississippi, convenient to some Rail Road, I will then buy me a small farm in Tennessee, and try at least to carry out what has so long been floating in my mind's eye. I hope I may succeed now as it is [a] matter that has become absolutely necessary for my crops here are not what 20 hands should make."[49]

Despite the reference to crops, Dent's more basic need was hope for survival in the event of the ultimate social revolution of emancipation. That hope was the yeoman's self-sufficient farm, separated, one assumes, from the black presence. Nor was Dent completely conscious of his despair for the Confederacy and slavery. In February, 1862, he ruminated on Union advances at Roanoke Island, North Carolina; Nashville and Ft. Henry, Tennessee; and Florence, Alabama, all the while telling himself, "our recent defeats" are "more beneficial than disastrous to our cause."[50]

More revealing of Dent's true mental state than false optimism was his strident abuse of speculator-traitors and Jews. In mid-February he raged in the journal: "Our worst enemies are a set of Unionists and Speculators among us that are numerous and doing vast injury to our cause and people. A sound discreet policy," he believed, "would be to imprison or hang the Union traitors and restrict the Speculators by severe penal laws. Such an Enemy at home and so formidable an enemy in the Yankee Armies must try the endurance and courage of our true men to the fullest extent. All people though, who have had to contend and fight for their liberties, have had that ingrate race to deal with; hence it should not discourage us in the least."[51]

That "ingrate race" reflected some anti-Semitism, another aspect of Dent's disgruntlement. In August, 1861, he had written to Minna that her sister "Liz spent the last two days with us; she came down on a shopping expedition, the stores in Clayton being empty. The Jews in Eufaula though smuggle in goods and supplies. I would not be surprised if many of them were not acting as agents for Yankees, but it is no matter as they will cheat them out of every cent they are entrusted with."[52]

Dent's epithet of speculator-traitor, however, included more than Jews. In December, 1861, he confided to Max Wellborn that the "Patriotism of some our most shineing lights seems to be embodied in Self. See Editorial of Spirit of South of Dec. 3d," Dent advised, "where 'some' are strongly suspected of being in alliance with Yankees and shipping Cotton North. Who are the parties, I have not yet learned, but it would not surprise me to hear Y[oung?] W[hipple?] & G[erke?] was . . . implicated. If so it is a large company engaged in it. . . . The severest punishment should be inflicted upon them. Corrupt men South are not few nor wanting, men who are more depraved than the meanest of Yankees. I often think to myself what is to become of the country?"[53]

Thus, Dent feared more than lower-class whites and free blacks. He also distrusted the successful business element of so-called Jewish and Gentile traitors. We can, of course, mark some of this down to the jealousy of a competitive businessman. There was also an element of scapegoating: the Confederacy was losing. Since Dent sold seventy-one bales of cotton in 1862 for sixteen cents per pound, perhaps he doubted his own loyalty and was covering himself with an outlandish attack on Semites and other business associates. [54]

There was also a relation between Dent's resurgent agrarianism and his growing distrust of speculators. Another piece of the puzzle that fits here was his need to believe that the war had obliterated his "fortune." In 1880 Dent recalled that only the most "long headed financiers" survived the economic catastrophe. The implication was that he had not, but of course he had, having weathered the war with at least $20,000 in assets, and probably twice that amount. [55] This relative prosperity required some rationalizing, and his self-image as a yeoman agrarian did nicely. Meanwhile, he was trying to collect on accounts whenever possible. In the same letter that attacked speculator-traitor "friends," Dent admitted: "I have too much to see after in January and February in my pecuniary affairs, not to be on the spot. Our pecuniary matters in Alabama are already unhinged by Legislative intervention, hence we must make the best arrangements with our Debtors possible, based on Honor and conscience." Some debts were paid, and these collections contributed to his solvency at the war's end. [56]

After February, 1862, Dent avoided comment on the Confederacy and War—or he removed it from the journals: there are numerous missing pages for the years from 1862 through 1865. The extant entries are irregular and sketchy, reflecting shortages of ink, paper, and hope. Numerous agricultural records are covered with paste and irrelevant clippings, reminiscent of the pessimistic journal of 1851-1854. Yet for all of Dent's self-conscious silence, we know that his vision of events was tragic, for on June 20, 1864, he allowed: "Black Roll...from Alpha to Omega. Battles, Murder & desolation the order of the day. Heaven and Earth seems Convulsed." [57]

Dent's caustic comment on the fall of Mobile somehow found its way into the 1858 journal. When Mobile Bay fell to Admiral D. G. Farragut in August, 1864, Dent attributed it to a lack of "resolution or courage" among the defenders of Forts Morgan and Gaines. The failings that he described, however, were more applicable to himself than to the Confederates on Mobile Bay. Dent had appealed all the way to Governor Thomas H. Watts in a futile attempt to keep the army from impressing his slaves for the defense of Mobile. Now, Dent preferred to identify with his native "Charleston and its defenders" where "resolution is stronger than ramparts" because "Charlestonians resolved never to give up their forts." When Charleston fell in 1865, the earlier comment became as meaningless as his readiness to admit of local crops, "Starvation in prospectus." [58]

For the Dent family in southeastern Alabama, hunger was never a threat. During the Civil War, John fed his immediate family and Negroes with ease, and he provisioned several members of his extended family and their slaves. Even then, there were enough foodstuffs for taxes in kind, for army impressment, and even for sale to neighbors who needed it and could afford to pay. Expecting to be reimbursed, Dent also issued some rations to indigents.[59] His business concerns had always included provisions. But now, with the stay laws disrupting moneylending, and with the sale of cotton so uncertain, not to mention family and community demands for food—the production of provisions was even more important than previously. After 1862 Dent's business, his family's needs, and patriotic interests converged in food production. In this activity, he was a loyal Confederate, a practical businessman, a responsible family man, and a doctrinaire agrarian who rather enjoyed the necessity of dramatizing self-sufficiency.

The plantation required more than foodstuffs, but those were the major concern. And the wartime prices, which Dent carefully recorded, indicate the scarcity of goods and the depreciation of Confederate currency. On November 1, 1862, he wrote: "Salt $150.00 a Sack. Bacon 60 cts per pound. Will have to send to Virginia for Salt. Shoes $12.00 a pair.... Cotton factory [cards] $13 pr bunch. Whiskey $12 per gallon." A sack of salt was rather large, because on November 8 Dent bought "8 Bushels Salt from the Coast companies for $180.00, equal to $22.50 pr Bushel."[60]

His price list of November, 1864, was more inclusive and inflated:

Sugar pr pound $5 to $12
Molasses pr gallon $6 to $8
Flour pr Barrel $90 to $120
Wheat pr Bushel $20 to $20
Potatoes pr Bu $5 to $8
Corn pr Bu $7 to $10
Chickens a piece $3.50 to $5
Turkeys   ''   '' $10 to $12 to $20
Ducks   ''   '' $6 to $10
Salt pr Barrel $75
Tobacco pr pound $5 to $8 to $10

At this listing, Dent believed that "The Scarcity of Articles and redundancy of the currency produces such prices and the tendency is upwards, in a short time 100 pr cent added."[61]

The omission of bacon from the 1864 list supports general indications that Dent produced a sufficiency of pork during the Civil War. While not all years' hog lists survive, the tables for 1862 reveal fifty-five head slaughtered, leaving sixty-seven stock hogs, which by 1863 had produced eighty-seven pigs "living." Dent's herd also survived two epidemics of cholera. In the record of July, 1863, he lost 37 of 156 head to this disease.[62] The weight of hogs slaughtered is not known. But by 1842 his hogs averaged about 150 pounds, and he tried to fatten wartime pigs. In July, 1861, he wrote, "Having Cotton seed put into a branch for the hogs to eat. Seem to thrive on them very well. Notice that a Mississippi Planter boils his Cotton Seed and feeds out which he says are as good as corn, and raises all his hogs that way."[63] Choking the hogs was a danger, and Dent's gin must have done for that time an unusually good job of cleaning seeds.

Because corn was dear and cotton was of uncertain value, Dent fed his cottonseed, conserved his corn, and borrowed the little seed he needed for a small cotton crop each year. The major drawback of this practice was the disuse of cottonseed for fertilizing the soil. Thus, in spite of his rigorous supervision of the planting routine, the corn yield per acre steadily declined during the war. There was no other significant variable to explain lower yields than declining soil fertility and, perhaps, inferior seed. The weather was rather constant. Labor and livestock forces were stable. Few slaves fled or were impressed, and Dent was careful to breed for enough horses and mules. He also continued to undercrop, with thirty-five acres per mule and fifteen per hand. He still preferred inexperienced overseers whom he could publicly boss and privately lambaste. Yet with these constants and the extra precaution of two separate plantings of corn each year, the yield per acre declined about 50 percent from 1861 to 1865. Dent maintained his yield of 3,000 to 4,000 bushels per year by doubling corn acreage.[64]

With the persons and beasts of Bleak House consuming about 2,800 bushels of corn each year, Dent's surplus was a saleable commodity and a welcomed currency. With corn he could buy newspapers, provisions, medical services, and even hire a tutor. His price for corn varied from one to three dollars per bushel, depending on the person and location. Locally he usually charged neighbors one dollar to a dollar and a half per bushel, probably in specie, and near the war's end he charged his financially embarrassed brother-in-law, R. B. Rhett, three dollars a bushel for corn shipped to South Carolina.[65]

As one would expect, Dent was quite concerned with foodstuffs other than pork and corn. For fresh meats, his plantation provided beef, poultry, and mutton. While poultry disease presented some problems, especially among turkeys, he had enough cattle to kill beef several times each year, whenever fresh meat was needed on the plantation or for donation to a "Barbecue at Eufaula." At the end of the war, he sold twenty-two head of cattle and valued his herd at four thousand dollars. To assure vegetable gardens in spite of the "non intercourse with the North," Dent saved "large quantities of Seeds" such as "Cabbages, Peas, Beans, Squashes," and the like. Again the self-sufficient agrarian, he believed his seeds "look if any thing finer than what Northern Seeds we are in the habit of getting." Yet he withheld comment on their relative productivity.[66]

And probably more important than garden vegetables were the additional acres in prewar staples such as yams, rice, wheat, and field peas. In 1864 Dent had 370 acres of corn land "sowed down" in peas. Aside from these traditional standbys, there was new wartime emphasis on ground peas for bulk and on sorghum, sugar cane, and watermelons for sweetening. Fanny Dent saw that the corn and wheat were ground on schedule. She also ran her own syrup mill and supervised the butchering and distribution of fresh beef. Tobacco was an item on Dent's price list, but coffee was not. Salt, as noted above, was a major problem late in the war. But if Dent could not buy salt, he could always borrow as much as 181 pounds from "McNab."[67]

Fabrics and clothing were also necessary. Dent continued to plant a cotton crop which from 1862 through 1865 averaged less than a hundred acres per year. The yield is unknown, but in this crop he possessed the raw staple for making some cloth. Although cotton cards were an "Extortion," he "Paid this day, 14 Sept 1863, $32 for a common pair Cotton cards, home made, and $77 for a bunch No 6 Cotton Cards."[68] Still the plantation probably bought more cloth than it manufactured. The price list of November 18, 1864 (in inflated Confederate currency), indicates that the Dents' wartime clothing was homemade from purchased materials:

Homemade Yarn pr yard $25
Homespun pr yard $5 to $8
Long cloth pr yard $5 to $8
Cloaks from $1500 to $2500
Common wool hats $40
Common shoes, Brogans $50
Fine shoes $75 to $100
Boots $250 to $300
Fine cloth pr yard $100 to $150

While this particular list concluded with "Man Wants but little here below," shoes *were* a special problem. Thus in September, 1864, Dent "Sent [Negro] Jack up to Clayton to work in Whit Clark's Shoe Shop, for the purpose of learning to make Shoes." The product must have been the rough common ones called brogans.[69]

Dealing in Confederate currency and specie, Dent provided goods and services for the general welfare. In addition to selling much corn for human consumption, he did a sizeable business in fodder. At three dollars per hundred pounds, he had no difficulty selling all of his surplus livestock feed. And during the war, he constructed for the county commissioners at least two major bridges on the Clayton-Eufaula road, receiving the contracts to maintain them as well. Dent's two-year tenure in the unpopular conscription bureau helped to prove his loyalty but was probably tedious, despite his having two sons in the Confederate military and his general indifference to public opinion, especially that of the "lower classes." Furthermore, Bleak House was open to at least one civilian refugee who was not a member of the family. And more than one Confederate soldier on furlough made this place his location for rest and recovery. When Dent provided sanctuary, he filed for reimbursement. [70]

Yet with all this activity, his primary concern remained business and family, that is, the plantation. Here, everyone was fed and clothed. A school of sorts was maintained for the children. And the father regretted the lack of entertainment and pleasures, especially for the "small fry." In 1864 he reported, "Christmas Sad & gloomy. Our once merry and prosperous days have past. War! with all its heroes, troubles, and sorrows has overtaken our land, and left its traces broad cast." By now Horry was dead; but there were others who deserved, and received, a "father's part." [71]

Until his death in July, 1864, Horry, like his father, did much to alleviate the family's discomforts and inconveniences. While at home on furlough in 1863, the oldest son fell naturally into his old role of responsibility on the plantation. Back on active duty, after experiencing the family's shortages, he sent treasures from the outside world whenever possible. These gifts occasioned some of the brightest spots in the father's wartime comment, and when he feared that Horry's "box" had gone astray, it was a "Heavy Loss," indeed. On May 24, 1864, "Horry sent me two boxes from Nassau containing Cotton Cards, Calicos, muslins, Hats, Shoes, thread &c. All lost by Express." But Dent was mistaken. A few days later, he rejoiced, "Boxes sent by Horry; one received on 24th May and the other on 29th, the last from Mr Eason of Charleston." The first box contained "5 pr Cotton Cards, 4 Bots Brandy, cloth...and several other articles." About a month later, Dent also "Received by express from Horry one Box Containing 8 yds Grey Cloth, 1 pr Shoes for Sally, 6 Bottles Whiskey." Even after Horry's death, the father received "2 boxes from Wilmington," in addition to his son's valise, trunk, and port money. [72]

Horry's gifts relieved needs and symbolized the family's interdependence and its members' commitment to one another. No sooner did Dent provide for his immediate family and Negroes than he began sending wagonloads of corn to Lizzie Clark in Clayton. He also assisted South Carolina relatives, especially during the war's last stages. Dent's beloved Emma, the unmarried sister, was living with his family by early 1865. In September, 1864, John was also assisting or encouraging Annie Dent Roper by sending her "Some dark Calico light muslins, 1 black felt hat, 1 boys light felt hat, 1 blue belt, 2 Small pocket knives." Three weeks later he "Sent to Annie Roper by Express two knives, 1 belt, bunch Shoe Strings." The items do not seem particularly significant, but while the journal for this period is too sketchy for one to infer the precise meaning of assisting the Ropers, Dent's role of provisioning the Barnwell Rhetts is clearer.[73]

In August, 1864, he shipped 586 bushels of corn to the Rhetts in Charleston. Pehaps sister Emma was with Kate Rhett at the time. The corn was priced $3.15 per bushel, making the bill almost $2,000, apparently in specie. But six months later, as General William Tecumseh Sherman moved from Savannah into Carolina, Dent wrote with misleading simplicity, "Mr Rhetts negroes reached here." It was February 4, 1865, that Dent assumed responsibility for feeding Rhett's blacks on a corn dole from his own cribs. The following June he tallied another "300 Bushels Corn Sold to R B. Rhett." This time no price was mentioned, probably because the second contract was "purchased and paid for in Confederate Bills."[74]

By April, 1865, the defeated Rhett had settled in or near Eufaula. Here he depended on Dent for corn, fodder, and various services. On April 23, the Alabamian noted resentfully, "Sent Bourbon to Mr Rhett by his orders." While no love was lost between these two, the "father of secession" was still a member of the family. It is possible the Rhetts stayed with the Dents temporarily before settling in Eufaula; the story is not clear. Once in Eufaula, however, the Rhetts had Emma with them for a while, because in July, 1865, Dent "Sent cart to town carrying box, gun and sword of Mr Rhetts and to bring back Emmas things from Mr Rhetts house. Herbert went . . . in Buggie to bring Emma back." Some of the Rhett Negroes remained at Bleak House until August 15, when the last of them left for Henry County, Alabama.[75]

In the meantime, the war was ending, and Dent was more than willing to assist the Lining refugees from Colleton District, South Carolina. "Dr Thomas Lining . . . and his Son John reached my house on 3d May from the C. S. Army in South Carolina." Dent's sister, Sarah Lining, and some of her children had already arrived at Bleak House. The modest farm residence in Barbour must have bulged at the seams, but Dent had always admired Lining and his profession. Thus he welcomed the family and wrote approvingly of the able physician's professional visits around the community. Lining's local income and his services on Dent's plantation would indicate less dependence than the Rhetts had imposed. And in August, the doctor returned to Colleton District to prepare for removing his family home.[76] The full extent of Dent's provisioning for South Carolina relations is not known, but he assisted at least four of his six brothers and sisters.

The United States' military victory over the Confederacy in April, 1865, convinced Dent that his worst fears of social revolution among whites and blacks had come to pass. Yet one can hardly accept the journals' indication that he completely repressed these fears from March, 1862, until April 29, 1865, when "4500 Yankees (army) under Genl .[B. H.] Grierson entered Eufaula . . . on raid from Mobile."[77] Legend has it that during this nondestructive raid, Grierson and Colonel Whitfield Clark had an interesting encounter in Clayton, but Dent did not confirm it. Instead, the Bleak House planter was concerned with Grierson's unsettling effect on blacks and lower-class whites. For example, on May 3, "Joe and Amos Ran away and went to the Yankees." And on May 4, the same day that "Grierson and his army left Eufaula for Montgomery," Jack and Clem also "ran away and went to the Yankees."[78]

While Dent actually lost few blacks during the summer of 1865, the running away was not yet over. On May 16, "Sophy went off to the Yankees." Three days later, "Brett, Tamlin, Alex [and] Scipio ran off this morning with the Yankee." But Dent was still the slave master, and with a vengeance. Now, he promptly "Sent for Jim Cunningham and his dogs to run them." Although the chase was to no avail, Union soldiers soon did Dent's work for him. On May 20, "Brett, Tamlin, and Alex returned. They went to the Yankees who gave them a good whipping and sent them back." Sophy returned on the same date, but no explanation was given in her case.[79]

Local law officers also acted as retrievers, even as they had before emancipation. One case of this, however, revealed the growing importance of the black family, which Dent was forced to acknowledge, seemingly for the first time. Here, he explained with less defensiveness than he would soon manifest toward the black family: "Toby left on [June] 19th, was taken up by the Marshall in Eufaula and imprisoned. Released today for $9 by his fathers request."[80] Apparently Dent paid the fine, and Toby came "home" to an antebellum status quo, at least for a little while longer.

In this context it was significant that Dent did not lament the demoralization of freedmen until July 6, two full months after the Grierson sweep through Barbour, which symbolized the demise of slavery. The journal's several accounts of blacks who quit the plantation after May, 1865, are conflicting ones. But the total number did not exceed twelve, and at least four of these soon returned, ingratiating themselves with Dent. For example on August 16: "Jack and Sam that went off with the Grierson raiders returned home last night from Montgomery. Both looking ill and used up. They ask pardon and promise to do better, saying they had their fill of the Yankees." This master experienced no immediate depletion of labor. In fact the bulk of his 137 "former" slaves continued on the plantation until December, 1865.[81]

If Dent articulated no concern over free-black behavior until July 6,

Grierson had barely departed in May when the planter took occasion to excoriate whites of the lower classes. In a journal essay, "The State of the Country," he insisted: "The lower classes are lawless. They are going round in mobs, breaking into Barns and taking corn. Their [f]ury and hatred to the rich is let loose, and their only object now is to show it by lawless violence. Nothing can satisfy them; the more you share out to them, the more they want and will have. In short, they who have bread or property are at the mercy of the mob. Never was a country so demoralized as this is, and such men when with [the] army swelled the list of deserters." As the conservative he was, Dent concluded: "Were it not for the Yankee troops in the country to keep down these wretches, anarchy would prevail." [82]

One would think the frightened Dent was in Jacobin France. But the fear was genuine, even if his reading of the facts was exaggerated. The important thing, however, is that his first postwar phobia was of unfortunate whites. Mindful of Negro theft in July, he admitted, "A large amount of corn is being stolen from out of the fields by the negroes and poorer class of whites." He also believed that whites incited blacks to steal. [83]

Within a year of Grierson's appearance in Barbour, however, an important shift had occurred in Dent's conception of the races and of their relative merits. In this later period, his memory of blacks' initial response to emancipation was exaggerated on the side of harshness. In May, 1866, he recalled:

> The freedom of the Negroes with us in this section begun with Griersons arrival. Thousands deserted the plantations and joined the Yankees.... Those that remained on the plantations, at least ¾ths of them, became disobedient, insolent and idle at once from disciplined, obedient, and faithful workers. They done but little work, and went and came as they pleased. Every thing was in confusion, and we had to complete the cultivation of the crop the best way we could. Some Negroes behaved admirably to their late owners, but ¾ths were wild and reckless with the idea of their freedom. [84]

Yet the detailed journal for mid-1865 shows no significant criticism of black laborers until July 6, two months after Grierson's departure. Even then, Dent was uncharacteristically vague when he observed: "Since the Negroes have been proclaimed free by the President of the United States, their demoralization is complete ... indifference and Idleness is their course. Obedience, contentment, and industry they have discarded; no longer do they exhibit their former cheerfulness and satisfied condition. But they are restless, easily excited, and go and come when they please." [85]

In this new theme of the happy, contented slave, Dent's concern for freedmen's welfare was already oblique and racist. "Their future will be want, misery and wretchedness with the larger number of them. [With] no one to care for them, guide and protect them, they will meet with ill treatment, rowdiness and many wrongs from the whites. Time will show in this great experiment whether as Slaves or Freedmen they were best off. Without being properly controlled, managed, directed and constantly employed, they will fast run into ruins, vagabondism and every species of vice." [86]

The comment of July, 1865, is the more ambiguous because it was the lay-by season of dead summer, when hands traditionally rested for the harvest. The comment is further undercut by Dent's failure to criticize the plowing and hoeing that preceded lay-by. There is also the large question of freedmen's incentive to work when there was no mention of wages or contracts or verbal agreements. One can only conjecture that Dent promised the blacks their usual provisions of food, clothing, shelter, and medical attention in return for completing the crop which was well begun before the laborers fully realized their free status. In fact the most revealing item in this July complaint was Dent's resentment of freedmen's right to travel and complain. There is also the barest suggestion of anxiety against the day of their departure.

Lest the Negroes appear too unselfish, however, it is well to remember that in these unstable times, there was certainty of provisions at Bleak Hill. Furthermore, Eufaula, only five miles distant, was close enough for an urban frolic and an easy return to bed and board. On August 5, with corn and cotton laid by, Dent vented his frustration in the matter of fodder, showing that more was at stake than winter forage: "Negroes are very restless [with] disposition to leave. All over the country they are leaving their former owners and leaving the fodder crop to dry up. This day I am 50 years of age." But Dent's freedmen did not leave in significant numbers, not yet. True, he had to "discharge" two or three for exercising the "impudence" of freedom, but his real worry was mass desertion. [87]

Faced with this as an inevitability, he tried to maintain a remote paternalistic dissatisfaction. "You cannot get more than half work out of the Negroes, hence so much fodder is being lost." Yet his real fear was expressed in a dream that he could barely bring himself to record. "Had an ominous dream last night—[I was] pulling fodder." [88] This vision of himself at so menial a plantation task must have been the ultimate shock to Dent's masterly sensibility and habit of command. With the blacks gone, he would be a type of slave. Meantime, more tangible developments troubled him and marked the changing scene. On August 15, he reported "Violets infant a hearty child found dead in bed this morning. Murdered by its Mother to get rid of it. Since fall, I have heard several say they did not wish to be troubled with Children." [89] The misleading implication here is that infanticide, like sullenness, was unknown in the so-called "happy" condition of involuntary servitude. And while slaves had occasionally stolen hogs for extra food, they did so clandestinely. Thus the planter was suprised on August 16 when freedmen "Tomlin, Alex, and Jim" were "detected at Killing a lot hog to day." [90]

If Dent had any particular difficulty harvesting his crops of corn and cotton in 1865, he never referred to it in after years, despite his penchant for reiterating comments on special agricultural problems. On the other hand, that portion of the journal covering mid-August to Christmas, 1865, was removed from the bound volume and lost or destroyed, which probably indicates trying experiences. One can surmise, then, that the crop was harvested with profit, though in a fashion that probably irked the meticulous Dent. More important, by Christmas Eve, the spectre of desertion had become reality. The master wrote dejectedly: "Most of the negroes have left the plantation without leave or license, but a few remaining." By this time, the freedman's demeanor was such a source of agitation that Dent's December 25 entry on blacks exhibited the mixed emotions of praise, grief, anger, and frustration: "Negroes behaved very well last night. Affy one of my negroes that left me died last night. She died in Eufaula." And, "Went to Eufaula. Negroes overrunning the town. So far but few making any contracts to hire next year." The social revolution now had reached crisis proportions, and the new year was at hand. Former slaves were still departing. And Dent "So far" had "not had the first application of a Negro to hire to me next year; prospects are gloomy indeed." [91]

Former chattels did not always depart in peace, a fact that causes one to wonder whether Dent made good his supposed promises to laborers for a crop profitably housed. Certainly there was plenty of room for misunderstanding on both sides in this fluid situation. Whatever the actual circumstances, Vurtur had been one of Dent's most trusted slaves, a long-time driver who required little, if any, supervision. On December 28, Dent fumed: "Vurturs family moves off to day—Insolent as they can be." On the same date, he was troubled by a former runaway: "Clem was here last evening—ordered him off the plantation and when at a distance of my reach [he] was very insolent. Patroled the Quarters last night. Kolts wagon was here at some clandestined plans: made it leave." [92]

By that year's end, all the blacks, save ten, were gone. This meant that a hundred persons of "ingratitude" gradually "abandoned" Dent, leaving him a life-long inability to understand the gesture of independence. In April, 1866, he tried but failed to comprehend why his skilled and most "indulged Negroes"—John, Alfred, and Bob—became "at once my greatest enemies and prevailed on every negro I formally owned to leave me. Such are the negroes, who have shown the most ingratitude to those who were their best friends and kindest masters." [93]

For Dent this inexplicable mass "desertion" required a psychological defense, even though it demeaned the ten blacks who remained at Bleak House. Thus by March, 1866, he had rearranged historical events to make them read as if he had purposely evicted the best laborers: "The [ten] negroes that have been retained [who were] formerly my Slaves," he wrote,

> are the hardest to get along with; they work very well, but are more surly and disrespectful in their way and manners. They do not seem satisfied; they think their remaining is an obligation on their parts confered, which should allow them privileges. The Strange Negroes do the best, and are more polite and accomodating. This is what I thought at first; that the planters had best get rid of their former Slaves and hire strangers. Every year a change will be best, keeping only such who have been tried and found true and faithful. [94]

That this statement was mere ego-massage is confirmed by Dent's reluctant admission in April, 1866, that he would have preferred his "former Negroes" over the "strangers" he was forced to hire in January. The process of losing former slaves and employing strangers required a painful adjustment. Yet on January 1, 1866, Dent joined the effort with hope and resolve:

> This is the year that free labor with the freedman is to be tried. The experiment is a great and hazardous one, involving millions of money and the fortunes of thousands. All depends on the negroes capacity to carry out faithfully the moral obligation of a contract as a freedman. Whether it will be done is the problem to be solved. It will require great segacity on the part of the White man in his management of the Negro to make him satisfied and labor to advantage and profitably. Patience and firmness is necessary to accomplish it. Without it, confusion and a failure is the result. As such, the new system must require a new policy exercised very discreetly. May God assist us all and crown our efforts with success. [95]

Still a man of hope, Dent would follow the old customs as closely as possible. On the other hand, he readily dispensed with the white overseer, because he had never liked that functionary and because, as he rationalized in 1880: "I was aware being just freed and intoxicated with the idea of freedom, they [black laborers] would never submit to being managed by a White Overseer. So I got an old experienced Negro driver who all his life had been accustomed to the management of negroes and was a good planter. My agreement with him was that I was to pay him $300 for his services, and he was to select the negroes and hire them for me. . . . My Man as Manager was named March Treadwell—he hired 30 Men, Women, and Children." [96]

There was not a little idealism in Dent's initial response to free labor. Early optimism, however, was soon awash in succeeding waves of disillusionment. The number of laborers varied from time to time. While Dent preferred paying money wages, he soon discovered that most blacks wanted a portion of the crop as pay. In an effort to meet government regulations and avoid misunderstanding, he devised a contract that probably evolved from experiences with freedmen in 1865. "This agreement witnesseth," Dent hoped,

> that Freedman A B. for himself has contracted with C D to serve him as a laborer on his plantation for the year 1866, for the following wage, to wit. That is, the said A. B. is to receive a hands portion of one third of the Corn and Cotton made on said plantation of the crop of 1866. And the said A. B. is to find himself with all the necessary rations, consisting of what is necessary to support and maintain a plantation Laborer for the year, and to cloth and shoe himself, which the said C. D. promises to furnish, and the said A. B. is to be charged for same as he draws it, at cost prices. The amount of said charges to be deduct out of the crop or value of same comeing to him. Further Stipulations are made in the Rules for the Government of the Plantation which have also been signed by the Contracting parties and made part of this agreement. Signed in Duplicate this 9th Day of January 1866 witnessed by....[97]

No copy of the "rules," which must have been detailed, is available.

While most of Dent's laborers worked under the above agreement during 1866, a few chose monthly wages at the rate of men $10, women $6, boys and girls $4. He also "provisioned" these laborers and subtracted costs from earnings.[98] As the new year began, inclement weather and the difficulty of securing hands conspired to put Dent to bed and keep him there through most of January. But the new system of planting got off to an encouraging start. Late in the month, the recuperating owner was forced to admit, "From what I have seen to day the 29th, the Freedmen seem to have worked very well."[99] But the year was young, and by planting time in mid-February, the former master "saw the first symptoms of insubordination, which gradually increased until they [freedmen] became nearly unmanageable. They commenced by walking off and leaving their work under the most frivolous pretexts. They would raise rows in the fields among themselves and have fights, turn out of mornings when they pleased to their Work, and deviled one as much as the Could."[100]

In short, the blacks were not obeying March Treadwell, and the Negro driver became increasingly inept. His "greates[t] fear was they would shoot him, for they all had pistols." Dent also paid grudging deference to armed blacks. And while he was less fearful than Treadwell, Dent avoided the Negro quarter at night and made frequent comment on the necessity of courage. He also secured "from Whit Clark . . . one of Colt's police pattern revolvers, price $13." [101]

At times he was even susceptible to false rumors of "Conspiracies getting up," conspiracies which never transpired, indicating that such plots were more imagined than real. The braver side of Dent realized this and saw no real danger when in May, 1866, "The girls (Miss Sternes, Annie, Sallie, Katy and Fanny) have gone to a picnic in Eufaula given by the United Sunday Schools to the Children." He concluded this aside securely and with pride: "Youth is full of hope and smiles and they enjoy such pleasures amazingly. After the stern realities of war, such peaceful and innocent recreations are blessings to our land." [102]

In 1880 Dent remembered more postwar fear than he had described in 1866. Thus it is not surprising that his initial response to free laborers' "insubordination" was to try to reason them into an understanding that they had a personal interest in producing a good crop. The futility of this effort shattered Dent's fragile faith in the free Negro laborer. With this disappointment, he began writing innumerable and repetitive short essays on specific labor problems. By distilling these statements, one can present his basic conception of the freedman as laborer.

Dent admired March Treadwell as "a very sensible and reliable Negro who has been a foreman for many years." But in May, 1866, the planter was forced to conclude of him: "He is now without energy or force of character, a perfect cyphor. He exercises no authority and seems destitute of energy and allows his hands to do as they please. The law gives him authority in his position, but he is afraid to exercise it; in short, the long habits of Slavery unfits him for the position" of foreman. [103]

Yet Dent was unwilling to apply the same rationale of slavery's limitations on his own management and on the shortsightedness of common field hands. Thus he "reasoned" with freedmen that "their wages is in the crop" and that "it stands them in hand to work it well, so as they can get more." Yet brief experience quickly convinced him that blacks' "interest in the crop as wages amounts to nothing." He ridiculed his laborers' narrow conception of self-interest: "If the Freedmen were as ready and punctual to turn out to work as they were to come home to meals and at night, the Army of Frederick the Great would be surpassed for discipline and regularity." [104]

Since the primary issue was the long-range crop, the owner had to ask, "What redress have we with freedmen who know not or care for their interest?" He regretted that the answer was coercion: "It resolves itself to this: if they take no interest in their own welfare can you expect them to take any in yours. The whole truth is this: when reason wont influence, fear must." Although Dent admitted: "I have no confidence in the integrity of the Negro or his disposition to labor without coercive measures," he hesitated to advocate or practice whippings for freedmen.

In fact he was firmly convinced that "The great error made in the management of my freedmen this year was in being too lenient and persuasive, instead of coercive." [105]   Although Dent abolished the office of white overseer in January, 1866, he was ready by May to concede: "The only Way to get Work out of the Freedmen—Have a steady reliable white man as foreman of the plows and another as foreman of the Hoes." While he finally employed a white overseer late in 1866, Dent was further convinced that the system was obsolete when his Negro laborers complained that "they were watched and made to work, which was not freedom. Freedom, they considered, was to work when they pleased and as they pleased, without white men superintending them; and that next year they would make no contracts, but do as they pleased." [106]   If this was a forecast of things to come, this planter would consider it. Meantime, he lacked an effective guarantee of diligence this year.

Because provisions comprised the Negroes' most identifiable "interest," Dent theoretically could have coerced them by withholding food. But that action was impracticable; it would weaken the laborers and simply invite more "Robbery" of "Corn, potatoes, hogs, poultry, and any thing they can lay their hands upon" quite easily in flimsy "log barns and cribs." Already, Dent exaggerated, "Nothing is now safe, and our losses by constant theft is endless." From this, he concluded the only effective means of coercion for free labor was regular money payment for services rendered. [107]   Along this line, he acknowledged a major flaw in the current "share" system: "We may anticipate some trouble at the end of the year, owing to the Negroes living up to his wages as fast as earned. When the end of the year arrives, and he finds he has nothing left from his wages, discontent will sure to follow. He will think he has been defrauded." [108]

Believing he had no means to protect his interest under the arrangements of 1866, Dent advocated the further capitalistic reform of the plantation system:

> The best policy I am convinced is to contract and hire them [freedmen] for money wages, and work them by time tables, deducting all lost time, negligence and misdemeanors. And when unmanageable discharge them from your service. The plan is in the Contract; let it be fully understood the working hours of the day, the holidays allowed. And if they do not come to time, and work up to time, they must pay for it, letting it be understood what they are to lose for each class of offences. System and regularity must be adopted and adhered to, to work to advantage and profit. The freedmen must be taught that time is as valuable as money, and he has hired his time to work faithfully and industriously. [109]

In Dent's case, neither the chronological nor the ideological gap between chattel and wage slaveries was very great.

When he foresaw that "large plantations will have to be abandoned under the freedmen system of labor," Dent knew that "Farming must be substituted in the place of planting—large plantations divided up into small farms." But he really could not envision tenants on his plantation; it was easier to see himself as a scientific farmer on fewer acres, using wage labor to "make the land produce three fold of what it now produces." Thus he would reduce his acreage, because hired labor was expensive and because "small farms" highly fertilized "seem to promise more success than large plantations half manured and half tended." [110]

Dent believed that free labor was more expensive than slavery. In the future, therefore, successful family farming would be intensive. Only large companies could afford the risks of plantation-size operations and numerous laborers. Somewhat inadvertently, he also explained why free labor militated against crop diversification: "This year I allowed the Negroes the privilege of having patches to plant for themselves. It wont do—as it conflicts with the cultivation of the crop; it causes dissatisfaction and trouble, and it is so much extra and hard labor on the plow teams. Besides these extra holidays" to work their patches "make the Negroes more reluctant to go to work after them." [111]

Dent's vision of a capitalistic revolution in southern agriculture also included the role of common whites. They should become willing and competent laborers for their social betters. "The great change wrought by our revolution," he admitted,

> has not yet opened the Eyes of our White laboring class. Whilst Slavery existed, they looked upon it as degrading to hire themselves out to labor. They would prefer destitution and nearly starvation before they would work out for a support that would be luxurious to what they are enjoying, that is, the poverty of false pride. Slavery is now abolished, and labor is free to all an honorable compe[ti]tion, and the demand for labor is great. Notwithstanding such, our poorer classes hang back, thinking it is degrading to hire out as laborers, particularly the female portion, who work in their own fields with the plow and hoe, not making scarcely the seed they plant, rather than hire themselves out to do house work, sewing or washing. Necessity in time will produce a change among that class of people; false stupid pride will have to give way to want and poverty and gradually they will undertake to labor as hirelings. [112]

Dent further believed that

> Example is needed to overcome this state of things. Hence, the sooner we can procure honest labor from the older free States, and show that the Whites are not ashamed to labor for an honest living, it will be better for all classes in the South. The negro is unreliable; the whites must be relied on and we must teach them that honest labor is respectable and will be

respected. I have seen white girls hired to sew in our house and as soon as Company would arrive, they would fold up their work and sit as dignified as possible, feeling ashamed to be seen working as a hireling. All this must be altered by a proper respect shown to the laboring classes and let them feel it.

Despite this optimism, Dent's one experience with white labor before he removed to Georgia was so discouraging that in another context he reiterated the need for immigrants "that will show" local whites "how to work, as heretofore they never have worked even for themselves." [113]

Such cautious hope for a competent white laboring force was rooted in disillusionment with freedmen. Recent disillusionment stemmed from a long-time habit of command. To say that Dent criticized freedmen for not being slaves is only a small exaggeration. A life of paternalism could not be discarded overnight like an old-fashioned garment. His intemperate sense of responsibility and habit of dominance caused most of the disappointments, many of which were petty. For example, the planter realized and genuinely regretted that the cane syrup that he bought for the Negroes was watery and inferior. But he expected the freedmen to suffer it in silence, as slaves would have done. When the blacks, understandably, complained of the inferior syrup and otherwise imperfect conditions, the one-time master sincerely, perhaps inevitably, believed them to be surly, dissatisfied, ungrateful, disrespectful, and basically "different" from his former "contented" slaves. There was no common ground for understanding. [114]

Dent's temporary abandonment of the white overseer also exposed him more directly to the frictions which that officer had previously absorbed. This was especially true in the matter of keeping order and quiet in the Negro quarter at night. Never very good at this, the former slave master would have been satisfied with nothing less than deathly silence at dusk, early sleep, and aggressive "hands" afield at day break. His habitual expectations were now unrealistic. The "peculiar institution" had left him ill-prepared for free labor of either color. In his thinking, any tardiness to work was linked to nocturnal dissipation, which he despised. Notice the reactionary tone of July 26, 1866: "All hands turned out very late this morning. Sun an hour high. Heard a drum beating at the quarter about 2 O clock a.m. They were up frolicking all night, hence their turning out so late this morning." [115]

Although the plantation rules for this year are not extant, it is clear that the blacks worked in gangs. Dent and March Treadwell set the time for work to begin and end. Nor was any laborer to deviate from the group's schedule except by Dent's permission. Failure to comply drew personal fines from fifty cents to five dollars, according to the violation, each fine to be charged and recorded against that hand's portion of one-third of the crop.[116] Dent enjoyed and exercised the illusion of "giving" some Saturdays to holiday or rest. But he "worked" hands through one Saturday after another whenever he could. Sunday work was the exception. Yet when freedmen determined to "take" a day on Saturday or during the week, Dent could do naught but decide to "give" it or declare an irresponsible "strike." He occasionally volunteered to give a Saturday, though not so freely as in antebellum times.

As one might expect, the Negro family was a major check upon Dent's continuing authority. And while he expressed no systematic analysis of this conflict, he sensed the challenge of the black family structure, resenting and even hating it. For example, Negro family ties stimulated travel and visiting, two practices that Dent found particularly irksome in freedmen. Nor could this former slave master appreciate the humanity of blacks' using funerals as an excuse to stop work and socialize. Dent considered his greatest burden to be the free Negro women who used their family's needs and personal health (pregnancies especially) to stay at home more days than they ever had as slaves. Free parents also limited his former use of the labor of Negro children. Although the quarter was more independent of Dent's control in 1866, his presence there was enough to evoke complaints to Treadwell and the open statement by blacks that they would not tolerate the quarter another year.[117]

While many of Dent's concerns were with harmless changes accompanying emancipation, there were more serious problems in the social realignment. As a sincere paternalist, he regretted these crises, especially the violence within some black families, which he described but could only attempt to explain: "We had great trouble throughout the year With the freedmen: the Men would beat their Wives and Children most unmercifully for the least causes. Their liberty as freedmen was too sudden from the discipline they were accustomed to as Slaves—hence they became barbarous and unruly."[118]

Violence in the cabin extended to the yard and field. On several occasions in this year, Dent and March Treadwell interrupted dangerous fights between Negro men who wielded knives, axes, and even pistols. While there is no evidence of any deaths arising from these encounters, Dent attributed such conflicts to jealousy over Negro women, a conclusion based on fact and his bias against free black families and black females. Dent also regretted that emancipation ended his prerogative of controlling black children in a day nursery of his making. He already perceived the altered Negro quarter as an unhealthy source of future problems. Occasionally, he could intervene there to appropriate a freedman's pistol for the good of the general welfare.[119]

In threatening situations, Dent's only sanctions were dismissal and imposing fines against an intangible income. Dismissal could disrupt the entire work force and was used only once as a final measure. In light of the absence of regular money payment, the second response seemed like no punishment at all, and Dent knew it. Still he made no note of threatening freedmen with whips and resigned himself to petty theft. In fact, when a servant "incendiary" set his house on fire (without serious damage), Dent had "no idea" who could have done it. Although he insisted he was too lenient with free labor, his inability to employ additional hands indicates a different view among blacks in and around Eufaula. [120]

Dent's ultimate criticism of freedmen was his low opinion of the crop they produced. He labeled it the poorest effort he ever saw. Throughout 1866, he consistently praised slave labor over free. On July 3, he wrote: "When cultivating with Slaves the crops were generally clean and in fine order and worked over the third time by the 4th of July. This year we (Free Labor) have only got through the Cotton but twice by the 4th July. And we have not been able to give the Corn crop its 3d plowing or 2d hoeing, which is the laying by working. The result is the crop has not been properly cultiviated, which is very evident from appearances and prospect." [121]

This evaluation, however, was patently unfair. In the first place, Dent always "undercropped" with slave labor, cultivating only about fifteen acres per "full" hand. In 1866 he admitted overcropping, that is, overextending his free laborers with about twenty-five acres for each full worker. With a total of thirty hands, he did well to have twenty full workers. Another factor was those black women who labored only one-half to one-third of their former schedule. Yet when Dent reduced his cotton acreage in 1866, it was because of the freedmen's insistence, not his concern. [122] His critique also failed to mention that 1866 was an unusually rainy summer. And though the fields were grassy, they were not as hopeless as Dent implied. The yields of this year were actually comparable to his wartime production with slave labor. In 1864 "under-cropped" slaves produced as little as six bushels of corn per acre; these freedmen produced ten. Seventy-five bales of cotton from 350 acres in 1866 was also equal to wartime production. Even after labor expenses, Dent netted $5,000 from this crop. [123]

Aside from "working" corn and cotton, the freedmen also performed many tasks which were formerly slaves' work. (This must have irritated them and probably contributed to their unwillingness to work in gangs the following year.) For example, on Bleak Hill plantation in 1866, freedmen "jobbed" when field work slackened, very much as Dent's former slaves had done. Now free blacks littered stock lots with straw, cleaned ditches, repaired fences, improved the public road, chopped wood for Dent's residence, and even gathered fodder for his animals. In these instances, the former slave master should have been glad that freedmen did not identify their self-interest with the crops of corn and cotton. There were, however, two menial tasks at which free blacks drew the line. These were tending the owner's swine and cultivating his family's garden. [124]

Another factor in Dent's unfair evaluation of free black labor was his early decision to quit Bleak Hill. Having decided by April, 1866, to move at that year's end, Dent's determination to succeed with free, gang-type labor was short-lived, to say the least. As the months passed, he expected the worst and was seldom disappointed. By July 19 he was already showing the plantation for sale: "Mr Holms came out with Henry Shorter today to look at the plantation with a view of purchasing." Being ready to move, Dent priced the place to sell quickly and on August 1 announced that he "Sold the Plantation Last evening...to Benjamin Morris—Terms: $10240 payable 1st January 1867. I am to throw in the Cottonseed, Gin, all the plows and plow gear, excepting 6 Set of gear which I keep for my wagon. I also throw in a old wagon." [125]

The Dents were leaving, and the planter's attitude was catching. Ten days after the sale, he wrote with uncharacteristic aplomb: "Notice that some of the Negroes are burning the shingles of[f] the houses. Will try and detect them at it." But he did not; there was no time for that problem or broken fences or general repairs. Now Dent's concern was harvesting the crop and purchasing another plantation, not necessarily in that order. The blacks undoubtedly sensed his intellectual abandonment of Bleak House. This does not mean that Dent left cotton and corn in the fields, for the crop was gathered and sold. But, as the journal shows, his mind was elsewhere, bent on fulfilling an old dream, or at least some part of it, as he determined to secure a "farm" in a mountain valley that would resemble, one supposes, his memory of neat and prosperous rural Vermont. [126] But he was a Carolinian who would remain in the lower South. Instead of Tennessee, he turned to north Georgia. Perhaps it was a step back toward his native state. Even as he priced the Alabama plantation to sell quickly, he also acted for an early purchase. The details of his initial contacts in Georgia are not known. Characteristically, however, he knew what he wanted and he proceeded to get it.

Dent's "Trip into the Cherokee Country of Georgia" was high adventure, to be recounted with loving detail, his first journey since war's end. This time he traveled alone, taking a new rail route to Macon. "Left home on Tuesday morning August 28th at 2 o clock in the morning," he wrote, noting that it was

raining and dismal looking for a start. Reached the R. Road Depot at Eufaula at 4, and the cars started at 5; few passengers until we reached Cuthbert when they flocked in more numerously; reached the Breakfast house at Smithville at 9 O clock—poor breakfast—charge $1. Dined at Fort Valley at 2 PM, where a large number of passengers came on board for Macon; reached Macon at 4 PM, and put up at the Brown house. Everything looked dull and gloomy; rainy weather in a strange place adds nothing to cheerfulness to one leaving home. $1 Dollar for Supper, 25 cents for a drink. Moderate charges for a bankrupt and ruined people. The idea is, the Necessities of some must enrich the others. So we go; misfortunes do not enlist charity, but get all we can is the motto.

The travelogue continues as Dent

Left Macon at 8¾ PM for Atlanta—fare $5.15; cars full, but not crowded; had a pleasant run that night and reached Atlanta at 4 am of 29th, raining. At this place we begun to see the effects of War. The ruins in many places are being rebuilt, and energy and progress seems to be the order of the day. Atlanta—left Atlanta at 8 AM for Kingston; reached Kingston at 11 AM, fare $3.50. Hired a Buggie at Kingston for $3 and went to Rome that evening, arriving at 7 PM.

On Thursday, August 30, Dent

went with Mr [J. R.] Stevens to examine the farms around Rome. Did not like them, being worn. PM. hired a Buggie and went down Cedar Valley and spent the night at Mr Marrns in 6 miles of Cedar town. Did not like that section of country as it was remote from market. Friday 31—Rainy morning. Left Marrns at 7 am and went to Cedar town; from Cedar Town crossed the mountain and went to Cave Springs in Vans Valley. 2½ miles from Cave Spring reached the Refugee farm belonging to Col [James G.] Harrison for which I offered $12000. [127]

In another context, Dent explained his liberal offer: "Vans Valley crops were very poor, owing to bad culture and a severe drought experienced. The people," he found

were in want of money, as the effects of the war and losing their present crops has caused much want and suffering. Notwithstanding their wants and poverty they ask very high prices for their lands, rangeing from $30 to $80 pr acre. The lands in that section of the country are no doubt overated, and are very much worn. After examining many farms, I made an offer of $30 pr Acre for a farm of Mr Harrisons in Vans Valley.... The offer was full up, more than what it was worth. [128]

Dent returned to Rome on Friday evening, and on

Saturday, 1st Sept, at 9 A M, left Rome in Buggie for Kingston, arriving at 12 O clock. And at 2 PM took the train for Atlanta, reaching Atlanta at 6 PM. At 8 PM, left Atlanta for Macon reaching Macon at 5 am, Sunday 2d. And at 8 AM, left Macon in the Eufaula train, arriving at 6 PM and comeing [home] that night. Cost of trip $63.80. [129]

Upon completing this strenuous journey, he found all well except for Mrs. Dent, who felt "badly." Although the "Negroes were quiet" in his absence, he believed them underworked and over-rested. Moreover, he was impatient to conclude the purchase. Thus on September 10, he observed: "Having sold the [Alabama] plantation [there are] no repairs to do. Water courses up, fencing washed away. Think of starting to Rome this evening as Mr Stevens writes he has confirmed the sale for the Refugee Cottage near Cave Springs." [130]

Dent left for Georgia the next day. The second trip followed the same route as the first and was less exciting. On completing the purchase without incident, he immediately set out for "home." On Saturday, September 15, he "reached Eufaula at 6½ PM, where my horse was awaiting me and arrived at home 8½ PM, finding all well. The trip was hurried but pleasant. Cost of trip—$63.15." [131]

"The Change," as Dent called this move, required an explanation, which he provided in mid-September: "Confirming my belief that large plantations and freed men as laborers are incompatible to ones successful interest, I have sold out my plantation of 1280 Acres in Barbour County Alabama and purchased me a farm of 400 Acres in Floyd County, Georgia." He sold a plantation and purchased a farm, because "At my time of life, all I can desire is peace, comforts and independence, Which I trust to secure by the Blessing of Almighty God by trying to lead a humble, industrious, honest, and economical life and by placeing my trust and Confidence in Him, through Jesus Christ and the Holy Ghost. Amen." [132]

In December, he reiterated the theme of renunciation: "In leaving Barbour County Alabama, to resettle in Floyd County, Georgia, I do not expect to benefit myself pecuniarily. But I have made the exchange to farm in a grain and stock Country, instead of Cotton planting where living will be cheaper, more abundant and less labor required than in a Cotton country making Cotton." Again he affirmed, "I place my trust in God, and my energies and prudence to make a comfortable liveing and support for my family. A fortune I am not in search of; all I desire is independence and comforts. Should I succeed in this, I am fully rewarded." [133]

This was Dent's positive motive for moving. In a negative vein, he could have been fleeing his unpopular past as conscript officer and creditor. He admitted trying to escape the blacks. "During the Summer [1866], from what experience I had with freedmen, I thought it best to remove from a Country where the Negroes were so numerous and becoming so lawless under the training of Radicals, Scalawags and Carpet Baggers.... My object in selling was to get to a Country where the Whites predominated, and the climate cooler, where the white man could labor, escaping the hot suns and malaria of the low Countries." This passage, written in 1880, telescoped the advent of Radical Reconstruction. [134]

In 1866 Dent actually believed that up-country blacks were more obedient than low-country Negroes: "The Freedmen in the upper country seem to be better managed and under better discipline than they are in the low countries; the only reason I can assign is: The up countrymen are less dependent on the freedmen than the low country people are, for they can get as much white labor as they need, whilst the low countrymen cannot get white labor that will work, and is entirely dependent on the Negro. The upper Countrymen makes the Negro obey him, and work hard or beats him and discharges him, Whilst the low country flatters and cajoles the negro, and gets but half work out of him." In 1871 Dent revised this statement: "My experience has been that the up country Negro labor is harder to manage. The reports on which that [above] was written is entirely erroneous." [135]

While holding to his agrarian dream of an independent, mountain farm of grain and livestock worked by competitive wage laborers, Dent was also exasperated with the average run of white people in the old cotton belt. Despite his several business interests, the postwar dispensation of Snopesism was a humiliating affront to his upper-class heritage and self-concept:

> A gentleman labors under all disadvantages in hireing freedmen as laborers, as he comes in compe[ti]tion with a class of [white] men unprincipled and dishonorable in extreme, who use every cunning and low device to induce the negro to work with them. They meet the negro in perfect equality, "hail fellow well met," flatter him up, and even drink with them, promising everything until the contract is ratified, when he drives him hard all the year, and cheats him out of his earnings. And strange to say, the negroes get along and are more satisfied with that class of men than they are with an honorable and high toned man. The only reason assignable is, "Birds of a feather flock togeather." [136]

The wellspring of Dent's "aristocratic" vision was not completely dry. The above critique also related to apprehension concerning the financial settlement at the end of the year. On December 3, he wrote "Freedmen and Settlements," explaining, "But few of the freedmen have made any wages to put up this year. They that contracted to find themselves in provisions and clothing have pretty well absorbed their wages in paying for the supplies, as provisions and clothing have been costly. Orders given them to trade in has also run up their accounts. And they who worked for money wages, and found in provisions, have also made but little, as they were extravagant with their money." Dent regretted freedmen's lack of "Calculation or thought about the past or future," for when they received "no money at their settlements, they take it for granted they are cheated."[137] He never intimated any sense of having short-changed these laborers.

Preparing to move to Georgia necessitated a quick harvest. Now Dent hired a white overseer named Howell, probably the same Turner Howell who was an overseer for him in antebellum years. It is possible that Howell reinstituted his earlier practice of whipping the blacks, but there is no evidence to indicate that he did, except for Dent's approval, in the abstract, of the practice. Blacks' expectation of a cash settlement probably assured the easy housing of corn and cotton. Dent realized a net profit of $5,000 from this crop.[138]

Aside from the harvest, Dent's numerous arrangements for the move included: selling corn, fodder, cotton, carriages, livestock, tools, and some furniture in Alabama; buying corn, wheat, and fodder in Georgia; closing the children's plantation school; collecting bills receivable (by suit when advantageous); paying his own bills; retrieving his money box from a friend; and visiting neighbors and family such as the Clarks, Claytons, Wellborns, Youngs, and General James Longstreet. Dent was also preparing a medicine chest, packing some possessions, planning a wagon train, saying goodbyes, and burning the correspondence of twenty years. He called the last "A sad Work Burning Letters. Having so much to move, I had to burn up to day a correspondence of 20 years. In those letters what a variety of thoughts, circumstances and conditions were expressed; the past and present were painfully striking."[139]

Meanwhile the future was pressing him hard. After December 1, Dent despised his almost total lack of authority over blacks. He also found Mrs. Dent's illness very inconvenient. She had been unwell since August, the month he sold Bleak House. On December 5, he wrote, "Mrs Dent quite sick which has frustrated all our plans and operations." Thus John Dent was "Doing anything and everything" in these days. At first he planned to accompany the wagon train of Billy Beasley. Instead, he sent his son, Charles, with the caravan to save "much loss and expense." On December 11 when the "Wagon train with stock left Bleak Hill at 1 PM for Refugee Cottage, Floyd Co. Georgia," the move had begun.[140]

The uprooting was apparently very difficult for Fanny Dent. Her husband's account was typically stoic. He had packed and sacrificed his presence with the wagon train. Surely she could ride the "cars." Following last goodbyes, he noted in mid-December: "My family and Self left Eufaula Ala in the cars for Rome, Ga. We left Bleak Hill Thursday 13th at 2 pm for Eufaula. Spent the night at the R. R Depot so as to take the Cars at 5 AM." The family was Mrs. Dent and "Seven Children, to wit, Annie, Charley, Katy, Fanny, George, Lucy, & Helen."[141]

As usual, Dent recounted the journey. "Had a pleasant trip from Eufaula to Macon, Cars crowded," he wrote.

> Left Macon at 8¾, night train, for Atlanta. Cars overcrowded, some persons having no seats; this crowd was owing to the Georgia legislature having adjourned and the members returning home. This train (of Wisdom) when about 30 miles from Macon, the Locomotive broke one of her Engines—lost 4 hours in fixing it. Proceeded after delay with but one Engine, and reached Atlanta at 9 am [December 15] just in time to take the Western and Atlantic train by their waiting 15 minutes on us to exchange Baggage. Had a very pleasant ride from Atlanta to Kingston, reaching there at 11½ am, and taking the Rome train—reaching Rome at 2 PM. Put up at the Chase Hotel. And on Sunday 16th left in the [morning] stage for Refugee Cottage (raining and Snowing); reached the cottage at 1 PM. cold.

The move by rail cost $159.75. [142]

It was five more days before Dent's "Wagons . . . 6 mules, 2 mares, and 3 Colts, and 14 head of Cattle, and my Buggie reached Refugee Cottage Friday Decr 21st 1866, at 2½ PM, with all things safe, except breaking a leg of my Secretary table." Still he was satisfied, and the five hands and Billy Beasley "started back for Alabama Saturday Dec 22d at 8 AM, with his wagon & 2 mules." It was only three days until Christmas, and the Dents' holiday was melancholy. [143]

Although the home was tight and warm, "a large brick mansion," the Dents had not moved all their furnishings and were quite uncomfortable for a "season." Still it was a beautiful place between the ridges, in a valley running north and south. The land was red clay, gently rolling down to the Big Cedar Creek, which lay several hundred yards away from the best house Dent ever provided. Its two stories contained nine large rooms and two enclosed halls. Yet on December 27, he complained mildly: "Up to this date confusion reigns supreme, no Servants as yet hired, house dirty, no comforts, our camp life must continue until we can buy Bedsteads, Chairs, and hire a cook and Servant. Annie and Mrs Dent are still cooking, nursing, and doing every thing else, but washing and Scouring." [144]

On the next day, however, conditions improved when he "Contracted with William Richardson (freedman) and Mary Jane his wife as laborers for the year 1867." He also employed the former owner's white laborer, Jeff Lemings. And on December 29, "at 12 O clock," it "commenced Snowing." By the next day "The face of the earth is covered with snow, 2 inches in depth." On the last day of this momentous year, life was settling down as Dent recorded, "Wagon hauling wood. Mr Lemings gone to hire hands if he can find any." And of course Lemings found them, for a total of six male laborers, which Dent thought a sufficient number. [145]

Finally this gentleman refugee from the antebellum South of low-country plantations, cotton, and slavery began the first day of the new year affirming a faith older than the trials of emancipation:

In commencing the duties of a new Year, Our first duty is to return to God our sincere thanks for His goodness and mercy to us—that He has brought [us] safely through the past year with many blessings undeserved on our parts. And although we have felt his Chastening rod, such chastening has been given us for some wise purposes. As such, we bow to His Will. We trust, with Christian resignation and Submission—Trusting He may vouch safe unto us Many Blessings and Divine dispensations for the year to come, as He may see fit to Bless us . . . in accordance with our conduct and merits. In the discharge of my Spiritual duties, We invoke His Blessings and Assistance; And in the discharge of our Worldly duties, I trust to do so by Gods assistance in an honest, upright and industrious manner, Hopeing He may reward my efforts with success and bless the works of my hands. As such, I undertake the duties of this year, Hopeing and trusting in God, through our Lord and Saviour Jesus Christ. Amen. Jno H Dent.[146]

EPILOGUE

As one of the advantaged few in the postwar South, "Major" J. H. Dent was as successful and influential in north Georgia as he had been in Barbour County, Alabama. Still advocating agricultural diversification and other reforms, he criticized the production of cotton with sharecropping procedures. Yet he felt obliged to follow these practices and profited from them, along with other business activities, like partnership in the local John Baker grist and flour mill.[1]

An amiable, popular, and civic-minded citizen, Dent was continually urged to run for the state legislature. But he consistently refused, preferring the quiet satisfaction of a business well-managed. He also believed that public office was an "unthankful" responsibility. Still, as a Bourbon Democrat, he was influential enough to serve as local committeeman, county commissioner, and long-time trustee and president of the board of the Georgia School for the Deaf in Cave Spring.[2]

While Dent continued to travel both locally and to great distances, the central concern of his waning years was family and friends. When his wife, Fanny, died in 1875, he soon married Elizabeth Anne Dowd of Edgefield, South Carolina. Becoming increasingly generous with his children and grandchildren in this period of chronic deflation and recurring national recessions, Dent nevertheless maintained assets of at least $30,000.[3]

Although a kidney disorder made his late years uncomfortable and even painful, he was under medical care and managed to remain active until December, 1891. Following a confinement of five months, during which Mrs. Dent kept the journal for him, J. H. Dent died on May 17, 1892, in his seventy-sixth year, and was buried in the family plot of the Cave Spring Cemetery.[4]

NOTES

PREFACE

1. Louis D. Rubin, Jr., "A Study in Pastoral and History," *Georgia Historical Quarterly*, LIX (Winter, 1975), 442-54, especially 450; Lewis P. Simpson, *The Dispossessed Garden: Pastoral and History in Southern Literature* (Athens, 1975), 34-64.

2. Carl Degler, *The Other South: Southern Dissenters in the Nineteenth Century* (New York, 1974), 125 *ff.*

3. Morton Rothstein, "The Antebellum South as a Dual Economy: A Tentative Hypothesis," *Agricultural History*, XLI (Oct., 1967), 373-82.

CHAPTER ONE

1. The problems inherent in defining an antebellum southern aristocrat are evident in W. J. Cash, *The Mind of the South* (New York, 1941), vii-18; Clement Eaton, *A History of the Old South: The Emergence of a Reluctant Nation* (New York, 1975), 390; Eugene D. Genovese, *The Political Economy of Slavery: Studies in the Economy and Society of the Slave South* (New York, 1965), 13-36; and *The World the Slaveholders Made* (New York, 1969), 137-50. For one influential Dent's view of the "elite," see Elizabeth Anne Dent Letters, *passim*, especially Aug. 8 [1853], and July 15 [1854], typescript copies in John H. Dent Papers, Troy State University Library, location of originals unknown.

2. Ray Mathis, Mary Mathis, and Douglas Clare Purcell, eds. of microfilm publication, *John Horry Dent Farm Journals and Account Books, 1840-1892* (University, Ala., 1977), II, 259; hereinafter cited as *DJ*.

3. Harry Wright Newman, *The Maryland Dents* (Richmond, 1963), 3-15. On pages 107-61 of this book, Newman traces the Eufaula family of Captain Stouten Hubert Dent (born 1833) as being descended from the seventeenth-century John Dent, reported to have been a nephew or cousin of John Horry Dent's paternal ancestor, Judge Thomas Dent, who is discussed in the present chapter. Thus the Eufaula families of John Horry Dent and of Stouten Hubert Dent were not directly related. J. H. Dent's granddaughter, Elizabeth Wellborn, married Warren Dent, a descendent of this second Maryland line; *DJ*, XXI, 14.

4. Newman, *Dents*, 15-25.

5. *Ibid.*, 18, 31-36.

6. *Ibid.*, 35, 47-50.

7. *Ibid.*, 48, 66-68.

8. *Ibid.*, 66, 83-84; Dudley W. Knox, *A History of the United States Navy* (New York, 1936), 47.

9. United States Navy Department, "John Herbert Dent, Record," abstract in M. B. Wellborn Papers, Auburn University Archives; Knox, *U. S. Navy*, 48-52, 58-78.

10. U. S. Navy, "J. H. Dent," in Wellborn Papers; Knox, *U. S. Navy*, 75; Newman, *Dents*, 67; S. E. Morison and others, *The Growth of the American*

Republic (New York, 1969), I, 352-55.

11. Jonah Horry-J. H. Dent-M. B. Wellborn Genealogical Chart, p. 1, type-script in Wellborn Papers; Elizabeth Schieffelin, typescript history of Jonah Horry-J. H. Dent Family, Los Angeles.

12. Horry Genealogy and Papers, in Huguenot Society of South Carolina and in South Carolina Historical Society, Charleston; Eaton, *Old South*, 11-12.

13. Horry Genealogical Chart, p. 1, in Wellborn Papers; Jonah Horry Will, in "Charleston Wills," vol. 32, book E, pp. 613-18, in South Carolina Archives, Columbia.

14. Jonah Horry Will, in South Carolina Archives, Columbia; Mrs. St. Julien Ravenel, *Charleston, the Place and the People* (New York, 1912), 384; Rev. J. Adams, *Eulogium 1835 on Elias Horry* (Charleston, 1835).

15. Ulrich Bonnell Phillips, *American Negro Slavery: A Survey of the Supply, Employment and Control of Negro Labor as Determined by the Plantation Regime* (New York, 1952), 249-50; Beulah Glover, *Narratives of Colleton County, South Carolina* (Brunswick, 1969), 48; Jonah Horry Will, in South Carolina Archives, Columbia; *DJ*, XXI, 1.

16. "Map of Colleton District, South Carolina, Improved for *Mills' Atlas*, 1825," in South Carolina Archives, Columbia; A. S. Salley, ed., "Journal of Gen. Peter Horry," *South Carolina Historical and Genealogical Magazine*, XL (July, 1939), 143.

17. E. A. Dent Letters, Sept. 17, 1854, in Dent Papers; Francis Pendleton Gaines, *The Southern Plantation: A Study in the Development and the Accuracy of a Tradition* (Gloucester, 1962), 143-72, especially 154, 157, 169.

18. Duncan Clinch Heyward, *Seed From Madagascar* (Chapel Hill, 1937), 62-72; Glover, *Colleton County*, 86.

19. William K. Scarborough, *The Overseer: Plantation Management in the Old South* (Baton Rouge, 1966), 178-94.

20. Elizabeth Anne Dent, "Diary," a fragment, typescript copy in Dent Papers, Troy State University Library, location of original unknown.

21. U.S. Navy, "J. H. Dent," in Wellborn Papers; *DJ*, XXI, 2; Ophelia Troup Dent, "Memoirs," typescript copy in Dent Papers, Troy State University Library, original at Hofwyl plantation, Darien, Georgia.

22. Ophelia Troup Dent, "Memoirs," Hofwyl Collection; the same legend is in Linton C. Hopkins, *Biography of Maximilian Bethune Wellborn* (1960), 11-12; and in M. B. Wellborn, Jr., "Dent Sketch," typescript copy in Dent Papers, Troy State University Library, original apparently lost.

23. Pierre M. Irving, *The Life and Letters of Washington Irving* (New York, 1863), I, 102-05, 111, 182. Elizabeth Schieffelin does a beautiful job of unraveling this tangle in her typescript history of the Horry-Dent Family. Also see Elizabeth Schieffelin to Ray Mathis, Oct. 24, 1975, in Dent Papers.

24. Ophelia Troup Dent, "Memoirs," Hofwyl Collection; italics mine. Jonah Horry Will, in South Carolina Archives, Columbia.

25. *DJ*, XXI, 2; Morison, *American Republic*, 354-86.

26. U.S. Navy, "J. H. Dent"; and Horry Genealogical Chart, p. 1, in Wellborn Papers.

27. E. A. Dent Letters, Sept. 17, 1854; and Wellborn, "Dent Sketch," in Dent

Papers; Hopkins, *Wellborn*, 12-13; *Birmingham News*, June 2, 1927.

28. *DJ*, XXI, 2; XIII, 252; Horry-Dent Genealogical Chart, p. 2, in Wellborn Papers.

29. *DJ*, III, 179; XIII, 252; E. A. Dent Letters, Sept. 17, 1854, in Dent Papers; *Directory for City of Charleston, 1831*, p. 69, in South Carolina Historical Society, Charleston.

30. *DJ*, XIII, 252.

31. Glover, *Colleton County*, 88, 106; interview with Beulah Glover, Walterboro, S.C., June 11, 1975; and the plot of the Dents' plantation which Glover prepared from Colleton County Records, in Dent Papers. Also see "Map of Colleton... for *Mills' Atlas*, 1825"; and Samuel G. Stoney, *Plantations of the Carolina Low Country* (Charleston, 1955).

32. Glover, *Colleton County*, 94-95; "Map of Colleton... for *Mills' Atlas*, 1825"; Beulah Glover, Maps of Colleton Families, copy in Dent Papers; *Directory for City of Charleston, 1831*, p. 69, in South Carolina Historical Society, Charleston; Lucretia Horry Will, in "Charleston Wills," vol. 40, pp. 305-06, in South Carolina Archives, Columbia.

33. E. A. Dent Letters, Nov. 24, 1839; Feb. 4, 1854, in Dent Papers; *DJ*, XIII, 282, 288.

34. *DJ*, XIII, 252-53.

35. *DJ*, XIII, 288-89.

36. Wellborn concretized the legend of President Andrew Jackson's offering J. H. Dent a naval appointment; Hopkins, *Wellborn*, 12-13; *DJ*, I, 218-19, 259-60, 264; II, 156, 207, 221, 236, 282, 314, 330, 332, 339, 349; IV, iv, 115; XIII, 253; XV, 288-92.

37. Interview with Beulah Glover, Walterboro, S. C., June 11, 1975; Charleston Chamber of Commerce, *Report... on Charleston and Hamburg Railroad* [Charleston, 1830s]; Eugene Alvarez, *Travel on Southern Antebellum Railroads, 1828-1860* (University, Ala., 1974), 7-8.

38. *DJ*, XIII, 253-54.

39. Dent's life-long attraction to and appreciation of New England was probably rooted in the circumstances of his birth in Newport, this 1833 northern tour, and his mother's sense of northern superiority, at least in education; E. A. Dent Letters, Sept. 10, 1848, in Dent Papers. Malachi Ford was a trustee of the Robert Morrison estate. Dent married a Morrison heiress; see note 44, below; *DJ*, XIII, 254-55.

40. E. A. Dent Letters, *passim*, especially, Jan. 4, 1838; Nov. 25, 1842; Feb. 21, 1846; Nov. 30, 1848, in Dent Papers.

41. Heyward, *Seed from Madagascar*, 3-44; Eaton, *Old South*, 221, 223.

42. *DJ*, XIII, 255.

43. Sarah Winston Lawton to Beulah Glover, May 7, 1975; and Beulah Glover to Ray Mathis [Spring, 1975], in Dent Papers; Morrison Papers and Genealogy, in South Carolina Historical Society, Charleston; see sketch of Leith in Emily B. Reynolds and others, *Biographical Directory of the Senate of South Carolina, 1776-1964* (Columbia, 1964); *DJ*, I, 34-35; II, 255; interview with Beulah Glover, Walterboro, S. C., June 11, 1975.

44. *DJ*, I, 218; XIII, 250, 255; Dent once lived with a man named Ford,

probably Malachi Ford, a trustee of the Morrison estate; J. H. Dent Marriage Settlement, in "Marriage Settlements," vol. 13, pp. 229-30, in South Carolina Archives, Columbia. A more detailed account of the property settlement is in J. H. Dent, "Trust Agreement with Morrison Estate," typescript copy in Dent Papers, original probably in possession of Mrs. Felix Rapp, Anniston, Ala.

45. *DJ*, I, 218; XXI, 2-10, 17-18; Horry-Dent Genealogical Chart, p. 2, in Wellborn Papers; Schieffelin's typescript history of Horry-Dent Families; interview with Elizabeth Schieffelin, Troy, Ala., Oct. 10, 1976; Schieffelin to Mathis, April 3, 1977, in Dent Papers; E. A. Dent Letters in entirety, especially, Nov. 24, 1839; Mar. 18, 1846; Sept. 10, 1848; Nov. 30, 1848; Feb. 10, 1853; June 5, 1854; July 15 [1854], in Dent Papers; Roper Papers, and *Charleston City Directory for 1856,* pp. 137, 155, both in South Carolina Historical Society, Charleston; Chalmers G. Davidson, *The Last Foray: The South Carolina Planters of 1860: A Sociological Study* (Columbia, 1971), 175; Laura A. White, *Robert Barnwell Rhett: Father of Secession* (Gloucester, 1965), 134.

46. E. A. Dent Letters, Nov. 24, 1839; Sept. 10, 1848; Nov. 30, 1848; Aug. 12 [1853]; Feb. 4, 1854, in Dent Papers; Ophelia Troup Dent, "Memoirs," Hofwyl Collection; Victoria Gunn, Brailsford-Troup-Dent Genealogy, copy in Dent Papers, original at Hofwyl plantation, Darien, Georgia.

47. Dent, "Trust Agreement," in Dent Papers; *DJ*, I, 34-35; Dent, "Memorandum to Trust Agreement," Jan. 20, 1882, in Wellborn Papers; "Map of Colleton . . . for *Mills' Atlas*, 1825."

48. Beulah Glover, ed., *In Memory of: Inscriptions from Early [Colleton County] Cemeteries* (Walterboro, 1972), 39; Wellborn, "Dent Sketch," 1, in Dent Papers.

49. *DJ*, II, 255.

50. *DJ*, XIII, 255-56.

51. *DJ*, XIII, 256.

52. *DJ*, II, 256.

53. *DJ*, I, 34-35; II, 255-56; E. A. Dent Letters, Aug. 8 [1853], in Dent Papers; Dent, "Memo to Trust," in Wellborn Papers. Hamilton Morrison was a taciturn man of pleasing personality, whom John Dent clearly liked. Anne Dent approved of Mary Elizabeth, but she disliked Hamilton and Julia Morrison; Schieffelin to Mathis, April 3, 1977, in Dent Papers.

54. E. A. Dent Letters, Jan. 4, 1838; Aug. 8 [1853], in Dent Papers.

55. There is a revealing view of rice planters' economic recession of the 1840s in Ophelia Troup Dent, "Memoirs," Hofwyl Collection.

56. See Eaton, *Old South*, 396, on the lesser gentry. Morton Rothstein's "Antebellum South as a Dual Economy" is more helpful in understanding Dent's complexity than Eugene Genovese's insightful, but rigid, thesis of the prebourgeois planter in his *Political Economy* and *World the Slaveholders Made*.

57. *DJ*, XIII, 256.

CHAPTER TWO

1. Henry Nash Smith, *Virgin Land: The American West as Symbol and Myth* (New York, 1950), 138-77, especially 161-64.

2. Clement Eaton distinguishes between frontier and mature plantations in *The*

Growth of Southern Civilization, 1790-1860 (New York, 1961), 98-124. In addition to Smith's *Virgin Land*, Gaines' *Southern Plantation, passim*, especially 143-57, assisted this analysis of Dent. Dent's real fear that the frontier would lessen his civility suggests that neither Cash's *Mind*, 3-14, nor Genovese's *World Slaveholders Made*, 137-50, has given this problem of gentry and frontier an intellectual base broad enough to build a convincing analysis.

3. *DJ*, II, 256; XIII, 256.

4. Margaret Pace Farmer, *One Hundred Fifty Years in Pike County, Alabama, 1821-1971* (Anniston, 1973), 26-33. Anne Kendrick Walker, *Backtracking in Barbour County; A Narrative of the Last Alabama Frontier* (Richmond, 1941), 36-58.

5. Albert Burton Moore, *History of Alabama* (Tuscaloosa, 1951), 10-33. For a briefer account, see Malcolm McMillan, *The Land Called Alabama* (Austin, 1975), 74-89, 117-19. Also see Donald B. Dodd and Borden D. Dent, *Historical Atlas of Alabama* (University, Ala., 1974), 24-30; Neal G. Lineback and Charles T. Traylor, eds., *Atlas of Alabama* (University, Ala., 1973), 20-21. Two new and helpful studies of Alabama which appeared in time to be read before this book goes to press are Daniel Savage Gray, *Alabama: A Place, a People, a Point of View* (Dubuque, 1977); and Virginia Van der Veer Hamilton, *Alabama, a Bicentennial History* (New York, 1977).

6. Green Beauchamp, "Early Chronicles of Barbour County," *Alabama Historical Quarterly*, XXXIII (Spring, 1971), 50-51; J. A. B. Besson, *History of Eufaula, Alabama, The Bluff City of the Chattahoochee* (Atlanta, 1875), 3-11; Mary Elizabeth Young, *Redskins, Ruffleshirts, and Rednecks: Indian Allotments in Alabama and Mississippi, 1830-1860* (Norman, 1961), 73-98.

7. Beauchamp, "Chronicles of Barbour," 51-58; Besson, *Eufaula*, 11-13; Farmer, *Pike County*, 26-33; Walker, *Barbour County*, 36-58; Young, *Redskins*, 73-98.

8. Hopkins, *Wellborn*, 14; Walker, *Barbour County*, 1-84, *passim*; Wellborn, "Dent Sketch," 1-2, in Dent Papers; Young, *Redskins*, 99-113.

9. *DJ*, II, 355; XIII, 256; Besson, *Eufaula*, 13-15; Walker, *Barbour County*, 1-84.

10. *DJ*, II, 256, 259, 275, 355.

11. *DJ*, XIII, 256-57.

12. *DJ*, XIII, 257; Lineback, *Atlas of Alabama*, 16-17, 22-23.

13. *DJ*, XIII, 258; Walker, *Barbour County*, 20.

14. *DJ*, XIII, 258; Marvin L. Harper to Ray Mathis, June 2 and June 5, 1975, and enclosures, in Dent Papers. Harper's material also shows that Dennis Dent built the Foster-Shirley-Cummings House in Tuscaloosa.

15. *DJ*, XIII, 257.

16. *DJ*, XIII, 257-58.

17. *DJ*, II, 256-59.

18. *DJ*, XIII, 259. This first plantation was actually on Johnson's Creek, a tributary of the South Cowikee.

19. Walker, *Barbour County*, 85-107; *DJ*, I, 1-3, 78, 79, 139, 157, 245-46; II, 355; III, 9; Charles S. Davis, *The Cotton Kingdom in Alabama* (Montgomery, 1939), 188. Dent patented some land; Marie Godfrey to Ray Mathis [Feb., 1977] in Dent Papers.

20. *DJ*, XIII, 259.

21. *DJ*, I, 108; III, xii; XXI, 4; Dent Genealogical Chart, p. 2, in Wellborn Papers; Hopkins, *Wellborn*, 14; Elizabeth Anne Dent Letters, typescript copies in South Carolina Historical Society, Charleston, location of originals unknown.

22. *DJ*, I, 82; XIII, 259.

23. *DJ*, III, 78; XIII, 254, 258, 260; also see Leo Marx, *The Machine in the Garden: Technology and the Pastoral Ideal in America* (New York, 1967), *passim*, especially 227-352.

24. *DJ*, I, 1-4, 14-16, 30, 37-39, 179, 245-46; III, xii; E. A. Dent Letters, Jan. 4, 1838, in Dent Papers; Dent also received $2,000 from South Carolina land sales in the 1840s.

25. *DJ*, I, 77-79, 245-46; V, 359; E. A. Dent Letters, Nov. 24, 1839, in Dent Papers.

26. Dent's criticism of speculators is treated in chapters two and six, below; *DJ*, I, 133; XIII, 275.

27. *DJ*, I, 104.

28. *DJ*, I, 133-34, 157, 245-46.

29. *DJ*, I, 176.

30. *DJ*, I, 256. For Dent's land transactions in Alabama, see Deed Books C, D, H, L, S, Probate Office, Barbour County Court House, Clayton.

31. *DJ*, I, 157; III, 79.

32. *DJ*, I, 162.

33. *DJ*, I, 157-58, 161, 205; Marie Godfrey to Ray Mathis, Feb. 28, 1977, in Dent Papers.

34. *DJ*, I, 175-76, 207-08:

35. *DJ*, I, 176; XIII, 256; XX, 3 *ff*.

36. *DJ*, I, 256; XIII, 260.

37. Wellborn, "Dent Sketch," 3, in Dent Papers.

38. *DJ*, I, 187-88, 192, 205, 207-08; III, xii.

39. *DJ*, I, 11-12, 176, 247-51; II, 103, 118; III, xii.

40. *DJ*, II, 361-65; George Dent is described in chapter one; in E. A. Dent Letters, *passim*, in Dent Papers; and in Ophelia Troup Dent, "Memoirs," in Hofwyl Collection. Family lore portrays him as a wencher and rake (perhaps in the tradition of his shadowy father?); interview with Elizabeth Schieffelin, Troy, Ala., Oct. 10, 1976.

41. *DJ*, II, 361-62.

42. *DJ*, II, 361.

43. *DJ*, II, 363. Dent made another positive reference to Cortes in *DJ*, II, 85. Also see William R. Taylor, *Cavalier and Yankee: The Old South and American National Character* (New York, 1969), 216; and see Eaton, *Southern Civilization*, 45-48, on Texas fever in the 1850s.

44. *DJ*, II, 365.

45. *DJ*, XIII, 260. This story is quite clear in the last pages of *DJ*, II, and in the early pages of III.

46. *DJ*, I, 205. Interestingly enough, Dent had a summer house at True Blue, but not at Good Hope-Millers's.

47. *DJ*, I, 256; XIII, 260.

48. *DJ*, II, 127.

49. E. A. Dent Letters, Sept. 8, 1854, in Dent Papers.

50. *DJ*, II, 255-59.

51. *DJ*, II, 162-63; III, xii; XIII, 260-61.

52. E. A. Dent Letters, May 9, 1854, in Dent Papers.

53. *DJ*, II, 264; III, 70.

54. *DJ*, XIII, 260-61.

55. *DJ*, XIII, 261, 283.

56. *DJ*, II, 354.

57. E. A. Dent Letters, Sept. 17, 1854, in Dent Papers.

58. *DJ*, II, 184; III, xiii. Dent's four large lots in the Sanford-Cherry St. area "joined" the fashionable "Hill District" of Eufaula society; Marie Godfrey to Ray Mathis, Feb. 28, 1977, in Dent Papers.

59. *DJ*, II, 234; III, xiii, xx.

60. *DJ*, III, 80.

61. *DJ*, III, 85-86.

62. Conservation was a dominant theme early in *DJ*, III; also see V, 212; and chapter four, below.

63. *DJ*, III, 70.

64. *DJ*, III, 252; V, 10.

65. *DJ*, V, 3.

66. *DJ*, II, 363; V, 26 *ff.*; XIII, 269 *ff.*

67. *DJ*, XIII, 271.

68. *DJ*, V, 256; XIII, 272.

69. *DJ*, IV, 72; V, 16; A-I, vii, 66, 84, 205, 212-13; A-II, 118; Davis, *Cotton Kingdom in Alabama*, 188; Professor William Smith of Troy State University School of Business assisted these calculations.

70. *DJ*, IV, 1.

71. See chapter six, below. This is another example of Dent's use of the Cavalier image, a separate story that I can only touch here, owing to its narrowing effect on the chapter.

72. In addition to Marx's *Machine in Garden*, Smith's *Virgin Land*, and Taylor's *Cavalier and Yankee*, I am indebted for analytical insights to R. W. B. Lewis, *The American Adam: Innocence, Tragedy, and Tradition in the Nineteenth Century* (Chicago, 1955).

73. *DJ*, XIII, 268-69.

74. *DJ*, III, 68.

75. *DJ*, I, 133-34.

76. *DJ*, II, 7; also see chapter three, below.

77. *DJ*, I, iii.

78. *DJ*, I, 50; Taylor, *Cavalier and Yankee*, 102-14, 249-54.

79. While Smith, *Virgin Land*, and others have ably argued the reality of image and symbol, I have tried to acknowledge the difficulty of getting at the reality of myth in my "Mythology and the Mind of the New South," *Georgia Historical Quarterly*, LX (Fall, 1976), 228-38.

80. *DJ*, I, 111-13, 86, 35. Dent's sense of failure as agricultural reformer was somewhat similar to Edmund Ruffin's; Avery Craven, *Edmund Ruffin, Southerner: A Study in Secession* (Baton Rouge, 1966), 60-72.

81. *DJ*, I, 53, 111-13; XVIII, 35; J. H. Dent, "Overseers and Their Employers," *American Agriculturalist*, IV (Dec., 1845), 368; Dent to Thomas Ewbank, Nov. 9,

1850, in *Report of the Commissioner of Patents, for the Year 1850: Part II, Agriculture* (Washington, 1851), 284-88; Dent to Thomas Ewbank, Commissioner of Patents, Nov. 5, 1849, copy in Dent Papers, original in National Archives, Washington, D. C. Professor James C. Bonner has observed that many of Dent's comments on agricultural reform (below) sound remarkably like articles from the *American Cotton Planter* (Montgomery) and the *Soil of the South* (Columbus); Bonner to Mathis, Feb. 24, 1977, in Dent Papers. Although cursory research does not immediately reveal Dent authorship in these or other regional journals, the problem deserves further investigation.

82. *DJ*, II, 76.

83. *DJ*, II, 28.

84. *DJ*, I, 31-32. Professor James C. Bonner observes that this system worked best on sandy soils like Dent's hammocks in Barbour County. Hooves would pack and clod clay soils too tightly for good cultivation the following year; Bonner to Mathis, Feb. 24, 1977, in Dent Papers.

85. The letters to overseers are introduced in chapter two, below. Some of the content of these letters is used here.

86. *DJ*, I, 61.

87. *DJ*, I, 19.

88. *DJ*, II, 91-92.

89. *DJ*, I, 19-20, 55, 62.

90. *DJ*, I, 59.

91. *DJ*, I, 60.

92. *DJ*, I, 60.

93. *DJ*, I, 233; IV, 44-46; also see chapter four, below.

94. *DJ*, III, 91; IV, 22; V, 141.

95. *DJ*, III, 155.

96. *DJ*, III, 83.

97. *DJ*, III, 39.

98. *DJ*, III, 89.

99. *DJ*, III, 52-53, 93.

100. *DJ*, II, 6.

101. *DJ*, III, 122.

102. *DJ*, III, 122.

103. *DJ*, III, 136; V, 16.

104. *DJ*, IV, 98.

105. *DJ*, III, 49.

106. *DJ*, III, 50.

107. Eaton, *Old South*, 273; Scarborough, *Overseer*, 16.

108. *DJ*, I, 24, 27-28; see Genovese on habit of command in his *World Slaveholders Made*.

109. *DJ*, I, 27-28.

110. *DJ*, I, 17-21, 50-56, 59-62; II, 91-92; III, xvii; W. Stanley Hoole, "Advice to an Overseer: Extracts from the 1840-1842 Plantation Journal of John Horry Dent," *Alabama Review*, I (Jan., 1948), 50-63.

111. *DJ*, I, 17.

112. Sources cited in note 110, above; and Scarborough, *Overseer*, 182.

113. *DJ*, II, 91-92.

114. *DJ*, III, xvii.

115. *DJ*, I, 20.

116. *DJ*, I, 20.

117. Scarborough, *Overseer*, 29.

118. Except for a partial list of overseers in *DJ*, III, xii, this list has been constructed from clues, hints, names, and accounts in each antebellum journal.

119. It is interesting to note that if Dent's three types of comment on overseers had a common denominator, it seems to have been his own early uncertainty of role status, an uncertainty which lessened with age and success. For example, his early rules for farming could be interpreted as "creative insecurity" in the habit of command. His second type of comment, the ironic combination of condescension and idealization of overseers, suggests a dualism that could have stemmed from Dent's youthful identification with old Bunting, his mother's admirable steward, who, as Dent's influential role model, was probably admired and feared. After all, Dent's instructions to overseers also included the master's own duties when he was a true resident farmer, duties not easily distinguished from those of a genuine steward. And, as we shall see, Dent never completely escaped the minor fear that somehow his overseer would dominate him. This last could have related to planters' commonly described practice of making the overseer a scapegoat, Dent's practice of which is discussed below. To generalize on Dent is useless, but interesting, especially when one speculates as to whether making overseers into scapegoats was more prevalent in the up-country, where former overseers might have a better chance to become large planters with overseers of their own.

120. Scarborough, *Overseer*, 6, 195-96.

121. *DJ*, II, 91.

122. *DJ*, III, 203.

123. *DJ*, III, 196.

124. *DJ*, III, 44.

125. *DJ*, III, 159.

126. *DJ*, III, 150.

127. *DJ*, III, 145.

128. *DJ*, III, 145.

129. *DJ*, III, 65.

130. *DJ*, III, 65.

131. *DJ*, III, 66.

132. *DJ*, III, 167, 175, 187.

133. *DJ*, III, 188.

134. *DJ*, III, 195.

135. *DJ*, III, 187.

136. *DJ*, III, 217; IV, 9, 52; V, 51, 90; Marie Godfrey to Ray Mathis, Feb. 28, 1977, in Dent Papers. Dent's view and experience of overseers contribute at times (as in the case of Turner Howell) to the more strict interpretation that this planter was generally correct on the incompetence of these white assistants; interview with Bertram Wyatt-Brown, Case Western Reserve University, [Feb., 1977].

137. *DJ*, V, 199.

138. *DJ*, IV, 13; V, 227; VII, 77-78.

CHAPTER THREE

1. The statistics are based on Rothstein, "Antebellum South as a Dual Economy," 376. This study of Dent as slave master draws analytical insights from the standard historical works on slavery in the United States. While cognizant of Stanley M. Elkins, *Slavery: A Problem in American Institutional and Intellectual Life* (Chicago, 1959), and of Ann J. Lane, ed., *The Debate Over "Slavery": Stanley Elkins and His Critics* (Urbana, 1971), my analysis of Dent has leaned more heavily upon Ulrich Bonnell Phillips, *American Negro Slavery*, and his *Life and Labor in the Old South* (Boston, 1936); Kenneth M. Stampp, *The Peculiar Institution: Slavery in the Ante-Bellum South* (New York, 1956); Eugene D. Genovese, *Political Economy of Slavery; World the Slaveholders Made;* and especially his *Roll, Jordan, Roll: The World the Slaves Made* (New York, 1976); John W. Blassingame, *The Slave Community: Plantation Life in the Ante-Bellum South* (New York, 1972); and finally, to bring what could be an endless list to a necessary close, Robert William Fogel and Stanley L. Engerman, *Time on the Cross: The Economics of American Negro Slavery* (Boston, 1974). A helpful introduction to several different interpretations of slavery is in Charles Crowe, *The Age of Civil War and Reconstruction, 1830-1900* (Homewood, 1975). William Styron's novel, *The Confessions of Nat Turner* (New York, 1967), has influenced my interpretation. I have also used, though to little advantage, James Benson Sellers, *Slavery in Alabama* (University, Ala., 1964).

2. *DJ*, I, 50.

3. *DJ*, I, 50-51.

4. *DJ*, I, 51.

5. *DJ*, I, 55.

6. *DJ*, I, 51.

7. *DJ*, I, 21.

8. *DJ*, II, 277.

9. *DJ*, V, iv.

10. *DJ*, II, 277.

11. *DJ*, III, 58.

12. *DJ*, III, 58.

13. *DJ*, III, 58-59.

14. *DJ*, III, 58.

15. *DJ*, III, 58.

16. *DJ*, IV, 17. His sense of guilt toward slavery developed long after emancipation; XIII, 290; XVI, 224.

17. *DJ*, IV, 57; for Dent's later comment on Grady, see *DJ*, XV, 130.

18. *DJ*, II, 7; a helpful study of white and black southerners' food is Sam Bowers Hilliard, *Hog Meat and Hoecake: Food Supply in the Old South, 1840-1860* (Carbondale, 1972).

19. *DJ*, I, 107; II, 278.

20. *DJ*, I, 76; III, 122, 155.

21. *DJ*, I, 77; IV, 51.

22. *DJ*, V, 236.

23. *DJ*, I, 42.

24. *DJ*, I, 13, 64.

25. *DJ*, I, 13, 43, 66.

26. *DJ*, II, 88, 147.

27. *DJ*, II, 146.

28. *DJ*, II, 182.

29. *DJ*, II, 198, 203, 205; IV, 82.

30. *DJ*, V, 229.

31. *DJ*, I, 132; II, 29.

32. *DJ*, IV, 101.

33. *DJ*, IV, 27.

34. *DJ*, II, 278.

35. *DJ*, III, 243; IV, 103.

36. Dent's disgruntlement with quarter noises is mentioned here and there throughout the journals.

37. *DJ*, I, 107; II, 185; III, 74-75, 252, 260.

38. *DJ*, II, 278.

39. *DJ*, XIII, 290-91; George M. Fredrickson, *The Black Image in the White Mind: The Debate on Afro-American Character and Destiny, 1817-1914* (New York, 1971), 161-64, 233, 236. Fredrickson's study has influenced other points of analysis in this chapter and throughout the book.

40. *DJ*, I, 132; V, 142; VI, 161.

41. *DJ*, I, 107, 235.

42. *DJ*, I, 81, 107; II, 185.

43. *DJ*, II, 185. Although Dent emphasized the matrifocal slave family, there are several evidences of strong black families on his plantations. For example, after emancipation, he despised the insulation of Negro women and children which their families provided. See chapter six, below, and Herbert G. Gutman, *The Black Family in Slavery and Freedom, 1750-1925* (New York, 1976).

44. *DJ*, II, 232; Fawn M. Brodie, *Thomas Jefferson: An Intimate History* (New York, 1974).

45. *DJ*, II, 185.

46. *DJ*, III, 29, 75.

47. *DJ*, III, 11.

48. *DJ*, III, 233, 261.

49. *DJ*, III, 180-81; also see E. A. Dent Letters for 1854 and 1855, in Dent Papers; and chapter five, below.

50. *DJ*, III, 186; IV, 27; V, 137.

51. *DJ*, II, 232; V, 158.

52. *DJ*, V, 158.

53. *DJ*, II, 150.

54. *DJ*, III, 64.

55. *DJ*, IV, 2; V, 133.

56. *DJ*, II, 278; XIII, 289; A-II, 118.

57. J. H. Dent to M. B. Wellborn, May 19, 1860, in Wellborn Papers.

58. *DJ*, I, 7; Sellers, *Slavery in Alabama*, 109-16.

59. *DJ*, I, 44.

60. *DJ*, I, 46-47.

61. *DJ*, I, 57.

62. *DJ*, I, 58, 137, 145.

63. *DJ*, I, 153-54.
64. *DJ*, I, 190; II, 126; IV, 40.
65. *DJ*, I, 138; III, 197, 202; IV, 43.
66. *DJ*, I, 190; and chapter five, below.
67. *DJ*, I, 203.
68. *DJ*, II, 78; III, 261.
69. *DJ*, II, 167.
70. John Duffy, "Medical Practice in the Ante Bellum South," *Journal of Southern History*, XXV (Feb., 1959), 53-72, especially, 60-61, would indicate that Dent's methods were not so archaic as those of many professionals.
71. *DJ*, II, 139; III, 124.
72. *DJ*, II, 139.
73. *DJ*, III, 105; IV, 42.
74. *DJ*, IV, 57, 60.
75. *DJ*, IV, 101.
76. *DJ*, III, 261; V, 164, 167, 186.
77. *DJ*, III, 87; V, 128, 182.
78. *DJ*, I, 57; V, 207.
79. *DJ*, V, 145-47.
80. *DJ*, V, 165-66; Marie Godfrey to Ray Mathis, Feb. 28, 1977, in Dent Papers.
81. He did not report blacks' injuring themselves to avoid work until after their emancipation; *DJ*, III, 105; IV, 54, 61; V, 235; VII, 46.
82. *DJ*, II, 39; IV, 17; V, 220, 247.
83. *DJ*, I, 131; III, 19, 81-83, 122.
84. *DJ*, V, 18-19.
85. *DJ*, IV, 42, 105.
86. *DJ*, I, 82, 195; II, 44, 114; III, 75; IV, 17, 39; V, 145.
87. *DJ*, II, 37; IV, 28; V, 181.
88. *DJ*, III, 74-75, 261; V, 197-98.
89. *DJ*, I, 178.
90. *DJ*, I, 63; II, 166; III, 191; V, 280.
91. *DJ*, II, 53.
92. *DJ*, II, 278.
93. *DJ*, I, 79, 130.
94. *DJ*, V, 171-73; also see chapters five and six on Dent's religious views.
95. *DJ*, II, 278.
96. His theme of the freedman's inferior labor is repetitious and tiresome from *DJ*, VII, into the last journal.
97. *DJ*, II, 12; III, 98; V, 24.
98. *DJ*, II, 87; IV, 92.
99. *DJ*, I, 51.
100. *DJ*, II, 91.
101. *DJ*, V, 90.
102. *DJ*, V, 82.
103. *DJ*, V, 83, 212, 214, 229, 237.

104. *DJ*, III, 85; VI, 97.
105. *DJ*, I, 51; V, 151.
106. *DJ*, I, 51-52.
107. *DJ*, I, 18-19, 52, 122.
108. *DJ*, II, 92.
109. *DJ*, III, 100-01; V, 157, 175.
110. *DJ*, V, 175.
111. *DJ*, III, 100.
112. *DJ*, I, 56.
113. *DJ*, I, 183; III, 71.
114. *DJ*, II, 31; IV, 21.
115. *DJ*, III, 177.
116. *DJ*, II, 44, 67.
117. *DJ*, II, 129.
118. *DJ*, IV, 53; V, 80.
119. *DJ*, II, 89; IV, 104.
120. *DJ*, IV, 95.
121. *DJ*, II, 106; IV, 104.
122. *DJ*, I, 76; III, 29, 185; IV, ii.
123. *DJ*, I, 110; III, 185; IV, ii.
124. *DJ*, I, 47, 78; II, 40; III, 109.
125. *DJ*, I, 150; IV, 60.
126. *DJ*, IV, 9, 18; V, 23.
127. *DJ*, I, 76; III, 185; V, 17, 264.
128. *DJ*, I, 53, 75, 84, 88, 110, 117, 198.
129. *DJ*, III, 60.
130. *DJ*, I, 84, 198; III, 60; V, 280.
131. *DJ*, I, 53, 85, 210.
132. *DJ*, IV, 56.
133. Genovese, *Roll, Jordan*, 116; *DJ*, V, 241.
134. *DJ*, I, 108; III, 180-81.
135. *DJ*, I, 113, 117.
136. *DJ*, I, 144.
137. *DJ*, I, 3, 144, 188, 247-51; II, 237; III, 106. After emancipation, Dent said
he had taken less than half of his skilled slaves' wages.
138. *DJ*, III, 86, 99, 106.
139. *DJ*, III, 180-81; IV, 16, 18; V, 161.
140. *DJ*, I, 178; IV, 17.
141. *DJ*, I, 102-03.
142. *DJ*, I, 103.
143. *DJ*, XVI, 129.
144. *DJ*, XVI, 129.
145. *DJ*, VI, 167; also chapter six, below.
146. *DJ*, II, 278.
147. *DJ*, III, 177.
148. *DJ*, V, 61-62.

149. *DJ*, V, 62.
150. *DJ*, V, 62.
151. *DJ*, V, 62.

CHAPTER FOUR

1. For a helpful analysis of the South's agrarian "mind," see Richard M. Weaver, "Aspects of the Southern Philosophy," in Louis D. Rubin, Jr., and Robert D. Jacobs, eds., *Southern Renascence: The Literature of the Modern South* (Baltimore, 1953), 14-30.

2. *DJ*, III, 135.

3. *DJ*, II, 8.

4. *DJ*, II, 254.

5. *DJ*, XIII, 280-81.

6. In addition to Perry Miller's works on New England Puritanism, see William Haller, *The Rise of Puritanism* (New York, 1957), 38, 96.

7. *DJ*, II, 138; III, xii; Weaver's "Southern Philosophy" also treats southern pessimism.

8. Fogel and Engerman, *Time on Cross*, 191-209, especially 203-04.

9. *DJ*, II, 62; also see V, 249. The organization and themes of this chapter were determined by Dent's concerns. In addition to those secondary sources cited in note one of chapter three, above, I have, in chapter four also, depended rather heavily on James C. Bonner, "Plantation and Farm: The Agricultural South," in Arthur S. Link and Rembert W. Patrick, eds., *Writing Southern History: Essays in Historiography in Honor of Fletcher M. Green* (Baton Rouge, 1965), 147-74; Davis, *Cotton Kingdom in Alabama, passim*, especially those portions on cotton production; Lewis Cecil Gray and others, *History of Agriculture in the Southern United States to 1860* (New York, 1941), I and II, *passim*, especially II, 691-720, 811-57, on corn, cotton, small grains, and livestock; and Weymouth T. Jordan, *Hugh Davis and His Alabama Plantation* (University, Ala., 1948), *passim*, especially chapters two and seven, on scientific farming and cotton production, respectively. I do not always cite specific dependencies in these or other chapters, but have acknowledged each source somewhere in the notes.

10. *DJ*, III, 151.

11. *DJ*, II, 235.

12. *DJ*, II, 5.

13. *DJ*, IV, 3-6.

14. *DJ*, III, xiv, 87, 90.

15. *DJ*, V, 1.

16. *DJ*, I, 177; IV, 3.

17. *DJ*, IV, 1, 5; V, 1.

18. *DJ*, IV, 2.

19. *DJ*, III, 87, 97.

20. *DJ*, III, 164-65; IV, 2, 5-8.

21. *DJ*, I, 52, 177; II, 13; III, 95, 121-22, 149, 152; IV, 3; V, 1.

22. *DJ*, III, 156; V, 12, 94.

23. *DJ*, II, 359.

24. *DJ*, II, 12; IV, 4; V, 1.

25. *DJ*, I, 208.

26. *DJ*, I, 207-08; III, 87.

27. *DJ*, III, 87.

28. *DJ*, I, 174, 177; II, 14.

29. *DJ*, I, 174, 238; III, 79, 95; IV, 4.

30. *DJ*, II, 12, 5; III, 94; IV, 18-19; V, 10; also see chapter three on undercropping.

31. *DJ*, II, 14, 264; III, 167, 262.

32. *DJ*, II, 14; IV, 2-4.

33. *DJ*, III, 164; IV, 7; V, 2.

34. *DJ*, III, 97, 173; V, 6.

35. *DJ*, II, 15, 20.

36. *DJ*, II, 20.

37. *DJ*, III, 95-96.

38. *DJ*, II, 106.

39. *DJ*, II, 107, 110; III, 172-73.

40. *DJ*, II, 25; also see Gray, *Agriculture*, II, 794-98.

41. *DJ*, II, 33; V, 201.

42. *DJ*, II, 110; V, 201.

43. *DJ*, IV, 12, 14, 16; V, 19, 148.

44. *DJ*, III, 174; V, 25.

45. *DJ*, IV, 18-20, 24.

46. *DJ*, II, 30; III, 99, 101; IV, 20-21.

47. *DJ*, I, 80.

48. *DJ*, II, 114; III, 100, 102.

49. *DJ*, II, 357, 360.

50. *DJ*, III, 100. He repressed his superstition, noting that he castrated colts without the proper "signs"; III, 230. He also argued against the policy of planting on the right "time" of the moon; XIV, 192.

51. *DJ*, I, 33; IV, 22. For more on these and other seeds used, see Dent's letters to Thomas Ewbank, Commissioner of Patents, in Dent Papers.

52. *DJ*, II, 359-60.

53. *DJ*, II, 114; IV, 23.

54. *DJ*, I, 63; II, 31, 114-15; IV, 37.

55. *DJ*, I, 82; II, 29, 115; III, 102; IV, 24.

56. *DJ*, III, 100.

57. *DJ*, I, 80; III, 103 *ff*.

58. *DJ*, III, 103-06.

59. *DJ*, I, 33.

60. *DJ*, III, 221; V, 44; also see Dent to Thomas Ewbank, Nov. 5, 1849, copy in Dent Papers.

61. *DJ*, I, 29.

62. *DJ*, I, 125, 143.

63. *DJ*, I, 91-92.

64. *DJ*, I, 91-92.

65. *DJ*, II, 35, 119; IV, 28-30.

66. *DJ*, II, 119

67. *DJ*, I, 98; II, 360; IV, 32.

68. *DJ*, I, 100, 105.

69. *DJ*, I, 203, 207-08.

70. *DJ*, III, 118; V, 55.

71. *DJ*, II, 41, 127; III, 109, 118; IV, 40.

72. *DJ*, II, 127, 129; III, 118, 234.

73. *DJ*, II, 126; III, 118, 193.

74. *DJ*, III, 109, 116, 229.

75. *DJ*, II, 127-28; III, 118, 194, 233; IV, 38, 41.

76. *DJ*, I, 40; II, 50; III, 112, 116, 123; IV, 36, 42.

77. *DJ*, II, 189; IV, 42.

78. *DJ*, II, 123, 127; III, 113; V, 53.

79. *DJ*, II, 360.

80. *DJ*, III, 194; IV, 46; do is "ditto."

81. *DJ*, III, 39, 121-22; IV, 46; also Dent to Thomas Ewbank, Nov. 5, 1849, copy in Dent Papers.

82. *DJ*, IV, 48, 50, 52; V, 360.

83. *DJ*, III, 125-26; IV, 48.

84. *DJ*, III, 200; IV, 49.

85. *DJ*, II, 59; III, 123, 125; IV, 56.

86. *DJ*, I, 40; III, 121.

87. *DJ*, I, 119; V, 69.

88. *DJ*, I, 121.

89. *DJ*, V, 80, 236.

90. *DJ*, II, 64.

91. *DJ*, III, 16.

92. *DJ*, III, 205; IV, 55.

93. *DJ*, V, 80, 85, 93.

94. *DJ*, II, 66; IV, 60.

95. *DJ*, III, 205-06; IV, 55-56, 61; V, 93.

96. *DJ*, I, 41; III, 128, 131, 206.

97. *DJ*, III, 206; IV, 60.

98. *DJ*, I, 142-43.

99. *DJ*, I, 143; III, 139.

100. *DJ*, III, 134; V, 94.

101. *DJ*, I, 48, 49, 53.

102. *DJ*, III, 208, 249, 250.

103. *DJ*, III, 139, 141, 209.

104. *DJ*, III, 53, 141; Phillips, *Negro Slavery*, 206.

105. *DJ*, III, 134, 136, 139, 209; V, 102. The monument was a large obelisk.

106. *DJ*, III, 139; Fogel and Engerman, *Time on Cross*, 203-04.

107. *DJ*, I, 53; III, 141.

108. *DJ*, I, 53, 54.

109. *DJ*, III, 141.

110. *DJ*, I, 150.

111. *DJ*, I, 54, 150; II, 46; V, 106.

112. *DJ*, I, 53; II, 78; Phillips, *Negro Slavery*, 209.

113. *DJ*, I, 53, 54; III, 141, 143, 211.

114. *DJ*, III, 214; IV, 81.

115. *DJ*, I, 159; III, 146; IV, 81, 86.

116. *DJ*, III, 146, 151, 214; IV, 79, 83, 91; also see the table on corn production in chapter four, below.

117. *DJ*, IV, 86, 87.

118. Eaton, *Old South*, 210-11; *DJ*, III, 148, 149, 151.

119. *DJ*, I, 33, 66, 159; IV, 90.

120. *DJ*, III, 148; IV, 94.

121. *DJ*, III, 151-52; IV, 97.

122. *DJ*, II, 3; V, 131.

123. *DJ*, II, 87.

124. *DJ*, II, 89; IV, 97; V, 131.

125. *DJ*, II, 4, 89; IV, 97, 99, 100.

126. *DJ*, II, 89; V, 89, 131, 132, 134.

127. *DJ*, III, 160; IV, 104.

128. *DJ*, I, 215.

129. *DJ*, I, 179; III, 89, 213; IV, 21.

CHAPTER FIVE

1. Anne Firor Scott, "Women's Perspective on the Patriarchy in the 1850s," *Journal of American History*, LXI (June, 1974), 52.

2. Bertram Wyatt-Brown, "The Ideal Typology and Ante Bellum Southern History: A Testing of a New Approach," *Societas*, V (Winter, 1975), 1-29; Anne Firor Scott, *The Southern Lady: From Pedestal to Politics, 1830-1930* (Chicago, 1970), 102.

3. *DJ*, XIII, 262. My perspective has also been influenced by John Demos, "The American Family in Past Time," *American Scholar*, vol. 43 (Summer, 1974), 422-46; by the several articles in Michael Gordon and Tamara Hareven, eds., *Journal of Marriage and the Family*, vol. 35, no. 3 (August, 1973), 393 *ff*.; and Theodore K. Rabb and Robert I. Rotberg, *The Family in History: Interdisciplinary Essays* (New York, 1973).

4. E. A. Dent Letters, Sept. 8, 1854, in Dent Papers; *DJ*, XIII, 282; chapter five, below, treats the education of J. H. Dent's children.

5. See chapter one, above,

6. E. A. Dent Letters, Aug. 12, 1853; Sept. 8, 1854, in Dent Papers.

7. E. A. Dent Letters, Sept. 17, 1854, in Dent Papers.

8. *DJ*, VI, 122.

9. E. A. Dent Letters, Feb. 4, 1854; March 30, 1855, in Dent Papers; *DJ*, XIII, 269; also see chapter five, below.

10. *DJ*, XIII, 281.

11. E. A. Dent Letters, May 19, 1853, in Dent Papers.

12. *DJ*, II, 191.

13. Walker, *Barbour County*, 73-84; *DJ*, II, 191.

14. *DJ*, II, 191-92.

15. *DJ*, II, 192.

16. *DJ*, II, 192.

17. *DJ*, II, 192-93.

18. *DJ*, II, 193.

19. *DJ*, III, 62, 63, 68, 119.

20. *DJ*, III, 161.

21. *DJ*, III, 160.

22. *DJ*, III, 160-61.

23. *DJ*, III, 161-62; also see E. A. Dent Letters, Jan. 3, 1855; and Elizabeth Schieffelin to Ray Mathis, Nov. 8, 1976, in Dent Papers.

24. *DJ*, III, 161.

25. *DJ*, III, 161-62.

26. *DJ*, III, 179.

27. *DJ*, III, 179.

28. *DJ*, III, 179-80.

29. *DJ*, III, 180.

30. E. A. Dent Letters, Feb. 10, 1853, in Dent Papers.

31. *DJ*, III, 180-82.

32. *DJ*, III, 182.

33. *DJ*, III, 182.

34. E. A. Dent Letters, March 30, 1855, and [June, 1855], in Dent Papers.

35. *DJ*, I, 218.

36. Frank F. Furstenberg, Jr., "Industrialization and the American Family: A Look Backward," in Marvin B. Sussman, ed., *Sourcebook in Marriage and The Family* (Boston, 1974), 38-39. I have used this excellent article for several points of analysis in chapters one, two, five, and six.

37. *DJ*, II, 257.

38. This composite of Mary Elizabeth Dent is based on all of the *Dent Journals*; and E. A. Dent Letters, in Dent Papers.

39. *DJ*, I, 218, 256; II, 201; XIII, 260-61; XXI, 4; E. A. Dent Letters, for 1854, in Dent Papers; and Scott, *Southern Lady*, 4.

40. *DJ*, III, 47; IV, 128.

41. *DJ*, XXI, 4; Sarah Lining Dent was fifteen when she died in 1866. Marie Godfrey to Ray Mathis, Feb. 28, 1977, in Dent Papers.

42. *DJ*, IV, 25-27.

43. *DJ*, IV, 22, 25, 27.

44. *DJ*, I, 114; IV, 20, 90; V, 6, 229, 233.

45. *DJ*, III, 172; IV, 76, 103; V, 48, 91.

46. *DJ*, IV, 78.

47. *DJ*, IV, 24, 77.

48. *DJ*, I, 105, 110; III, 147; IV, 6; V, 94.

49. *DJ*, V, 151, 156, 219.

50. By the late 1850s Dent estimated family expenses at $3,500 per year, and usually managed with a thousand dollars less; *DJ*, III, 252; IV, 12, 31, 32, 81; V, 352; A-I, *passim*.

51. *DJ*, IV, 3, 54, 104; V, 4, 76, 83.

52. *DJ*, III, 160; IV, 97, 103.

53. *DJ*, I, 82; and III, IV, V, *passim*.

54. *DJ*, IV, 26; V, 23, 46, 49, 52, 87, 94.

55. *DJ*, III, 119; IV, 63.

56. *DJ*, V, 227, 231, 236; Welborn, "Dent Sketch," 2, in Dent Papers.

57. Hopkins, *Wellborn,* 73-82; see Dent's letters in Wellborn Papers; *DJ*, IV,

iii, 2, 29; VII, 50; XIII, 286.

58. *DJ*, V, 59.

59. E. A. Dent Letters, in Dent Papers; Minna Dent Wellborn Letters, in Wellborn Papers; *DJ*, V, 115, 158.

60. *DJ*, III, 91; IV, 56; V, 64.

61. *DJ*, V, 26, 65, 70, 92.

62. *DJ*, III, 144, 161; IV, 6; V, 220, 241; for more on Dent's sons, see chapter six and the postwar *Dent Journals*, especially XIII, 286-87.

63. *DJ*, XIII, 289-90.

64. *DJ*, III, 92; IV, 64.

65. *DJ*, IV, 8; XIII, 276.

66. *DJ*, IV, 25, and *passim*. Dent was kinder to Methodists in the postwar period.

67. *DJ*, IV, 91-92; V, 12, 18, 63, 141.

68. E. A. Dent Letters, Sept. 10, 1848, in Dent Papers.

69. *DJ*, II, 42, 96, 122, 212; III, 22-23; E. A. Dent Letters, Feb. 4, 1854, in Dent Papers.

70. E. A. Dent Letters, Jan. 23, 1855, in Dent Papers. The Dent girls' attendance at the Union is based on record of tuition paid to "McIntosh," who was at the college; *DJ*, IV, 36; also see III, 12, 31, 36, 46, 106, 119.

71. E. A. Dent Letters, Feb. 4, 1854, in Dent Papers.

72. *Ibid.*, and *DJ*, III, 8.

73. *DJ*, III, 46.

74. *DJ*, III, 46.

75. *DJ*, III, 46-47.

76. D. Harland Hagler, "The Ideal Woman in the Antebellum South: Lady or Farmwife?: The Agrarian View," unpublished paper delivered at the forty-second annual meeting of the Southern Historical Association, Atlanta, 1976.

77. *DJ*, III, 46-47.

78. *DJ*, III, 46-47.

79. *DJ*, III, 47.

80. *DJ*, III, 175, 220; IV, 10, 14, 36, 44, 60, 124; V, 46, 79, 110.

81. *DJ*, IV, 3, 23, 49, 77, 124; V, 22, 103, 150, 234. "In Memory of John Horry Dent, Jr., C. S. Navy," typescript copy in Dent Papers.

82. *DJ*, V, 141, 150-51.

83. *DJ*, V, 190, 243.

84. *DJ*, XIII, 260-61.

85. Furstenberg, "Industrialization and American Family," 35; Fanny Whipple Dent's gravestone, Cave Spring Cemetery, Cave Spring, Georgia; *DJ*, XIII, 283.

86. *DJ*, XIII, 283-84.

87. *DJ*, V, 95.

88. *DJ*, V, 51, 116.

89. *DJ*, III, 118, 170, 173; IV, 3, 65-71, 83, 84, 86.

90. *DJ*, III, 149; IV, 26, 90; V, 43, 132, 352.

91. *DJ*, IV, 7, 12, 26; V, 10, 43, 90.

92. *DJ*, IV, 3, 7; Dent to Minna, Feb. 25, 1861; and note on Minna to Dent, Dec. 4, 1864, in Wellborn Papers.

93. *DJ*, IV, 3; V, 71, 75, 131, 141-42.

94. *DJ*, V, 162; XIII, 262.

95. *DJ*, III, 148; IV, 1-2, 6, 40, 84; V, 157, 231.

96. *DJ*, V, 83; XIII, 262; for more on the plantation as the "garden" or "life" of the mind, see Simpson, *Dispossessed Garden*, 1-33, especially 23-25.

97. *DJ*, IV, iii, 29; V, 83; VII, 82.

98. See chapter two, above; and *DJ*, III, 11, 27, 31, 55; IV, 81; A-I, 54, 76, 100, 104, 118.

99. *DJ*, I, 163, 180; II, 323, 330, 339, 343-44, 357; III, 268; V, 261-62; VII, iii; Dent to Minna, Feb. 25, 1861, in Wellborn Papers.

100. *DJ*, IV, 22, 23; V, 20.

101. *DJ*, III, 160; IV, 30, 40, 54, 63, 77, 91; V, 116-17.

102. *DJ*, III, 163; V, 41, 58, 59, 60.

103. *DJ*, I, 150; II, 13; IV, 52, 60; V, 69, 134, 228.

104. *DJ*, IV, 88; V, 82.

105. *DJ*, V, 172, 181, 184.

106. *DJ*, V, 185.

107. *DJ*, V, 145, 159.

108. *DJ*, IV, 55-56.

109. *DJ*, IV, 57.

110. *DJ*, IV, 105; XXI, 5; on the abolition issue, see chapter five, below; and Hopkins, *Wellborn*, 15.

111. *DJ*, IV, 57-63; XIII, 261.

112. *DJ*, IV, 128.

113. *DJ*, IV, 128; XXI, 4-5.

114. *DJ*, IV, 63-65.

115. *DJ*, IV, 65.

116. *DJ*, IV, 65.

117. *DJ*, IV, 65.

118. *DJ*, IV, 65.

119. *DJ*, IV, 66.

120. *DJ*, IV, 66.

121. *DJ*, IV, 66.

122. *DJ*, IV, 67.

123. *DJ*, IV, 67; XIII, 273; Dent's admiration for Yankees was characteristic of that trait among southerners as described by John Hope Franklin, *A Southern Odyssey: Travelers in the Antebellum North* (Baton Rouge, 1976); also see note 39 of chapter one, above.

124. *DJ*, IV, 67.

125. *DJ*, IV, 67.

126. *DJ*, IV, 68.

127. *DJ*, IV, 68.

128. *DJ*, IV, 68.

129. *DJ*, IV, 69.

130. *DJ*, IV, 69.

131. *DJ*, IV, 69.

132. *DJ*, IV, 69.

133. *DJ*, IV, 70.

134. *DJ*, IV, 70.

135. *DJ*, IV, 70.

136. *DJ*, IV, 71.

137. *DJ*, IV, 71.

138. *DJ*, IV, 71.

139. *DJ*, IV, 71.

140. *DJ*, XIII, 273.

141. E. A. Dent Letters, Sept. 10, 1848, in Dent Papers.

142. *DJ*, V, 77; Dent to Max, May 19, 1860, in Wellborn Papers.

CHAPTER SIX

1. In this chapter and preceding ones, I have relied rather heavily on Minnie Clare Boyd, *Alabama in the Fifties: A Social Study* (New York, 1931); Lewy Dorman, *Party Politics in Alabama From 1850 Through 1860* (Wetumpka, 1935); Walter L. Fleming, *Civil War and Reconstruction in Alabama* (New York, 1949); Lucille Griffith, *Alabama: A Documentary History to 1900* (University, Ala., 1972); Malcolm Cook McMillan, *Constitutional Development in Alabama, 1798-1901: A Study in Politics, the Negro, and Sectionalism* (Chapel Hill, 1955). Helpful general studies of the 1850s and 1860s have been David M. Potter, *The Impending Crisis, 1848-1861* (New York, 1976); and J. G. Randall and David Donald, *The Civil War and Reconstruction* (Boston, 1961).

2. *DJ*, I, 136; XIII, 262.

3. *DJ*, IV, 25.

4. *DJ*, II, 193.

5. *DJ*, III, 57; Dorman, *Politics in Alabama*, 128, and Roy Franklin Nichols, *Franklin Pierce: Young Hickory of the Granite Hills* (Philadelphia, 1969), 450-69.

6. *DJ*, III, 56.

7. *DJ*, III, 56.

8. *DJ*, III, 253.

9. Walker, *Barbour County*, 165; Glover, *Colleton County*, 22, 90-91; *DJ*, III, 205, 209.

10. *DJ*, III, 58-59.

11. *DJ*, V, 72; the term "conditional Unionism" is from Degler, *Other South*, 125 *ff.* For a good view of South Carolina Unionism among Dent's distant kinsmen and of the type of Charleston society he eschewed, see Margaret L. Coit, *John C. Calhoun: American Portrait* (Boston, 1950), 222-25, 236-37.

12. *DJ*, V, 133.

13. Dent to Max, Aug. 28, 1860, in Wellborn Papers.

14. *Ibid.*

15. *DJ*, V, 204.

16. *DJ*, V, 205.

17. There are several accounts of a Cato secession party; *DJ*, V, 205; Walker, *Barbour County*, 174; Eufaula Heritage Association, *Historic Eufaula: A Treasury of Southern Architecture, 1827-1910* (Eufaula, 1972), 20.

18. *DJ*, V, 205, 206, 210.

19. *DJ*, V, 212; and Dent to Minna, Feb. 25, 1861, in Wellborn Papers.

20. Dent to Minna, Feb. 25, 1861, in Wellborn Papers; White, *Rhett*, 194 *ff.*

21. Dent to Minna, Feb. 25, 1861, in Wellborn Papers.

22. *DJ*, V, 196, 206.

23. Dent to Minna, Feb. 25, 1861, in Wellborn Papers; Walker, *Barbour County*, 165-67, 170, 175.

24. *DJ*, III, xix.

25. *DJ*, V, 196.

26. *DJ*, V, 222-24, 226, 257.

27. *DJ*, V, 222-23.

28. *DJ*, V, 224-25.

29. *DJ*, V, 225-26.

30. *DJ*, V, 234.

31. Minna to Dent, Dec. 4, 1864, in Wellborn Papers; *DJ*, VI, 144; VII, 56. There was also brief mention of transient wartime tutors named Leavel, Hudson, and Whigham; VI, 179; A-I, 77.

32. *DJ*, V, 235, 237, 242.

33. Dent to Minna, Aug. 22, 1861, in Wellborn Papers; *DJ*, IV, 56; V, 261; VI, 80; XXI, 4: also see "In Memory of John Horry Dent, Jr., C. S. Navy," typescript copy in Dent Papers.

34. Minna to Dent, Dec. 4, 1864, in Wellborn Papers; *DJ*, V, 243; VI, 181. See postwar *DJ*, especially XXI, 13.

35. *DJ*, V, 243-46, 256-58; Dent to Minna, Aug. 22, 1861, in Wellborn Papers.

36. *DJ*, V, 242-43; Taylor, *Cavalier and Yankee*, 270-97.

37. *DJ*, V, 118.

38. Dent to Minna, Aug. 22, 1861, in Wellborn Papers.

39. *DJ*, XIII, 272.

40. *DJ*, V, 249-50; Dent to Max, Dec. 4, 1861, in Wellborn Papers.

41. *DJ*, V, 256, 258.

42. Dent to Max, Dec. 14, 1861, in Wellborn Papers.

43. *Ibid*.

44. *DJ*, V, 266, 268.

45. *DJ*, VI, 176; XIII, 262; A-I, 212-13; A-II, 118.

46. *DJ*, V, 239.

47. *DJ*, V, 263.

48. Dent to Max, Dec. 4, 1861, in Wellborn Papers.

49. Dent to Minna, Aug. 22, 1861, in Wellborn Papers.

50. *DJ*, V, 271.

51. *DJ*, V, 272.

52. Dent to Minna, Aug. 22, 1861, in Wellborn Papers.

53. Dent to Max, Dec. 4, 1861, in Wellborn Papers. Dent continued this theme in 1880; *DJ*, XIII, 262.

54. *DJ*, V, 269.

55. *DJ*, XIII, 275; A-I, 186; A-II, 118.

56. Dent to Max, Dec. 4, 1861, in Wellborn Papers. At the war's end, Dent had $14,000 in secure loans; *DJ*, VII, 61; A-II, 118.

57. *DJ*, VI, 76.

58. *DJ*, IV, 121; VI, 65-66, 76; Thomas H. Watts to Dent, April 14, 1864, T. H. Watts Executive Papers, in Alabama Department of Archives and History, Montgomery. On the little evidence of impressment of slaves in Alabama, see

Griffith, *Alabama*, 439. At least three of Dent's slaves were impressed, perhaps more.

59. *DJ*, VI, 64, 71-73, 78, 184; A-I, 63, 107.

60. *DJ*, VI, 6; A-I, 107, 128-29.

61. *DJ*, VI, 85.

62. *DJ*, VI, 6, 13-14, 36.

63. *DJ*, I, 169; V, 245.

64. *DJ*, V, 246, 265, 283; VI, 87.

65. *DJ*, I, 209; VI, 88; VII, 76; White, *Rhett*, 240-41.

66. *DJ*, V, 245; VI, 76, 86, 150, 181.

67. *DJ*, VI, 12, 69, 75, 88, 94, 147; VII, 78.

68. *DJ*, V, 279; VI, 37.

69. *DJ*, VI, 80, 85.

70. *DJ*, VI, 21-22, 38, 65, 82, 89, 186; XIII, 262; A-I, 107, and *passim*.

71. *DJ*, VI, 80, 83.

72. *DJ*, VI, 9, 64, 68, 69, 78, 79, 80.

73. *DJ*, VI, 80, 103.

74. *DJ*, VI, 79, 88, 89.

75. White, *Rhett*, 240-41; *DJ*, VI, 90, 94, 103, 118, 124.

76. *DJ*, VI, 94, 108, 109, 123. John Dent seemingly aided his brother, George Columbus, and family during the Reconstruction period.

77. *DJ*, VI, 94.

78. Walker, *Barbour County*, 199-208; Marie Godfrey to Ray Mathis, Feb. 28, 1977, in Dent Papers; *DJ*, VI, 95.

79. *DJ*, VI, 97.

80. *DJ*, VI, 106.

81. *DJ*, VI, 73, 126, 175.

82. *DJ*, VI, 99.

83. *DJ*, VI, 116.

84. *DJ*, VII, 13.

85. *DJ*, VI, 111.

86. *DJ*, VI, 111.

87. *DJ*, VI, 120-21, 175.

88. *DJ*, VI, 120-21. Another irritation in this period was the necessity to apply for military pardon, which Dent (unlike his brother-in-law Barnwell Rhett) requested. He did this in August through his friend Eli S. Shorter. The request was duly recorded in September, and he took the oath of loyalty February 2, 1865; *DJ*, VI, 120, 135; "Military Record Register of Applications for Amnesty and Pardons," I, 291 (entry 868), in Alabama Department of Archives and History, Montgomery; White, *Rhett*, 241.

89. *DJ*, VI, 124.

90. *DJ*, VI, 126.

91. *DJ*, VI, 127.

92. *DJ*, VI, 128.

93. *DJ*, VII, 7.

94. *DJ*, VI, 148.

95. *DJ*, VI, 130; VII, 6. This analysis of freedmen owes much to Peter Kolchin,

First Freedom: The Responses of Alabama's Blacks to Emancipation (Westport, 1972).

96. *DJ*, XIII, 263-64. This number did not amount to more than twenty "full" hands, about half of Dent's wartime force.

97. *DJ*, VII, 2.

98. *DJ*, XIII, 264.

99. *DJ*, VI, 131, 134.

100. *DJ*, XIII, 264.

101. *DJ*, VII, 7, 13; XIII, 265.

102. *DJ*, VII, 13, 22.

103. *DJ*, VII, 28.

104. *DJ*, VII, 11, 17, 49.

105. *DJ*, VI, 166; VII, 4, 11, 36.

106. *DJ*, VII, 20, 22.

107. *DJ*, VI, 74, 145.

108. *DJ*, VII, 4.

109. *DJ*, VII, 74.

110. *DJ*, VII, 5-6, 46.

111. *DJ*, VII, 5-6, 19.

112. *DJ*, VII, 75.

113. *DJ*, VII, 75, 78.

114. *DJ*, VI, 143. Now the myth of happy slaves was full-blown.

115. *DJ*, VII, 52.

116. *DJ*, VII, 27, 31, 42, 56.

117. *DJ*, VI, 144, 151, 155-58; VII, 15, 22, 33, 265.

118. *DJ*, XIII, 265.

119. *DJ*, VI, 163, 165, 169; VII, 47, 80.

120. *DJ*, VI, 152, 167; VII, 36, 42.

121. *DJ*, VII, 42.

122. *DJ*, VI, 149; VII, 1-2, 49.

123. *DJ*, VII, 76; XIII, 266; A-II, 118.

124. *DJ*, VI, 110, 121, 125, 139, 140, 153 *ff.*, 162.

125. *DJ*, VII, 50, 54. Deed Book S, 83-84, Barbour County Courthouse, Clayton, shows Dent sold 1280 acres at $8.00 per acre.

126. *DJ*, VII, 54.

127. *DJ*, VII, 64.

128. *DJ*, VII, 61.

129. *DJ*, VII, 65.

130. *DJ*, VII, 62.

131. *DJ*, VII, 65.

132. *DJ*, VII, 65. Dent kept at least forty acres in Barbour County for several years and had other business dealings with Whit Clark and the Pettys.

133. *DJ*, VII, 86.

134. *DJ*, XIII, 266.

135. *DJ*, VII, 87.

136. *DJ*, VII, 80.

137. *DJ*, VII, 83.

138. *DJ*, VII, 77-78.

139. *DJ*, VII, 67-83, especially 82.
140. *DJ*, VII, 82-84.
141. *DJ*, VII, 84, 86.
142. *DJ*, VII, 85.
143. *DJ*, VII, 88.
144. *DJ*, VII, 88.
145. *DJ*, VII, 88-89.
146. *DJ*, VII, 89.

EPILOGUE

1. An article based on limited sources, which nevertheless spans Dent's antebellum and postbellum experience is Thomas A. Belser, Jr., "Alabama Plantation to Georgia Farm, John Horry Dent and Reconstruction," *Alabama Historical Quarterly*, XXV (Spring, 1963), 136-48.

2. *DJ*, VII-XXI, especially XX, 3 *ff*.

3. *DJ*, A-I–A-IX.

4. *DJ*, XX; also see Ray Mathis and Mary Mathis, *Introduction and Index to John Horry Dent Farm Journals and Account Books, 1840-1892* (University, Ala., 1977), *passim*, especially ix-xxxii.

AN ESSAY ON UNPUBLISHED SOURCES*

The major source for this study has been the twenty-nine volumes of John Horry Dent journals which are deposited in Troy State University Library, Auburn University Archives, and University of Alabama Library. Thomas A. Belser, professor of history, Auburn University, is in possession of one J. H. Dent Journal for 1876-1877 (XII). The bulk of these journals, twenty-five in number, are in Troy State Library and include volumes II-XI, XIII, XIV, XVI, XVII, XX, XXI, AI-AIX. Two journals, volumes XVIII and XIX, are in the Auburn Archives; and two more, I and XV, are in the University of Alabama Library. Hard copies of all the above journals, including Belser's, are deposited in the Troy State Library and Auburn Archives.

The set of copies at Troy State has been paged according to Ray Mathis, Mary Mathis, and Douglas Clare Purcell, editors, *The John Horry Dent Farm Journals and Account Books, 1840-1892* (University, Alabama, 1977), 30 volumes on four reels of positive microfilm, with a separate book of *Introduction and Index*. In researching Dent's Alabama period, I utilized the copy of his journals in Troy State Library; but in the notes above, I cite the microfilm edition of *Dent Journals* (abbreviated *DJ*), because of its accessibility.

The volumes most pertinent to this study are I, 1840-42; II, 1851-54; III, 1855-57; IV, 1858; V, 1859-62; VI, 1863-65; VII, 1866-70; XIII, 1878-80 (contains the most extensive autobiographical statement); XX, 1891-92 (another memoir); XXI, "Family Record" (genealogy); A-I and A-II, personal account books of J. H. Dent's Alabama period.

Because Dent destroyed most of his correspondence in 1866, supposedly to lighten the burden of removing to north Georgia, the Wellborn Papers in Auburn University Archives have been especially helpful; they contain about thirty Dent letters to and received from the M. B. Wellborns, who were his daughter and son-in-law. This correspondence dates from 1860 through 1891. Other helpful items in the Wellborn Papers include a genealogical chart for the Horry-Dent-Wellborn families, the United States Navy Department's abstract of Captain John Herbert Dent's naval career, and a Memorandum to the Dent Trust (marriage agreement with the Robert Morrison estate, 1835). The later Memorandum is dated 1882.

The J. H. Dent Papers in Troy State University Library (aside from the Dent Journals) include copies of Dent materials in the Wellborn Papers and in other depositories listed below. There are also a few letters, clippings, excerpts, and other fragments which were loosely inserted in the bound Dent journals and therefore removed as irrelevant for microfilming. Most of these pieces (which include Dent's will) are from the later Georgia period and are not directly pertinent to this study. One exception to this is the memorial to "J. H. Dent, Jr., Confederate States Navy"; he died in 1864. This collection's largest value for the Alabama years are copies of Dent family papers for which the originals have been

---

* The notes, above, will serve as a guide to the published sources I have used.

lost or which remain in private possession. Elizabeth Schieffelin of Los Angeles, California, permitted me to copy the few extant excerpts from Elizabeth Anne Dent's childhood "Diary" and also E. A. Dent's letters to J. H. Dent in Barbour County, Alabama. Although the location of these originals is unknown, Anne Dent's letters are one of the richest sources for this study. Mrs. Schieffelin also placed a copy of the J. H. Dent-Morrison Trust, 1835 (which she made from one owned by Mrs. Felix Rapp, Anniston, Alabama), within the Dent Papers. Julia B. Hodges, Lewisburg, West Virginia, provided a copy of the same excerpts from E. A. Dent's "Diary." And J. H. Beury, also of Lewisburg, allowed his copy of M. B. Wellborn's "Dent Sketch" to be recopied for the Dent Papers; the original is apparently lost.

The Dent Papers also contain all of my notes, correspondence, and jottings of interviews conducted in person, by telephone, and by correspondence throughout the course of my research on this project since 1970. The most important correspondents and subjects for interview have been Professors James C. Bonner, Bertram Wyatt-Brown, William K. Scarborough, Aubrey C. Land, and Barton Starr; also Anne Boucher, Marie Godfrey, Beulah Glover, Sarah Winston Lawton, and Elizabeth Schieffelin. Mrs. Schieffelin's several letters to me, along with my notes of a day-long interview with her and of a rapid reading of her typescript history of the Jonah Horry-J. H. Dent family, compose a mine of information on family legends which she has spent years demythologizing. Mrs. Schieffelin also provided me a copy of the elusive Linton C. Hopkins, *Biography of Maximilian Bethune Wellborn* (1960).

The "Deed Books" in the Probate Office of the Barbour County Court House in Clayton, Alabama, contain a complete and helpful record on each plantation bought and sold by J. H. Dent from 1837 through 1866. Marie Godfrey of Eufaula, Alabama, a local historian and professional researcher, has an impressive collection of Barbour County records from which she answered numerous questions relating to early settlers and men of power and influence like Whitfield Clark. I also gleaned some information from the small manuscript and rare book collections in the Shorter Mansion and Carnegie Library, Eufaula, Alabama.

The Thomas H. Watts Executive Papers and the "Military Record Register of Applications for Amnesty and Pardon," both in Alabama Department of Archives and History, Montgomery, yielded two Dent items relative to his wartime and Reconstruction activity. Douglas C. Purcell provided these pertinent pieces. The Tuscaloosa County Preservation Society, Tuscaloosa, Alabama, contains information on J. H. Dent's uncle, Dennis Dent. Marvin L. Harper provided copies of this. The cemeteries of Clayton, Alabama, and of Cave Spring, Georgia, bear mute but clear testimony to the family's stature, and to Dent's devotion to wives and children. The first wife and some earlier children were buried at Clayton. Dent, his second wife, and some later children were interred at Cave Spring. The early deeds and papers belonging to James C. Culver (owner of former Dent home in Cave Spring) are revealing of his land transactions in north Georgia.

Holdings of the Georgia Department of Archives and History, Atlanta, and of the Georgia Historical Society, Hodgson Hall, Savannah, while containing some useful items, were not as helpful as the collection of Brailsford-Troup Genealogy and Ophelia Troup Dent's "Memoir," which are in the Hofwyl plantation near

Darien, Georgia. Copies were provided by Victoria R. Gunn. The museum at Fort King George, near Darien, has a map which shows "Rhett," R. Barnwell, as successor to E. A. Dent at Cedar Hill plantation near Darien. Elizabeth Schieffelin provided this information.

At the South Carolina Department of Archives and History in Columbia, the volumes of "Charleston Wills" and "Marriage Settlements," as well as copies of early maps proved to be of inestimable value. The genealogical files of the Huguenot Society of South Carolina in Charleston were helpful on the Horrys, Hugers, Roberts, and Sarrazins. The same was true of genealogical files and personal papers of the Morrisons, Ropers, and Linings; of early *Charleston City Directories*; of typescript copies of a few additional Elizabeth Anne Dent letters not in the Schieffelin file; and of nineteenth-century maps of Colleton District, all in the holdings of the South Carolina Historical Society, Fireproof Building, Charleston. In the Charleston Library Society, I found a few very early and helpful books on Elias Horry (the businessman) and his Charleston and Hamburg Railroad. The deeds in the Colleton County Court House, Walterboro, South Carolina, enabled my friend and researcher, Beulah Glover, to plot E. A. Dent's plantation known as Fenwick. Glover's personal holdings include her unpublished historical maps of family plantations in Colleton which I copied, used, and deposited in the Dent Papers.

The National Archives in Washington, D.C., has thus far yielded one unpublished Dent letter to the Commissioner of Patents; it is dated November 5, 1849. Professor Allen Jones of Auburn University provided this. And Professor Grady McWhiney, of the University of Alabama, directed me to Dent's letter of November 9, 1850, which is published in the *Report of the Commissioner of Patents* (1851), 284-88. After thorough research in the National Archives, John Douglas Helms (in a letter of April 14, 1977) suggests that even if Dent's correspondence with the Commissioners of Patents and Agriculture was voluminous, it was apparently destroyed in 1935.

ACKNOWLEDGMENTS

Acknowledging those persons who have been of special assistance is one of the few pleasant tasks in the final stages of completing a book. Having a long list of helpers, I shall, in most cases, limit my comment to the type of assistance rendered. I am deeply indebted to each person named, as well as to others who, for practical reasons, cannot be credited here.

Members of the Dent family who have made journals and papers available and granted permission for publication are Edmund D. Dent, Jr., Miami, Florida; John Horry Beury, Lewisburg, West Virginia; Julia B. Hodges, Lewisburg, West Virginia; Mary Hopkins, Atlanta, Georgia; Julia W. Daugette, Atlanta, Georgia; and Elizabeth Schieffelin, Los Angeles, California. Local historians who have helped keep me on the path of fact are Beulah Glover, Walterboro, South Carolina; Marie Godfrey, Eufaula, Alabama; Margaret Farmer, Troy, Alabama; and Martha K. Lindsey, Cave Spring, Georgia.

Librarians and others having special collections who have assisted are Allen W. Jones, professor of history and archivist, Auburn University; Frances P. Barton, Special Collections, University of Alabama Library; Grady McWhiney, professor and chairman, Department of History, University of Alabama; the South Carolina Department of Archives and History, Columbia; the South Caroliniana Library, University of South Carolina, Columbia; the Huguenot Society of South Carolina, Charleston; the South Carolina Historical Society, Charleston; the Charleston Library Society; Mary W. Martin, Carnegie Library, Eufaula; Hilda C. Sexton and Peggy Abraham, Eufaula Heritage Association; Probate Office, Barbour County Court House, Clayton; Marvin L. Harper, president, Tuscaloosa County Preservation Society, Tuscaloosa; Milo B. Howard, director, Alabama Department of Archives and History, Montgomery; Lilla M. Hawes, director, Georgia Historical Society, Savannah; Victoria R. Gunn, Georgia Department of Natural Resources, Atlanta, and Hofwyl Collection, Darien; Len G. Cleveland, Georgia Department of Archives and History, Atlanta; John D. Helms, National Archives, Washington, D. C.; Mr. and Mrs. James C. Culver, Glenn House (Cottage Home), Cave Spring.

I owe special thanks to Kenneth Croslin, director, Troy State University Library, and to his cooperative staff, especially Ethel Sanders, director, Readers and Special Services; Nell Bassett and Martin Kruskopf, Reference; Pam McGee and Gloria Moseley, technical assistants; Patricia Porter, Circulation; Rebecca Howell, Periodicals; Thelma Mershon, Betty Chancellor, and Frankie Muller, Acquisitions. I have also received much help from the Troy State Communications Services, James W. Hall, Jr., director; Dale Moseley and Thomas J. Seal, staff members. Patricia Duke, art instructor, Troy State University, taught me how to dissolve the paste on journal pages.

Those who reduced my teaching responsibility so that I could complete this study are Duane C. Tway, chairman, Department of History and Social Sciences; John M. Long, dean of Arts and Sciences; W. T. Wilks and Edward F. Barnett, deans of Academic Affairs; and Ralph W. Adams, president, Troy State University. Nor would this have been possible without the willing support of my departmental colleagues. Doris Jennings, secretary, deserves special thanks for her help, interest, and faith.

Students in my classes of southern history have been helpful, testing my ideas and doing some research. Cecil W. Hurley, J. R. Buziuk, and Jessie G. Echord went beyond course requirements to locate important unpublished sources. Student assistants who made notes, filed, typed, and checked references are Judy Dorman Helms, Sharon Blalock, Deborah Ridgeway, Debra Mixon Wiggins, Jo Ann Lindsey, Anida Oglesby, Denise Coleman, Janet Fuller, Debora Benton, and Wanda Smith.

In the project's early stages, before the Historic Chattahoochee Commission began sponsoring it, some expenses for research, travel, and copying were defrayed by the Troy State Research Committee and Library. This initial underwriting, however, was soon replaced by the Historic Chattahoochee Commission, whose wise and adequate support could serve as a model to any foundation-assisted research and publication. Those persons most directly involved in the commission's assistance of the study are Allen W. Jones, professor and archivist of Auburn University, who recognized the subject as a viable one for the commission; H. Floyd Vallery, assistant to the president of Auburn University, who as a member of the commission recommended the study to Florence Foy Strang, projects chairperson, and she to the members, for their subsequent approval; Douglas Clare Purcell, executive director of the commission, who has attended the book's publication with interest and vision; and Jean Robinson, secretary to the director, who has cared for details with courteous finesse.

Among other good things, the commission supported my search for competent critical readers, whose keen perceptions of errors and misemphases have saved many embarrassments. Readers who have done yeoman service in improving these pages are Bertram Wyatt-Brown, Case Western Reserve University; James C. Bonner, Milledgeville, Georgia; Aubrey C. Land, University of Georgia; William K. Scarborough, University of Southern Mississippi; Ann Boucher, Huntsville, Alabama; Douglas Clare Purcell, Historic Chattahoochee Commission; Marie Godfrey, Eufaula, Alabama; Elizabeth Schieffelin, Los Angeles, California; and Barton Starr, Troy State at Fort Rucker, Alabama.

Nor would this volume have been possible without the careful attention of The University of Alabama Press, especially F. P. Squibb, editor. Finally, my wife, Mary, has been a constant researcher and critic. Providing much good help, she has preferred the first role to the second. Still she and our sons, John and Charles, have lightened both the mood and burden of the book by refusing to take me or J. H. Dent too seriously. Of course, I accept full responsibility for the errors and shortcomings herein.

Ray Mathis
Troy, Alabama

INDEX